Autobiography of
AUGUSTUS
HOPKINS
STRONG

Autobiography of AUGUSTUS HOPKINS STRONG

Crerar Douglas, editor

Judson Press ® Valley Forge

AUTOBIOGRAPHY OF AUGUSTUS HOPKINS STRONG

Copyright © 1981
Judson Press, Valley Forge, PA 19481

Unless otherwise indicated, Bible quotations in this volume are from *The Holy Bible,* King James Version.

Library of Congress Cataloging in Publication Data

Strong, Augustus Hopkins, 1836-1921.
  Autobiography of Augustus Hopkins Strong.

  Includes bibliographical references and index.
  1. Strong, Augustus Hopkins, 1836-1921.
2. Theologians—United States—Biography.
3. Baptists—Clergy—Biography.   4. Clergy—United
States—Biography.   I. Douglas, Crerar.
BX6495.S7985A32   230'.61'0924 [B]   81-5970
ISBN 0-8170-0916-7   AACR2

The name JUDSON PRESS is registered as a trademark in the U.S. Patent Office. Printed in the U.S.A. ✿

*This autobiography
is dedicated to
my children and my grandchildren.*

Contents

Autobiography of
AUGUSTUS
HOPKINS
STRONG

AUGUSTUS HOPKINS STRONG

Preface

But the continuous toil of those who have tried to find a union, a "synthesis," has kept theology alive. Without them traditional Christianity would have become narrow and superstitious, and the general cultural movement would have proceeded without the "thorn in the flesh" which it needed, namely, an honest theology of cultural high standing.

Paul Tillich[1]

I

Augustus Hopkins Strong (1836–1921) was one of the most influential Calvinist theologians in America when, on his sixtieth birthday, August 3, 1896, he began to write for his children and grandchildren "the simple story of my life." His *Autobiography* bears the marks of the Gilded Age in which it was written: wealthy and pleasure-seeking, yet analytical, unapologetically cerebral. And it has its share of Gilded Age social ironies: it is the story of a

---

[1]Paul Tillich, *Systematic Theology* (Chicago: University of Chicago Press, 1951), vol. 1, p. 7.

man who was equally close to the Rockefellers and the Rauschenbusches; a man who, like his father, had been converted by Finney and, like his son, was intrigued by the thought of Einstein.

The story is Jamesian in its intense concern with the transmission of mighty patriarchal heritages from one generation to the next and in its setting on the boundary between bumptious young America and old Europe. It is Gothic Revival in its magnitude, its eclecticism, its cheery enthusiasm about past and future.

But Strong's story is also more homespun than the Gilded Age. In its anecdotal moralism, its unpretentious biblical realism, its unpompous sobriety in the face of disasters, its recognition that there are such things as tragedy and Providence, sin and atonement, the story is almost Lincolnesque.

Why has Strong's story lain in manuscript, largely unknown, for more than eighty years? One reason is its extraordinary candor. Just four years before starting the *Autobiography*, Strong had been at the height of his influence. He had just completed twenty successful years as president of Rochester Theological Seminary; he had just been elected to a three-year term as president of the American Baptist Missionary Society; and his *Systematic Theology* was recommended by leading Baptists, Presbyterians, and others on both sides of the Atlantic as one of the best orthodox Calvinist theologies of the century. For reasons which most of his friends and associates never understood, Strong broke with the conservatives by announcing that he had become an "ethical monist." Many of his followers could not understand Strong's new ethical monism, and many others who did understand it did not approve of it.

In his *Autobiography* Strong set out to show that ethical monism was, in fact, the goal toward which his spiritual life had been moving all along. Even more than a *Bildungsroman* or an *apologia pro vita sua*, both of them common enough genres of Strong's day, his *Autobiography* became a *confession*, reaching back to the Augustinian-Puritan exercises in spiritual self-examination which were, in fact, preparations for meeting Him who searches every heart on that day when no secrets will be hid. The *Autobiography* gradually became more sacred than a public document: like the family worship services which meant so much to him, Strong's *Autobiography* became a private witness to those who knew him best. It was his way of telling his family that he knew he was far from perfect but that his life had shown him how to trust the everlasting love of God.

As his father's literary executor, John Henry Strong had the right to publish Augustus H. Strong's *Autobiography* after the latter's death in 1921. Three extant versions of the manuscript show the younger Strong's effort to edit the *Autobiography* in such a way as to remove references which might be embarrassing to anyone still living. He seems to have concluded, however, that it was better not to publish the book at all than to make deletions in a story which his father had so carefully unified.

John Henry Strong kept the manuscript until his death in 1960. During the 1960s his second wife, Nadine Strong, made a typescript of the *Autobiography* available to the Strong family. Six photo-offset copies were made, and Richard B. Sewall, a son of Kate Strong Sewall, gave one of the photo-offset copies to the Colgate Library of the American Baptist Historical Society on the campus of the Colgate-Rochester Divinity School.

Upon the death of Nadine Strong in 1976, Emilie Strong Smith, a daughter of John Henry Strong, inherited the *Autobiography* and her father's collection of Strong papers. When it became evident that there was widespread interest in the *Autobiography*, Mrs. Smith, Professor Sewall, and Elizabeth de Cuevas, a granddaughter of Charles Augustus Strong, joined efforts to make possible its publication in its entirety. Other members of the Strong family, including Margaret Lewis Crosman, a daughter of Laura Strong Lewis; Alan S. Cook, a grandson of Mary Strong Cook; Robert S. Cook, a son of Mary Strong Cook; and John M. Smith, a grandson of John Henry Strong, also brought their knowledge and able assistance to the project.

II

The ethical monism which created so much turmoil for Strong in his later years has only recently begun to receive the attention which it deserves.[2] Many monisms were popular during the 1890s, the harvest time of Hegelianism and British Hegelianism. Strong and his Calvinist colleagues had for decades condemned all monisms, both materialist and idealist, as pantheistic and finally atheistic—a blurring of the distinction between God and his creatures to such an extent that both lose the power of independent action and thereby lose also their moral accountability.

But Strong came to the conclusion about 1892 that the gospel itself is a kind of monism, though not a simple monism. When it proclaims that, in Christ, God is both participating in our suffering and lifting us out of our suffering, the gospel is, in fact, setting forth a kind of monism which at first seems contradictory—an *ethical* monism—in which God is totally immanent in our brokenness and yet totally transcends our sinfulness, hence setting us free by binding us to himself. The gospel's ethical monism, said Strong, is a personalist monism or even (as he sometimes called it, straining paradox almost to the breaking point) a dualistic monism because it proclaims that, in Christ, God not only suffers in our suffering but also, in a manner visible only to the eyes of faith, triumphs over all suffering even in the most contradictory of circumstances. Strong put it this way in a sermon in 1902:

> God is passible, or capable of suffering; that is the first truth. God suffers in proportion to the breadth of his being and his nearness to his creatures; that is the second truth. And now recurs our problem, how can such suffering consist with blessedness? The answer is the third truth which I would inculcate: God is the ever-blessed God, because this suffering is the condition of joy and is swallowed up in joy. . . . If even a child can submit to a surgical operation gladly, for the sake of the health that will accrue; if the patriot can endure exile for liberty and

[2]Carl F. H. Henry, *Personal Idealism and Strong's Theology* (Wheaton: Van Kampen Press, 1951); LeRoy Moore, Jr., "The Rise of American Religious Liberalism at the Rochester Theological Seminary, 1872–1928" (Ph.D. dissertation, Claremont Graduate School, 1966); Irwin Reist, "Augustus Hopkins Strong and William Newton Clarke: A Study in Nineteenth Century Evolutionary and Eschatological Thought," *Foundations: A Baptist Journal of History and Theology*, vol. 13 (January-March, 1970), pp. 26-43; Crerar Douglas, "The Cost of Mediation: A Study of Augustus Hopkins Strong and P. T. Forsyth," *Congregational Journal*, vol. 3, no. 2 (January, 1978), pp. 28-35; *idem*, "The Hermeneutics of Augustus Hopkins Strong: God and Shakespeare in Rochester," *Foundations*, vol. 21 (January-March, 1978), pp. 71-76; Grant Wacker, "Augustus H. Strong: A Conservative Confrontation with History" (Ph.D. dissertation, Harvard University, 1978); Winthrop S. Hudson, *Baptists in Transition: Individualism and Christian Responsibility* (Valley Forge: Judson Press, 1979).

country; if the martyr can find the fires of the stake a bed of roses—surely He who sees the end from the beginning can endure suffering for the sake of what is to come thereby. Here too, the key to the mystery is furnished by our Lord Himself, who in prospect of his sufferings rejoiced in spirit, and for the joy that was set before him endured the cross.[3]

Strong's ethical monism can look at times like the neoorthodoxies of the twentieth century in its sharp focus on the atonement, its Christocentric Biblicism, its uncompromising insistence on original sin, its Calvinistic critique of *Kulturprotestantismus* (especially evident in his *American Poets and Their Theology*, completed in 1916 when he was eighty).[4] Yet Strong has more interest in idealist metaphysics than most of the neoorthodox theologies, and he is more interested than most of them in the immanent God's gradual self-manifestation through the products of human culture.

His ethical monism can also look like the European kenotic theologies of the nineteenth century and Anglo-American process theologies of our century in its concern with the costly immanence of God in creation, its rejection of metaphysical dualism, its organic philosophy of nature, and even its proximity to the panpsychism of Strong's elder son, Charles Augustus. Yet Strong's God has more freedom than the kenotic or process Gods to speak and act independently of humanity, and Strong's humanity is more ensnared than the kenotic and process humanities in traditional Christian concepts of original sin.

The difficulty of categorizing Strong's theology is one reason for its importance. Strong's thought forces us to sharpen the categories in which we write the intellectual history of his epoch.

III

Strong's influence was as diverse as the interpretations of his controversial theology. As president and chief theologian of one of the most important Baptist seminaries in America for forty years

---

[3] Augustus Hopkins Strong, *Miscellanies* (Philadelphia: The Griffith and Rowland Press, 1912), vol. 2, pp. 348-350.
[4] Augustus Hopkins Strong, *American Poets and Their Theology* (Philadelphia: The Griffith and Rowland Press, 1916).

(1872–1912), Strong personally shaped the moral and theological outlooks of hundreds of Baptist ministers, missionaries, and denominational leaders. Most of his students followed Strong's lead in attempting to take the best from both conservative and liberal views, but some of them pursued more radical implications of Strong's ethical monism. The death-of-God theologian George Burman Foster was one of Strong's students. The panpsychist Charles Augustus Strong was both Strong's son and his student. Social ethicist Walter Rauschenbusch's life and thought were inextricably bound up with Strong's from the beginning of his life to the end. All of these thinkers had to reject a portion of Strong's vision before arriving at their own mature theologies, but the very intensity of their dialogue with him and the diversity of their debts to him are, in fact, a tribute to Strong.

A generation which has inherited a Protestantism in which the diverse forces held together by Strong have somehow blown apart can learn much by listening to him. Valuable theologies, even the greatest of them, are often overlooked by the generation which most needs to hear them, only to be rediscovered by a later generation. Augustine was lost in the shuffle while Augustinians were drawing up handbooks clarifying his theology. Aquinas was condemned for teaching the Aristotelianism which he had spent his life refuting. Luther and Calvin were succeeded by scholastics who could not bear the thought of an uncodified reformer. Jonathan Edwards was succeeded by gray Edwardseans (including his son) who were restless until they could reduce the master's vision to manageable proportions, and Kierkegaard was succeeded by no one.

Less famous theologians, also, have entered into a kind of theological limbo before the full dimensions of their thought could be appreciated. John W. Nevin and Philip Schaff with their Mercersburg theology, Walter Rauschenbusch with his theology of the kingdom of God, Peter Taylor Forsyth with his theology of the cross, and Augustus Hopkins Strong with his ethical monism all called into serious question the prevailing attitudes of the Reformed churches of their time, and all had to pay for their boldness by being misinterpreted soon after their deaths.

A debt of gratitude is owed by many to Judson Press for

keeping Strong's *Systematic Theology* in print for many decades, even when it seemed useless to some because it was neither "fundamentalist" nor "modernist." A debt of gratitude is also owed to the family of Augustus Hopkins Strong for their preservation of Strong's candid story in its entirety, even though its candor was not always pleasant, and especially for their willingness to authorize the publication of the *Autobiography* in its entirety. While doing research on Strong, I became curious about his descendants' response to such a mammoth ancestral summons as the *Autobiography*. I asked one of Strong's grandchildren, Professor Richard B. Sewall of Yale University, to write a personal response to his grandfather's story for inclusion in this first published edition of it, and I am grateful to him for consenting to do so. The *Autobiography* has, to be sure, a solemn theological purpose, but it is also a human document showing us that even the ethereal abstractions of ethical monism have their rootage (and indeed their only value) in the vicissitudes and joys of life in community, including that most delicate of communities, the family.

Many people have provided special assistance in the preparation of Strong's *Autobiography* for publication. I would like to express special thanks to the members of the Strong family listed above and to William H. Brackney, many Douglases, T. Michael Elliott, Christina E. Fessler, Phyllis A. Frantz, James Goss, Howard J. Happ, Janet Hazlett, Winthrop S. Hudson, William M. Kramer, Thomas T. Love, Yoshimichi Masaki, Mokusen Miyuki, F. Patrick Nichelson, Faye Pullen, R. S. Ramakrishna, Michael P. Samartha, Robert D. Shofner, Edward C. Starr, Amzi and Elma Belle Toops, Richard Torgerson, Richard A. Underwood, Peter VandenBerge, and especially Harold L. Twiss of Judson Press, who has guided the publication of the *Autobiography* with skill and kindness.

Crerar Douglas
California State University, Northridge

A Grandson
Responds

The name "Grandfather Strong" was early associated in our family with Deity. I confused him with God. Before his one visit to our house, I thought of him, like God, as quite out of the reach of small boys. I was about ten when he came, and I remember his presence in our parlor (immaculate for the occasion) as somehow sanctifying the whole house. He was august—no one was ever better named—and yet benign. I found that I *could* approach him, and did. The fear and trembling (a phrase you will meet often in the ensuing pages) departed at his welcoming smile. But if I hoped for more, I never got it. He didn't intend to spend his time talking to children. August, yes, and benign; but removed, certainly, from my world. Not quite human?

That was my question until the *Autobiography* came my way in 1962. A swift leafing through brought all kinds of reassurances: boyhood scrapes; a harebrained and adventurous brother; the trials of early schooling; two broken engagements; Yale days, refusing Skull and Bones (even at the invitation of, among others, Chauncey Depew); ill health through overstudy in the seminary, followed by a

19

worldly and colorful year abroad to recover, when he learned to drink wine, talk German and French, listen to music, respond to art, and walked up to thirty-five miles a day in the Swiss Alps; his early ministry in Haverhill, Massachusetts—that "little shoe-town," which was "dead-alive" when he came there ("I could hardly breathe," he wrote) and which wept when he left; his life in the big church in Cleveland where he demanded discipline and hard work from his flock—and got both; his acceptance of the presidency of Rochester Theological Seminary on the condition that he not have to raise money for the first two years ("Begging I hated almost as much as being hanged"), only to find that he had to raise money to pay his own salary. (Necessity being the mother of necessity, he did it—and became the greatest money raiser in the Baptist church.)

And so it goes—anecdote after anecdote, crisis after crisis, personality after personality. Rereading the *Autobiography* now, I am more impressed than I was at first with my august grandfather's *style*. The anecdotes are told with a fine sense of narrative; they have pace and pungency. The crises (mostly spiritual), though often somewhat attenuated in the telling, are presented with a sense of form and even drama. The confrontations are as fresh as if they had happened yesterday. Here's one with John D. Rockefeller, whom he was trying to interest in founding a Baptist university in New York City. The going had been rough. Finally, Strong could hold his fire no longer:

> . . . I concluded to speak some plain truth. I told him that the Lord had blessed him with financial prosperity greater than that of any other man on the planet—he had made more money in a single lifetime than any other man that ever lived; and if he did not do more for God than any other man that ever lived, he could never stand in God's judgment. He turned red, and he looked very angry. But I had delivered my message, and I left the result with God.

Whether it was divine intervention or the effect of Strong's courageous assault, the result is a matter of history, even though (to Strong's disappointment) the money went to the University of Chicago.

The parade of personalities in the *Autobiography*—sketches of the lives and characters of the men and women with whom he was associated at every phase of his career—is, at the very least, an interesting phenomenon of the period. It was the day of the pious eulogy, whose guiding principle was *nil nisi bonum.* Biography was free from the now current obsession with the underside of human personality. Strong made no attempt to psychoanalyze his subjects; though aware of their defects, he presented his characters to illustrate aspects of Christian leadership, intellectual power, or spiritual dedication. Though he noted some few failures, his people, like Chaucer's Pilgrims, had striking qualities. Each was in some way remarkable. Strong learned from them all—sometimes (and here is where the reading gets more interesting) how *not* to do it. Like Tennyson's Ulysses, he was a part of all that he had met, and he was generous in admitting his indebtednesses.

Clearly, he was born to command, and latterly the role he enjoyed most was that of patriarch. An anecdote has come down about the rearrangement, by his then-adult children, of the furniture in the living room of the parental home in Rochester. The aim was to freshen up the place. Returning from a trip, the patriarch viewed the results benignly and uttered his verdict: "Isn't that nice! *Now we'll put everything back just where it was.*" The painstaking care with which he sketches the characters and budding careers of not only his children but also their spouses and then his grandchildren indicates the seriousness, I take it, with which he viewed his patriarchal obligations. The unity of the Family was of first importance. Indeed, the *Autobiography* is as much a monument to that as it is to his labors in the service of the Lord.

To the modern reader, his uncluttered, well-paced style and, above all, his humor are his saving graces. Writing at age sixty, Strong reminisces about the hairbreadth escapes of his brother Henry:

> Father and Mother had a sort of admiration for a boy who could survive so much, and I think they concluded at last that the mere fact of his being alive was *prima facie* evidence that Providence had something for him to do in the world. When he gave me five thousand dollars of Kodak stock the other day, I thought I saw clearly one of the things he was preserved for.

At his first pastorate in Haverhill, Strong, with a wife and child, felt cramped on a salary of $1,200 a year. He knew himself then as he knew himself during his exciting year in Europe after the seminary: he was a worldly young man, all too worldly. Looking back at Haverhill, he writes: "Truth is, I was originally intended for a millionaire. I have a natural taste for splendor. Largeness pleases me." (His gold-headed cane is still one of my prized possessions.) He got a raise. When he left Haverhill, his departure was abrupt, to the consternation of his flock. "But," writes Strong, "I never believed in cutting off a dog's tail by degrees." On one of his later trips abroad, he was careful not to drink wine until the ship was well out to sea. "I drink wine abroad," he writes, "but not at home. I once told Theodore Bacon that I had to draw the line somewhere, and I drew mine in the middle of the Atlantic ocean. Whereupon he remarked that that explained to him for the first time the meaning of the phrase 'Half-seas-over.' " He gloried in being president of a seminary—that is, a graduate school—and not a college with its unruliness and turmoil. "I have always thought," he writes, "that there must be a future life for canal horses, washerwomen, and college presidents; since they do not get their deserts in this life, there must be another life, to justify the ways of God."

All in all, this is a rich book, even for one whose main interest is neither in American theology nor the Baptist church nor the Rochester Theological Seminary nor the Strong family. For all his piety and soul searching, Strong was fully aware of the seething and yeasty life of his time: the famous Table Knockings in Rochester and the story of the "Spiritualist Bank"; the oratory of Emerson, Henry Ward Beecher, and Wendell Phillips that thrilled him; the Civil War; the sight of Lincoln's funeral cortege as it came up Broadway, which moved Strong to propose a Lincoln monument "over against the Washington Monument"; the impact of the new science on his thinking, which led him, on his own, to undertake systematic study of botany, geology, meteorology, and metaphysics; his unabashed—and successful—efforts to channel at least some part of the great new fortunes, like Rockefeller's, into the work of the Lord. (The concept, though not the phrase, of "God's gold" might well have had its start with him and his colleagues.)

But, as Rev. Crerar Douglas has brilliantly pointed out, ultimately the *Autobiography* stands as a record of the spiritual progress and intellectual development of an important figure in the history of theology—and not just American. All other matters, delightful as they are, must be viewed as secondary. I can only thank Dr. Douglas for his invitation to point them out.

Richard B. Sewall
Yale University

1

Early
Memories

On this third day of August in the year of our Lord 1896, on my sixtieth birthday, I begin to write the simple story of my life. For many years I have purposed to do this when the time should be convenient, and Providence seems to make it convenient now. By mistake the railway serving-men have sent my portmanteau to Canada instead of Canandaigua, and I am stranded here at Cook's Point, away from my family and without books. I cannot write about Goethe as I had intended, for notes and papers are lacking. It is a good day for retrospect. I begin with small hope of soon completing. But by devoting odds and ends of time to the task, I may at least hope to put down something that otherwise would be forgotten and to get on toward finishing an account of myself; whereas, without beginning, there will certainly be no ending.

I am not possessed of the notion that the record of my days will contain anything of extraordinary value or that my life itself has been a distinguished life. I do not write with any design or expectation that this autobiography will be printed. My aim is merely to preserve for my children and my children's children a statement of facts that may interest them. Heredity is very potent; perhaps what they read may throw light upon tendencies to good or evil which they feel within them. My example may to some appreciable extent warn or inspire: I would be of as much service to them as I may. When my father had retired from active business and come to be seventy years of age, I urged him in a similar way to write out his reminiscences. This compliance with my request has left to us a little manuscript book that will be precious to all his descendants, not only because it has historical value but also because it tells the plain story of an honest, industrious, and godly life.[1] I have had greater opportunities than my father had, but I shall be satisfied if those who read my story shall be persuaded that I was as good a man as my father was. However that may be, my writing is intended as a sort of example to those who come after me. As my father's story has helped to draw his children together, to increase their sense of family dignity, and to convince them that they cannot without guilt live a life below their father's level, so I would by this account of my own life lead my children and their children after them to esteem and love one another and to set before themselves a higher standard of living than that with which they might otherwise content themselves. And as I write out my story, I could wish that each of my children might also at a fitting time write out his own story. These reminiscences of successive generations would in time become a family treasure.

There is a special reason why I take interest in the task at this particular time. As I reach the age of sixty years, I am impressed more than is usual for me with the brevity and solemnity of our earthly life and the importance of making it a preparation for the life that is to come. I remember reading in 1860 the biography of Dr. Thomas Chalmers. The first six decades of his life Dr. Chalmers called his weekdays, and the seventh decade he regarded as his earthly sabbath, to be spent in special communion with God and in

[1]Alvah Strong, *Autobiography of Alvah Strong* (n.p.: Privately printed, n.d.). All footnotes in this book, unless otherwise indicated, are the editor's. Although Strong's lengthy genealogical appendices and index have been abridged, the narrative of the *Autobiography* appears in its entirety. The editor has modernized spelling, punctuation, and usage where appropriate. The manuscript from which this edition was made is in the Samuel Colgate Library of the American Baptist Historical Society, Rochester, New York, bound in four volumes by Augustus Hopkins Strong.

anticipation of the eternal sabbath of heaven. It is true that our modern age has somewhat antiquated Dr. Chalmers's distinction between sabbath days and weekdays. We are inclined to look upon all good secular work as sacred and to admit into the Sunday much that would once have been thought incongruous with religious thought or devotion. Yet there is a grain of truth after all in the scheme of the great Scottish preacher. So long as we are children of time and sense and so long as sin has any remaining hold upon us, fixed times of worship will be of value, and the same rule that applies to the seventh day of the week will apply to the seventh decade of life. The special observance of it may serve to detach the mind from what is merely worldly and to fasten the thoughts and affections more closely to things above. As Dr. Chalmers did, so I would, with the present year and the present day, begin a more definitely consecrated life. When I am tempted to do evil, I would say, "My soul! not today! This day belongs to God!" And I would make the present writing a beginning of this new consecration.

I have always thought the *Confessions* of Rousseau and the *Confessions* of Augustine, respectively, to be good illustrations of the spirit with which the saved on the one hand and the unsaved on the other will at the last meet God. Rousseau, with a flippancy and conceit which amount to blasphemy, declares that when he is called to answer before God's bar, he will simply present to the Judge a copy of his book as evidence that his soul is pure and that he has done his duty in this mortal life. Yet the book upon which he relies for justification is a record of treachery and licentiousness. Augustine, on the other hand, while he frankly acknowledges the passion of his early days and the deeply rooted evil of his heart, seems ever breaking into sobs of contrition and ever casting himself upon the divine compassion. With every confession of sin there is a prayer for mercy and an appeal to God for help and for salvation. I, too, would mingle with my writing a continual prayer that God would be merciful to me a sinner. Even the slight review of my life which I take today convinces me anew that for me there is forgiveness and deliverance only through the mercy and love of God in Jesus Christ, my divine and atoning Savior.

"How can a man get away from his ancestors?" says Emerson. We might reply that when they are good people, he does not need to get away from them. The Strong family can point back to a thoroughly respectable and stalwart lineage. The instances of outcropping physical strength which appear along the line of our past history make it probable that these are survivals of an original vitality and prowess which gave the family its name. It was a wonderfully prolific family, as Professor Benjamin W. Dwight of Hamilton College found to his cost. Having married a Strong, he became interested in the question of his wife's ancestry. Collecting a little material, he determined to write the *Genealogy of the Strong Family*. He little knew what a task he was undertaking. It proved to be an elephant upon his hands. For Elder John Strong, of blessed memory, who landed at Plymouth in 1630 and from whom nearly all who profess and call themselves Strongs are descended, had no fewer than eighteen children, and it is scarcely a hyperbole to say that all of these eighteen had eighteen apiece. As matter of sober fact, I find that the next in the line of descent from Elder John Strong to me had fifteen children; the third in the line had eight; but, as his excuse for having so few, it is said that he was killed by the Indians at the early age of forty-two, or he would doubtless have had many more. The fourth in the line had twelve children and the fifth, fifteen. From that point in the genealogy down to my own day the stock grows gradually less prolific until the list of my own offspring reaches only the meager number of six. I trust, however, that the family is not dying out and that my children will not permit it to die. Let them read Professor Dwight's *History*, in two octavo volumes of eight hundred pages each, one of the most voluminous family records yet published in this country, and as they see what their progenitors have accomplished in the way of multiplication, let them go and do likewise.

An examination of Professor Dwight's record will show that my ancestors were not only prolific but long-lived. Elder John Strong died at the age of ninety-four and his son at the age of ninety-six. After Jedediah Strong, Jr., whom the Indians killed at Woods' Creek, New York, come four in succession who lived respectively to the ages of eighty-three, fifty-two, sixty-nine, and seventy-five. Rhoda Payne, the wife of Philip Strong in the fifth generation, died at the age of eighty-six, after having borne fifteen children. She was a woman of prodigious strength. Before her marriage, as her betrothed approached her, she raised a large tub of clean water standing near her to her mouth and playfully drank his health, asking him in a bantering way to return the compliment. At another time, seeing two young men tugging ineffectually to put a barrel of cider into a wagon, she offered, if they would stand aside, to do it for them and then did it with ease. Honest endurance rather than brilliancy appears to have characterized my forefathers. And yet some branches of the family have their heraldic insignia. I have fancifully combined the arms of one branch with the motto of another to make my own crest. The eagle, the symbol of aspiration, soars from the mural coronet, the symbol of victory, with the motto: *Tentanda est via,* "The way must be tried." It teaches the success of courageous endeavor.

I have but slight recollection of my paternal grandfather, Ezra Strong. I just remember him and the house in which he lived on Exchange Street. There rises before me the faint image of a large, heavy, and lame man, with a physician's case of medicines. He had come to Rochester from Auburn, where he was one of the last surviving illustrations of imprisonment for debt—debt in his case accompanied by no defect of honesty and meriting no such penal infliction. It may be questioned, however, whether Ezra Strong's imprisonment did not have the effect upon his children of making them less sanguine and more cautious in business and giving them a salutary horror of debt. I am sure that my own eagerness to discharge all my pecuniary obligations and my success in preventing even my extravagance from going beyond the limit of my means in hand has been partly due to the story of my grandfather's misfortunes. My grandmother I remember far better; for while my grandfather died when I was only ten years of age or in 1846, she survived until I was over fifteen, or until 1852. I recall a quiet, sweet-tempered, uncomplaining, little old woman, in a plain black dress, knitting in a rocking chair by the fire. When my brother Henry and I made a tower of tin pans in the sitting room and brought them suddenly down with fearful clangor to the floor by knocking out the undermost, I seem even now to hear Grandma peacefully remarking to my mother, "Catherine, your boys are very active critters!" I remember Grandma's peaceful death—the first death-scene of the very few that I have witnessed. Father brought my brother Henry and me into the lean-to sleeping-room of the house on St. Paul Street where she had been for some weeks ill, and there, after a few gasps for breath, Grandmother died, while we stood wondering and awe-stricken by the bedside. It is my impression that both my father and I inherited from Grandmother Strong our evenness of temper and calmness of judgment, while Grandfather Strong perhaps furnished us with something of his enterprise and largeness of outlook.

My father, Alvah Strong, was surely never named from the Duke of Alva. My grandparents had probably never heard of the duke. Alvah Strong, at any rate, was a man whose whole disposition, character, and life presented characteristics precisely opposite to those of the blood-thirsty persecutor and tyrant of the Netherlands. He was a most peaceful, patient, generous, hospitable soul. He had a steady will, but he did nothing by jerks. He had healthy emotion, but he was not oversensitive. In the government of the family and the management of his business there was often much to annoy him, but in all his life I never knew him even once to show anger. He inflicted corporal chastisement when his children deserved it, but the calmness of his demeanor made the infliction judicially impressive. His good nature and willingness to oblige led him to endorse the notes of other people. He was sometimes imposed upon and met with heavy losses. There were several fires by which the savings of years were swept away. But my father never uttered objurgations; he never cherished bitterness; and he never seemed depressed. One night the alarm bell roused us, and a messenger brought the news that our newly equipped printing office, on the site of the present Wilder Building, was on fire. The weight of presses and type-metal on the upper floors soon precipitated this valuable material into the cellars, and up through the funnel, as from a veritable crater, a pillar of fire ascended to heaven. After all hope of saving anything from the wreck was abandoned, I saw my father standing on the opposite side of Exchange Street and quietly viewing the scene. I drew near to his side with such sorrow and sympathy as a boy could show and said, "Oh, Father! what shall we do?" But Father only replied, "Wait till tomorrow morning for that. It will be all right. Isn't that a fine sight?"

Augustus Hopkins Strong in his early years

My father had no education but that of the country school and the compositor's case, but he had a natural refinement and a good judgment which generally answered in place of training. He loved knowledge, and the printing office, in which he went through all the grades from roller boy to proprietor, served for his university. The counting room in those days was a sort of Exchange. Men of all pursuits and from all parts of western New York met there, and there they discussed every kind of subject, from the wheat crop to the Atlantic cable and from the nomination of Henry Clay to the differences between Old and New School in the Presbyterian Church. Father was open-minded, courteous, inquiring, conciliatory, and he drank in information continually. Without being a great talker or debater himself, he set others to talking or debating, and he learned from them. He liked to have interesting people at his house that he might hear them talk. If he had had his own way and my mother had permitted, he would have had a constant succession of guests. His candor and kindness made him the confidant of multitudes. He was the friend, adviser, and encourager of rising young men. He tried to reclaim the wayward from evil courses; he helped his employees to set up in business for themselves; he relieved the destitute; he freely forgave great wrongs when there was any sign of repentance. His influence for good was very wide, for as a newspaper publisher he came in personal contact with as large a number of people as any other single man in this part of the country. And all who knew him respected him and loved him for his unfailing suavity and kindness. Many since he died have said to me that, take him for all in all, Alvah Strong was the best man they ever knew.

He was not a profound thinker or a skilled writer or a practiced speaker or a master of social usages, but he was a plain and honest man, careful of the feelings of others, with great persistency of purpose, some inventive and organizing ability, and the determination to use what gifts he had for the glory of God and for the good of the world. He was a Christian man, with no brilliant experience, but with the disposition to be frank about what religion he had. In 1830 he was converted during Mr. Finney's first visit to Rochester. He sought the great evangelist at his room in the hotel. Mr. Finney bade him be seated by the door until he had finished a letter. At length my father, then a young man of twenty-one, perceived a towering form approaching him and heard a searching voice: "Well, what is it?" Father stammered out that he thought he ought to be a Christian, but he could not *feel*. Mr. Finney reached down for the iron poker that lay beside the stove and raised it fiercely as if he would beat out my father's brains. Father naturally dodged, whereupon the great evangelist simply said, "Ah, you feel *now*, don't you?" and returned to his writing. Father went away indignant at such a reception. But then he began to reflect. He concluded that Mr. Finney meant to teach him a lesson. If he was afraid of a poker, he had far greater reason to be afraid of hell. He soon had feeling enough. At least he expressed his sense of duty by giving himself to Christ and joining himself to the Baptist church.

My father was always afterwards an active Christian. He talked to others concerning their duty to serve Christ. He was early made a deacon of the church, and for forty years he was a faithful visitor of the poorer members, a seeker after the neglectful, for a long time a teacher, and for a little time a superintendent of the Sunday School. When he was himself worth no more than $10,000, he subscribed $1,000 to the University of Rochester, and though he died possessed of only about $50,000, he left $5,000 to the theological seminary, thus giving a tenth, not of his income but of his property, to the Lord. His benevolent contributions, however, were systematic and continual, and they would have been far greater if his financial schemes had prospered. But in the newspaper business the day of advance payments had not yet come, and bad debts swallowed up the profits. Accumulation was mainly in the increasing value of the plant and goodwill of the concern. Yet my father narrowly escaped being rich. In 1857 he held telegraph stock enough to have made him worth half a million if he had only retained it. But after a long struggle to keep what he had, he sold to Hiram Sibley just at the time of the combination and organization of the Western Union Company, and though so many others became millionaires, he remained comparatively poor. Yet he was never really poor. He always paid his debts, lived in comfort, educated his children, gave to every good cause, and had the reputation of being five times as well off as the facts would warrant. God knew what was best both for him and for his family. In spite of many disappointments and losses, I believe he was, when judged by the highest standards, far happier than if he had been the selfish possessor of a great fortune. And his children may themselves be better off today than if they had been born to wealth.

It touches me deeply when I remember that the sale of telegraph stock to which I have alluded was made while I was a senior in college and in large part, as I believe, for the purpose of meeting the expenses connected with the close of my college course. But it was of a piece with my dear father's perpetual generosity to his children. No cost was too great if they might only be educated. His mingling with men had given him a due appreciation of the value of a liberal training, and it was his ambition to give his children greater advantages in the race of life than he himself had had. It was for them that he strove to make money. He made sacrifices that they might see the world by travel. Father and Mother gave up their own house and took a small one when I came to Rochester to be president of the seminary, in order that I might have a better opportunity to do my work of instructing and entertaining. And whatever he did was unostentatiously done. He was a quiet and simple man, but for his station he had large views and a liberal heart. My great regret is that while he lived I was so absorbed in my own work that I did not sufficiently notice and commend his loving but undemonstrative care. Since Father and Mother have gone, the beauty of their lives has grown upon me. They did not receive their deserts in this world. I have sometimes felt an impulse to pray for the dead and to ask that God would in heaven reward them for all the goodness they showed me here. And as we ask our friends here to forgive us and to pray for us, so I have sometimes almost believed in the intercession of the saints and have felt like asking Father and Mother in heaven to forgive me and pray for me.

If I owe to my father my imperturbability and cheerfulness, my breadth and persistence, it is from my dear mother that I inherit anything I may possess of vivacity, humor, and power of expression. The substance comes from my father, the form from my mother. Father furnished the staying qualities, Mother the showy qualities. I cannot write of my mother's ancestry from any personal knowledge, for she was an orphan long before she was married. I only know from others that she came of an extremely bright though a somewhat eccentric stock. The Hopkins family had social and political distinction, as the *Memoir* of Samuel Miles Hopkins which we still preserve in manuscript abundantly testifies. It was a family of talent, wit, imagination, gifts for poetry, oratory, and literature. Four sisters and one brother, after the early death of their parents, were distributed among near relatives. They differed from one another in their fortunes and surroundings. Aunt Janette found a congenial home and social culture in Geneva; Aunt Almira a more meager living in Mount Morris; Aunt Jane and my mother, Catherine Hopkins, came to Rochester to earn their own support by the millinery business. My mother and Aunt Janette were the handsome pair among the sisters. I was always fascinated by Aunt Janette's regular and expressive features, as well as her sprightliness and kindness. My mother lacked the early social advantages of Aunt Janette, and her nature was far more shy and retiring. Indeed, she was almost morbidly seclusive. In this she resembled her brother Augustus, for whom I was named, but in this she was unlike all her sisters. Here was the most marked difference between my father and my mother. She was a woman of the home, fearing society, wholly devoted to her family, while he was a great lover of his kind, eager to see and converse with all who came within his reach. But, with all her reticence and timidity, my mother had a depth of sensibility, a keenness of conscience, a vein of humor, a gift of expression, which quite surpassed the endowment of my father and were in my judgment very unusual. When Mother's reserve was broken down and she felt free, she was charming and witty and eloquent. But she was known to very few. When she died, I wished to put away conventionalities and speak at her funeral because I felt that a precious treasure had been entirely hidden from the world and that I ought in gratitude to tell how much the Lord had done for me in giving me such a mother. And though I did not then follow the prompting of my heart, I rejoice now that there is another life in which character shall be seen in its real beauty and the secrets of all hearts shall be revealed.

Like my father, my mother had a high opinion of the advantages of education, and in her girlhood she had tried to secure them. Before coming to Rochester, where she sang in the choir and fascinated my father, she managed for a little time to attend the

Female Seminary at East Bloomfield. I have still in my possession
an octavo volume of Paley's *Works*, bound in yellow sheepskin with
the title on green leather, which my mother told me she bought with
the earnings of her own labor to study at the East Bloomfield
seminary. Her maiden name in pencil was once upon the flyleaf, but
as I cannot find it now, I think she must have erased it when she gave
the book to me in September, 1856. Nothing could induce me to
part with that volume, and I trust my children will never let it go out
of the family. I take shame to myself for my small estimation of my
many books when I think how much this one book cost my mother
and how precious it was to her. It was the beginning of her library.
Others were added to it, and the love of books and reading was
easily communicated to me by my mother's example. But as my
mother's life was for a dozen years of my childhood and babyhood
so bound up with my own, I think it best now to pass to the story of
my own life and speak of my mother and her influence in connection
with that. I can do this with the greater propriety for the reason that
my father during those early years was, through all the waking hours
of each day with the exception of mealtimes and Sundays, from
early morn till late at night, away from home and actively engaged in
his printing office or counting room. I can remember the long
evenings after supper was over, my mother's habit of beginning
them with a nap upon the sofa, the many times we waked her by our
noisy play, her rising to read to us or tell us Bible stories before we
went to bed. Then I learned that Adam was the first man, that
Samson was strong and Moses meek, and that Jesus Christ died on
the cross for me, a sinner.

But before all this, I was born. I am told that the eventful day
was the third of August, 1836. The locality was a little frame house,
No. 105 Troup Street in the city of Rochester, on the south side of
the street and three doors west of what is now South Washington
Street. The little frame house has long since been removed or torn
down, but the site is at present occupied by the brick dwelling of Mr.
H. H. Pyott. I remember little more than a spinning wheel and a
garden along the side of the fence, where I sowed seed and then
pulled up the plants to see how they grew. There was a front gate,
and this was ordinarily fastened to keep me in. But one day at the
age of three I in some way got out and made my first independent

excursion into the town. When my anxious parents found me a half mile away and asked me where I was going, I replied that I was going to hear Mr. Church preach. Rev. Pharcellus Church was a pastor of the Baptist Church. He was a solemn but excellent man, in a suit of spotless black and about his neck a preternaturally high white stock. When he made a pastoral call, I vanished, for I knew that if I were found, I should be obliged to sit bolt upright while he read the Bible and prayed. I probably needed prayer, for about this time I narrowly escaped death by hanging. Father had been reading after breakfast the account of the execution of a murderer. It occurred to me that it would be a fine thing to rehearse the scene. A rope was hanging from a beam in the woodshed; I put a tub bottom side up just beneath it, mounted the tub, and tied the rope tight about my neck. I then said to my innocent brother Henry, who gladly assisted me, "Now, Henry, when I say, 'One, two, three!' then you pull out the tub!" Henry obeyed, and I was suspended by the neck between heaven and earth. Not, however, till I was dead, for either my wriggling or Henry's screams called in an interested spectator in the person of my dear mother, who saved me to the world by cutting the rope. I had a scar around my neck so long after this that I never felt inclined to repeat the experiment.

These are reminiscences connected with the house on Troup Street. But they are not the first things I remember. It has been an interesting question with me how far back in one's life memory extends. I suppose it depends somewhat upon the other question—whether there are any striking events to remember. In general, I think people remember only what they have language to express in words; that is, we remember only what happened after we learned to talk. However this may be, I am sure that the earliest of my recollections dates back no further than to my third year. A great event then took place: my father and mother took me to Michigan. I remember the railway car in which we rode to Batavia and Buffalo and especially the storm on Lake Erie, in which the steamboat rocked very unpleasantly and I finally lost my power of self-control and, sitting up in the berth, said energetically, "This boat sha'n't go so!" Whether the elements paid any attention to me, I do not remember. At any rate we reached Edwardsburg, in Michigan, where my Uncle Myron lived. We fished one morning in the little lake on whose bank his house was situated. My older cousin "Hop," or Hopkins, pulled up his hook injudiciously and caught himself in the nose, which necessitated a surgical operation, with a jackknife, to deliver him. And I, being entrusted with a small kitten, grasped it so fondly around the neck that it was of no use as a kitten thereafter, and the only thing left to do was to have a public funeral, which the whole family attended.

My entrance upon political life was at the age of four, when my father, with his usual desire to put me in the way of seeing the world and getting new experiences, took me to a great mass meeting in the Extempore Log Cabin which was erected as a means of promoting the election of William Henry Harrison to the presidency. The great barnlike structure, lit only by circlets of oil lamps, the song of "Tippecanoe and Tyler Too" with which the building rang, but especially a captive coon that tried in vain to escape from his hanging cage impressed my youthful imagination and made me a violent Whig. In fact, my father's connection with a party paper and his deep interest in the success of Harrison, Clay, Taylor, and Fremont in successive presidential campaigns did much to interest me in politics and made me, when I was a pastor, take considerable part in political matters. When William H. Seward visited Rochester, my father took pains to introduce me to his notice, and I remember the governor's kindly taking me upon his knee and talking to me. And when Daniel Webster, fresh from his advocacy in the United States Senate of the fugitive slave bill, came through Rochester to defend the Compromise Measures of 1850, my father saw that I had a place in the arcade where I could hear the great defender of the Constitution, with his Olympian brow and cavernous eye sockets, as he spoke to the hushed and listening crowd from the gallery.

Those were days of regular churchgoing. Father was a most methodical man himself, and the household was expected to follow his example. The weekly prayer meeting was to be attended by all who had reached the age of twelve; the Sunday morning service was to be attended by all over the age of four or five. The younger members of the family sometimes made complaint. But there was no discharge on that account. Rain or shine, the children had to go. When I was about ten years of age, I waked on a winter morning and to my great delight found that a great snow had fallen. It was Sunday, and the thought immediately occurred to me that the streets would be so blocked as to make it impossible to go to church. Whether rightly or wrongly, the drifts to my imagination seemed mountain-high; Alp upon Alp arose as I looked out the window. I came downstairs in great glee, exclaiming, "Father, we can't go to church today!" "Why so, my son?" "There won't be anybody there!" "Won't be anybody there? Well, if there isn't anybody else there, it will be very important that *we* should be there!" So he trotted me out through the drifts. Sure enough, when we reached the church, we found but a half dozen people, and there was a prayer meeting instead of a preaching service. But then *we* were there, and I had learned a lesson never to be forgotten. I believe in accustoming children to regular attendance upon divine worship. As a means of education it is as valuable as the school, and the habit once formed is hard to break, whereas the formation of the habit of regular attendance after long and persistent neglect in childhood is very difficult. Father had his trials with my brother and me at church. Henry in particular could never be relied upon for quiet or reverent demeanor. Father usually sat between us to prevent mischief. But when he got interested in the sermon and his attention grew lax, Henry would cut up some dido that was memorable. On one such occasion my brother laid himself out flat upon the cushion and, as he observed that father did not notice him, gradually worked his body round till his head was hanging backwards over the edge of the seat, while his feet were hoisted up like liberty poles above the back of the pew. Father's attention was suddenly called to this very unecclesiastical spectacle, and he was seized with a sudden impulse to give Henry a good shaking. But the trouncing was of no great duration, for Henry had a bell in his pocket, which began to ring out over the congregation. I do not remember what Henry caught when we reached home, but my impression is he got no pie for his dinner. Sunday School was as regular an exercise as church, and I have been in the Sunday School as a scholar or teacher ever since I entered Mrs. William N. Sage's infant class as a little child in short dresses.

A somewhat larger and broader life began with our change of residence. My father's business prosperity seemed to warrant removal to a larger house. He purchased the dwelling on South

Saint Paul Street, just opposite the present laundry of Mr. Elwell. The moving interested me. It was springtime. The trees were full of blossoms. There was a great attic where Henry and I could play. There was a barn and a buggy and a black horse named Old Turk and a dusky native of the Sandwich Islands named Pooley to take care of him. Pooley was a great swimmer, also a great drinker. He had been thrust into the water when he was a babe and been forced to swim or drown. This seemed to give him, through his after life, an aversion to water as a beverage. Father was after a time compelled to dispense with his services. He had been brought to this country by missionaries, but the change of scene did not change his heart, and he died a miserable death. Old Turk, however, survived his care. He was about twenty years of age and submitted to all sorts of indignities. Pooley made him go through all the antics of the circus ring. Old Turk would stand on his hind feet and kiss his master for a lump of sugar. Henry and I made him gallop within an inch of his life. But we learned to ride, and many an excursion into the country and to the bay enlivened our days.

My good mother endeavored to train her children for usefulness and to make them equal to any possible exigencies of their future lives. She told me that many a missionary had been obliged to go ragged because he could not mend his clothes. She enticed me to learn the art of sewing, and at the same time cultivate my missionary spirit, by making a patchwork quilt for the heathen, and for this benevolent work she paid me at the rate of one cent a patch. I began also to knit, but I got the yarn so much tangled that Mother thought the trouble and expense worth more than it came to. Father insisted that sawing and splitting wood was good exercise for boys, and many a cord had Henry and I to cut and pile up neatly in the shed. Whether the thinking was high or not, the living was certainly plain. It was not till I was twelve years of age that our meals were prepared by a servant. Cornmeal mush, with milk or molasses, formed our common breakfast. Potatoes baked or boiled, mashed or warmed over, served for dinner. Soda biscuit often appeared at tea. Meat of any kind was rare and, except in the form of dried beef or codfish, was visible only once a day. There was a prevailing impression in our family that animal food was inflammatory and unhealthful and that its place should be taken by graham bread. My mother had derived this impression from reading her two large volumes of Graham's *Lectures on Anatomy, Physiology and Hygiene*, illustrated with plates and diagrams of all the internal organs of the human body. The fact that Dr. Graham, the author, died of starvation did not affect Mother's confidence in her guide, and she still continued to make unleavened cakes of simple graham flour and water and to commend them to her offspring by giving them the name of "gems." She enticed me to read through the two books of lectures by giving me twenty-five cents a volume, and my first knowledge that I had a stomach and the awful perils therewith connected was gained from this reading. Not even the fifty cents which Mother so lavishly expended, however, could alter my honest dislike for graham bread, and I never look upon it now without a protest against the quantities which I was compelled to consume in my childhood.

Mother was accustomed to say that we would see the good of it in after years. If a very sound digestion is any proof of good diet, Mother's prophecy has been fulfilled. We were never coddled. Candy and sweetmeats might be marked *non est inventus*—except on holiday occasions. On Christmas and Thanksgiving there was mince pie. Mother tired of our importunities, for in spite of her instructions we persisted in thinking that mince pie was good. One day she unguardedly promised to give us all the mince pie we could eat. I ate a whole one and had the colic, but, strange to say, this experience did not cure me, and I like mince pie to this day. In a similar way Mother on another occasion consented to give brother Henry all the pancakes he wished. Henry succeeded in disposing of nineteen when the batter gave out and my brother was saved. This suggests to me the long series of hairbreadth escapes which Henry experienced, and as I fear he will never give the record of them to posterity, I put them down here in order that the memory of them may not be lost. I always had a certain feeling of envy as I thought how many things Henry could do that I could not. He was more physically active than I; he could swim and play ball better. The result was that he met with more accidents and got into more scrapes. Father and Mother had a sort of admiration for a boy who could survive so much, and I think they concluded at last that the mere fact of his being alive was *prima facie* evidence that Providence had something for him to do in the world. When he gave me five thousand dollars of Kodak stock the other day, I thought I saw clearly one of the things he was preserved for.[2]

Our woodshed had a long ridgepole. Henry thought it an admirable course to run races on. The track was straight and level, though it was narrow. Henry succeeded well, until one day he stumbled, rolled down the roof, fell off the eaves, and landed below, near the kitchen door, with a broken arm. Henry was carried into the house; the surgeon was called; the arm was put in splints; and in a few weeks he was well and ready for something new. This something was a bobsled, which had brought wood for our winter fires. After the wood was unloaded, my brother caught a ride on the sled as it took its departure. Sitting on the crossbar with his legs dangling to the ground, one of these legs naturally came in contact with the central post to which the double gates were ordinarily hooked, and a couple of bones snapped. Henry was taken into the house a second time for repairs. After he had recovered, he attempted to monkey with Old Turk, and the horse kicked him in the side and deprived him for a time of what life he seemed to have left.

He and I were required daily to saw and split a certain amount of wood. As I raised the axe, I remarked, "Out of the way, Henry, or you'll get hit!" Henry did not get out of the way, and without my intending it or knowing how it was done, the axe came down into his skull—at least it looked as if a slice had been cut out of his head. But the doctor sewed him up, and within a few days Henry was as lively as ever. Opposite our house on the street was a blacksmith's shop, and the windows of the shop looked out upon the Erie Canal. One day the blacksmith saw a commotion in the water and concluded that it was a small boy—in fact, it proved to be Henry, sinking the third time. The blacksmith jumped in, pulled out my brother, held him up by the heels to let the water run out, resuscitated the boy, and took him home to his mother. Henry subsequently skated into an airhole in that same canal in the winter, but that time he clambered out without help.

[2]After several other careers, Henry Alvah Strong met the young George Eastman and decided to fund his experiments in photography. H. A. Strong was president of the Eastman Kodak Company from 1881 until his death, July 26, 1919.

The "perils of waters," however, did not end here. To make more realistic the narrative which follows, I shall be obliged to say that Henry was a natural musician. While I tried to learn the piano and could not, Henry picked up music by instinct. The trouble with me was partly that I had a lenient and smiling young woman for a teacher. If she had had a rod in her hand and had used it, I should have learned more. I tried the accordion and the violin as well as the piano, but I never got further than to play Schubert's "Serenade" on the last-named instrument. At times, when I am in good form, I can even now play the "River Waltz" and "God Save the Queen," and there seems to be some trace of these ancient melodies in my fingers' ends, though Laura seems for some reason to be thrown by my playing into convulsions of laughter.

But there was no joke about the playing of my brother Henry. He was to the manor born. He was an active and well-dressed young man, with a turn for adventure. Father secured him a position as clerk in the American Exchange Bank in New York City. Henry had hardly gotten a start in his work, however, before he telegraphed to Father that he had shipped before the mast to Japan. Father thought this rather too rough and extensive a beginning, and he went down to New York to beg Henry off. He succeeded in substituting a voyage to Havre. The captain of the vessel was a friend of our family, and it was thought that this would secure a soft thing for Henry. Unfortunately the captain was only a figurehead, and the real commander was the first mate, who gloried in putting the novices through. The new beginner must be duly initiated. The result was that Henry was set to perform all sorts of ugly tasks and had to face all sorts of danger. Several times he came near being swept overboard by great seas and went down to his hammock with hands covered with blood after he had been compelled to climb the icy rigging. There is a story that he wrote his name in letters of blood on the woodwork over his hammock as a warning to all who should come after. The time of year was not favorable for a first voyage, for it was winter. The captain at the close of the voyage told my brother that he must go to the hospital until his hands were cured. Henry regarded the hospital as a kind of almshouse and preferred to run away from the vessel. He hid himself until the ship had discharged her cargo and had sailed again. Then he hired himself out to an

English woman who kept a sailors' boardinghouse. There he peeled potatoes and waited on the table until he earned enough money to pay his passage home. At intervals in his duties he played the piano in the parlor, to the great astonishment of the guests, who had known him only as a handsome young waiter.

Henry was mightily glad to get home from a foreign shore. But he had hardly landed before he arranged to go to Pike's Peak in the Rocky Mountains. Father set him up in the shoe business with Cousin Hop in Denver. The business was a failure. Henry furnished the capital and Hop the experience. At the end their positions were reversed: Hop had the capital and Henry had the experience. Henry was obliged to return to civilization. Without money this was difficult. He therefore procured a canoe, and, having stocked it with food, he proceeded to sail down the river. The canoe, however, struck a snag and was upset. Henry had to swim to overtake it in the rapid current. He found this impossible and, to save his life, made for the shore. But the bank rose precipitously and gave him no chance to land. At last he espied the projecting branch of a tree, made a spring, caught it, and was saved. Again he reached home, but only to enlist in the navy. Secretary Seward obtained for him the position of assistant paymaster. All through the War of the Rebellion [Civil War], Henry served his country by paying off sailors and making reports to the Navy Department. He passed the forts at Mobile with Admiral Farragut. On furlough he got acquainted with Nellie, and that did the business for him. He married a good Christian girl, settled down, became a first-class businessman, and the other day the *Democrat* called him a millionaire.

I cannot vouch for the truth of all these details about my brother. I tell the story only as I have heard it. For corrections and for further interesting particulars, I refer the reader to him. It will be readily believed that, with such a brother, life in the old house on St. Paul Street was not devoid of incident. The attic witnessed many thrilling scenes. There I secretly read the *Thousand and One Nights* and very improperly and unnecessarily hid the book for fear that my parents would not approve of it. There all sorts of shows were enacted, some in imitation of a celebrated necromancer whom we had been permitted to see and some in imitation of a circus and menagerie which we had attended. We had magic lantern exhibitions—admission one cent. We blacked our faces and gave entertainments as Negro minstrels. And we held religious services, at which Henry was sexton and I preached. We filled a large tin bathtub with water from the well, and while Father and Mother were absent at the real church, we baptized the cat in the orthodox way and administered communion to her, the elements being water and pickled codfish. One of Father's methods of punishment was to tie us up in this attic. He was too merciful to make the rope short—in fact, the rope was a whole clothesline. This permitted a considerable degree of freedom, and these periods of imprisonment, with the help of the "hired girl" in the kitchen, were almost as diverting as going to school.

If I have seemed to speak humorously of Mother's physical training, I wish now to prevent any misinterpretation of what I said. She was right in believing that no very high degree of mental or spiritual health could be attained apart from a healthy body. Hence we were encouraged to play, to use our limbs, to walk, to ride, to live in the open air, and even to saw wood. Exercise in the gymnasium and the sight of the experts who practiced on the bars or the trapeze and used the boxing gloves or the fencing foils gave me an idea of the value of a good muscular development, which I acted upon to some extent afterwards in my college course and in the ministry. But those days were almost prehistoric as far as athletics were concerned. I now feel that I got only the first faint beginnings of a proper physical training. It was largely my own fault. I inclined more to reading than to bodily exercise. I too often remained indoors while Henry was playing ball or chestnuting. In college I was a member of a boat club, but I seldom rowed. For years in my early ministry I was the victim of lassitude and felt unequal to my work. I am sure that if the bicycle had been then in existence and I had used one, I should have doubled my efficiency as preacher and pastor. Yet with all my sins of omission, I must credit my mother with much of the general good health I have enjoyed, for it was her insistence upon the needs of the body that prevented me from giving up physical exercise altogether. I attribute my gradual gain in health and in power to work ever since I began to preach very largely to the fact that I have from year to year taken more regular walks and have every summer spent some weeks in the country either fishing or boating.

My first knowledge of letters was gained from picture blocks upon the floor. I have a sort of impression that I talked before I was two years of age and read before I was four. But my first schooling was when I began to attend the District School Number Twelve. John W. Adams was the principal. He first taught me in the upper room of the old stone building opposite our house on St. Paul Street. After Mr. Wadsworth of Geneseo made to the city his gift of land and apparatus, the primary department was transferred to the new and, as it then seemed, magnificent schoolhouse which now bears the name of the Wadsworth School. Here I went through all the grades, got feruled for coming in late, was occasionally admonished, but on the whole showed myself a ready scholar. The parsing of Milton's *Paradise Lost* in a class of boys and girls much older than I, my first study of Anthon's *Latin Lessons*, and my earliest acquaintance with chemical retorts and electrical machines were epochs in my mental history. A boy named Stephen Charles, who had a turn for science, induced me to join with him in making a waterwheel, a magnet, and an electrical machine. We produced hydrogen, carbonic acid, and, I believe also, oxygen gas. A few years afterwards, just before I went to college, this same Stephen Charles was captain of an engineering party for the construction of the railroad from Batavia to Attica. I spent three summer months as rodman in his party and learned the beauty of the woods and skies as well as the mathematics of surveying. Evenings we spent singing with the Attica girls or reading Robert Burns. The delight of that first communion with nature was something which I shall always remember with gratitude. It approached to ecstasy. The brilliant color of a flower and the singing of a brook as it wound its way through the forest thrilled me, as they did Wordsworth:

> There was a time when meadow, grove, and stream,
> The earth, and every common sight,
> To me did seem
> Apparelled in celestial light,
> The glory and the freshness of a dream.[3]

[3]William Wordsworth, "Intimations of Immortality from Recollections of Early Childhood," 1. 1-5.

Much poetry besides that of Wordsworth has been intelligible to me because I had that summer out-of-doors. And my conceptions of heaven have taken their tone in large part from those experiences of pure and rushing emotion in view of God's beautiful works.

There were two striking episodes in my school days which in all honesty I must mention. When I was eleven years of age I was, perhaps for the purpose of getting me away from bad boys in the district school, transferred for a little time to a private school on Adams Street, a long way from my home. It was kept by a tall stiff pedagogue named Foster. The walk to and fro was tedious. It occurred to me that a carriage to convey me and a slave of the lamp to summon the carriage, à la Aladdin, would be very convenient. Alas, I had no lamp like Aladdin's! But I had seen in my father's counting room a drawer with money in it which might serve the same purpose. One day, when Father left his key in the drawer, I conceived that my time was come. I took some five dollars in bank bills and hired a hackney coach and two horses to bring me and a couple of my schoolmates home. I do not remember that the sin of this robbery was impressed upon my mind until the ride was over. Then I was filled with fear and hid the four dollars of change under the doorstep. I had a restless night and a still more restless day after the night was gone. The incident of my sailing through Main Street in a hackney coach came to my father's ears. The shortage in cash at the office awakened his suspicions. There was an investigation, a trial, a confession, a bringing forth of the stolen money from its hiding-place, and a most memorable application of the rod by way of punishment. My own remorse and shame before discovery, my positive gladness when at last my sin had found me out, my father's combined affection and severity, the justice and solemnity with which he pleaded with me and then chastised me gave me a permanent and valuable understanding of the folly and misery of sin, and of the mercy as well as the righteousness of God.

A year later I was sent to the school of Mr. Miles, on the corner of Troup Street and Plymouth Avenue. The school was in the basement of an edifice which at that time occupied the site of the present Plymouth Church. In the yard in front of this building was a stout pole twenty feet high, with a revolving iron top to which ropes were attached for the boys to swing on. Mr. Miles was the best teacher of geography I have ever known. He had an eye to form. With him map drawing was an art. He taught his scholars to repeat in topographical order the names of all the towns in the county of Monroe, all the counties in the state of New York, all the states in the Union, all the counties of England, Wales, Scotland, and Ireland, all the countries of Europe, and all the important cities of all these countries. But of all the teachers I have had, he was most nearly a savage. Partial, arbitrary, passionate, he was in discipline a model of all that a teacher ought not to be. He had great physical strength, black hair like the mane of a lion, and a sort of ferocity which struck terror into the heart of every pupil who managed to displease him. He would kiss the good boys before the whole school, and he would flog the bad ones within an inch of their lives. His methods of punishment were unique. A boy named Vespasian or Vespucius Robins was accustomed to "suck his tongue," though I confess to this day I do not know the exact nature of this offense. Mr. Miles tried to correct this bad habit by sending the boy to the druggist's for a bit of asafetida, tying the asafetida in a rag, and then compelling Robins to suck this bitter plum as he sat upon the platform. If a scholar was inattentive upon the other side of the room, he would be brought to a sense of duty by having a ruler or an inkstand hurled at his head. Robins was the special object of Mr. Miles's wrath for no particular reason except that the boy was stupid and afraid. One day he was ordered to lie down flat upon the floor while the teacher mounted a bench and from that elevation deluged the boy's face with water from a sprinkling pot. On another occasion Robins was compelled to draw a pail of cold water from the well and set it down at the end of the bench. Mr. Miles took the boy by the heels, held him with his head downward, mounted the bench, and then repeatedly let his head down into the water and withdrew it till Robins was nearly drowned.

My brother Henry and I took turns in carrying our books home from school. Henry and I got on very well together except that occasionally Henry would call me names, and I would throw stones at him. There came to be a controversy as to the question whose turn it was to carry home the books. I left them to Henry, and Henry left them in the street. Mr. Miles whipped Henry to make him confess it was his turn, but Henry, instead of confessing, only ran away from school. Mr. Miles made an example of Henry by turning his coat inside out, painting his cheeks with stripes of red ochre, marking RUNAWAY upon his forehead, and standing him up on a barrel in the yard so that the boys could dance an Indian powwow around him. Henry showed himself thoroughly consistent by running away again the next day. The only time in my life when I was profane was as I returned from Mr. Miles's school. As I was coming home over Court Street Bridge, I was seized with the impulse to swear. I had but a single companion, and without any immediate provocation and with no motive but to see how it would sound, I took the name of God in vain. I shall never forget the effect both on my companion and on me. It was like a clap of thunder from a clear sky. The world seemed suddenly to grow dark. God seemed to frown upon me. My companion was frightened. And as for me, I slunk home in terror and never swore again. I wish I could extenuate my fault by saying that I swore at Mr. Miles. That was not the fact, though he richly deserved it. In lieu of swearing, I have always taken a sort of satisfaction in remembering that he spent his last days as a convicted bigamist in a western state's prison.

A third select school must be added to the list. It was that of Mrs. Greenough on North Avenue. This lady was a person of great social gifts and genuine refinement. I think it quite possible that my parents thought my conversational powers in need of cultivation, for I was unusually reticent. Mrs. Greenough was a born talker, and she had seen the world. I remember only two things about her school. One is the impression made upon me by her correct and elegant pronunciation. Her son, a boy two or three years older than I, had caught from his mother this fine use of words. When he said "Do not trouble yourself" and "I will not need your help" instead of using the contraction "don't" and "won't," he seemed to me a superior being. But when, on failing to hear what was said to him, he used the phrase "I beg your pardon" instead of simply saying "What?" I saw that I had been brought up in a lower social stratum than he, and I determined to speak my native tongue with accuracy. The boys with whom I had formerly associated had accustomed me to regard propriety of speech as indicative of conceit. I now made up my mind that it was a beautiful thing and a thing to be cultivated. If I have ever learned to talk well extemporaneously in public, it is because I have tried to speak correctly in private conversation. But little Mademoiselle Perabeau! Shall I ever forget her? She first taught me German. She made the exercises of Ollendorf positively delightful by her sprightliness. I have just had bound, for a memento, the *Illustrirte Zeitung*, which constituted my first German reading book. Compared with modern illustrated weeklies, it is an archaic sort of production. But it stimulated my love for language. I made up my mind that I would master the German. It led me a little later to buy the *Complete Works* of Schiller in one volume and, before I went to college, to read through his *Thirty Years War* and his *Song of the Bell*. And I have kept up my reading of German ever since.

My literary development I attribute in part to a thorough course in dime novels. One of my fellows at the district school had a pile of yellow-covered literature, such as *The Phantom Ship* and *The Pirate's Bride*. He was also a subscriber to the weekly journal called *The Star-Spangled Banner,* which contained the thrilling stories of "Ned Buntline." Before I was fourteen years of age, I must have read a hundred such novels. They were incredibly silly and worthless, but they gave me a love for reading. It matters not so much what one reads, provided he learns the art of reading at all. I have sometimes thought that a young woman who read absolutely nothing but novels might get from them a good education if only the novels were well chosen. The novels I read were not well chosen, but in the bushels of chaff there were, after all, a few grains of wheat. An occasional quotation of poetry took my fancy and led me to wish that I had more from the same author. A historical allusion moved me to read sober history. Little by little I learned to discern between good and evil; I sloughed off the evil; I read good books as omnivorously as I had previously read the worthless or the bad. My father's great generosity in permitting me to buy pretty much what I chose at the bookstores and so to gather a little library of my own greatly strengthened my literary bent. A reading circle composed of teachers and older scholars of the Wadsworth School met one evening of each week, and I received great stimulus from it. Side by side with my scholastic training, and in fact outrunning it, was this constant reading of books. Before I went to college, I had become familiar with Shakespeare and Milton, Dryden and Gray, Tennyson and Longfellow, Byron and Burns; I had read Macauley's history of England and Gibbon's history of Rome; and from many sources I had gathered quite a stock of literary and historical material which afterwards proved of the greatest service. My college course was especially successful simply because I had larger resources at my command in competitive writing and prize debates than most of my classmates possessed.

My love for public speaking in a similar way was developed rather early. School declamations helped to inspire it. When I was about thirteen years old, a compositor in my father's printing office, O. B. Powers by name, boarded at our house on South St. Paul Street. He had been editor of a newspaper, and he had a large stock of information about politics. He took a fancy to me and thought me a promising boy. With him I went to hear John B. Gough at a time when his oratory was in its first freshness and power. Nothing that I have heard in later years has so entranced me as did the music and pathos of his eloquence. With this same Mr. Powers my father permitted me, merely for the sake of experience, to hear a rendering of *Macbeth* at the theater. I was sent alone to Auburn to hear Kossuth. It was the day of lyceum lectures, and I listened to Emerson and Curtis and Thompson and Beecher and Wendell Phillips. On a certain Fourth of July—being fourteen years of age—I was invited to deliver a Fourth of July oration in our backyard, to a congregation composed of my own family and our immediate relatives. Mr. Powers gave me some help in the preparation of the oration, but it cost me much labor and anxiety. The applause of my friends made me think that I could become a public speaker. The Orion Debating Society, which I afterwards joined, though I was its youngest member, gave me excellent opportunity to acquire confidence, and this, too, proved a great advantage when I entered upon the competitions of college life.

Before I tell the story of my immediate preparation for college, I must add a word with regard to the multiplicity of my early experiences. My father believed in variety of environment and in the stimulus of travel. He was forever stirring me up by putting me into new and strange scenes. I can remember my first ride to Lake Ontario. I remember the first distant momentary glimpse of its far line of blue and the feeling of mystery and awe which that glimpse inspired within me. From the summit of the last hilltop as we pressed onward I remember the yet more solemn feeling with which I looked upon the great waters that stretched away before me, now so deep and cold, so fathomless and illimitable. But when we came down to the water's edge and I was led out into the rolling waves, there seemed to be nothing but the sea—the solid shore had vanished. I was overwhelmed and lost but for my father's voice lifted up to encourage and my father's hand stretched out to help. I love to turn all this into a parable. As I go on in the journey of life, as youth grows into manhood and manhood into age, death and eternity assume larger and larger significance to me. The first distant glimpse of them in my childhood overawed my soul; the sins of my youth made them fearful; even to me a Christian the final stepping down into the flood will be a unique experience—it cannot be anticipated. Yet, since I have accepted Christ as my God and Savior, death has no terrors. I have heard his voice saying, "When thou passest through the waters, I will be with thee; and through the rivers, they shall not overflow thee." Death is mighty, but Christ is the Conqueror of death, and his pierced right hand will help me through the flood and open to me the gates of paradise upon the other side.

When I was older by several years, Father took me to Niagara Falls. We dined at the Cataract House while an orchestra played in a gallery and an army of waiters brought in each course in solemn procession and at a given signal deposited their dishes upon the table all together with one mighty thump. We walked around Goat Island, went to the top of the tower that then stood on the edge of the fall, put on waterproofs and passed under the cataract, steamed up to the descending torrent of water on the little *Maid of the Mist.* But the climax of all was our crossing the river from one high bank to the other upon a rope of wire. They were making the first preparation for the suspension bridge. A kite had been flown across the great chasm; when the kite came down, the string was used to pull across a heavy cord; that in turn served to bring over a wire; the wire dragged after it a cable about the thickness of one's finger; pulleys ran upon this cable; from the pulleys was suspended a little iron car; this car the superintendent invited my father and me to enter. The prospect was appalling. The cable sagged down into the abyss; at a little distance it looked like a thin wire; farther off it was a mere hair; as it approached the opposite shore, it was absolutely lost to sight. Only after many tears was I induced to commit myself to the car; the swift descent to the middle of the river took my breath away; when gravitation ceased to carry us farther and we hung suspended between heaven and earth waiting for the windlass to draw us up to the other side, the suspense was terrible. But it was a lesson of faith which I have utilized many a time since. Launching out on the promises of Christ is a more safe adventure than my committing myself to that wire, for Christ knows more than any superintendent. He is in the car besides, and if I go to destruction, He must needs go with me.

My father did not always go with me. Little by little he accustomed me to go alone. When I was only twelve years old, he sent me on the packet boat—a night ride on the Genesee Valley Canal—with my cousin Hop to visit relatives in Moscow, La Grange, and Mount Morris, and the cordiality with which I was received won my heart and taught me something of true hospitality. On this visit, too, I learned nearly all I ever knew about farming and was afterwards willing to take it in homeopathic doses. A buggy ride with Hop to East Bloomfield was still more memorable because the entertainment given us was to our youthful minds unspeakably elegant. For the first time, moreover, I was treated with marked respect and was made to feel as if I and my opinions amounted to something. Like my mother, I was naturally lacking in self-confidence. Society was for years a burden and trial to me. The kindness of the good people whose very names I now forget but who laid themselves out to make that visit pleasant can never be forgotten. It made a social epoch in my history. It gave me hope that I might make my way in the world. It taught me that one of the best services any human being can do to the Lord Jesus Christ is to be kind to a boy.

A long series of excursions followed these which I have mentioned. I went to the State Fair at Albany at the age of thirteen. To walk up to the register at Stanwix Hall and amid the crowd to secure a room was no small achievement. The journey thither, by canal as far as Utica and thence by rail, was the longest I had yet undertaken. Uncle William H. Spencer was the pastor of the First

Presbyterian Church of Utica, and my week there was full of interest. But the canal ride, with the chances of bad company and bad books, was hazardous for so young a boy. Afterwards I went with a companion, Theodore Whittlesey, to New York City and learned the wonders of the Astor House and the great metropolis, and I know of no harm that came from the trip. Fishing excursions to Rice Lake in Canada and the Thousand Islands and railroad rides to Portage Falls and Buffalo are specimens of the way in which I was constantly thrust out to try my hand in contacts with my fellowmen. My father was determined that I should learn something of the world. I think he went to the extreme limit of propriety when he sent me to the courthouse to hear a man tried for murder and to the county jail to see another man hanged. Yet the intense earnestness of the closing arguments of counsel showed me how direct and energetic preaching ought to be; the solemnity with which the judge put on the black cap and pronounced the sentence of death became to me a type of the final judgment, and the pallor and trembling of the poor wretch in view of the gallows enabled me afterwards to picture to myself and to others the hopeless misery of the damned.

When I had reached the age of thirteen, the "Rochester Knockings" began. Mrs. Fox, the originator of these novel entertainments, rented of my father the old house we had formerly occupied on Troup Street, and her daughters furnished the manifestations. Among many who were drawn in from the surrounding country to hold converse with the spirit world were Mr. and Mrs. Sleeper of Mount Morris. Mr. Sleeper was a Presbyterian elder of means and influence, a reputable and cultivated businessman, and Mrs. Sleeper was a woman of more than ordinary character and social gifts. They came to Rochester to investigate, and they stayed with us as our guests. One morning my father unfortunately offered to accompany our friends to the house of Mrs. Fox, and I was permitted to go with the party. We found the house absolutely full of people. Mrs. Fox and one of her daughters met us at the door, told us that the house was too full at that time to receive us, but asked the spirits whether they would appoint a future interview. The question was immediately answered affirmatively by raps upon the piazza floor, and these raps continued after we all had descended to the brick sidewalk. "And where would the spirits meet us?" Answer: "At Mr. Strong's house, that same evening." This was more than Deacon Strong had bargained for. As an officer of the church, as well as proprietor of the Rochester *Democrat*, he had desired to keep somewhat aloof from what he feared was a work of the devil. But he must please his guests. He finally consented, and Mrs. Fox and her daughters promised us an evening visit.

The evening came at last and with it the Fox girls and their mother. Our heavy mahogany table was rolled out into the center of the room. Mother tried to put Henry to bed, but he was thoroughly frightened at the idea of going to sleep in the dark when Satan and all his angels were let loose in the house; so Mother was forced to permit him as a spectator. The company sat in silence about the table with hands stretched expectantly upon it. Soon we began to hear raps upon the under side, then upon the floor, then upon the doors and walls of the room. Katy Fox was a pretty young girl, and she sat opposite me. I was at a susceptible age, and as she shook her curls, I thought that she smiled upon me. I was so irreverent as to wink at her, and strange as it may seem, she winked in return. From that moment all sense of solemnity left me, and I was unable to persuade myself that the whole performance was not a piece of hocus-pocus, played off upon us by the girls. Not so with Mr. and Mrs. Sleeper. Though the answers given by the spirits to our questions were vague and unsatisfactory, except in one or two instances, our guests were profoundly impressed. Mr. Sleeper got down on his hands and knees, in order that he might put his head under the table a little nearer to the source of the knockings, but he rose even more bewildered than he had been before. At last the séance ended. Mr. and Mrs. Sleeper returned to their home in Mount Morris. But my father was shocked and never could forgive himself for his connection with the affair when he learned that our friends had left the Presbyterian church and had become Spiritualists.

Miss Allen was an aged spinster, who had taught school and had had Katy Fox for one of her scholars. She, too, investigated but with a very different result. Going one morning to Mrs. Fox's house, she asked if she might be permitted to converse with a dear departed friend. Mrs. Fox assured her that the spirits were ready to talk to her and inquired who it was that she wished to communicate with. Miss

Allen asked to talk with her grandmother, long since deceased. And what question would Miss Allen like to ask? She replied that she wished to know how her grandmother spelled the word "scissors" now that she had reached the heavenly state. And the answer was spelled out letter by letter: "S-I-S-S-E-R-S." "Ah," exclaimed Miss Allen in her high, piping voice, "that's just the way Katy Fox used to spell scissors when she was at my school!" It was as beautiful a demonstration of the truth of spiritualism as the spirit of Daniel Webster gave when he said that if he were to live his life over again, he would wish to correct some mistakes he had made in his *Dictionary*.

The critical time in a boy's education is the time when he begins Latin. Unless he is well grounded in the elements, it will be almost impossible to make of him a scholar. This crisis of my scholastic history came when I was fourteen years of age. I was transferred from private and inferior schools to the Collegiate Institute. A great three-storied stone building on Cortland Street occupied the site of the present Unitarian Chapel. There were several teachers, but only one made his mark upon me. This was the principal, N. W. Benedict. He was a genuine pedagogue, somewhat stiff and pedantic, but a lover of the classics, a man of learning, and entirely devoted to his calling. He was not enough of a grammar grinder; he was not an adept in modern methods of instruction; if a scholar translated well, the processes by which he reached his results were not severely scrutinized. But he impressed all whom he taught with the idea that Latin and Greek were liberal and delightful studies, and he inspired an ambition to secure the best possible college training. When I entered college and measured my attainments by those of men from Exeter and Andover, I found that I was lamentably deficient in classical technique, but I found also that I had more of the classical spirit. My college courses were greatly handicapped by my imperfect knowledge of Greek and Latin grammar; but when I entered college, I had read not only the authors required for admission but also something of Horace, Herodotus, Aeschylus, and Aristophanes besides.

I never should have gone over all this ground had it not been for a young man named Chester Wright Heywood. He was ten years older than I and was earning his way by sweeping the schoolrooms and ringing the bell. With my cousin Hopkins and me, he was beginning his Latin. When we had completed about six months of work, had finished the early exercises in the Latin reader, and had reached the fables, the spring vacation came. Heywood was in earnest to secure an education, and he proposed to Hop and me that we should see what we could do, should spend the three vacation weeks in study by ourselves, and should try to enter an advanced class when the next term began. My cousin loftily declined the proposal: he declared that he would do no vacation study but would have a good time. A kind Providence moved me to decide differently: I fell in with the plan, rose up early and studied late, and when the next term opened, had read nearly through the Latin reader and was promoted to a class of older boys that was reading Cicero. That self-sacrificing effort and its result convinced me that I could do something if I tried. I began to be ambitious—I fear I was also somewhat vain—but from that time I gave myself no rest. Whatever industry could do I accomplished. I had a poor training in grammar, but from the Latin I learned the meaning of English words, and a new delight in sonorous and noble speech took possession of me.

If I were to make an inventory of my mental resources at the close of my preparatory course, I should name first a love for study; secondly, a fine rhetorical sense; thirdly, a considerable knowledge of literature; and, fourthly, an overwhelming ambition. My thinking powers were not developed to any such extent as my powers of expression. I had a quick sensibility; I kindled easily; there was genuine oratorical excitability. Every occasion when an essay was to be written or a speech to be made in debate seemed to me a great occasion: I was in my element when preparing for it and when delivering what I had prepared. Though I was not at home in society, I was quite at home before an audience. I had great faith in my ability to persuade with the living voice. But I now perceive that my ideal of public speaking was somewhat declamatory. I believed too much in great orations. My fluency was in danger of running away with me. I needed more reading, more study, more contact with able men, and especially more thought. These defects were to some extent remedied by my eighteen months' experience in the counting room, and by my four years' experience in college.

As far as classics and mathematics were concerned, I was warranted as prepared for college when I had completed my fifteenth year. Both Professor Benedict and my father, however, thought me too young to begin a college course, and I was therefore admitted to my father's office for a while to learn something about business. I am sure that the time I spent there was as useful as any other period of equal length in my whole course of education. I have already spoken of the printing office as my father's university. It was also to a large extent my own. It was the gathering place for all sorts of people, and a confidential clerk like me could get an inside view of many kinds of life—commercial, political, and religious. In eighteen months I had learned bookkeeping so well that I kept all the books of the establishment by double entry; I made deposits at the bank; I wrote down telegraph reports of the markets and the news as the operator dictated them from the wires; I learned to set type, correct proof, work a press; I got the whole run of the concern from buying paper to paying off the employees. It was during this time—1852 and 1853—that the University of Rochester and the theological seminary were doing their second and third years' work. My father was treasurer of the seminary, and all the funds of the institution passed through my hands. I little thought, as I paid the beneficiaries their appropriations, that the time would come when I should myself be president of the institution and teach theology to the sons of the very students to whom I then gave aid. I learned from these students and their professors much about education; election excitements made me feel that it was my business to have decided views as to politics, but I was chiefly benefited by acquiring business habits, learning to keep accounts, and gaining knowledge of practical administration.

2

College Days

At last the time came to leave business and take my college course. After the brief vacation which I have already described as spent with an engineering party in the country, I went down to New Haven, passed my examinations, and began my college life. It may seem strange that, when my father was so interested in the new Baptist institutions at Rochester, I should have been permitted to enter at Yale. There were two reasons: first, the influence of a friend in the preparatory school and, secondly, the broad ideas of my father. Theodore Whittlesey's father was a graduate of Yale. The son descanted to me on the glories of the ancient eastern college until I could be content with a course at no other. Theodore fully expected to go with me. But at the last moment his finances seemed to fail, and he went into business while I was left to go to Yale alone. My father did not seriously oppose my wish. He believed that new surroundings and large classes would give me a stimulus which Rochester could not afford. And in this he was true to himself and faithful to me. I am sure that the broader life of New Haven, its noted names, its greater thoroughness of instruction, its old traditions, the better preparation of my classmates, and the large number of bright men among them induced in me a quicker and larger growth than I could have gotten in my native town. All my life long I have looked back to my college days as halcyon days. I have never since found such friends as I knew then. The currents of life were fresh and strong. Though there was some evil, there was a preponderance of good. I owe most of my subsequent success in life to the teaching and the associations of old Yale.

Something of this good influence consisted in the taking down of my self-esteem by the higher standards which prevailed around me. I can never forget my first recitation under Professor James Hadley. The lesson was the first four lines of Homer's *Iliad*. I learned it with a cheerful confidence which was born of ignorance. The first man called up was an Andover man. Professor Hadley put questions the very meaning of which I could not understand. The analysis of the verb, of which I knew nothing, was assumed to be a familiar thing. One question followed another with the regularity of clockwork; each question was as clearly and concisely worded as if an hour had been given to putting it into form, but the Andover boy gave the answers so quickly that he almost seemed to slap them back into the professor's face. And the number of them! A hundred questions were asked upon a single line. In two or three minutes I had learned what was meant by absolute thoroughness of investigation, study of all the ins and outs of a subject, precise understanding of it, and precise expression. If I had learned nothing else in all my college course, that acquisition would have been worth all the cost. But as this new light dawned upon me, all my hopes of excelling in scholarship at Yale were dissipated. I saw that with my imperfect preparation, I had before me a long struggle. I was handicapped in the race. Not only had my conceit vanished, but also I was greatly discouraged. I concluded, unwisely as I now think, that I would put my energies, not into the regular studies of the curriculum, but into writing and speaking. I do not mean that I did really ill in the matter of scholarship, for I took a Dissertation at commencement, and with a very little additional care in making up omitted recitations I could have taken an Oration. In such studies as Horace with his elegance and grace, Tacitus with his brilliancy and intensity, solid geometry with its absolute certainty of demonstration, the history of civilization with its great principles and its breadth of outlook, I attained a very respectable rank. But I counted scholarship a thing of secondary importance. I did not hold myself to a perfect learning of my lessons. My verbal memory was never of the best, and I contented myself with getting what seemed to be the substance while I was careless of the form. In this I now see that I made a great mistake, and I afterwards urged my sons in their college work to make sure first that they mastered the regular curriculum before they devoted themselves to literature and debate.

But the course I marked out for myself had its advantages. It was the day of prizes at Yale. Prize compositions, prize declamations, and prize debates held a large place in the minds of the students. From the very beginning I entered the lists, and I was almost uniformly successful. In two Linonian Prize Debates in the freshman and sophomore years, I took the first prize; I won the first prize twice in the sophomore year for composition and once for declamation. In the senior year I took the Yale Literary Gold Medal for the best essay and the Deforest Gold Medal for the best oration, receiving the latter, however, by lot after the faculty had found themselves unable to decide between the merits of my oration and that of my competitor, John Milton Holmes. My speaking and writing gave me an acknowledged position in college politics. I was the first class president, was in two successive years elected by the Linonian Society to represent my class at the annual Statement of Facts, was honored in the senior year by being made Class Orator. When just before graduation I delivered, within two or three days of each other, both the Class Oration and the Deforest Oration and my father and mother came down to New Haven to see my triumphs, I felt as if hard work had been rewarded. For though I did not put my best work into the studies of the course, I did put my best work into these contests. All that industry and patience could do in the way of investigation and elaboration, both literary and elocutionary, I can honestly say that I did. And as a preparation for the subsequent struggles of actual life, it constituted no mean training.

I have already intimated that I was intensely ambitious. The title of my graduating essay at the Rochester Collegiate Institute was "Born to Conquer," and I was determined to illustrate the theme in my own person. It was a selfish ambition in large part, and there were those who knew how to use it for their own purposes. When I entered college, Edward C. Billings had just graduated. He was an adroit and unscrupulous politician, though he was at the same time a man of most persuasive manners and of very considerable ability. He espoused the cause of Ike Clark and sought to win for him the first presidency of Linonia. For this purpose, though he himself was a student in the law school, he made friends with the prominent freshmen and, among them, with me. It amuses me now to think of the many visits he made me and the arts he used to win me over to Clark, his friend. He taught me elocution, and I can never be sufficiently grateful that as the result of his advice my voice was changed from a high head tone to the lower register and my delivery from the declamatory style to that of elevated conversation. But the influence of Billings was not wholly salutary. He was devoid of principle. He was Machiavellian to the core. With him the end justified the means. I will illustrate only by mentioning a single instance. He persuaded me that success in the Freshman Prize Debate would rest, other things being equal, with the contestant who first succeeded in getting the necessary books. He therefore either stole the keys or borrowed them with the connivance of the assistant librarian and induced me, at dead of night, with a dark lantern, to make a raid upon the Linonian Library. The expedition was so needless, so hazardous, and so idiotic that it has often made my blood run cold to think that I could have been inveigled into it. He urged it in order to get me into his power and make me his tool. It succeeded for a time, only because I was a simpleton. But it took no long time to see through his design, and when I once learned to know him, I detested him forever after.

"Instruction is the best part of education," so said Bishop Butler. But Yale College had not learned this lesson. In those days there was almost no instruction. Professor Hadley and President Woolsey were almost the only exceptions to the rule—and they are the only teachers whom I remember to have given actual information to their pupils. The system was a different one—it consisted simply of learning lessons from a textbook and reciting them to the tutor or professor. No discussion was permitted at any time. I do not recall that a single question was asked by any student of an instructor during the whole four years of my college course. It was a dead-alive system, which of itself did much to make scholarly work a drudgery and almost nothing to make it attractive. Great as Professor Hadley's merits were as a drillmaster and an example of thorough investigation, he never so much as intimated to us that Homer was a poet, that there was a mythical theory of the authorship of the so-called Homeric poems, or that those poems had had any influence upon the literature and liberty of Greece or of the world. Tim Dwight taught us Plato, but he never told us that Plato had a system of philosophy, that there was a difference between the philosophies of Plato and Aristotle, or that either of these had a following down the ages. Never was it suggested to us that a subject might have light thrown upon it by side reading; never were we referred to books for illustration; never was the history of a science spoken of. A narrow accuracy was cultivated—breadth was ignored. When I think what might have been done in the way of making study interesting and how completely the student was left to his own devices, I feel that I was treated hardly, and I thank a good Providence that prevented me from utterly despising the regular studies of my course.

As it was, I suffered in other ways than in scholarship. Birds of a feather flock together, and my own small sense of the value of the curriculum brought me naturally into contact with those of a similar turn of mind. Looseness of scholastic habits has a moral side to it, and I formed associations which were not of the best. There were bright men who cared more for a gay time than any sort of work. I fear I was something of a Bohemian. I learned to smoke and I began to drink. There were brilliant evenings when conversation was much enlivened by sips from the flowing bowl. Some of the best scholars of the class encouraged me by their example and presence on these convivial occasions. Yet I must say, in all sincerity, that I did not run riot. Never in my college days nor in all my life have I been intoxicated. Nor did I associate with any of the worst of my classmates. I had a natural delicacy which was shocked by coarseness or obscenity. The vice which attracted me had to be at least refined. I attended the theater only two or three times during the four years. I never played cards for money. But for two and one-half years I was edging toward evil. I was gradually losing my sense of restraint. The attractions of a vicious life became more and more strong. My power to resist grew weaker. If I had gone into New Haven society and had come in contact with cultivated women, it would have been well for me. But my very laxity in matters of scholarship and perhaps my rather indiscriminate associations prevented my being invited where I could have gotten the most good. Until the last year I was left to work out my problems for myself. The result was that I had a growing sense of badness and helplessness which, as I now see, was a providential preparation for better things.

The good which I got from my college course consisted very largely in the acquaintance which I formed with men, both among the faculty and among the students. First of all, and towering above all the rest, was President Woolsey. Tall and bent, pale and thin, he was the very image of a scholar. He had coal-black eyes, that could flash with indignation and pierce you through. Indeed, he was by nature a man of passionate impulses. The story was that in his youth sudden anger would sometimes lead him to fling an inkstand at an opponent. The mastering of his temper had been the work of years. Yet even in his later days temper sometimes mastered him. At evening prayers, after the first snow, the students came into chapel stamping their feet. The exercise was contagious and soon the whole place resounded. When the president made his way to the pulpit through this uproar, it was evident that he could not contain himself. Once in the pulpit, he began a violent harangue. But he suddenly recovered himself. Stopping short in the middle of a sentence, he opened the Bible, read a penitential psalm, and made a most humble and contrite prayer. One morning in his lecture room a young man who did not know his lesson ventured to make a mock recitation and, when challenged, to give an impertinent answer. I saw the president's face turn white; he bowed his head upon the desk before him; there was a half-minute's silence like the silence of death; he raised his head, called upon another man, and the recitation went on. He knew that if he spoke to the offender, he would speak too much; so he said nothing. We knew what a lava flood was pent-up there; self-repression was not a sign of weakness but of power. No man whom I have ever met has so ruled me by his mere character. He was modest yet courageous, candid and

Charles Augustus Strong

cautious, yet inflexible when he had reached conclusions, a born disciplinarian, yet so simple and so just that his discipline had an air of inevitableness about it. Above all he hated a lie, and his own Christian manhood reflected itself and reproduced itself in his pupils. It was worth going to Yale College to sit for four years under the influence of President Woolsey.

Noah Porter, who afterwards became Dr. Woolsey's successor in the presidency, was in my day professor of intellectual and moral philosophy. He was noted for lack of discipline, as President Woolsey was for the opposite. An easygoing good nature made him popular. He was full of learning, but he was as poor a teacher as I ever had. He added no suggestions of his own to the lesson from the textbook, and I finished my course in metaphysics with the impression that the subject was dry and dull. There was one exception. He gave us a brief course of lectures on ethics. It was one of the few bits of actual instruction which were given to us during our four years. I became deeply interested in his contention that conscience was not a separate faculty like intellect, sensibility, and will but rather a mode in which these faculties act—in other words, man's consciousness of his own moral relations, together with a peculiar feeling in view of them. For the first time in all my college experience I went to Dr. Porter after the lecture, told him that I was interested in his doctrine, and asked in what books I could find the view stated and elaborated. To my surprise the professor, like a young schoolgirl, blushed to the roots of his hair, and in an embarrassed way said he was afraid I could not find anything written in that line, for the view was original with him. Many years afterwards I visited him in New Haven. He had served as president and had resigned. He was feeble in body, but his mind was still alert. I said to him, "Dr. Porter, I have come to ask you whether you have apostatized from the true faith." His eye flashed, and he inquired what I meant. "Yes," I continued, "I wish to know whether you have become an idealist." "Never!" he answered. "Never! If idealism be true, what is the world but a dream?" His published work on *The Human Intellect* did me far more service than any instruction I received from him in college, and in my *Systematic Theology* I have mentioned his name with gratitude as one of the three who did most for my intellectual development. I count it an honor that he was my friend, and I recognize the debt I owe to him as the first example I ever had before me of real philosophical thinking.

George P. Fisher was chaplain, or pastor, of the college church. He was fresh from Andover, a pleasing writer and preacher, yet so utterly devoid of oratorical gifts that I have seen students sleeping by the score around me while he was reading his sermon and tears were trickling down his cheeks. His lectures on pantheism gave me a taste for theology. The characteristic of his thought and style was its lucidity. In arrangement and expression he was a model for all who treat difficult themes. If I myself write clearly, I owe it largely to Professor Fisher. But I owe to him more than this. When the crisis in my religious history came, as it did soon after, Professor Fisher took interest in me, invited me to his room, talked with me, read to me from John Calvin's *Institutes* and showed me that they were conceived as orations, and set me at a higher order of philosophical and theological reading than I had known before. All my life long Dr. Fisher, too, has been my friend, and I take great pleasure in recognizing my great indebtedness to him and to the books he has written. When in October, 1896, I stood with him at the Princeton Sesquicentennial to receive the Doctorate of Divinity, I regarded it as one of the greatest honors of my life.

I will not delay to speak at length of Tommy Thatcher, who gave me a little inkling of comparative philology when he pointed out the common roots in the Latin and the Greek; nor of William D. Whitney, the Sanskrit scholar, who taught me German and gave me in three months more of an insight into the structure of the language than I had learned in seven years before; nor of pompous old Professor Olmsted, whose definition of wisdom, as the choice of the highest end together with the choice of the best means to attain it, I remember better than any of his disquisitions on physics; nor of Benjamin Silliman, Jr., whose vanity was so conspicuous as he performed his experiments in chemistry before the mixed audience of college boys and of girls from Miss Dutton's School; nor of James D. Dana, that noble specimen of a Christian man of science, whose faith in God's special revelation in the Bible was just as frankly avowed as his openness of mind to all the facts of God's revelation in nature. The mention of these names is enough to show that no young man could leave New Haven without having fixed in his mind many an object lesson to influence his whole intellectual and moral life. If the student carried away nothing he had learned from books, his college course would not therefore be in vain. Personal influences are the strongest forces in education. The man is greater than his teaching, and character counts for more than learning. I am glad that my ideals were elevated by contact with such scholars and such men.

I was influenced almost as much by my own classmates. Some of them were noble fellows, highly endowed intellectually, socially, and morally. Norman Carolan Perkins was my most constant companion; in the senior year he was my chum. He had a kindliness of spirit which amounted to genius. The very soul of good humor, he won the confidence and affection of all. He had great acuteness as well as delicacy of mind and a great power of logical reasoning. He took a first prize in English composition and a Townsend Prize besides, more because he could not help it than because he tried for it. But he was too indolent to use his abilities except on the rarest occasions. He was poor, but he had unlimited assurance in borrowing money, and he seemed to succeed best in borrowing from those to whom he owed most. His tailor furnished him not only with clothes but also with funds to pay his college bills, having some faint hope, I suppose, that Norman would recompense him in the distant future. And so Norman intended to do, though hope delayed often made the hearts of his creditors sick. An easygoing companion like my chum did much to reconcile me to an easygoing life. Yet my friend's sad after failure is a sufficient commentary on the wild oats theory. Indolent habits played mischief with him. Though at one time in his senior year he made a brief attempt to live a Christian life, his love for smoking and drinking led him soon to abandon it. He was class poet at the same time that I was class orator. He studied law and began practice of his profession in Chicago. For a time he was successful, but he was extravagant in his expenditures. He built a beautiful house, and he collected an extensive library. To meet some heavy bill of expenses, he appropriated to his own use money which he had collected for a client. He was disbarred; he lost his house and library; he was forced to leave Chicago; he spent his last years as assistant librarian of the

Public Library of Detroit; he died, I fear, without a Christian hope. But why should I say this? May not the mercy of the Savior, to whom at least once he turned in penitence, have given him before he died a renewal of those religious aspirations and resolves which he disclosed to me when in old North College he waked me at dead of night to tell me that he wanted to be a Christian?

John Milton Holmes was my chief competitor in college. It was he with whom I divided the Deforest Prize Medal. He was much older than I—in fact, he was the oldest but one of the members of our class. He was tall and stalwart, with an air of rollicking good humor that was irresistible. He had had all sorts of experience. He had been cashier of a bank, editor of a newspaper, daguerreotype artist, contributor to magazines, teacher of country schools. He had an endless stock of comic stories. He would regale for hours a company in a parlor or a literary society in its hall. He had read, as it seemed to his college mates, the whole circle of English literature. He talked with confidence, and even with eloquence, on every conceivable subject, educational, political, or religious. He was a good deal of a poet, and some of his effusions, like the "Battle of the Ball," which celebrated the first football game of our college course, had the swing and lyric spirit of Macauley's *Lays of Ancient Rome.* Withal he was a man of industry and a first-class scholar. While I took only a Dissertation, he took a High Oration. Everlastingly popular, with abounding health, and confident that he could work without limit, he burned the candle at both ends and wasted his strength. He was as poor as Perkins, and through most of his course he paid his way by tutoring a backward classmate. The days were spent in teaching or in recitations; the evenings were devoted to smoking, drinking, and endless storytelling; after all others had taken to their beds, Holmes would spend a large part of the night in preparing his own lessons for the succeeding day. As we were obliged to be at prayers at half-past-five in summer and at half-past-six in winter, his time for sleep was often reduced to one hour or two. And yet he was preparing for the ministry. The truth that the laws of our physical nature are laws of God had not yet dawned upon the student world. Holmes never seemed to suspect that his Bohemian life, his example of dissipation, or his abuse of his own strength was wrong either to God or man. (So Edward Payson would preach and pray like a seraph on Sunday, eat pound cake and mince pie before retiring to rest, and then wonder that Satan was let loose upon him on Monday.) Holmes graduated with many honors. His early ministry was most promising and successful. But he soon developed disease of the lungs, broke down utterly, traveled for his health, but in vain. He died after a very few years, the victim of his own unconscious folly. And yet I do not know but I myself would have met the same fate had it not been that early weakness taught me to husband my energies. Poor Holmes! His was a rich and luxuriant nature, taken far too soon from the world he might have blessed.

Before I permit John Milton Holmes to vanish from the stereoptic screen, I feel inclined to tell over again one of his stories. John Milton's stories were always founded in fact, but the drapery was not always so trustworthy as the figure which it hid. A half dozen of us were in New York on our way home after a term had ended, and we spent the night at the Metropolitan Hotel. After a late supper, we got to spinning yarns in a large room with several beds. Holmes was in his glory, and he made it a memorable night. He told the story of a Spiritualistic Bank of which he had been cashier in Chicago. The president was half crazy and under the influence of a medium determined to invest his whole fortune in this practical demonstration of the truth of spiritualism. At the request of the president's wife, Holmes went into the bank to save what could be saved from the approaching wreck. At first the only peculiarity of the institution was that its larger operations were conducted entirely at the dictation of the spirits. Every question of discounting a note was referred to mediums who sat for regular business in a room above the office and secured appropriate advice from the supernatural world. After this feature of the concern was noised abroad, there was naturally a larger number of notes presented for payment than was desirable. The question whether payment should be granted or refused was also referred to the spirits. People were likely to be indignant at being compelled to wait: two stalwart Irishmen were stationed before the counter whose business it was when any of these people made trouble to snake them incontinently out the back door. The president's conception of the mission of the bank grew larger as time passed. He came to believe that the institution was called upon to land a great reform in the matter of diet. Human nature required nothing but vegetable food: a meat diet was a sign of the fall and was distinctly demoralizing. And as beans contained the greatest amount of nutriment in a given compass, the race of man was to subsist upon beans. All the employees of the bank were therefore required to confine themselves to this article of food. Barrels of beans were stored in the cellar; quantities were baked daily; there was a special table on which beans were served in the shape of soup; they were boiled, scalloped, and fricasseed; indeed, no method of preparing them known to culinary science was ignored. Holmes could stand the discounting of notes and even their payment at the will of the spirits, but he drew the line at beans. His soul abhorred that meager diet, and he one day rebelled and took a generous beefsteak at a restaurant around the corner. On his return the president met him with a revolver, accused him of being a traitor, and was about to blow out his brains. Holmes thought it a poor rule that would not work both ways, told the president it was all a mistake, that the spirits themselves would testify that he was all right. They went together to the upper room; the spirits were consulted; they declared that Holmes had done no such thing as the president had accused him of. John Milton had learned the art of securing communications from the spirits on his own account.

Soon after this, the president received a message from the spirit world informing him that the bank was to introduce a great reform in the matter of dress. Mankind had departed largely from the simplicity of Eden, and that simplicity was to be gradually restored. He appeared at business therefore in a garment resembling a long white nightgown, tied with a blue ribbon around the waist. All the employees of the bank were ordered to don garments of the same sort. As time was manifestly needed to prepare these garments, Holmes secured a brief respite and took his opportunity to make known the condition of things. At night he removed all the funds from the vaults and put them in a secure place. When the bank opened the next day, there was a howling mob and the office was wrecked, the president appearing on the balcony, which opened out of the upper room, and haranguing the crowd. He was taken into custody, was adjudged insane, and the drama was over. But it was

not over for Holmes. He had become entangled in the toils of
spiritualism. Beginning by producing raps and feigning to write out
communications from the other world, he ended by being beset with
raps which he did not consciously produce and finding his hand
compelled to write communications which were utterly strange to
him. Some of these communications were so true as to frighten him.
To test the matter, he asked the spirits one Sunday afternoon what
text his father was preaching from a hundred miles away. A text was
written out which he did not remember even to have been in the
Bible. But with the help of a concordance he found the text and on
writing to his father found also that he had preached on that
identical text that Sunday afternoon. But Holmes concluded that
the whole thing was too uncanny to be continued. That night as the
spirits began to knock upon the head of his bed, he commanded
them in the name of God to depart and never return to him. The
rappings ceased, and he was never again disturbed. Let some old
resident of Chicago give testimony in this case. It would be
interesting to know how much of truth there was in Holmes's story.
Si non è vero, è ben trovato.

Frank Butler entered college at the beginning of the
sophomore year. He was older than Holmes—was, in fact, the
oldest man in our class. He had made preparation for college ten or
twelve years before, but ill health or insufficiency of funds
compelled him to go into business. He attained a good position and
made money, but he wished to preach the gospel and to secure a
classical education so that he might preach. When he came among
us, he must have been thirty-five, if not forty, years of age. But he
was a born gentleman; he put on no superior airs. The modesty and
humility with which he bore himself in presence of teachers and
scholars was worthy of all praise. He had a fund of practical
information which no one else possessed. He was *au fait* on all
matters of etiquette and society. His essays, read in class, were
models of mature sense as well as of elegant expression, and there
was a delicate humor about them which provoked universal
admiration. Although the essays were not profound in thought, all
recognized their excellent level of ability. Butler infused into the
class just the element which it lacked—a high tone, a gentlemanliness which never condescended to be rude, a superiority to

underhanded ways in politics, and a humorous contempt for splurging in public speech. But his most important influence was religious. To many of us, Francis Eugene Butler's example of Christian living rectified our mean ideals and made it impossible any longer to say that religious life in college was an impossibility. I believe that from my first contact with him I felt the necessity of being a gentleman and a Christian. I do not remember that he ever directly addressed me on the subject of religion, but I do remember times when his delicate criticisms, half hidden in a veil of genial and affectionate talk, made me feel that my whole life was wrong and that I must change or die. He was a truer friend than most of my associates. He stood by me when I became a Christian, strove to help me in the forming of new associations, got me invited into some of the best society of New Haven. I owe him more than I can tell. Yet he too met an early death. After studying theology at Princeton, he became a chaplain in the army. After an engagement he was carrying help to the wounded. A rebel sharpshooter, unmindful of his chaplain's uniform, picked him off with a bullet, and Frank Butler died, a knight without fear and without reproach.

When I come to speak of the men who still live and are doing their work in the world, I feel that I must be more sparing of description. Moses Coit Tyler was always a jolly good fellow. The word "Coit" had somehow never been introduced into his name in college days. In scholarship he was just one notch ahead of me, but in speaking and writing he did not rank so high until the very close of the course. In his commencement oration Moses blazed out like a new star. When he satirized the preachers who denounce the sins of the Amorites, the Girgashites, the Hivites, and the Perizzites but speak very softly of such modern sins as avarice, drunkenness, and slaveholding, the audience burst out in thunders of applause. We thought in college that Moses was something of a crank. There were times when he shut himself up in an unaccountable way and came out only after a sort of bombardment of his apartments. But he was always good-natured and never dissipated. In our freshman year I remember his asking me what I proposed to do in the world. When I said that I was going to be a preacher, he was greatly taken aback. That, he declared, was his own purpose. That an ungodly youth such as I was at that time should have any such plan of life must have been a mystery to him. Indeed it seems now almost as much of a mystery to me. Moses has since blossomed out into a charming preacher, a professor of history, and a famous writer on American literature. I count him one of the noblest and best of my surviving classmates, if indeed I would not put him at the head of them all.

Arthur Wheeler was a curious compound in those days. He, with Butler and Holmes, was a High Oration man, while I took a Dissertation and Tyler only a First Dispute. Accurate scholar as he was, Arthur had a heart in him, and Perkins and I soon found it out. Between Wheeler on the one hand and Perkins and me on the other there grew up a peculiar tie, more like the romantic attachment of Damon and Pythias than anything else. Perhaps Wheeler never realized the affection he inspired. At times indeed he seemed to repel it. He had very strong antipathies, and the vocabulary of objurgation which he employed was more varied and startling than I have ever heard from any other human being. His imagination seemed occasionally to run to spiders and snakes, and we conceived a salutary fear of his maledictions. But we always cherished respect for his opinions and believed in his friendship. When we reached the end of our junior year, Perkins and I made a compact that we would never be separated from Wheeler and that either all three of us would go into Skull and Bones together or none of us would. One night about two o'clock I was roused from my slumbers by heavy rapping on my door in old South Middle. Fifteen men entered and ranged themselves like a *Vehmgericht* around the room while I stood in nightshirt and trousers before them. They solemnly informed me that I had been elected a member of their society and asked for my acceptance of the election. I replied that this depended upon who my associates in the society were to be. They said this must be left to them. I answered that I was willing to leave most of the selections to them but I desired at least to know whether Wheeler was to be included. They declined to give further information. I then declined the election, and they filed out of the room in the same order in which they had entered. They proceeded immediately to the room of Norman Perkins, which was directly above my own, and there precisely the same drama was enacted. I retired to rest, supposing that the end had come. But about four o'clock in the morning there was another knocking at my door, and the fifteen Skull and Bones men entered once more. This time their leader, who was none other than Chauncey Depew, condescended to argue with me. But I stuck to my resolve, and they once more departed, only to meet with the same reception in the room above. So Norman and I were left out of Skull and Bones, all on account of our devotion to Wheeler. Whether Wheeler ever learned of it, I do not know to this day. But the result of our declination was that the class turned to us as one man, and I was elected class orator and Perkins, class poet. I have never been sorry for our chivalrous espousing of Wheeler's cause, for he has proved himself in these later years an able and even a briliant teacher of history in his professorship at Yale; more than any other man he has secured the array of splendid buildings which now adorn the campus, and both in my visits to him and in his visits to me he has been always the same strong and acute, yet gentle and tender friend.

Secret societies at that time were all class societies. In the freshman year I was a member of Delta Kappa; in the sophomore year, of Kappa Sigma Theta; in the junior year, of Psi Upsilon; in the senior year, but for the compact I have just described, I suppose I should have belonged to Skull and Bones. Besides this last organization, the only other senior society was Scroll and Key. No one of the societies to which I belonged had in it any element of dissipation. All were literary in their purpose. They promoted sociability, but the nearest approach to drinking was a bowl of weak claret punch, which appeared on special occasions only. Smoking was usually indulged in after the literary exercises were over. There was a good deal of effort to make the secret societies useful in college politics; perhaps the worst effect they had was that they made their members clannish and indisposed to recognize the merit of men in any other society than their own. It is amusing now to remember how many bacchanalian songs we sang and how exceedingly little we drank. The air of mystery and good fellowship was very enticing, and without being a member of some society a man had no great standing in his class. The initiations were remarkable affairs. On one occasion the medical college was secured as the scene of operations, and candidates were drawn up by a rope through the flue through which corpses were raised to the dissecting room. On another occasion the candidate was court-martialed on some specious charge, condemned to die, and shot by a file of soldiers, of course with blank cartridges. At the same moment that the soldiers fired, the floor gave way underneath the victim; he was seized by fiends, put into a coffin, and carried out for burial. The story is that a tall westerner endured his initiation very complacently until his tormenters attempted to nail down the lid of his coffin, when he sprang out, laid about him right and left, reached the open air, and exposed the whole business. My personal knowledge extends to nothing so bad as this. We did have chapel rushes and considerable hazing. In my freshman year one of my class was smoked out and then ridden on a rail. Those who were thus treated had usually made themselves obnoxious to the sophomores by superior airs unbecoming a freshman.

In our sophomore year Kappa Sigma Theta dissolved, and a proposition was made to establish a secret society upon a new basis. Hitherto, however good a society might be and however delightful its associations, these associations came to an end with the year, and its members were then scattered. The new society was to continue through the whole course. It was to include eleven men from each class, and these were to be the brightest and the best, the men who had taken the highest honors in scholarship, composition, and debate, and who had shown themselves to have marked social gifts besides. Our standard was certainly higher than that of any existing society, and we succeeded in making our selections conform to our standard. The men who composed the society were Frank E. Butler, Edward W. Hitchcock, John Milton Holmes, Levi Holbrook, Joseph C. Jackson, Norman C. Perkins, Moses Coit Tyler, James Marshall, Smith Harris Hyde, Joseph P. Buckland, and I. I doubt if so noble a set ever gathered before in any secret society of Yale. The society was to be not only the *crème de la crème* but secret of the secret. It had no name, no officers, and no records. But it did have a hall, with a big iron door and an enormous brass key. The resources of the society were exhausted in paying for the door, so that after the door was passed, the hall had the aspect of the holiest place of the temple at Jerusalem when the Emperor Titus entered it—it was pretty nearly empty; but for a rough table and eleven cane-seat chairs, there was absolutely nothing. But behind that iron door there were readings and talks that would have done credit to the *Noctes Ambrosianae* of Christopher North. There Holmes and Perkins and Jackson and Holbrook were in their glory, and friendships were cemented which have lasted through all our after lives. We sported a wonderful pin, a winged globe surrounded by a golden serpent which was engaged in devouring its own tail. The serpent had a ruby for its eye, and both serpent and globe had for a background a Maltese cross in the corners of which were eight minute diamonds. The law of the society was that no member was ever to answer any question about it propounded by an outsider and never to speak of it except to a fellow member. When the pins were "swung out," there was a sensation. It was at once perceived that this society was a self-constituted aristocracy, and this drew upon its members the envy or the hatred of many who had not been so fortunate as to be invited to join it. It was suspected, moreover, that our intention was to make it a course society instead of a class society, and everybody could see that this plan, if successful, would undermine and ruin all the existing secret societies of the college. The result was that not only our own class but also all the other classes combined against us. All that ridicule and argument could do, combined with threats of social ostracism, was done to discourage and frighten our men. The pressure became too great for some of our members to bear. We folded our tents like Arabs and silently stole away. The society had a farewell meeting, disbanded as quickly as it was formed, sold its iron door. Each member gave his pin to the girl he loved best—I gave mine to Cousin Carrie Hopkins—and the places that had known the *Innominata* knew it no more forever. It was a bold but a vain attempt, ideally praiseworthy, but beset with practical difficulties, to found a secret society upon grounds of merit only.

I cannot conclude my reminiscences of the *Innominata* without a brief account of Levi Holbrook, for he and I are its only surviving members.[1] I have said that he was the valedictorian of our class. He was certainly our most thorough and finished scholar. Indeed, I believe that when we graduated, he was reckoned, upon the ground of his marks in examinations, the best scholar Yale had yet produced. He had a well-to-do father, who took pride in his son and

---

[1] Strong added the section on Levi Holbrook later, probably in 1917.

paid his way generously through his college course. Holbrook took the first rank in Williston Academy, his preparatory school. He came to Yale with the ambition to carry everything before him. And he did it, but so quietly and easily that he disarmed envy and was popular with all but those who hated work and discipline. Even the lazy had to confess that Holbrook's past faithfulness in study had made his after course easier than theirs.

He was one of my earliest and best friends, in spite of the fact that my scholastic ambitions were not the same as his. I admired the quickness, accuracy, and elegance of his mind, and our common love for literature was a bond of union between us. Let me give a single instance of his scholarly ability. One day I called on him just before a recitation. To my surprise, he said, "I have not yet looked at my lesson. Sit down while I read it over." It was a whole page in Greek prosody, with extracts from the Greek poets for illustrations. In ten minutes more the bell rang; we ran over to the recitation room; Holbrook was the first called up, and he reeled off every word of that difficult lesson, Greek verses and all, as perfectly as if he had had hours for preparation. Such mastery gave me a sort of awe; I never could attain to it. Holbrook and I have been fast friends through all these following years. Failing eyesight and failing health turned him from teaching to finance. He went into Wall Street, became an expert in railway securities, a member of the Century Club, and the owner of a great apartment house on 59th Street and Central Park. In 1917 we visited him at his summer home on Lake Winnipesaukee. We communed together of the days that are no more and resolved that we two surviving members of the *Innominata* would stick together till we died.

I do not know that the secrecy of these college societies was of any real use. Whatever good they accomplished might have been better without the oaths and the flummery. The secrecy was essentially puerile and pretentious. There was really nothing to be reticent about. Or if there was, it was only some discreditable scheme of college politics, some plan to poll all the votes of its members in a contest for the presidency of Linonia or The Brothers, which would not bear the open daylight. I believe that college secret societies have prepared many men for the stratagems and spoils of Tammany. It is better for college men to act in the open as they will have to act when they get out into the world. And this leads me to say that the government of a large college like Yale is a better object lesson to the student than the government of a small college like Rochester, for the reason that in the small college personal government is more common, while in the large college the government is conducted according to general principles. It is a good thing for a young man to learn in college that there is a reign of law and that law will be executed impartially without fear and without favor. Let him be treated in college just as he will be treated in the world; let him be judged according to his deeds; let social position or wealth count for nothing if he does wrong; let poverty count for nothing if he does right. This was the spirit of Yale in my time. The faculty had a democratic form of government. Not the president, but the faculty, by majority vote, decided cases of discipline, and general laws were rigidly enforced. And the student body was democratic also. No one asked whether a student was rich or poor—the only question was whether he came up to a proper standard of scholarship, honesty, and good nature. A man was found studying in bed on one of the coldest winter days because he had no money to buy coal, but he was as much respected as any man in the class because he was a first-class scholar. A subscription was quietly circulated; money was raised; while he was absent in recitation, coal was put in his bin; he never knew where it came from.

Perhaps some note ought to be taken of surroundings, customs, and expenses. For the first two years of my college course I roomed out of the college buildings, at No. 10 West Chapel Street. In those days it was difficult for a freshman to secure a room in college. But I was chiefly influenced to room outside by the example of Luther M. Lee, a senior from Meadville, Mississippi, to whom I brought a letter of introduction when I entered. He had boarded and roomed at No. 10 West Chapel Street for the three previous years. For my board I paid $3.50 and for my room, fire, and lights $1.50 more. There was a pretty little daughter of my landlady, Miss Sallie Collins by name, who made herself very agreeable and to whom I might have become permanently attached if she had only had more of education and social advantage. As it was, I managed to while away in her company altogether too many evenings that might have been better given to study. Now that she is a grandmother, I can safely praise her bright and cheery ways and wish her all manner of blessings both for this world and the world to come. Her home and table were places where Holmes and Perkins, Wheeler and Southwick continually met. In my junior year I felt the need of getting in with the current of college life, and I roomed at 54 South Middle; in my senior year I was transferred to 124 North College, and for that year only Norman Perkins was my chum. The last time I was in New Haven, I revisited these scenes of the past, but everything seemed changed and desolate. The merry faces were gone, and youngsters were occupying my ancient haunts. I noticed that smoking had become far more nearly universal than it was in my time. Then I think that no more than one-third of the students smoked. Now it would be within bounds to say that two-thirds of the student body are smokers. My college expenses were $550 for the freshman year, $650 for the sophomore year, for the junior year $750, and for the senior year $850. These sums included traveling and books. I fancy that the modern youth spends from 50 to 100 percent more than I did.

I have reserved the account of my religious awakening until this point of my narrative because some knowledge of my college surroundings and companions is necessary to the understanding of it. In fact, to make my conversion intelligible, I must go back to my childhood and tell something about my mother's influence upon me. She was a deeply religious and a most conscientious woman. I doubt whether any mother ever lived who sought more continually to train up her children in the nurture and admonition of the Lord. One of the earliest things I remember is her taking me into a dimly lighted closet every Saturday afternoon after the day's work was done and kneeling with me beside a chest while she taught me how to pray. I remember her suggesting to me the thoughts and, when I could not command the words, her putting into my mouth the very words, of prayer. I shall never forget how, one day, as I had succeeded in uttering some poor words of my own, I was surprised by drops falling upon my face. They were my mother's tears. My mother's teaching me how to pray has given me ever since my best illustration of the Holy Spirit's influence in prayer. When we know not what to pray for as we ought, he, with more than a mother's skill and sympathy, helps our infirmities and makes intercession within us while Christ makes intercession for us before the throne.

Mother taught me very early the verses of familiar hymns, and after she could afford a piano, she used to sing and play these hymns to my great delight. It was simple music. On weekdays it was

> Flow gently, Sweet Afton,
> Among thy green braes!

On Sunday afternoons it was

> Mary to the Savior's tomb
> Hastened ere the break of day.

She had a soft, sweet voice, and the tender words sank into my soul. My mother was not demonstrative, and words of affection were rare, but I knew that she loved me, and in my childish way I returned her love. One day I was bitten by a dog. There had been much talk of hydrophobia, and mother was alarmed. I shall never forget how she uncovered the place, laid me upon the bed, and with her own lips she sucked out what she feared might be the poison. I have no manner of doubt that she would have sacrificed her life for mine. She was deeply interested in my early religious impressions. When I was ten or twelve years old, I attended a prayer meeting with her and became so thoughtful that after reaching home I took refuge behind the stove and meditated upon my duty to God while my mother walked softly lest she might disturb me. On more than one New Year's Eve I went to my bed solemnly impressed with my sinfulness and convinced that I ought not to begin another year without giving my heart to God. At the age of fifteen, I came under the influence of Charles Hibbard, a theological student whom my parents had consented to board. He warned me against sins of impurity in a gentle and affectionate way for which I have always been grateful, and he gave me a sort of desire to follow his example and be a missionary to the heathen. As I have already said, I entered college with the impression that I should someday be a minister of the gospel. And yet in spite of all my early education, I was at heart very far from the kingdom of God. I had had many convictions of duty, but the will and the power to obey were yet lacking.

Two letters which I received about this time are treasured up in my mind as among the influences which contributed to my conversion. One was from Cousin Jenny Farr. She had always exercised a sort of fascination over me by the mere fact of being older and being a woman. When she wrote to me urging me to be a Christian, I felt deeply grateful. Though I did not at once change my course, I could not forget her interest or her prayers. And the other letter was one from Cousin Lillie Fowler. I remember my surprise that a young lady of my own age should be interested in my religious welfare. The very fact that I cared so much for her as a correspondent and friend gave her words a peculiar impressiveness and meaning. She never will know how much she did for me. But I did not then sufficiently feel my need. As I now view it, my selfish, ambitious, reckless life for three years in college was permitted by God in order to convince me that I was a great sinner and helpless in my sins unless God should have mercy upon me. My moral standard was rising every day as I saw before me in the faculty and among the students good men and true who lived a different life from my own, while at the same time my estimate of myself was falling till at times I was hateful to myself. I was subject to great temptations, and though I was preserved from the worst sins, I became increasingly fearful that I might ruin my soul for time and for eternity. It was at the close of the second term of my junior year, in April, 1856, that I stood one spring-like afternoon in front of the old college chapel while the bell was ringing for evening prayers. My thoughts were wandering to the ends of the earth, when I felt a hand laid upon my shoulder, and a trembling voice uttered the words, "Strong, I wish you were a Christian!" I turned and saw Wilder Smith, the man who had sat for nearly three years next to me in the recitation room. He was a plodding student but not a man with whom I had been intimate, or whom I greatly liked. But this was the first word anyone had spoken to me upon the subject of religion since I had entered college. I saw that it had cost Wilder an effort to utter the words. They struck a chord in my soul that had not vibrated before; I replied, "Thank you. I ought to be a Christian, I know; I will think about it." It was the only word he spoke, and I had no time to say more, for the bell began to toll its few last strokes, and we both passed rapidly in to our seats at prayers. It was the only word he ever spoke to me, and yet it haunted me until I closed with God's offer of pardon and began an earnest Christian life.

I must tell the rest of this story about Wilder Smith. He and I both became ministers of the gospel. I was a pastor in Haverhill, Massachusetts. One day I was surprised by a visit from Wilder. I invited him to stay with me over the Sunday. He preached for me in the morning, and I preached in the afternoon. After the second sermon we returned to my house on the hill, and we talked about old times. I had long ago resolved that when an opportunity came, I would thank Wilder for what he did for me. So I began, "Do you know, Wilder, that you did me the greatest service I ever received from any mortal man?" "Why, no," he replied, "what do you mean?" "Don't you remember," I continued, "how you spoke to me, about being a Christian that afternoon in our junior year?" "No," said he, "I do not remember it." And I could not recall it to his memory. It was probably one of many words for God which he had spoken to his classmates, and he had spoken them so often that he had utterly forgotten them. But God did not forget them, nor did I forget the word he spoke to me. It was a little thing to him—it was much to me, for the salvation of my soul seemed to turn upon it. I have often thought of it as an illustration of the question of the righteous at the judgment: "Lord, when saw we thee an hungered and fed thee?—When did we anything worthy of notice or reward?" But the Lord shall answer, "Inasmuch as ye did it unto one of the least of these, my brethren, ye did it unto me."

The spring vacation of 1856 began on the eighth day of April, and as I usually had done, I made my way homeward to Rochester. I reached the house on South Clinton Street late in the afternoon. Father and Mother were glad to see me, but I noticed that they did not propose to stay at home that evening to visit with me. Their interest was in the meetings of Mr. Finney. The great evangelist, who had revolutionized the town in 1830, and under whose preaching my father had then been converted, was now, twenty-six years after, conducting another campaign. The converts of the first revival had grown up to be the foremost men of the place, and they now stood round him like a bodyguard. A second revival was in progress, of even greater power than the first. I knew much about Mr. Finney, for I had visited my relatives in Oberlin, where he was monarch of all he surveyed. I had a salutary fear of him, for he had once looked down upon me with his eagle eye and had confounded me with the question why I was not a Christian. At the supper table after my arrival home all the talk was of the meetings, and although I had had little thought of spending my first evening of vacation in church, curiosity to see what all were talking of, the fact that all the others were going to hear Mr. Finney, and perhaps also some subconscious conviction that the concerns of my soul were decidedly the most important all moved me to go with the rest. The meeting that evening was held in the Bethel Church on South Washington Street, which afterwards was removed and became the Central Presbyterian. The house was packed with eager listeners, even the aisles being filled with chairs. My cousin Jenny, who married Mr. Farr, had walked to the church with me. I remember with gratitude a letter which I had previously received from her urging me to begin a religious life. We somehow got separated from the remainder of our household and were shown seats in the middle aisle, halfway back from the pulpit and at the end of the pew.

I remember nothing of the sermon or the service, until the very close. The novelty of the occasion and of my surroundings probably occupied my attention more than the truth that was uttered. I had no thought of personal responsibility or of being forced to a decision. But Mr. Finney evidently had a different view of the case. I saw his tall form bending over the congregation, and I heard him, with solemnity and authority, ask all who were convinced that they ought to submit themselves to God to rise from their places, pass through the aisles, and go into the room below. To me it was like a thunderclap from a clear sky. I knew that I ought to submit myself to God. I knew that to sit still was to deny this. For the first time in my life I felt compelled to act. For a moment I sat as if petrified. Then I said to myself: I will for once try to do my duty. I turned to Cousin Jenny, asked her if she could get home alone, and when she gladly said that she could, made my way out of the pew, through the crowded aisle, and down the stairs until I reached the room in the basement which had been kept for inquirers. There I found perhaps fifty persons scattered about, who, like me, had taken at least one step toward following out their convictions.

I sat at a distance from the rest, half ashamed of myself for what I had done and still more perplexed as to what still remained to do. Rev. Frank F. Ellinwood, the pastor of the church, came to me and asked me if I was a Christian. I told him that I was very far from it. "You have some feeling on the subject of religion?" "No, I have no feeling at all." "But, by your coming here you have virtually said that you know you ought to submit yourself to God?" "Yes," I replied, "I know I ought." "Will you, then, submit yourself to God, now?" "That is a great question," I answered. "I do not know what it means, and I do not know how." "But you know that you have been doing wrong all your life; will you begin now to do right? You have been living for self; will you now begin to live for God?" This simplified matters very much. But still the sacrifices and humiliations of a Christian life cast their shadows before me, and I responded, "I cannot tell what I should have to do; I do not know whether I am willing to promise." "You do not need to know beforehand, and it is impossible that you should know beforehand all that you would have to do. God knows, and God will tell you as fast as you need, if you are only willing to do his will. Nobody can see the whole way through the woods at the start. Follow the path, and the way will open before you. Will you submit yourself and your whole life to God, expecting him to teach you what your duty is?" I could only say again: "That is a great question. I do not know whether I am willing or not." "Well," Mr. Ellinwood replied, "you must decide that question for yourself. If you are ever saved, you must come to this point of submission, and you have more knowledge of the way now than you may ever have again. I will leave you for a few moments, and I will come back for your answer." So he left me to myself.

It was very wise treatment. God must have given him wisdom. The moments that followed were moments of struggle. I reviewed the past. I saw that I was a miserable sinner, that I had been living a wicked life, that I was in danger of being given over to my wickedness, that if I was ever saved there must be a change, that the chance to change was now given me, that the chance might never come again. I shuddered when I thought of going back to my old sins; I felt that a life of truth and righteousness was the only life to live; if that was to be the final life for me, why not begin it now? I could not see the future or tell what God wanted of me, but this one thing I did see, that he wanted my heart, my service, my life. Gradually the determination was formed within me that I would put myself into God's hands to do with me what he would. I could do nothing else, and I had a vague conviction that I should know, if I only followed on to know, the Lord. It seemed a long time before Mr. Ellinwood returned. But when he put the question once more: "Will you now submit yourself to God, expecting that he will teach you what to do?" I replied simply, "Yes, I will!" I do not remember that the pastor prayed with me or said anything further except to express the hope that I would soon find the light. I went out from the inquiry room, and the darkness outside seemed the very image of the darkness of my soul. All the way home I was saying to myself, "What a fool I have been to promise I know not what!" But then the good Spirit within me led me to respond, "God knows, and God will show me." And God *did* show me. When I reached the house, the family had retired to rest. I went into my room. The gas was lighted. I saw a Bible on the table. Then it occurred to me that God had pointed out the first duty. I had never read the Bible regularly. Now I resolved to study the Word of God and every day to make a portion of it my own. I read a chapter; I do not remember where. Then a second duty presented itself. I had never formed the habit of daily prayer. I resolved to seek God every day upon my knees. I bowed before him at my bedside, renewed the vow I had made to serve him, asked for wisdom and direction from above. But I had no feeling that God heard or that my prayer was answered. All I knew was that I had done the best I could. The rest I was compelled to leave with God. I lay down to sleep. The most critical day of my life was over, and my decision had been made aright.

I had no idea that night that I was a Christian, nor was I even sure that I had truly turned to God. But I now believe that night to have been the night of my conversion. It was indeed a very unintelligent conversion. I do not remember that I had any thought of the Lord Jesus Christ as the way to God or as the sacrifice for sin; much less did I regard myself as having come into any definite relationship of union or fellowship with him. Nor did I think of the Holy Spirit as in any way influencing me, nor of myself as dependent upon the Holy Spirit for wisdom or renewal. My associations at Yale and at Oberlin had been with those who magnified the human element in salvation, and my conversion was a purely New School conversion. To my mind, coming to God was an affair of my own will alone, and conversion was simply the giving up of my sins and the beginning of a life of obedience. Yet I now see that here were repentance and faith in the germ. I did hate my sins and wanted to turn from them. I did cast myself upon God for help and salvation, and though I did not realize it, this was a casting of myself upon Christ, who is none other than God manifested to help and to save; this was implicit reliance upon the Holy Spirit, who is none other than God manifested to enlighten and to regenerate. I had not enough faith to be *assured* of salvation, but I think I had enough faith to be *saved*. If I had died that night, I believe I should have had a place at God's right hand. It has often been very affecting to me that God could accept so ignorant and so self-dependent a consecration as I then made. It is an illustration of the great truth, on the one hand, that He will not break the bruised reed or quench the smoking flax, and, on the other hand, that He will lead the blind by a way that they know not.

I had made a decision to submit to God. What that involved I was yet to learn. As I went on, God taught me. When I rose the next morning, I told my parents what I had done the night before. There was a great union prayer meeting held at half past eight in the basement of the old Brick Church. It seemed a duty to attend it. When there, I heard those who desired to be Christians invited to rise. I rose with many others. I gave audible utterance to my desire that all should pray for me. And though I could not see that I made any progress, though in point of fact I seemed to myself to be getting more conscious of my darkness and helplessness every day, I continued every day to attend the meetings, both morning and evening, and every day to respond to the invitations that were given. I think I must have risen a score of times to ask for prayers. I felt that I owed a duty to my relatives and associates who were not Christians. Though it cost me a great struggle, I went to my cousin Hop Strong and urged him to go with me. In our own family, I remember a prayer meeting in which Father and Mother prayed, and I followed. Dear brother Henry then tried to pray but could not find words and broke out into crying. Oh, if I had only then had grace and sympathy enough to put my arms around him and encourage him to persevere! But I had no light or peace myself, and I could give none to others. I was seeking my own salvation, but selfishness was largely mingled with my efforts. I had not yet the love of Christ in my heart, and so I failed to win my own brother. But I have always believed that these tears of his were evidence that he wanted to be a Christian, and I have even hoped that the last great day might show that he had the broken and contrite heart. Though I did not do my duty to him then, I have not ceased to believe that he would yet confess the name of Christ before men and be at last confessed by Christ before his Father and the holy angels.

So the days went on until the three weeks of the spring vacation were over and the time came for me to return to college. I had read my Bible and prayed; I had asked Christians repeatedly to pray for me; and I had tried to influence my friends to take the same course I had been taking. Yet the favor of God seemed further from me than ever, and at times I began to doubt whether there was any use of further effort. God was teaching me my first lesson in Christian doctrine. I was learning the depth and enormity of sin. With all my striving, my sins seemed blacker and blacker. Might it not be that I had sinned away my day of grace and could never be saved? I went to the railroad station to take my departure. Father and Mother both accompanied me to the train. They were full of anxiety about me. Without a Christian hope, how could I safely encounter the temptation of college life? Would not all my good intentions and resolves vanish like a morning cloud? So they feared. But, thank God! *my* fear was greater still. I felt that the summer was past; the harvest was ended; and my soul was not saved. I said good-bye to my parents with a solemnity that I can hardly express. The conductor said, "All aboard!" The train moved out of the station. I took my seat, buried my face in my hands, and said to myself, "This train is taking me to hell!"

Then I began to meditate. Was God at fault or was I? It must be I. Had I done the right thing in breaking away from my sins and seeking my salvation? I knew I had done right. Was the promise of God to be trusted? I knew that it was. What had been the effect in my seeking? Then it flashed upon me that, after all, I had only been making an experiment with God. I had been unconsciously saying, "I will try this thing awhile, and I will see how it will turn out. If my effort fails, I can still go back and be as well off as I was before." No, I saw that this was unbelief and was giving the lie to God. It was not an experiment that he asked of me but the final and total consecration of my whole being and life to him. Even if he should never give me evidence that he accepted me, my duty was nonetheless clear to serve him as long as I lived. Though I never should have a moment of joy on earth, the only right thing for me henceforth was to be the Lord's, for time and for eternity. And God enabled me then and there, as the train rushed on, to give myself, not tentatively and partially, but finally and wholly, to him. I had no thought of Christ; I had no thought of the Holy Spirit; I thought only of God, and of surrendering myself to him. Nor did I have the slightest evidence, even then, that God accepted me. I only had the satisfaction of knowing that I had done all I could. To be out of hell was more than I deserved. Even though I never had a ray of light upon my path, I would serve God now and forever. I gave up looking for comfort and trusted God to give it or withhold as he pleased. I set my face like a flint to go back to New Haven a servant of God and to stand for him through thick and thin, whatever the consequences might be.

I have read of a certain young woman who found that a gold necklace was tempting her to vanity and ruining her soul—she therefore gave the necklace to her sister. In a similar way when I opened the door of my college room and saw a box of cigars upon the mantel, I perceived that these cigars might be my ruin, and I gave them to Norman Perkins. The humorous aspect of the gift did not occur to me till long afterwards. At the time I was only intent upon untying the cords with which Satan had bound me. I knew that smoking brought other things in its train—bad company, drinking, and a habit of self-indulgence. So I made short work of the matter by giving up tobacco altogether. Only twice have I smoked since that spring of 1856—once on our Class Presentation Day, when long pipes were handed round to all of us, and once in Paris at the great restaurant of the *Trois Frères Provençaux* when, in the summer of 1860, Elisha Mulford, Sam Scoville, and I had twenty-five cent cigars at the end of a famous dinner. It was well for me that I gave up the habit when I did, for I am sure that with my sedentary habits smoking would have been a great hindrance to my health and influence.

Norman Perkins, who roomed just above me in South Middle,

and the next year, when we became seniors, was my chum in North College, had first to be informed of the change in the purpose of my life. He received my communication gently and respectfully; only afterwards did I learn how deep an impression it made upon him. But I felt that I must make a clean breast of it to the college world. I therefore attended the Sunday morning class prayer meeting. It was the last place where I was expected, and my entrance caused surprise. But when I rose and told those present that I had come to the conclusion to change my ways, that I wanted to be a Christian, and that I begged them to help me and show me how, there was an unmistakable sensation. My classmates took me by the hand, encouraged me, prayed for me, and I felt that the Rubicon was passed—now I must go on, and conquer or die. It cost an effort to go into that room and tell my story there, for I had no triumphant tale to relate. I had no idea that I *was* a Christian, and I told them so. But then I was determined to be a Christian if I could only find the way. I went out of the meeting more downcast than when I went in. It seemed to me that every new effort only increased my darkness. It certainly made me feel intensely my dependence upon God. I had come out before the whole college, relying solely on the word and promise of God. If that failed me, I should be a fool indeed.

But I was not destined to fail, for God's word was pledged to me. I felt every day that I must search the Scriptures. There alone I hoped to find comfort. But my old habit of reading without reflecting was upon me. Chapter after chapter passed under my eye, but all seemed like an idle tale that signified nothing. One afternoon in May, however, I read the sixth chapter of Second Corinthians. The early part of the chapter made no impression upon me. But when I got to the last three verses, the word of the Lord came to my inmost soul. There I read, "I will dwell in them, and walk in them; and I will be their God, and they shall be my people. . . . saith the Lord, and touch not the unclean thing; and I will receive you, and will be a Father unto you, and ye shall be my sons and daughters, saith the Lord Almighty." The outer word seemed to become an inner word; God himself seemed to be speaking; light and power were communicated to me; I listened and believed. I said to myself, "I *have* come out from among them; I *have* bound my soul not to touch the unclean thing—sin. And here God himself declares that he will receive me and be a Father to me and that I shall be his son. The promise is mine; God, who cannot lie, has spoken it; I *am* a child of God!" And as I said the words, I felt that a tie was established between me and God more close and dear than any tie of blood. A thrill went through me as I realized my new relationship to the Eternal One. I could no longer keep from pouring out my soul in prayer. I shut up the book and knelt by my bedside, praising God for his mercy to me, a sinner. But the best was reserved for the evening. I sat at the open window. A soft low hum of insect life was in the air; the lights from the college rooms gave to the great elms a mysterious dignity and glory; the world outside seemed somehow elevated to the planetary spaces above and to be a part of a mighty universe in which dwelt and reigned a present God. Peace was mine, like a river that overflows its banks in spring. It was a calm joy the like of which I had never known before. At last, and for the first time in my life, I was right with God, and right with my own conscience. Now I had the right to live, and I felt within me the clear instinct of immortality. I was joined to God forever, and as I looked up to the stars that shone through the trees, I said to myself, "When those shall grow old and die, I shall dwell with God and shall partake of the life of God!"

I cannot describe the sweetness and beauty of living during the few weeks that followed. As I walked out in the early summer mornings, the warm sunshine that enveloped the earth and transfigured every meanest stick and stone seemed to me the very image of the all-encompassing love of God embracing and transforming even the miserable and the vile. I wandered into the woods. In a little clearing was an apple tree in full blossom. Strangely enough, an old man emerged from the thicket and, as he saw me gazing with admiration on the blossoming glory before me, simply said, "How like a Christian, adorned with the Christian graces!" And then, without further words, he departed as quickly as he had come. I felt as if it were the message of one of God's prophets to my soul. To be a true Christian became my highest ambition. I was offered the first presidency of Linonia, one of the great honors of a college course, but I declined it, wisely or unwisely, because I did not wish to turn my thoughts away from God and religion to the strifes of college politics. With Cady Eaton, afterwards professor of botany, I roamed through the forests and climbed East and West Rocks, collecting specimens of plants which I analyzed and preserved. It was a summer spent with nature and with God.

I tried to influence others to begin a Christian life. Often it cost a severe struggle to conquer my diffidence and address certain of my classmates. I remember starting with Buckland to go the post office. I went with the determination to speak with him about his soul. But, strangely enough, I could talk about everything else; when I tried to broach the subject of religion, words failed me. We walked all the way down and all the way back. Just as we were parting, in a sort of agony I blurted out, "Buck! I want you to go with me!" He knew what I meant. He had been expecting this all along. He answered most gratefully and kindly, but I was ashamed. Why could I not be frank about these matters of greatest concern? I have learned that the only way to make sure of doing our duty to others is to embrace the first opportunity and then to be instant, in season and out of season.

On the third day of August, my twentieth birthday, I was baptized by Rev. J. R. Scott in the First Baptist Church of Rochester. I was not at that time fully convinced that Baptist doctrine was absolute truth. But I knew that I must make a public profession of religion and must connect myself with some body of believers. I argued that, if I were immersed, I certainly should never be obliged to be baptized again, whereas other modes might prove to be insufficient and the profession might have to be made over again. I therefore related my experience, such as it was, to the First Baptist Church, and they accepted me. I had no particular joy in my baptism. Indeed, it was a disappointment to me that I derived no conscious benefit from my act of obedience. But I had an ever-increasing satisfaction in doing what I knew to be right and an ever-increasing abhorrence of the wrong. When I returned to college for my senior year, I went with the determination to do my duty and to be of use. I prayed that God would make me the means of converting others. And I had some success. On the Annual Fast Day, after a powerful sermon by N. W. Taylor, who looked as if he had risen from the sepulcher to preach to us and who declared that the sinner could turn to God whatever the Holy Spirit did do or did not do, I felt strongly moved to call upon two of my friends in their rooms and to urge them to give their hearts to God. I went to Sandys. I had hardly begun to talk to him when he yielded, said he wanted to be a Christian, and asked me to pray with him. We knelt, and he seemed then and there to surrender himself to Christ. I went to Hodge, and a similar scene took place there. Both these men, I think, began a Christian life. I was most concerned, however, for my chum Norman Perkins. One night, in the middle of the night, I was awakened by the opening of my bedroom door. There stood Norman in tears with broken voice saying that he was a great sinner and begging me to pray for him. I did pray, and he prayed for himself. I thought he gave himself to God. In meetings that were held in our rooms and even in meetings of the whole college my chum spoke and prayed. For a time he seemed to run well. But he did not give up smoking, and after a little his old habits of self-indulgence came back upon him. He gradually lost his interest in religious things, and when, several years after, I preached in Chicago where he was practicing law, I could not persuade him to come and hear me preach. Did he see inconsistencies in my life which turned him aside? May God forgive me if it was so! At any rate, his Christian course seemed to come to an end. But I still hope that under the ashes a spark of the divine fire continued to smoulder and that before he died, even though at the last hour, God brought him back from his wandering.

I wish I could say that my own Christian life grew more vigorous and joyful to the end of my college days. But I must confess with shame and sorrow that the light became clouded. I was disobedient to the heavenly vision of a few months before. Perhaps the very elation of success prepared the way for religious declension. I had begun with altogether too great confidence in my own strength of will, and I was left to discover that my own strength was weakness. Although my ambition was gratified by winning some of the highest prizes of the college course, I took little pleasure in them. I knew that there were nobler honors which I had missed. I had lost the quick sense of God's favor. The joy of his salvation had departed, and all because of my willful departure from him. I have come to believe that God permitted this in order to teach me my second great lesson in doctrine. I learned that God alone can regenerate. And the process was this: my willful transgression, after such experience of his forgiving mercy, wrought in me a profound conviction that I was not sufficient to myself. Only God could keep me true to him. My complete dependence upon him for *preserving* grace threw light upon my earlier experience and taught me that I then must have been the subject of *regenerating* grace. If without the help of God I could not *keep* myself in the Christian way, how without the help of God could I ever have *gotten into* that way? Yet in spite of my sins, I still believed that I had begun a Christian life. Nor had I any doubt what my calling in life was to be. From the moment I was converted, I knew that I must preach the gospel. All the more was I filled with despondency as I contemplated my own unfitness. The responsibilities of the ministry began to loom up before me. I knew that I must make a new consecration of myself to God. I longed to get away from New Haven and to have a quiet time for retrospect and prayer. When one of my classmates proposed to several of us that we spend six weeks immediately after our graduation in the woods of Maine, I welcomed the opportunity and eagerly accepted the invitation. It promised to be a retreat with Jesus in the wilderness.

I made my way to Boston where I was greatly impressed with Bunker Hill Monument, the State House, and Music Hall with its great organ and its bust of Beethoven. From Boston I proceeded by train to Skowhegan and thence by stage to Newport on Moosehead Lake. I can never forget my first sight of that wonderful sheet of water. It spread out its arms in every direction into the forest like the horns of a moose, and this gave it its name. The outlet into the Kennebec River some years before had been obstructed by a high dam. As a result the level of water in the whole lake had been raised many feet; myriads of trees along the banks had been killed; their trunks had fallen, and the bark had worn away until the whole shore, for all the forty miles of the lake's length, was thickly strewn with their whitening skeletons. On the afternoon when the stage descended the hilly road to the rude inn and steamboat landing at Newport, the sun was just setting, and a tremendous storm was coming on. The heavens were black as ink, and the waters of the lake reflected the blackness above them. Just two things remained to lighten up the landscape. One was the spectral arms of the skeleton trees that swarmed like ghosts along the shore, and the other was the fierce radiance of the setting sun that poured out a lurid light upon the inky blackness of lake and sky. I have seen many fearful aspects of nature in my lifetime, but never before or since have I seen anything that looked so like the very mouth of hell.

At the little hotel I met the men who were to constitute our party. They were Levi Holbrook, the valedictorian of our college class; Robert Brown, who now superintends the college observatory; Warren Southwick, whom Holmes coached through college; George S. Gray, who afterwards married the sister of Robert Brown; and a cousin of Holbrook's, named Longfellow, who was experienced in woodcraft and was soon recognized as commander of the party. At Kineo, halfway to the northern end of the lake there was a piece of level ground projecting from the eastern shore, and upon it was situated a hotel. Back of this promontory was a rocky bluff several hundred feet in height. The morning after our arrival we clambered to the top, having ordered boats to meet us at the northern end of the bluff where it sloped down to the water. We had gotten halfway down to the boats when one of our number proposed that we should do what never had been done before, namely, make our way to the hotel along the precipitous face of the cliff. There were ledges of rock that furnished a foothold, and there were occasional bushes on which we could secure a grasp. All assented to the proposition, and we made the start. There was no accident or difficulty till we came to a place about ten feet wide where the rock made a sheer descent of 150 feet to the water below. I was the last of the party. When I came to the spot, I was told by the men in front of me that the only way to cross safely was to turn my back to the rock and, with my heels, sidle along the narrow ledge. The path was certainly not as broad as one's hand; the water at the foot of the precipice looked deep and cold. I was entirely unused to such places, and my first impulse was to turn back. But my friends had gone before me and had succeeded—why should not I! To go back was to be a coward; so I pushed on. All went well till I reached the middle of the dangerous stretch; then my heel struck a smooth stone and in an instant slipped off the edge. The horror of the situation comes back to me as I think of it. A moment more and I should have plunged into the water below, had not a merciful Providence inspired me to throw up my hands and grasp a twig that waved above my head. It was just strong enough to prevent my fall. I slowly drew myself up to my place again and got a firm hold for my heel. When I knew that I was safe once more, my strength completely departed; I was white as a sheet; I could hardly make my way back to the hotel, though the rest of the path was easy. Strange to say, I told nothing of this experience to my companions. Perhaps the reason is that, at the moment that I recovered my foothold, I had an overpowering sense of the presence of God. It seemed to me that the Almighty had interposed for my deliverance by putting his own right hand underneath my foot and lifting it to a place of safety. I have had no manner of doubt since then that the Christian in his best moments, and the unregenerate man in his times of peril, may have a presentative intuition of God.

I felt after that experience, all through my wanderings in the wilderness, that I owed my life to God, that only his mercy had preserved me, that I belonged to him as never before. My companions were all Christian men. In the solitude of the forest or while sitting in my canoe I meditated much about my miserable past, and I made many resolves for the future. Nature was grand, but lonely also, and I threw myself much upon God in silent prayer. There were many incidents to enliven us. One evening just after sunset, at the mouth of a stream that emptied into the lake I saw the whole surface of the water alive with leaping trout—several times we caught three of them at one throw. At the dam over the outlet where the River Kennebec takes its beginning, I looked down into the deep water below and saw scores of great trout lying side by side as thickly as sardines in a box, but though we let down baited hooks under their very noses, not one of them would favor us even with a nibble. We went across the carry at the northern end of the lake to the River Penobscot, and then we made our way down the river to Mount Katahdin. The rain poured as we shot down the rapids; we sat all day in the water that filled the bottom of our canoes; we lay down in wet clothes on a few twigs cut from the hemlocks, with our feet to the campfire and with nothing but a bit of canvas over us. But we took no colds, and we slept soundly. We made the ascent of Katahdin, saw from the summit a vast wilderness with no visible human habitation—a sea of green, broken only by dazzling patches of water, by actual count forty-two different bits of lake and river—a sight such as I expect never to see again; camped out on the mountainside the same night without food or covering, but though hungry and chilled to the bone, we still caught no colds and went down next morning to the river as merry as larks. All but Robert Brown. He stirred up a nest of hornets and in fighting them lost his spectacles in the long marsh grass; as he was very nearsighted, life was a burden to him afterwards; to see Bob follow his leader and make random jumps from one stepping-stone to another over a rushing stream was a sight so funny that even the painfulness of it to him could not prevent our inextinguishable laughter. And so at Bangor association with my college classmates ended; they went their several ways, and I betook myself to Rochester, my early home, to pursue my course of study for the ministry.

I have one addition to make to the record, and that is a brief account of the class meetings that have taken place since we graduated. We were 107 men, counting 3 who afterwards received their degrees. The class of 1857 had a great reputation for scholarship, ability, and character. Our largest reunion occurred in 1860, and I reached home from Europe just in time to attend it. Almost all the old boys were there—Butler and Holmes and Perkins and Tyler among them. I find by looking at the printed report included in my volume of *Miscellanies, Collegiate and Literary* that I made a good speech at that meeting, though it entirely passed from my memory afterwards.[2] Ten years after graduation a second meeting was held, but how different was that! Our Civil War had been fought. Ten of our class had fallen in battle or had died as a sacrifice upon their country's altar. We met at Cady Eaton's beautiful home in New Haven. After supper, which lasted a couple of hours, the roll of the class was called. Those present responded for themselves in speeches and gave account of their doings. Letters were read from many of the absent, and of others report was made by their friends. When the names of the dead were called, tributes were given to their memory. A multitude of touching incidents were related, and the interest increased to the very end. The meeting held on till the morning light shone in at the windows and the chapel bell

[2] In his manuscript, Strong added a note indicating that this volume should not be confused with his later volumes entitled *Miscellanies* (Philadelphia: The Griffith and Rowland Press, 1912).

began to ring for half-past-five o'clock prayers. We formed in procession, walked into chapel, and listened to divine service as we had done in the days that were gone. Then we came out and separated with three rousing cheers for the class of fifty-seven.

And now I have just attended my fortieth class meeting. On June 29, 1897, thirty-six men gathered at Robert Brown's residence, in the grounds of the Yale Observatory of which he is director, for a luncheon party at noon. As many as could do so brought their wives and children. John and Lide came from New Britain, Connecticut, where they had just settled, and I had no reason to be ashamed of them, for they were both much admired. At nine in the evening the members of the class met for their class dinner. Sixty-six are living, and of these thirty-four sat down. After dinner, the roll was called as usual. But this time there was nothing like formal speech making. It was too serious an occasion for that. Each man told his own story simply or answered for the departed. I had greatly feared that the meeting would be gloomy, and I dreaded to attend it. There were indeed some sad features. Sam Scoville tried to lead us in some of the old rollicking songs. But our voices could not reach the high notes as they once did, and the merriment seemed rather hollow. The long list of forty-one dead, so many of them noble and precious souls, looked ominous enough, especially when every head was gray or bald and each man felt the pressure of some infirmity that witnessed that he had in him already the sentence of death. Some of my classmates assured me that I looked the youngest of the whole lot, but I attributed much of their good opinion to a kindly disposition. I was asked to preside and naturally reserved my own remarks to the last. The result was that I made my address at half-past-four in the morning, after the day had begun to break, and it was after five when I retired to rest at my hotel.

But such a meeting I shall never attend again. The old boys had wonderfully grown. Frankness, freedom, confidence, and character had developed. They were no longer afraid to speak their minds. In the case of many, their speaking was like the lifting of a veil—for the first time I looked into their hearts. Indeed, I felt that I had never known some of them before. Their accounts of struggles and successes, afflictions and achievements went to my soul. I felt ashamed that I had known them so ill. My heart went out to them all, in pride and sympathy and prayer. I appreciated the words of Tennyson in "In Memoriam":

> Regret is dead, but love is more
>   Than in the summers that are flown,
>   For I myself with these have grown
> To something greater than before.[3]

With all the rest of my class I had learned to love, and it was a delightful thought that love shall live and shall grow forever. Yet I could not have had this hope if I had not put my trust in Christ. The greatest decision of my life was that one which I made when I determined to stop short my career of selfishness and begin the service of God. My whole life turned upon that decision. From that moment I seem to myself to have been under the special care and leading of a divine Providence. I have been enabled to accomplish something in the world when, left to myself, my life would have been wasted. It was with gratitude to God that I reviewed the past the other day at New Haven. And among the things for which I was most grateful were the friendships that I formed at Yale. College men are together long enough to permit such friendships to crystallize. The average man absorbs himself in his family or business, but he has no time to make friends. Beyond all the discipline of college life, its broad outlooks, its noble examples, its acquisitions of knowledge, I put the value of college friendships. They grow upon me with every passing year. They teach me the immortality of love. The ties that are broken here shall be knit again in the great hereafter. Christ is preparing our mansions for us in the other world by gathering there one by one the friends we love best. Thackeray asks, "If we love still those we lose, can we altogether lose those we love?" The answer came to me the other night when we sang again at our class meeting these two old songs:

> Around the walls Yalensian the fleeting
>   years shall flow,
> But never bring the equal here
>   of fifty-seven, O!

---

[3] Alfred Tennyson, "In Memoriam," 131. 29-32.

and

> Soon shall we meet again,
>   Meet ne'er to sever
> Soon shall peace wreathe her chain
>   Round us forever;
> Our hearts will then repose
> Safe from all earthly woes
> Our songs of praise shall close
>   Never, no, never!

3

Seminary Days

My course of theological study was pursued at Rochester, and this was for several reasons. In the first place, Rochester was my home, and I felt it due to my parents that, after having so generously carried me through college, they should have the benefit of my time and company while I was studying for the ministry. Though I was not yet a firm Baptist, I was not sure that I could conscientiously unite with any other denomination of Christians, and I felt it safer to make my theological preparation at a Baptist seminary. This constituted the second reason for studying at Rochester. But there was a third, of greater weight than either of the two I have mentioned, namely, that Dr. Ezekiel Gilman Robinson at Rochester would be my teacher. He had begun his teaching in the seminary about the time I entered college. I had heard him preach in my vacations while I was visiting at home. His tall and commanding form, his clean-cut extemporaneous utterance, always thoughtful and incisive, sometimes rising into passionate eloquence, gave him a striking resemblance to Wendell Phillips and seemed to me the very ideal of a pulpit orator. As soon as I determined to be a Christian, I also determined to be a preacher, and I felt that I could have no instructor in theology or homiletics half as competent as Dr. Robinson.

He taught both of these branches, for the seminary was still in its infancy, and there was as yet but little division of labor. I count it an advantage that I came thus early under the doctor's influence. His dictations in theology had the forms of Princeton, but these were merely tentative—he himself was criticizing and inquiring and gradually working his way out from these forms into a realistic system more true to the facts and to Scripture. He encouraged us to criticize and to inquire, seemed to care little whether we agreed with him, as long as we formed opinions for ourselves, and never was so happy as when he stirred up a hot debate. This method of teaching was so utterly unlike anything I had known at Yale that it found me unprepared to make the most of it. I was very silent and timid in ordinary conversation; to mingle boldly in class discussions, to challenge the doctor and hold my ground was something I was quite unequal to. Fortunately we had older men than I in the class, men who were not afraid, and I drank in courage from their example. Little by little I accustomed myself to think, or rather I was compelled to think, and I regarded the two years I spent in Rochester under Dr. Robinson, in spite of the fact that I kept my mouth so tightly closed, as the real beginning of my intellectual history.

I had studied psychology and ethics in college and had taken some interest in them. But their relation to the great problems of existence had not been pointed out to me, and they had seemed to have no great practical value. Under Dr. Robinson all my ideas with regard to metaphysics were changed. I began to see that it alone dealt with realities, that, in fact, one could have no firm footing in any other department of knowledge unless he had reached a good metaphysical foundation. I was stimulated to read Sir William Hamilton. I studied in private his criticism of Brown and his *Philosophy of the Conditioned.* As Dr. Robinson himself was a convert to the doctrine of relativity propounded by Kant and taken up by Hamilton and Mansel, I naturally regarded this as the ultimate philosophy, and for many years it shaped my theological thinking. It took me more than a quarter of a century to see my way out of it. When I discovered that in knowing the phenomena we also know the thing in itself and that, instead of seeking to know the reality apart from the phenomena, we should be content to know the reality in and through the phenomena, it was a wonderful relief to me. Then I saw that God is not concealed by his manifestations but that in his manifestations we know him. But in those days all this was hid from me, and in some respects my philosophy became a fetter to me. Yet I came to see the inestimable importance of such studies, and I owe my interest in this fundamental work very largely to the influence of Dr. Robinson.

Besides our theological discussions, the class was required to construct and criticize plans of sermons. Here Dr. Robinson's acuteness was preeminent. His insight was quick as lightning. He could point out the weak spot in a skeleton with such precision and could so concisely state the needed amendment that these class exercises afforded a remarkable discipline of thought. The nearest approach to this work at Yale had been the requirement that every composition should be accompanied by an analysis of the course of treatment. But there had been no criticism upon the work after it was done, either as to its substance, its arrangement, or its literary style. This lack Dr. Robinson to a considerable degree supplied. He was a sharp critic. He abhorred vagueness of thought and vagueness of expression. He was himself a model of simplicity and directness. His few remarks by way of criticism were always illuminating and always practical. And the class supplemented his remarks by their frank and thoroughgoing exposure of the defects of the plan or the sermon which had been presented. Nott and Wilkinson and Sheppard, in particular, were mature men. They had had considerable experience in preaching as well as teaching. Their criticisms often cut deep. But they were given and received in good part, and they were of vast service to me. If I have ever attained clearness of thought and expression, I must give the credit largely to those hand-to-hand fights in the homiletical classroom. Dr. Robinson raised up a generation of strong preachers, and he did it by adding the teaching of homiletics to his teaching of theology. And how did he teach homiletics? In two ways: first, by compelling his students to production under criticism and, secondly, by compelling his students to criticize one another.

The classes of the seminary during my course of study from 1857 to 1859 were not large. My own class had only sixteen men connected with it. But among them were men of mark. I must mention three of them: Richard M. Nott was the older brother, the half brother, I think, of Kingman Nott, whose brilliant course as a preacher and pastor in New York City came to so early and sorrowful an end. Richard was an acute thinker. He was cold in temperament, but he was a great logician and a very able, just, and noble man. He knew the defects of his good qualities, and he lamented them. He could pursue a long course of subtle reasoning and present the results with unsurpassed clearness and cogency. But it was difficult for him to kindle with his theme. He dealt too much in abstractions. And yet he was a most godly man. He would have gone to the Hottentots, or he would have gone to the stake, at Christ's call. His piety and his intellectual grasp induced the First Baptist Church of Rochester to call him for its pastor even before he had finished his seminary course, and he served the church for six years. On a certain Sunday after I myself had been ordained, I was at home during a vacation, and I heard him preach. He gave a very clear, subtle, and able discussion of an important theological theme. But there was not the slightest indication in voice or manner that he had any but an intellectual interest in it. At the close of the sermon I spoke some words of commendation. He almost broke down when I uttered them. In a most mournful voice he said: "Oh, Strong! I can only discuss subjects! I cannot persuade myself that they have relation to anybody. I cannot put my *heart* into them!" And that was the fact. He could not get *en rapport* with his audience. He could not rouse or inspire them. He was a born thinker but not a born preacher. His work wore upon him. His health failed. He was compelled by signs of consumption to go south, and though he afterward took small pastorates, he never fully recovered. After fifteen years, crowded with many trials, which he bore with heroic patience, he died in Wakefield, Massachusetts, a man of whom the world was not worthy.

Nathan Sheppard was a man of precisely the opposite sort. He had not a grain of logic in his composition. There were no joints to his mind. Yet he had a most original and even startling power of observation and a great fund of undigested learning. He was a southerner from Baltimore. His mother had died early, and he never felt that he had a home. He was the most moody and variable of all men. There was no *juste milieu* with him. He was either on the mountaintops of felicity or in the depths of despair. He was so witty that in one of his good humors he would keep the dinner table in a roar. But often a bad humor would seize him, and no artifice could extort from him anything but silence or a gruff response. He had a brilliant imagination. He was a picturesque writer. But he had no sense of proportion, and his views of doctrine were hazy in the extreme. I have never met a man whose impulses were so unaccountable. At times he would take delight in saying the most brusque and rollicking things; then he would repent and confess himself a heartless idiot. Occasionally he took me into his confidence. He had great ambitions; yet he had great self-distrust. He wanted to be a spiritual man, but the routine of piety was very irksome to him. He had striking gifts as a speaker, and his little book *The Use of the Will in Public Address* is full of useful suggestions. But he was a sort of Bohemian, and it became a great question even in our seminary days whether he would ever consent for any long time together to be tied down to the regular work of the preacher and pastor.

At the end of our first year in the seminary my father asked him to accompany us on an excursion to Lake Superior. He was to meet us at Oberlin. Aunt Mary Hopkins invited him to spend the night with us at her house. Sheppard, however, was in a bad mood, and he made himself disagreeable from the start. He criticized the bed and the table, in spite of the fact that he was a guest. When we reached the steamboat at Cleveland, he was displeased with the stateroom we had provided for him. I suggested mildly that we must all try to make the best of possible discomforts and that this was essential to a pleasant journey for others as well as for him. Whereupon my friend simply closed his mouth and for two weeks spoke not a word. There was one exception. The lake was rough; Sheppard became seasick; this did not improve his temper. When we reached Marquette, he decided with the rest of the party to go ashore and lodge at a hotel. Father, Sheppard, and I were shown to a large room with three beds. Before retiring, Father proposed that we should have prayer. "Those pray that want to!" responded Sheppard, and while Father and I kneeled down, Sheppard divested himself of his clothing and jumped into bed. This insult to my good father was more than I could endure. I said as little to Sheppard thereafter as Sheppard said to me. With this single exception he was dumb as an oyster until we got back to Detroit, and there, without a word of farewell, he left us to go East. After a while I reflected that it would be unpleasant to have Sheppard's fit continue through the next seminary year. It occurred to me that I might possibly have provoked him by my criticisms. I wrote him a note expressing regret that our journey had been marred and hoping that our disagreement might not be permanent. Shortly thereafter I received from him a most brokenhearted letter of penitence. He accused himself of selfishness and perversity and ingratitude and begged me to forgive him. Of course I did so, and we were friends forever after. But he was careful from that time on not to expose me to any of his tantrums.

Mr. Rathbone of Albany was once entertaining Sheppard. It was a Sunday morning, and Sheppard was to preach. Breakfast was over, and the time for family prayers had come. But Sheppard had picked up a novel and had gotten interested in it. Mr. Rathbone took down the family Bible and said, "Mr. Sheppard, we will now have family prayers." Sheppard did not move. "Mr. Sheppard, we will now read the Scripture." Sheppard kept on reading his novel. "Mr. Sheppard, it is time for worship." Sheppard flung down his book, said, "Let us pray!" and got upon his knees. It was doubtful whether Mr. Rathbone or his family were edified by the prayer that followed. But in spite of these peculiarities, the young man had great gifts, and he became pastor of Tremont Temple in Boston. There he ran a brief and brilliant course. He was a sensationalist, and for a while he attracted attention. He exchanged pulpits with Charles Bridgman of Jamaica Plain. Rising in his friend's church to offer the invocation, he observed that the majority of those present did not bow their heads but sat bolt upright. When he came to the next prayer, he bent benignly over the pulpit and said, "As the congregation does not seem to make much of prayer, we will omit that part of the exercises." So he gave out a hymn instead. But one of the deacons did not sing. He walked down the aisle and out the door in great wrath, and Sheppard was never invited again.

Rockefeller Hall, the main building of the Rochester Theological Seminary in Strong's time.

The pastorate at Tremont Temple soon came to an end on account of Sheppard's instability and eccentricity, and my friend became a wanderer upon the face of the earth. He took to lecturing; he was professor of elocution; he lived in London as correspondent for American newspapers; he was shut up in Paris during the siege and wrote an account of it which was published by Tauchnitz; he returned to America and led a literary life. He became more and more morose; he lost his faith, or at least he ceased to cherish his old form of belief; he fell suddenly dead in the corridors of the post office in New York City. He had a warm heart, but his affection was wayward and impulsive; his love did not abound in knowledge and in all judgment; his talents were not under control of sober reason; lack of balance prevented him from using his gifts to permanent advantage. If he had only been able to put himself under discipline and submit to limitations, his brilliant gifts would not have been so nearly wasted.

And now I come to a seminary classmate to whom I owe so much and for whom I still cherish so warm a friendship, in spite of a great breach between us, that I must give more than usual time and pains to describing him. I refer to William C. Wilkinson. From the first day that I met him in class, I was drawn to him although there was a superior air about him that at the same time provoked me. He was the most natural critic I have ever met. The niceties of language were to him matters of most serious concern. At the same time he had a sublime confidence in his own judgment. Wilkinson was never so sure he was right as when the whole civilized world thought him wrong. The calm and self-sufficing air with which he would propound unpopular opinions was enough to take one's breath away. On a certain occasion a considerable company of ministers were discussing the custom of exposing the face of a deceased person to public view at a church funeral. One after another expressed himself in disapproval. The custom pandered to the vulgar curiosity of mere strangers; it wounded the feelings of sorrowing friends; it dissipated the effects of the preceding religious service. All were unanimous in wishing the custom abolished—all but Wilkinson. Though he was young and though he spoke last, he proceeded with cheerful confidence to declare his opinion that the custom was a salutary and impressive one; it was well for the living to become familiar with death; friends of the deceased should concede something to the religious welfare of strangers; the object lesson was better than the sermon. The calm dogmatism of my friend always reminds me of Whewell's remark: "We are none of us infallible—not even the youngest of us."

I remember his taking me in hand as we walked away from the seminary one day. Some little impropriety in my demeanor had attracted his attention, and he wished me to correct it. He could have gently intimated my fault, and I would have thanked him. But he treated a peccadillo as if it were a crime, and the *de haut en bas* manner of his reproof was such that I was tempted to self-justification and resentment. He was amazingly subtle and elaborate in his attacks upon error. He preached in a country village. He wished to show the nature of the influences that kept men from confessing Christ. He began by saying that his text was so peculiar a one that he would for once reserve it for the close instead of announcing it at the beginning of the sermon. Then he went through a long series of approaches—evil was present in many hearts at once. It was not the result of collusion; yet there was plainly, in it all, an intelligence and a design. The intelligence and the design were superhuman in their subtlety and malignity. It must be the intelligence and design of some evil being. And so he ended the sermon with his text "Ye are of your father, the devil." I am not sure that this ended his ministry in that community, but I almost think it ought to have.

The same oversubtlety and overelaboration marked his style. There was much thought but also much indirection. The roundabout was preferred to the direct, the complicated to the simple. I could give some extraordinary specimens, but I forbear. When Wilkinson afterwards came to teach homiletics in our seminary, the needs of his students to some degree opened his eyes, and he inculcated plainness of speech. Indeed, his own style was considerably modified and improved. He was a good teacher for men who were born with a rhetorical sense. Woe to the pupil who had no rhetorical sense! My friend made some fine point by way of criticism. The dull man could not see the point. The more blind he was, the more determined Wilkinson was to make him see. At last the man got angry; Wilkinson grew sarcastic; the man ended by losing all faith that his teacher was either a gentleman or a Christian.

Incapacity to take another's point of view and to make friends of his students spoiled the professor's work as a teacher and at last roused the whole seminary to such a pitch of opposition that we had either to dismiss the seminary or dismiss him. *Hinc illae lacrimae.* I did the best I could to save his feelings. But I had to side against him. And so a long friendship was broken, at least on his part. And now the Jew has few dealings with the Samaritan.

To Wilkinson, however, I owe very much in the way of minute criticism. With all his circumlocutions and qualifications, he was widely read in the best literature, particularly that of the poets. And he was himself a poet. I used to think he reveled in the form more than the sense. But he compelled you to weigh each word and justify or condemn the place each word occupied. The mechanism of verse was a matter of the deepest interest to him. Whether a dactyl or a spondee would best help the effect was a subject for an hour's discussion. He used to call me a purist because I always demanded the simplest and plainest speech. I used to call him a stylist because the style in his writing was too obviously an end in itself. But he set me to thinking more carefully about my ways of expression. He taught me that *c'est le dernier pas qui coûte.* Classic finish, completeness, clearness—how much they cost! Yet they are worth all they cost, and we should never be content without them. While Wilkinson was an ultraconservative on such subjects as dancing and inspiration, believing that inspiration is verbal and dance is essentially immoral, he was a wonderful liberal when it came to certain characters like Daniel Webster. Nothing could convince him that Daniel was addicted to drink, and his defense of the great statesman's course in advocating submission to the Compromises of the Constitution, fugitive-slave bill and all, was a model of shiftiness and special pleading. In the Pundit Club, which I once characterized as an association of gentlemen who could state their suspicions as opinions and their opinions as facts, Wilkinson was exceedingly popular. His quiet insistence upon the most astonishing proposi-tions, and the fine fencing with which he would defend them, always challenged a fight and made it interesting. But it was in private conversation that I got the most good from him. Both during our seminary course and when we were together afterwards as professors in the institution, a large part of our life and recreation consisted in walks and talks together. We were friends and counselors who never saw precisely alike but derived good from mutual contact and stimulus. After he broke with me in 1881, my world lost one of its treasures. I long tried in vain to reunite the broken bond. As I never gave up my affection for him or my respect for his courage and candor, I did not doubt that we should one day come again to understand one another.

Fortunately, the understanding came about—not in the next world but in this. After fifteen solid years of labor, Wilkinson produced his two poems, *The Epic of Saul* and *The Epic of Paul.* I did not for a long time read the first. I was indeed determined not to read it until he sent me a copy and gave me thereby a mark of restored friendship. In the autumn of 1896 I went to Chicago to deliver the convocation address before the university. He called upon me, and we had a pleasant talk. On returning home, I wrote to him that life was short and I could not be satisfied without making one effort for reconciliation before either of us died. He replied that he was of the same mind but that before complete reconciliation was possible some past matters must be explained. I told him I had not wronged him in any way and therefore had nothing to confess but that I would be glad simply to forget the past and begin anew. He accepted my proposition and sent me his first book. When I read it, I wrote him a letter congratulating him upon having written a great Christian poem, a poem that would live to bless the world. My commendation was none too high, for the psychology of Paul's conversion was never more accurately grasped nor the nobility of his character more grandly exhibited. I have yet to read *The Epic of Paul,* but I regard my possession of it as a proof that I have regained one of the best friends of my life.

Before I leave Wilkinson, however, I must tell about a former visit to Chicago. It was the time of the World's Fair. The University of Chicago had just started, and Wilkinson was professor of poetry. It was the first professorship of poetry since the schools of the prophets in ancient Israel in which the pupil was set to grind out poetry under the very eye and criticism of the professor. Oxford and Cambridge have professorships of poetry, in which the professor lectures and tells his pupils how and how not to do it. But actual production under criticism—this was left for Wilkinson to set agoing first in modern times. I asked him how the thing worked in practice. He gave me an encouraging answer. "What sort of poetry do they write?" I asked. "Why," he replied, "you would be surprised to see how good some of it is. The subjects, though, are often peculiar." "What sort of subjects?" said I. "Well, the other day a young man put on the board a poem entitled 'Ernest D. Burton.' Professor Burton was his teacher in exegesis, and the young man was so taken with his instruction that he wrote a poem about him." Wilkinson called to take me over to afternoon chapel service on Sunday. As we passed through the campus, I observed that workmen were hammering away in the erection of the new Kent Laboratory. "Professor," said I, "is this a Christian institution?" "We are not responsible for this," he replied. "The contracts were let without conditions, and the contractors are working on Sunday after the Chicago fashion." When we had found our seats in the chapel and President Harper's exposition of the prophet Joel was well under way, a great express wagon loaded with trunks thundered up under the windows, and the delivery began. After the interruption was over, I turned to Wilkinson and said, "Professor, is this a Christian institution?" "Oh," he replied, "Divinity Hall has been let to visitors for the World's Fair, and they come and go, just as at an ordinary hotel." In the evening we heard Professor Shorey in that same chapel talk to the Young Men's Christian Association of the university. His subject was the common element of the religions. He maintained that the Greeks had all that was important to religion and, in fact, that Socrates and Plato were in some respects in advance of Christ. Wilkinson was there, and I said to him, "Professor, is this a Christian institution?" But this time he did not answer. I could see, however, that the Chicago atmosphere had considerably toned down his early orthodoxy. He did not denounce and objurgate as he would have done twenty years before.

It was Wilkinson who, in our undergraduate seminary days, first induced me to preach a sermon. The schoolhouse in Irondequoit was used as a gathering place for Sunday evening worship, and for once there was no supply—would I consent to conduct the service? I consented, spent a Sunday afternoon preparing the outline of my remarks, and in the evening walked with Wilkinson to the place of meeting. It was a novel experience. I had talked to debating clubs, but never before had I attempted to expound a passage of Scripture so as to awaken and save men's souls. I have in my papers, written in lead pencil, the plan of those remarks. It is a model of all that a plan ought not to be. But my purpose was good. I sought the help of God. I did not enjoy the effort, but Wilkinson kindly said that the people did. The next Sunday I was asked to go out to the Rapids to superintend a little Sunday School in the afternoon and preach in the evening. I did not understand at the time how important a matter this was. But now I see that God meant me to serve an apprenticeship to my trade. There at the Rapids I preached for a year and a half, and there I gained an experience the effects of which will be lost "not till earth, and not till heaven, pass away."

The Rapids, as everybody knows, is the name of a knot of houses on the bank of the Genesee River, three miles south of Rochester. In 1858 the Genesee Valley Canal at this point ran parallel to the river, and here a large number of boats lay high and dry during the winter. The boatmen were men of the roughest sort. They spent their leisure in fighting, drinking, and playing cards. There were three grogshops, no church, and only one dilapidated schoolhouse. Into this schoolhouse on Sunday afternoons were gathered a forlorn set of children and a rude set of young people. Unwashed, low, and often bad, their needs touched the heart of at least one good woman. That woman was Mrs. Charlotte Stillson. She, with her husband, Mr. George Stillson, lived in the only decent house in that vicinity and cared for her aged parents, Mr. and Mrs. Turner. On Sundays after I had attended morning service at the First Baptist Church in town and had taught my young women's Bible class in the church Sunday School, I walked my three miles, often through rain and mud, to Mrs. Stillson's house at the Rapids. There I had a cold lunch and soon after went a little farther out on the Chili Road to the tumbledown schoolhouse, where I led the singing and superintended the school. We came back to Mrs. Stillson's for supper. After supper, and often with a lantern to light us along the miry road, we repaired again to the schoolhouse, which was dimly lighted with tallow candles and was crowded to its utmost capacity with an audience of seventy-five. There were fellows outside to throw stones through the windows and fellows inside to create every possible disorder. Somehow I managed to secure their goodwill, and they made me no positive trouble, though it was hard for the young women, without a guard, to get back unmolested to their homes. But all the while there was one quiet little woman whose influence was gradually subduing the community, and that was Mrs. Stillson. On weekdays she visited the parents and induced them to send their children to the Sunday School or to come themselves to preaching service on Sunday evening. Nor was it all talk. She made clothes for ragged urchins, got the mothers together and taught them how to sew, gave medicine to the sick and Christmas presents to the poor. If ever God sent an angel of mercy to a disreputable and ill-deserving neighborhood, he sent such a one to the Rapids in the person of Mrs. Stillson.

It was a good thing for me that I began my first continuous preaching of the gospel in such a place and with such a helper. My tendency in college was in the direction of rhetorical display. If my first sermons had been delivered in churches and to cultivated people, I fear that they would have been artificial and stilted performances with little power to move the heart. But at the Rapids, it needed only half an eye to see that rhetoric would be thrown away. Moreover, I had no time to construct elaborate discourses. My seminary studies occupied almost the whole week; only Saturday was left to prepare my address for Sunday evening. As a result, I wrote out nothing in full. I put down a brief analysis of my subject, taking the most evangelistic themes and treating them in the simplest and most illustrative way. But I felt that the souls of those people were laid as a burden on my heart and that before God I was responsible for them. I prayed for God's Spirit to help me, and I preached as a dying man to dying men. As I look back to that little schoolhouse and remember the hushed and awestricken way with which many of my auditors sometimes regarded me, their faces only faintly visible in the dim candlelight, I feel persuaded that God was there and working with me. I tried at any rate to preach the simple gospel of Christ and to bring those who heard me to immediate repentance and to faith in Jesus as their Savior. My observation of the methods of Mr. Finney was very valuable to me. I used a simplicity and a boldness that I should hardly have dared to use if I had not remembered his example. And many became interested in religious things. Some of the young people were soundly converted and grew up to be teachers of others. The foundations of the present church at the Rapids were being unconsciously laid. The power of the gospel has been demonstrated in the transformation of that ungodly and drunken community that gave our police more trouble than any other into an orderly, prosperous, and churchgoing suburb of Rochester.

All this would have been impracticable if Mrs. Stillson had not continually seconded my efforts. On a certain evening she invited some twenty young women to her house for talk and prayer. I read them the fifty-third chapter of Isaiah and told them about the suffering Savior who had died for them. I asked them one by one if they would not then and there submit themselves to him. Almost all of them declared that they would. We knelt in prayer. They prayed for themselves. It was a scene of weeping and crying for mercy. I think several found peace in believing before they left the house. Others gradually came into the light. Some went back to the world and to hardness of heart. But my experience in this little revival of religion taught me my third lesson in theology, namely, that the atonement of Christ is the effective and the only persuasive to faith. I had learned at my conversion the guilt and helplessness of sin. My subsequent instability had taught me that only God can regenerate. Now I learned the lesson that no man had a right to believe in God as a Savior except upon the ground of the sacrificial death of Jesus. And the way of it was this: the more thoughtful inquirers in my meetings were troubled about the way of salvation. It was not enough to tell them that God would forgive them; they needed to see *how* God could be just and yet justify.

I told them that God would change their hearts and make them new creatures: that did not provide for their past sins. Then I told them of a debt paid and a penalty borne for them upon the cross. That usually gave relief to the troubled soul. I remember the first case of a person who, under my very eyes, seemed to pass from death unto life. It was Miss Mary Monroe, who afterwards married Ves. Robins. She had been under deep concern for weeks. Her sins seemed to her very great, and she had begun to think there was no mercy for her. How could God ever accept so great a sinner? As I was talking with her, there came into my mind Dr. Candlish's hypothesis of a deferred atonement. I said to her, "Suppose Jesus had just come to earth but had not yet died. Suppose he should speak to you and say, 'I have come in pity to take upon me the guilt of all who will accept me as their substitute and trust me as their Savior. I will bear your burdens, pay your debts, suffer your penalty, if you only let me. But it is for you to decide whether you will have me bear your iniquities or whether you will bear them yourself. Will you now take me as your substitute, trust me as your Savior, make me your representative, put all your affairs into my hands?' " And even while I was uttering the words, a change passed over her face like the change from darkness to light. She said, "Now I see it! Yes, I will; I do take Jesus as my Savior! He has died for me, and I accept him!" So she learned that it was not a question whether Jesus would accept her but whether she would accept Jesus. Because of his finished atonement she could at once rejoice in forgiveness and salvation. I believe the Holy Spirit made the truth of Christ's sacrifice the means of her renewal and did this even as I spoke.

I am not sure that I did not learn more theology at the Rapids than I learned at the seminary. I now know that it was Christ who taught me my first lesson about sin and my second lesson about regeneration. He was with me even in my earliest experience, though my eyes were holden so that I did not see him. Here at the Rapids I seem to myself to have got my first glimpse of Christ as a conscious factor in my religious experience. I began, as I have described, by recognizing that his atonement constituted the only ground for my acceptance with God. A thorough study of the Epistle to the Hebrews which I conducted in preparing for my Bible class at the church Sunday School mostly enlarged my conceptions of Jesus and his work and showed me that he was not only the ideal priest but also the ideal sacrifice, because he was himself divine and because he offered up himself. I have ever since regarded the study of the Epistle to the Hebrews as affording the best introduction to theology. The unique significance of Christ as the substance of which the Old Testament dispensation was the shadow, as the one and only Mediator and Savior, as the appointed sacrificial victim by whom the world was to be reconciled to God shines out there in wonderful distinctness and beauty. I might have learned all this as a matter of theory, and it would have not deeply impressed me. My responsibility in directing inquiries, whose fate seemed put into my hands, made it all a matter of practice. I learned that the human conscience as well as the justice of God declare that without the shedding of blood there can be no remission.

I learned from Mrs. Stillson another lesson about Christ. She was the first person I had ever met who made upon me the impression that she lived every day and every hour in conscious and intimate communion with the Savior. I think it a great blessing ever to have seen one such man or woman. I think it a great pity that so many people have never come in contact with such a one. For when you have seen one, you can have no more doubt of the truth of Christianity than you can doubt the shining of the sun. Such a sight of lives lived by the faith of the Son of God kept Schleiermacher true to Christ long after he had gotten out from Moravian influences. Of course I had previously known many good Christians; my father and mother were good people; I had college friends who were faithful to me. But in Mrs. Stillson I had for the first time an example of constant companionship with Christ. Her faith was almost sight. The Savior was her joy and her song, and that all the day long. She had many cares and many trials. Neither her husband nor her son nor her brother was a Christian. She was almost alone in that heathenish neighborhood. Often she could not command her time for a minute, from morning to night, to read her Bible or enter her closet. But she prayed without ceasing. A smile of heavenly peace irradiated her face. The word of the Lord was always in her heart. Christ was ever with her as her counselor, and in his strength she went about in the household and in the community evermore doing good. I learned from her example the doctrine of a present Christ. And though I had still much to learn about this present Christ and conceived of him as external rather than as dwelling within the heart of the believer, I could not thereafter either live or preach as if Jesus were a theoretical or distant Redeemer. Before this I had addressed my prayers to God the Father; now I began to pray to Jesus my elder brother, my human companion, my present friend.

My whole after ministry was so greatly affected by this influence of Mrs. Stillson's example that I wonder now how I could have refrained from telling her what she had done for me. I think there was a sort of holy humility and reserve about her which made it difficult to speak to her anything that might seem like words of praise. But afterwards I was sorry I had not broken over this barrier. For she had a long succession of sorrows. Her aged parents lingered on in extreme weakness to tax her utmost strength for many years. Her husband and brother both died without having made confession of faith in Christ. Her son married a hardhearted and wicked woman who persecuted her mother-in-law and at last drove the son to suicide. By the wiles of this same daughter-in-law and her lawyers, she was defrauded of a large part of the little property which her husband left her. And last of all, heart disease confined her for years to her house, and accumulated troubles weakened her mind. When I last called upon her, I tried to comfort her by telling her that it was she who first made me acquainted with my dear wife and taught me one of the best lessons of Christian experience that I ever learned. She shrank back as if I had shocked her with some dreadful news. She protested that she had done nothing for me, that to suppose it was absurd because she had never been a Christian, she had sinned away her day of grace, and God had forsaken her; in short, she had committed the last and worst of sins, the sin against the Holy Ghost, for which there is no forgiveness either in this world or that which is to come. When I prayed with her, it was with a sort of horror that she knelt. When I told her that whosoever will may take the water of life and that him who cometh Christ will not cast out, she only replied that those things were for me but not for her. She must look forward only to the blackness of darkness forever. What could I do but commend her in my heart to the Savior of infinite pity and rejoice as I thought of the rapture and surprise which will be hers when that same Savior welcomes her enfranchised spirit to the abodes of glory and bids her take one of the highest seats in his kingdom! For neither the cruelty of man nor the oppression of Satan, neither decay of the body nor alienation of the mind can separate us from the love of God which is in Christ Jesus our Lord.

During my course in the seminary I preached only two or three times in town, and then I read written sermons. I somehow got the idea that a city congregation must have very fine—that is, very elaborate—preaching. *Memoriter* preaching, which I could have easily managed, seemed disingenuous. To extemporize, I was afraid. Therefore I read. I am sorry I did so, and if I had my life to live over again, I would never take a manuscript into the pulpit. But I wrote two or three elaborate sermons—sermons into which I crowded all my knowledge and experience. The first one was a class sermon on "Likeness to Christ," aimed to show that *likeness* comes from *liking,* and that *liking* comes from *looking.* The texts were two: "Beholding as in a glass the glory of the Lord, we are changed into the same image" and "We shall be like him, for we shall see him as he is." My preaching of this sermon in the First Baptist Church, before my father and mother and all the professors of university and seminary, was a critical and momentous occasion. How I prayed for grace to overcome my fears! And I did have grace and liberty—until I got two-thirds through the sermon. Then it occurred to me—I think the devil himself suggested it—that I was doing famously. Immediately I became self-conscious and embarrassed. There was a sudden slump. The rocket came down a mere charred and broken stick. I longed for a trapdoor to open in the platform to let me through. I received many compliments for my sermon, but they were very gall and bitterness to me. That I might not be exalted above measure, God gave me a secret thorn in the flesh.

My second sermon was on the text "Who is made priest, not according to the law of a carnal commandment, but according to the power of an endless life." Of course I had to give in one sermon the substance of the whole Epistle to the Hebrews and the whole doctrine of the atonement as I had learned it at the Rapids. The sermon might well have been expanded into a half dozen. Still, the essence of the gospel was there, and when I came to preach it to the same audience that had heard the former one, I held on to God with a death grip, and said through the whole service, like sinking Peter, "Lord, save, or I perish!" So I got through, with not only a whole skin but also with so much joy and spiritual exaltation that preaching began to seem the glory and ambition of my life. Since then I have had many varied experiences; I have preached in all sorts of ways and with all sorts of success. But I profess that the greatest enjoyment of existence, the very acme of honor and dignity, is to stand before a company of your fellow beings bound to the judgment seat of Christ and proclaim to them the message of divine love and mercy. One single experience in which you forget yourself in the word of God and are so taken possession of by God's Spirit that you hold your audience in the hollow of your hand and do with them what you will is worth all the struggles and trials and humiliations of the Christian ministry. The Lord mercifully gave me a few such experiences when my work began. Otherwise, I hardly think I should have had courage to press on through the discouragements of ill health that beset the first years of my ministry.

I have said nothing thus far of any other member of the seminary faculty than Dr. E.G. Robinson. In fact, he towered above all the rest both as a preacher and as a teacher. His personality was of more value than his instruction. He gave us very little in the way of definite system, but he did inoculate us with his scorn of laziness and meanness, and he taught us how to think. He had a tender heart, but it was usually hidden underneath a brusque and even threatening manner. He would be so moved at the funeral of a little child that he would be unable to go on with the service, but he would also be rasping and sarcastic in the extreme when his students were inattentive or dull. We had a salutary fear of him, and none of us were admitted to intimacy until we had proved our mettle in the actual work of life. Coming back in after years, we were astonished to find the doctor gentle, and even familiar. Little by little it would appear that he had been our best friend all the way through. But he never spoiled us by compliments. If he ever showed warmth or enthusiasm, he soon retracted it all, as if he were ashamed of himself. His worst fault was perhaps his everlasting spirit of criticism. Many a book "was not worth the paper it was written on." It was hard to draw from him words of praise for any man or any thing. He taught us to use our eyes, to judge fearlessly, to speak manfully. But it would have been well if he had had more of generosity, more of kindness, more of love, more of faith. Yet he bowed reverently before Christ. Like Stein, the great German statesman, he was proud toward men but humble toward God.

Dr. Velona R. Hotchkiss taught both Hebrew and Greek. He was a man of learning, and considering the fact that he was fresh from the pastorate, he was a very good teacher. His learning, however, was of the rabbinic sort, and an extraordinary sensitiveness interfered somewhat with his teaching. He and Dr. Robinson could never fully agree. Dr. Robinson was a radical, while Dr. Hotchkiss was a conservative. Dr. Robinson was always questioning the sufficiency and correctness of the old views; Dr. Hotchkiss thought it sacrilege to disturb them. Particularly as to inspiration, Dr. Hotchkiss would yield not one jot or tittle. He believed that the world was created in six days of twenty-four hours each, and he believed in the universality of the Noachian deluge. He was greatly scandalized when I read an essay in which I took Hugh Miller's view that the days of the first chapter of Genesis were periods of indefinite duration. But the climax came when Nathan Sheppard read his essay on the deluge. It was a mock attempt to show how all the animal kingdom could have been stowed away in the ark and the different species collected for that purpose. The kangaroos, for example, came over on an isthmus from Australia, and the polar bears were floated down from Greenland on chunks of ice. As Sheppard gravely proceeded, the twitching of the doctor's face was pitiful to behold; we should have exploded with laughter if Dr. Hotchkiss had not been so fearfully angry. But Sheppard made a lame apology, and amity was restored. Dr. Hotchkiss was a good man at heart, though he was somewhat narrow. He put his learning and faith to good use in his expository preaching. He knew the art of constructing a sermon, of weaving into it a mass of varied information, of bringing out the subtle suggestion of a text. The transfiguration of Christ and the Twenty-third Psalm—in fact, any one of a dozen passages that have unity in themselves— were made so luminous and so intensely interesting that they could never afterwards be forgotten. And there was always an evangelical conclusion into which the doctor put his heart. I tried in after years to imitate this expository preaching, but it was never so natural to me as to Dr. Hotchkiss. I will say no more about him here for the reason that I have given full expression to my admiration and regard in my book entitled *Philosophy and Religion*.[1]

Dr. George W. Northrup was not yet a Doctor of Divinity at that time. He had just finished his undergraduate work and was

[1] *Philosophy and Religion: A Series of Addresses, Essays and Sermons Designed to Set Forth Great Truths in Popular Form* (New York: A. C. Armstrong and Son, 1888), pp. 344-346. Hereafter abbreviated *Philosophy and Religion*.

beginning his teaching as professor of ecclesiastical history. He was a stalwart and impressive figure, but comparative ill health and a naturally melancholy disposition gave him an air of weakness. Yet he was a clear and vigorous thinker. He was deeply conscientious, and he was trying, at the same time that he was teaching others, to settle some of the most important theological problems for himself. He was more of a mystic than either of our other professors. He longed for a closer walk with God. His prayers often seemed like wailings. In a company, where he had become abstracted and unconscious of his surroundings, he suddenly broke out with the exclamation, "Oh, that I could be like God!" There was something uncanny and abnormal about him that prevented either his piety or his thinking from getting the firmest hold upon students. But his method of teaching history was admirable. He would analyze a movement like the Crusades or Scholasticism in such a way that the main questions about it would be suggested and the student would be led to work out his own answers. There was no dictation and no reading of lectures. All was discussion. The professor put himself on a level with his class, and it was a free fight. I did not fear Dr. Northrup as much as I feared Dr. Robinson, and in his department I more nearly let myself loose. I had the misfortune in after years in his presence at one of our alumni dinners to say that Dr. Northrup had never given as good instruction as he did when he was a beginner. The doctor seemed a little offended. But I meant it well. And what I meant was simply this, that he never afterward could have done so well by any class as he did for ours because at that time his very inexperience compelled him to put himself by our sides as a fellow student, and that stimulated us to think for ourselves as we never would have been stimulated by more advanced and dogmatic instruction.

A debating society among the students set us to thinking also. We discussed the freedom of the will and the relation of the race to Adam. But we also discussed practical questions. And this was one of them: "Has the foreign field or the home field the greater claim upon young men preparing for the ministry?" I was appointed to speak for the foreign field. I entered upon the discussion with little thought of its personal relation to me. But as I reflected upon it, it occurred to me that I ought to go where the need was great and the laborers few. The presumption was that we should go abroad; the burden of proof rested upon the man who would stay at home. I made a great speech—so they said—but the impression made upon me was deeper than any that was made upon others. I became greatly agitated as to my own duty to the heathen. I found that a thousand selfish motives had mingled with my desire to preach the gospel. Comfortable living and the gratification of my love for oratory were by no means left out of view. I was startled to see how far I was from being willing to say, "Here am I, send me!" In the struggle I almost began to doubt whether my Christian profession had been sincere. But at last I concluded that if I was not willing to go abroad, I had no right to expect the blessing of God at home. I put myself anew into the hands of Christ, to do with me what he would. And he gave me such a new sense of his love that I would have gladly stayed all my life at the Rapids, or at his bidding I would have gladly gone to the Kamchatkans or the Hottentots. But when I was once willing to go, he put an obstacle in the way.

Those two years in the seminary—for the course had not yet been lengthened out to three—were very quiet years. I went very little into society. I devoted myself almost altogether to study and to my work at the Rapids. My father's house was a most comfortable home. Though we had taken possession of our residence on South Clinton Street in the spring of my sophomore year in college, the house had not seemed large enough to furnish a study for me. So just before my college course ended, in anticipation of my studying theology at Rochester, Father had added a wing to the main structure that furnished a new sleeping room for my parents above and a commodious room for me below. Those two years were very pleasant, both to me and the rest of the family. Henry had started off on his adventures; Kate was at school at Farmington; Belle was a little girl at home, to whom I was much attached and for whose benefit I invented fairy stories innumerable. Father and Mother were well, and everything seemed to prosper. But toward the spring of 1859, either because of my journeys to the Rapids through mud and snow or because of general indifference to physical culture in my previous college course, I began to have a bad cough. The cold seemed to settle upon my lungs. One morning I was surprised by an expectoration of blood. This was repeated several times. Dr. John

Reid was our family physician. When I told him the whole story, he fairly turned pale and declared that I must stop study at once and be in the open air for a whole year. No brain work but plenty of bodily exercise was his specific, and he warned me and my parents that if I did not heed his injunctions, I might enter the kingdom of heaven sooner that I wished. We all became greatly alarmed and set about devising a plan of relief. Just at that time Theodore Bacon concluded that he would go to Europe for a pedestrian tour. I had known him as a Yale graduate of older standing than I, and we had been jointly deputed to found the chapter of Psi Upsilon in the University of Rochester. He proposed to me to join him in his European travels. I consented, provided my father would furnish the necessary means. Father promptly did this, and on May 6, 1859, leaving my seminary course unfinished by two or three months, I set sail in the steamer *City of Washington* from the port of New York for Liverpool.

Theodore Bacon was so striking a personality and he had so much influence upon me that I must give some account of him. He came of good stock. His father was Dr. Leonard Bacon, pastor of the Centre Church at New Haven and afterwards professor of ecclesiastical history in the Yale Divinity School. Dr. Bacon was a good deal of a statesman—in fact, he seemed to some people to have more interest in politics than in religion. He was an admirable platform speaker. He would have done nobly in the Senate of the United States. When I was at Yale, he occasionally preached in the college chapel. He usually took some politico-religious theme, and he commanded our rapt attention. But his ordinary discourses were quite uninteresting. Young Tutor Hadley, when he wanted to characterize a man as extraordinarily dull, would say, "Why, he is as dull as Dr. Bacon when he hasn't anything but the gospel to preach!" Delia Bacon, the ardent and unbalanced advocate of the Baconian authorship of the plays commonly attributed to Shakespeare, was Dr. Bacon's sister. If Dr. Bacon was ever dull, this could hardly be said of his children. And he had many of them. I once asked Theodore how many brothers and sisters he had. It seemed a painful question to him. He began to count them up on the fingers of one hand: "There is Susan, and George, and Leonard, and William, and I." Then he began on the fingers of the other hand until he had exhausted them. He took the first hand over again until he had got up to thirteen. Then he stopped, saying, "I believe that is all." All those thirteen were as like each other as peas in a pod. They all were opinionated to the last degree; they all liked to fight better than they did to eat; they all were accurate scholars, and what they knew they could tell at a moment's notice. They were astonishingly well read in history and politics, and they were critical, irritable, overbearing, dogmatic, and, above all, sharp-tongued. Woe to the man who provoked their wrath, for they could lash him within an inch of his life. They carried in their belts the scalps of many enemies, and they were always making enemies. Yet they were also very true and valuable friends.

Theodore knew much more than I, for he was older and had had some preliminary experience in the law. He also knew that he knew more, and he was bound that I should know it. I learned a great deal from him. I should have learned more if he had not so insisted upon being instructive. Ordinarily I was humble and submissive. But when he showed contempt for my ignorance and declined to consider my counterarguments to his opinions, I had to draw the line and cease talking with him. His temper was not improved by the fact that he had just been jilted by Miss Selden, the young lady whom he afterwards married. Her perfidy was the subject of his malediction. He had at first tried to soothe his blighted affections by studying for the ministry. But he soon concluded that he was not called to preach the gospel. Europe and travel then promised to restore him. I became the victim of much of his sourness and discontent. As we stood in the mausoleum of Burns at Ayr, we saw at the foot of the poet's statue the Bible which he had presented to Highland Mary as they clasped hands over the running brook and vowed to each other to be faithful.

> Till a' the seas gang dry, my dear,
> And the rocks melt wi' the sun.[2]

The Bible lay open, and in it passages were marked referring to the solemnity of an oath. When Bacon saw these, he took out his notebook and copied them. "What are you doing that for?" said I.

---

[2] Robert Burns, "My Love Is Like a Red Red Rose," lines 9-10.

"I am going to send them to *her,*" he responded. The end of this romance needs to be told. Bacon remained two years in Europe. He returned to America to enlist in the Federal Army on the breaking out of the Civil War. He served bravely. On a furlough, he came to Rochester. He called on Miss Hattie Ward. Miss Hattie told him that out of mere respect he ought not to leave town without visiting Miss Selden. Theodore refused but finally consented to make a formal call if Hattie would go with him. In the course of that call something occurred to summon Miss Ward from the room. What happened after her exit no man, except Bacon and Miss Selden, knoweth to this day. But the result was that the long quarrel was made up; the wedding cards were sent out, and Mr. and Mrs. Bacon have been living in peace and quietness these many years with a noble family of children around them—Mr. Bacon, the first lawyer of Rochester, and Mrs. Bacon, one of the most esteemed of women.

I cannot tell the whole story of my fourteen and a half months abroad—nor even the story of my two months pedestrianizing with Bacon through the Lake Country of England and Scotland and down the valley of the Tweed to Berwick, Durham, and York. Yet there are a few scenes which shine out through the mist of memory and which I cannot omit to mention. First let me speak of some foreign preachers. On our first Sunday morning we attended the church of Dr. Hugh MacNeill, afterwards Bishop of Carlisle. It was in the west end of Liverpool. The attire of the congregation impressed me—not the plain black of our American men nor the silks and satins of our American women but rough tweed business suits for the men and simple muslin for the women. Yet it was a noble congregation both for number and for character. The service was plainly rendered, but when Dr. MacNeill rose to speak, I found my expectations raised to the highest. Tall and slender, the very type of a university man and a born gentleman, he also seemed a devout and evangelical Christian. He held a limp-covered Bible in his hand, and in the most conversational manner he proceeded to expound the doctrine of the Holy Spirit. His clear-cut extemporaneous utterance resembled that of Dr. Robinson, but it had in it more of culture and more of kindliness. He told us that in the Holy Spirit we had Christ himself, no longer confined to a single locality but omnipresent with all his scattered followers throughout the world.

And at the close he put down his book, and stretching out his hands as if in benediction he congratulated all who loved the one Lord and Savior, that by one Spirit they had access unto the Father.

In Glasgow we heard John Caird, a man of leonine head and shaggy black locks, rush through a sermon with such energy and intensity that he did not permit the auditor to intermit his attention from the beginning to the close. I asked an intelligent Scotchman how it happened that all the Scotch preachers had this tremendous flow and fervency. His reply was, "Why, don't you know? It's Doctor Chalmers!" Sure enough, Dr. Chalmers, being dead, was yet speaking in hundreds of Scotch pulpits. In Edinburgh Dr. R. S. Candlish greatly interested us. He gave an afternoon exposition of the "heavenly places" of Ephesians. Two thousand people all turning the leaves of their Bibles at the same moment in order to keep track of the doctor's subtle Scripture references was a sight not to be forgotten. At Kelso we heard Horatius Bonar expound the latter portion of the sixth chapter of Ephesians: "Our warfare is not with flesh and blood, but with principalities and powers—the world—rulers of this darkness." "A gude mon, and the women like him!" was the description one of the parishioners gave of this preacher. He had not yet become famous as the writer of hymns. At Kelso, the church officers waited in the vestibule with their big platters to receive contributions as the people went out and seemed to frown when the contributions were too small.

London, however, was the great place for preaching. We heard Frederick Denison Maurice twice—earnest but vague—I understand him better now than I did then. He was chaplain of Lincoln's Inn, and the afternoon congregation of barristers was something unique. We learned that all men are saved and all men children of God; all they need is to know this, and the gospel is the proclamation of an already accomplished redemption. We heard Dr. John Cumming, the great expounder of prophecy. After standing near the door through all the introductory service, though the pews were only half-filled, the keys were brought out and the pew doors were unlocked to receive us just before the sermon began. We were greatly instructed when Dr. Cumming arose and in his most mellifluous way spoke as follows: "My dear hearers, permit me, before I enter upon the sermon of the evening, to give you a practical exhortation. It has been reported to me that certain ladies of my congregation have been devoting so much time of late to the study of prophecy as to neglect their ordinary household duties. Now, you will bear me witness that I have urged you to the study of prophecy. But I would bid you also remember that there is a limit beyond which study is not useful." About his exhorting them to the study of prophecy there could be no manner of doubt. He had been preaching every Sunday evening for many years on the seven heads and the ten horns, and I was surprised at his surprise at their devotion to prophecy. I have never known people to spend much time in the interpretation of the book of Revelation without also losing their interest in the conversion of souls. Lord Brougham was nearly right when he said that the study of prophecy either found men crazy or it left them so.

Charles H. Spurgeon was at this time preaching on Sunday mornings at the little chapel in New Park Street, while afternoons and evenings he addressed great audiences in Surrey Music Hall. The morning service I remember little about. It was followed, I know, by the Lord's Supper, to which I was admitted upon securing a ticket from the committee of deacons in the vestry. In the afternoon I heard Mr. Spurgeon in Surrey Music Hall. There were only rough board seats, and that for a part of the audience; hundreds were standing. The preacher looked youthful; he had a jaunty and self-confident air; he ran up the steps to the pulpit and gazed over the great congregation, as if to say, "I think I can do the business for you!" The sermon made little impression upon me, and I doubt whether it made much impression upon others. I went away disappointed. But I came again. On the next Sunday Mr. Spurgeon's manner was entirely different. He seemed to feel his responsibility. He seemed to cast himself upon God. His text was: "Kiss the Son, lest he be angry, and ye perish from the way, when his wrath is kindled but a little." It was the greatest popular sermon I had ever heard. The voice was rich and musical; the utterance perfectly flowing and unconstrained; clear, simple, persuasive speech; yet so full of energy, pathos, and unction that it riveted attention and deeply moved every hearer. Best of all, it was the very gospel of Christ. I heard Spurgeon many times afterwards, in 1872, 1874, 1887. At each succeeding visit, I could see that he was growing mellower and more spiritual. His prayers especially came to be more noticeable for lofty and self-forgetful eloquence than were his sermons. But as for preaching, pure and simple, by which I mean the warning of the sinner and the offer to him of Christ's salvation, I never afterwards heard from Mr. Spurgeon a sermon so powerful as this.

Cathedrals interested me almost as much as preaching. Here I was fortunate in having Bacon with me. He had studied Anglican architecture, and he knew the history of England. He would burrow around the ancient structures and find out all that guidebooks could tell him. The determining of the date of such and such an arch or window, the deciphering of such and such a monumental inscription, the connection of such and such an erection with its proper bishop or monarch was an engrossing pursuit to him. He was a born archaeologist, epigraphist, numismatist. And I was a tyro. I did not know how little I knew, and I did not know how much he knew. I have no doubt I bothered him with my simpleminded questions, and still more with my shortsighted objections. Yet on the whole we got on well together. If I did not become as much of an authority on architectural details, I think I appreciated quite as much the grandeur and beauty of those relics of the past. The cathedral at Chester was the first that we visited. The crumbling stone, blackened with age and smoke, gave me a profound impression of antiquity. Melrose Abbey and Fountains Abbey showed me the splendor of the old monastic establishments. But Durham and York capped the climax. They are witnesses to medieval wealth and art. I afterwards saw Lincoln and Peterborough, Worcester and Salisbury cathedrals, besides St. Paul's and Westminster Abbey, but I was never so awed by a pile of architecture as when I first stood at evening before York Minster and saw the great dim arches lift themselves into the region of "sailing birds and silent air."

I must only mention my attendance at the Handel Festival in the Crystal Palace, where all of Handel's masterpieces were produced by the greatest organ in England, an orchestra of a thousand instruments, and a chorus of three thousand voices, all before an audience of thirty thousand people; my visit to the House of Commons, where the debate had the air of a business conversation between gentlemen instead of the spread-eagle oratory at that time so common in America; or my excursion to Aldershot to witness a sham battle in which twenty thousand troops engaged and I narrowly escaped being overwhelmed by a charge of cavalry and infantry—escaped by taking refuge behind a carriage which opportunely had halted upon the eminence where I stood. At the close of the fight, General Knollys, standing between the Queen and Prince Albert on the one hand and the Prince of Wales and the Princess Alice on the other, reviewed the columns as they filed by. I ought to say that, five minutes after the fight began, the field seemed covered with smoke, and how anyone could determine the result passed my comprehension. Bacon and I visited Oxford and were entertained by Mr. Warne, a Baptist, and yet postmaster of that high church town through half a dozen changes of national administration—an example of the blessings of a good civil service. We went to Warwick, Kenilworth, Stratford-on-Avon, Stonehenge, and the Isle of Wight. Here we separated for a time. I wanted to see the mountains, and I knew that Switzerland must be seen in August or not at all. Bacon disliked mountain scenery because the neighborhood of a precipice made him dizzy. We parted amicably, he returning to London and I taking the steamer from Southampton to Havre.

My first experiences in France were too interesting to be passed over. They illustrated phases of French character. On arriving in Havre, a gendarme took my passport, and I was required to apply for it at the Hôtel de Ville, where I found myself in a long line of passengers. One after another we approached a mighty official seated at a table. I mustered up my best French and asked for my passport. The official then propounded to me a question. Alas, I could not understand him. Again I asked for my passport, with the same response. I began to despair, for the train to Rouen was just about to leave and I had no time to lose. I turned around and espying a gentleman, who seemed to be English, I besought him to interpose in my behalf. He asked as I had done, received the same response, and then turning to me interpreted it in the words "What is your name?" I was covered with confusion, but I got my passport and caught my train. On the way to Rouen, in the midst of a lot of voluble Frenchmen, a gentleman who sat apart noticed me and asked if I were not an American. He introduced himself as M. J. J. Appleton of Boston. He had been minister to Sweden and to Naples. He was now United States Consul at Rouen. He gave me all manner of information, ordered me a dinner at Rouen, provided me with a guide to the cathedral, and instructed me how to find a quiet French hotel near the station in Paris. After seeing the wonders of Rouen, I again took the railway and reached Paris at ten on Saturday night. Portmanteau in hand, I emerged from the station to make my easy way to the Hôtel Tronchet. But I somehow lost myself. I walked on and on along a brilliantly lighted thoroughfare, but there was no hotel. I concluded that I had taken the wrong one of two streets diverging from the station and that I could reach the right one by going cross lots. That only involved me in greater difficulty. I reached a region of warehouses, where there was not a soul stirring. I began to be beset with fears of highway robbery. At last two gentlemen in evening dress approached. They had evidently come from the theater or opera. I addressed them in the best French I could command and told them my perplexity. "Ah, sir," they replied, "you are very far astray! Permit us to conduct you." And so saying, though it was after eleven at night, they turned round from the way they had been going, took me what seemed a fifteen minutes walk, put me down in front of my hotel, politely doffed their hats, and wished me a very good night. I began to believe in French politeness.

I stayed only over Sunday in Paris and immediately proceeded to Basel, in Switzerland, by way of Troyes. Here was an old cathedral which I wished to visit. Not a soul at the hotel could speak a word of English. At the *table d'hôte* dinner I was put at the right of the gentleman who served as master of the feast. He devoted himself entirely to me, and the twenty or so other guests were all absorbed in listening to our conversation. I protested that I knew little French, but he drew me out. With all sorts of delicate compliments, he encouraged me to be entirely free. He asked all manner of questions about America and my travels. I thought I was getting on famously. At the close of the dinner my entertainer insisted on being my guide through the town. He showed me the cathedral, gave me a quantity of valuable local information, treated me with the utmost kindness. At last he brought me back to the hotel and saluted me in departing as gracefully as the two gentlemen whom I had so fortunately met in Paris. But the *dénouement* was not so pleasant. I went to my room and was disrobing myself before retiring when I heard laughter from the court below. Opening my window slightly, I discovered the tall form of my gentlemanly guide. He was entertaining a constantly increasing company of eager listeners. I began to understand that he was retelling to them, with all sorts of fantastic exaggerations, the conversation which he had had during his walk with me. All my slips in the use of French, all my mistakes and blunders, were set forth with a drollery and grimace which amused even me. Of course I still felt indebted to him for his courtesy, but ever since then I have wondered whether I ought to be wholly content with the sequel. His politeness was evidently not entirely disinterested.

On the terrace of the cathedral at Basel, I met a young Englishman whose plans seemed to be much like my own, and we agreed to take our inexpensive pedestrian tour in Switzerland together—most of the time for ten francs, or two dollars, a day. We went to the house of Erasmus, but the occupant told us that no such gentleman lived there, though it possibly might be well for us to inquire at the next door. We saw the Holbeins in the museum. But the greatest wonder of Basel was the blue, arrowy Rhine. The rail brought us to Schaffhausen and the noble falls of that same river; to Constance, with its memorials of Huss and his martyrdom; to Ragatz, the baths of Pfeffers, and finally to Zürich and Zug. At Zug, our pedestrian tour actually began. Up and down the Rigi, then to Lucerne, Fluelen, the Furca Pass, the Rhone Glacier, the Grimsel, Meyringen, Rosenlaui, Grindenwald, Wengern Alp, Lauterbrunnen, the Staubbach, Interlaken, Thun, Freiburg, Geneva. It was a wonderful panorama that passed before us. By this time I had attained a high state of health and spirits, and I saw everything with the enthusiastic eyes of youth. I have always advocated the taking of Europe in early life when the pulses beat quickly and all great things are a wonder and delight. These sights of one's youth sweeten all one's after years.

My young Englishman was a treasure. Modest but well informed, he was also full of life and talk. By dint of inquiry I learned much of English customs and ways of thinking. And here was one of the main uses of my year abroad. My range was widened. Hitherto my horizon had been narrow and academic. This young businessman gave me a new outlook. But I met many other men in my travels who did me the same service. I gradually learned freedom in conversation. Mingling with men of the world who were not afraid to say that their souls were their own, I came to think that I might possibly have opinions and express them. The extreme timidity which had hitherto distinguished me in society began to give place to ease and confidence. And the first conscious beginnings of this freedom came from my talks with my companion in Switzerland. Unfortunately, he was compelled to leave me at Geneva, and I went on alone. I climbed to the Tête Noire on the way to Chamonix. I shall never forget the ecstasy with which I was filled as from the mountainsides above Martigny I looked off eastward upon the long vista of the valley of the Rhône. Chamonix disappointed me, but when I went to Zermatt, crossed the St. Théodule Pass, and saw the snow wreaths upon the summit of Mont Blanc from the opposite peak of the Cramont, the height and grandeur of the monarch of mountains dawned upon me. The descent into Italy, from the savage desolation of the glacier at the foot of the Matterhorn, was another memorable experience. The description of Sir Henry Taylor in *Philip Van Artevelde* only expresses my feeling as with knapsack on my back I strode down the valley:

> Sublime, but neither bleak, nor bare,
> Nor misty, are the mountains there;
> Softly sublime, profusely fair;
> Up to their summits clothed in green,
> And fruitful as the vales between,
> They lightly rise, and scale the skies,
> And groves and gardens still abound;
> For where no shoot can else take root,
> The peaks are shelved and terraced round.

My ability to walk grew with practice. I began by accomplishing only ten or fifteen miles a day. Then twenty to twenty-five was the regular amount for a month. My last two walks were thirty and thirty-five miles respectively. It was on a Saturday afternoon that I reached the Hospice of Grand Saint Bernard from Morges on the

Italian side. Here I spent Sunday in the clouds. The snow, the dogs, the monks, and the service were all interesting. I was not long without companions. On reaching Freiburg in Breisgau from Geneva, I found W. P. Bacon and F. W. Stevens of the Yale class of 1858 and made an arrangement to travel with them to Berlin. Together we visited Strassburg with its great cathedral, Baden-Baden with its splendid gambling halls, Heidelberg with its ruined castle, and then we sailed down the Rhine to Cologne, taking Speyer, Frankfurt, Mainz, Bingen, Coblenz, and Königswinter on the way. It was the time of the vintage. We filled a big basket with grapes every morning and devoured them all before night. "The castled crag of Drachenfels" and all the old robber fortresses that frown from their heights upon the "wide and winding Rhine" had a meaning of their own derived from my reading of *Childe Harold*. Bacon and Stevens were not literary, but they were good fellows, and it was pleasant to be with Yale men once more. The crane was still swinging from the top of the unfinished tower of Cologne Cathedral, but I bought a picture entitled *"Der Dom zu Köln, in seiner zukünftigen Vollendung."* I am glad that this prophecy has since been so magnificently fulfilled.

Düsseldorf, Hanover, Brunswick, Berlin. Friday evening, October 7, found me installed in my own apartments at 1 Neu-Wilhelm's Strasse, 2 Treppen, overlooking the Spree, with swans sailing upon the narrow stream. For ten dollars a month I obtained two furnished rooms, a parlor and a bedroom. My breakfast of coffee, rolls, and butter cost me about ten cents. Herr Künstler gave me an hour a day of German instruction. I attended lectures at the university—Hengstenberg, Twesten, and Nitzsch—but soon concluded that for me, as for most young American theologians, studying theology in Germany must practically mean studying the German language. This I made considerable progress in, but I should have made more if I had separated myself entirely from my American friends and boarded in a German family. As it was, though I bought and read German books and attended German lectures, I dined and supped with Americans, and most of my conversation was with them. But among them were fine men. J. K. Paine, a Harvard man, and afterwards professor of music at Harvard, sat by my side at concerts and interpreted symphonies.

Elisha Mulford came to my room two or three evenings of each week and talked till ten or eleven or twelve or one o'clock, as the spirit moved. Mulford was of the Yale class of 1855, too lazy ever to be a scholar, too deaf to be a preacher, but an omnivorous reader, a born conversationalist, with a Coleridgean vagueness and a Coleridgean fluency. He had a way of ingratiating himself into the interest and affection of his hearer. The profound respect with which he treated your least suggestion was flattering in the extreme. His wildest flights of heresy were so reverently and humbly uttered that they seemed the breathings of a saint. His pipe was never absent, and there was a halo of smoke about his head which in his moments of inspiration gave him the air of one of the glorified. Here was another piece of my education. Mulford encouraged me to talk, though he did most of the talking himself. He had been advised to leave Andover because he was a disciple of Maurice and was instituting a Mauricean propaganda which was obnoxious to Professor Edwards Amasa Park. He finished his theological course at the Union Theological Seminary, but even there the doctrine of Maurice was not popular. A bishop of the Episcopal church got hold of him, and Mulford became an Episcopalian. In Berlin he was learning German and reading Hegel. It was Hegel's philosophy and Maurice's theology which he afterwards tried to popularize in his two books entitled *The Nation* and *The Republic of God*. His friend Dr. T. T. Munger has described to me the chaotic condition in which the manuscripts of these books came to him and the endless labor that was needed to extricate the grains of wheat from the bushels of chaff. But for all that, Mulford was a man of rich and rare mind. His personality was greater than his literary productions. Thoughtfulness and refinement were manifest in his most casual remarks. He made many friends, among whom I am glad to be able to number myself as one. The New Theology represented by Lyman Abbott, George Gordon, A. H. Bradford, and A. M. Fairbairn is foreshadowed in Mulford's books.

Berlin was the scene of my education in painting and music. The Royal Museum, with its pictures of all the schools and centuries arranged in historical order, was a noble place for studying art, and there I spent many an afternoon. Liebig's orchestra played three times a week in a great hall the masterpieces of the great composers, and the price of admission was only two and a half groschen, or seven cents. You could buy a glass of beer, and that would bring your bill up to ten cents, and a cigar would make it fifteen. The orchestra numbered eighty performers; and yet before the concert was over, it was sometimes difficult to see the fiddlers for the smoke. There I heard in succession all the great symphonies of Haydn, Mozart, Beethoven, Schubert, Mendelssohn, Schumann, and some of the overtures, like *Lohengrin,* with which Wagner was just beginning to astonish the world. With my friends Bacon, Stevens, and Mulford I bought tickets to the entire series of symphony concerts by the Royal Orchestra, chamber concerts by a stringed quartet of which Joachim was the leader, concerts of the Sing-Akademie and the Domchor in which were rendered such compositions as Handel's *Messiah,* Mozart's *Requiem,* and Rossini's *Stabat Mater.* Occasionally I went to the opera, but this was in general too expensive. Once or twice I heard a German play, like Schiller's *Maid of Orleans,* but I was not familiar enough with spoken German to get the full advantage of it. The music was my greatest source of enjoyment in Berlin, and I shall never in this world hear so much of it again.

As Christmas drew near and the cold increased, I felt Goethe's drawing toward the South, and I prepared to leave Berlin and journey toward Italy and the East. On December 26 an early train carried me to Wittenberg, with all its memorials of Luther, including the university where he lived with his wife, and the Schlosskirche to whose door he nailed his ninety-five theses. Then came a day in Leipzig and a couple of days in Dresden. The Dresden gallery, with its *Sistine Madonna,* was of course the great attraction. From Dresden I went to Prague and returned. The half oriental city, with its mementoes of Wallenstein, filled me with enthusiasm. Then I went to Nuremberg, where I seemed transported to the middle ages, their antique dwellings, and chambers of torture; to Ratisbon, where I saw the Rathhaus and the rack, as well as the great cathedral; to Munich, where the Pinacothek and the Glyptothek impressed me; to Salzburg, the most romantic place for situation that I had yet seen; and thence by *diligence* or *Schnellpost,* since there was as yet no rail, to Vienna. The capital was at that time still encircled with its ancient walls, and it was by no means the bright and airy city which modern architects have made it. Trieste, Venice, Verona, Mantua, Parma, Bologna, and Florence followed in quick succession, Florence being reached by a *diligence* ride of eighteen hours from Bologna to Pistoia over the Apennines—a freezing ride on January 24. But Florence rewarded me. The Uffizi and Pitti Galleries were glorious, and in the Boboli gardens the roses were blooming in the open air. I feasted on Raphael and Michelangelo and Fra Angelico for a week, living at the Pension Suisse and finding pleasant Americans for companions. Then on to Pisa, Leghorn, and Rome.

The Eternal City was my home for more than three weeks. I found Theodore Bacon once more, now apparently recovered from all his moroseness, and, with Bacon, Samuel Scoville, my college classmate, who was tutoring the son of Henry Ward Beecher and engaged to the daughter of the same dignitary of the church. On the Piazza San Carlo, 433, 2^d piano, we four and, I believe, six other young Americans rented from an impecunious count and his countess the whole floor of a Roman palace, each of us having to himself a superb, great sleeping apartment and all together having our breakfasts and dinners served in a vast frescoed salon by the keeper of a neighboring restaurant, the total cost of this sumptuous living to each person being $1.25 a day. Sam Scoville took us occasionally of an evening to call on Mrs. Harriet Beecher Stowe, who had apartments on the Pincian Hill and was chaperoning Miss Hattie Beecher, as well as her own exceedingly disagreeable daughters. Mrs. Stowe was a pleasant woman, and with her we subsequently made a famous tour of the Catacomb of Sant'Agnese under the conduct of Dr. Smith, professor in the Jesuit College, in which Dr. Smith was plainly intent upon making proselytes of his Protestant visitors. We heard the pope conduct a simple mass in a Chapel of St. Peter's, and we saw the cardinals, with their scarlet hats and robes and coaches, driving through the streets in all the splendor of princes of the church. The carnival was celebrated after the old-fashioned style with the racing of horses through the Corso and the scattering of flowers and confetti. Twenty-three days were all too short to see the antiquities and the art of Rome, and ever since that time I have almost longed for a good settled bronchitis which would compel me to spend a whole winter in this most instructive and fascinating of all the cities of the world.

Mr. and Mrs. Frank Wayland of New Haven were then taking their wedding journey abroad, and they invited me to join them in a carriage ride from Rome to Naples. Mr. Goddard of Providence was also of the party. In four days of eight hours each our *vetturino* brought us safely through. We passed the lakes of Albano and Nemi, lodged at Velletri, where Augustus was born, and lunched at Appii Forum, where Paul's good brethren came to meet him   і where Horace embarked on his journey to Brundusium. We spent the second night in Terracina, the frontier town of the Papal States, and lunched at Mola, on the beautiful bay of Gaeta. Here one of our party amused himself by cutting off a lizard's tail to see it wriggle when separated from the body and by heating copper coins in a candle flame and then throwing them to the beggars who thronged the front of the hotel. After a third night, at Sant' Agata, we passed over the edge of Monte Massico, the region famous for Massic wine, and over the Falernus Ager, the source of the Old Falernian, lunched at Capua, and reached Naples by four o'clock in the afternoon. In Naples I spent nine of the most delightful days of my life. Bacon joined me, having walked all the way from Rome. At the Pension Anglaise, we found Mrs. Bowne and her two daughters from Staten Island, and with them Bacon and I saw all the sights of Naples and made excursions to Salerno, Amalfi, Paestum, and Pompeii. The bay of Naples, with its curving shore and the twin peaks of Vesuvius looming up across the blue and sunlit water, formed the loveliest picture my eyes had yet rested upon. But I had soon to leave it, for on March 11 I took a French steamer to Messina and Malta and from Malta a steamer of the Peninsular and Oriental line to Alexandria in Egypt.

My experiences in Eypgt and Palestine are described in the lecture "Recollections of the East," published in my book *Philosophy and Religion.*[3] Here again I found good company, especially L. Clark Seelye, who has since become president of Smith College. With him and an Andover classmate of his I twice traversed the Holy Land from end to end and along the coast of the Mediterranean from Beirut to Jaffa and again through the country northwards from Jerusalem to Damascus.

[3] *Philosophy and Religion,* pp. 468-483.

A part of the time we joined the party of General Cotton, an English officer who was returning from China, and our company then numbered twenty gentlemen and ladies, with eighty animals to carry our luggage and camp equipage. We had precisely a month of Palestinian travel, for we left Beirut on March 27 and reached Beirut again on April 27. Who can tell the delights of rest upon the deck of the French steamer as we sailed from Beirut in the balmy air past Cypress and under the lee of Asia Minor with its snowcapped mountains looking down upon us, to Rhodes and Smyrna and Syria and Athens! I reached Athens on May 7, 1860, the anniversary of my sailing from New York. Here I explored the city and surrounding country as I had explored Jerusalem. I ascended Lycabettus and Pentelicus, and as I looked off upon the blue Aegean with its islands, I thought Greece was manifestly designed by Providence to educate the human race in beauty and in freedom. And the Acropolis, crowned with the wonderful Parthenon, was just as manifestly the appointed fortress and sanctuary of a bold and enterprising people. I conceived a love for Greek independence, and though I had not been able to see the Turk in Constantinople, his capital, even then, from what I heard of his unspeakable depravity, I learned to pray that his empire might perish and that the Greeks might rule the East in his place.

After a week in Athens—confined to Athens because there was then not even a carriage road for more than ten miles in any direction from the city—I took Seelye, though he was more or less ill of fever contracted in Palestine, and sailed in a small Austrian-Lloyd steamer for Corfu, Trieste, and Venice. It was a stirring time. The unification of Italy had begun. In Venice on a Sunday afternoon crowds of well-dressed people would throng the Piazza di San Marco, but as soon as the Austrian military band appeared and prepared to play, the crowd would silently scatter until not a soul was left to hear the music. The scowl on every face showed hatred of Austria and determination to be free. On the way to Milan news came of the successful descent of Garibaldi upon Sicily and the progress of the revolt against the Bourbon Ferdinand II. At every station along the railway after we entered the dominions of Victor Emmanuel were signs of frantic excitement. Speeches and martial music were summoning men to volunteer. Through all this I made my way to Milan—where I saw the great cathedral and Leonardo da Vinci's *Last Supper* in its sad deterioration—to Lakes Lugano and Maggiore, and by the Simplon Pass to Geneva and Paris. In Paris I found Scoville and Mulford and Clarke, who had been for a time chaplain at Yale and was taking his vacation. We made a merry and a lively party. I had not really seen Paris on my way to Switzerland, and I now spent two weeks exploring the wonders of the city. The greatest sight was the review of sixty thousand troops on the Champs de Mars by the Emperor Napoleon III and the Empress Eugénie. In my notebook I have the jotting: "He looked every inch an Emperor, and she was all grace." How little I foresaw Sedan and the siege, the abdication and the exile! In fact, no one else foresaw these things. Paris was on the top wave of gaiety and lavish expenditures. Our party determined to signalize our departure by a *fin de siècle* dinner at the Trois Frères Provençaux, then the most noted restaurant in the world. We asked the proprietor what a dinner would cost. The reply was: *"Pour dix francs, un dîner ordinaire; pour vingt francs un très joli dîner; mais pour cinquante francs par personne un grand dîner."* All this was of course *"les vins apart."* Including these, and concluding that *in medio tutissimus ibis,* our dinner cost us just eight dollars apiece. We drove up in a first-class carriage, attired in evening dress, were ushered into a beautiful little apartment hung with silk tapestry, had a service of porcelain and silver, three waiters, an artistic menu, and plenty of flowers. The first course was yellow melon, the second, a red soup with a little red shrimp in the center of each plate. Then came a variety of French dishes, with Roman punch served in between. Ice cream was brought in checkerboard fashion on a silver salver, each one of the sixteen squares being a different color and a different flavor. Great strawberries came next, and we wound up with coffee, cognac being burned upon it, and with cigars for a franc each. I do not think this example of extravagance worthy of imitation, but perhaps for once it was pardonable, as it gave us an idea of French cuisine in its perfection. The dinner, moreover, was a flow of reason and wit as well as a feast of the sense. Four toasts were proposed and four speeches made. I only wish I could recall them all. The single one I remember was "The four homes that are to be."

With Scoville and Mulford I left Paris for Brussels on June 13. Together we visited Antwerp, Amsterdam, and The Hague. On June 23 we were in London, and on June 30 Mulford and I sailed from Liverpool on the steamer *Arabia* for Boston, where we arrived on July 11. I had been absent from my native land one year, two months, and four days, and the cost of it all had been about twenty-four hundred dollars. Summing up the gains and the losses of my tour, I can gratefully acknowledge a vast improvement in my health. The symptoms of lung trouble had wholly disappeared. I seemed in full vigor of body and mind. I had learned a great deal about foreign languages and foreign life. My observations in Palestine and the East enabled me ever afterwards to treat Scripture scenes and events in a vivid and accurate way. Above all, I had found my tongue, had acquired ease in conversation, and had learned to mingle with men. A proper knowledge of the world is essential to confidence in one's own powers. I am sure that my various experiences not only made me a broader and more effective preacher, but also they added indefinitely to the richness and interest of my after life. I have a store of memories upon which to draw both for solace and for illustration. While I was abroad, I did not realize all the advantage I was getting. A halo clothes all the places of famous story as long as you have not visited them; when they stand actually before your eyes, the halo vanishes, and you have a temporary feeling of disappointment; but when you leave such spots again behind you, the halo fortunately returns, and there it remains forever after.

But there is something to offset all these advantages of foreign travel, especially of travel so prolonged as was mine. True it is that if I had not gone then, I probably never afterwards could have gone—both time and money would have been lacking. But so long an absence threw me, more than is common, into the currents of foreign life. I was much of the time in the company of pleasure-seekers, people who have no strenuous purpose in life. Human nature is self-indulgent. It can persuade itself that it is *getting* good without the least effort on its part to *do* good. The noble American idea, that life which accomplishes nothing had better not be lived at all, is easily and quickly outgrown in the midst of people who are absorbed in the pursuit of new sensations and laugh at the suggestion that they owe anything to others. I must confess with sadness that though I left America full of eagerness to preach the gospel of Christ and ready to go to China or Japan for Christ's sake, a year without a prayer meeting left me with little love for Christ or for men's souls. It was with a heavy heart that I landed in Boston. My work in the ministry loomed up before me, not invitingly as a year before, but threateningly. It took me a whole year to recover my spiritual tone. Anxiety and perplexity were the price I had to pay for peace. I now have my doubts whether it is well for any young candidate for the ministry to interpose a year of travel between his preparatory studies and his actual work of preaching. Better go at once into the pastorate and take the foreign travel afterwards in brief spells of vacation. The pleasure-seeking spirit is a terrible foe to spiritual life and spiritual work.

4

First
Pastorate

But God did not leave me to myself. I found questions arising which drove me to my knees. There was first the question of my denominational relations, and there was secondly the question as to the proper place to begin my labors. In Germany I had settled one serious matter—that of the form of baptism. I found absolutely no difference among scholars with regard to the meaning of the word "baptize," and I began to see that the symbolism of the ordinance required that its form should be immersion. What other form could set forth the merging of the believer into Christ and the believer's participation in the death and resurrection of his Lord? But when it came to the matter of Communion, I was at sea. Most of my relatives upon my mother's side and all my college friends and acquaintances were Congregationalists or Presbyterians. How could I consent virtually to disfellowship them? These questions became mixed up with the other question of my future location. I had not been long at home before Dr. Robinson asked me to go to New York City and preach as a candidate for the First Baptist Church there, of which the lamented Kingman Nott had been the pastor. As I had been born and bred in a city, it seemed to me quite natural that a city should be the place of my first pastorate, and of all cities New York City seemed to furnish the best chance of success. I preached very well, so I thought; in fact, I questioned whether my sermons were not too good for the people. In one way they were too good—they were too elegant and too literary. The hardheaded, plain, and pious members of the old First Church thought that the simplicity of the gospel would please them better than fine rhetoric. The result was that to my great surprise the church did not give me a call to become its pastor. Dr. Robinson then sent me to Haverhill, Massachusetts, a village of ten thousand inhabitants. A staid and conservative church of three hundred members had been served for twenty-three years by its pastor, Dr. Arthur S. Train, and had only surrendered him when Newton Theological Seminary demanded him for its professor of homiletics and pastoral theology. The town was beginning to manufacture shoes, but the traditions of an aristocratic past were still rife. There was an artistic church edifice, in the Gothic style, though it was of painted wood, and there were pleasant social surroundings. Yet all my first impressions were unfavorable. The place seemed dead-alive. I could hardly breathe in it. But after my depressing experiences in New York City I was reasonably humble. The people were pleased with my preaching, and when the evening service was over, a large committee of deacons and members filed into the parlor of the house where I was staying and presented their earnest request that I would accept the pastorate of the church.

I suppose I should have fallen in at once with their offer and begun my work but for the fact that I was still unsettled in my mind with regard to the question of Communion. I said to them that while I was a thoroughgoing Baptist in the matter of immersion, I could not yet say that I believed in restricted Communion. If I came to them, they would have to give me liberty in that respect. This startled them like a thunderclap out of a clear sky. They replied that the church had stood in Haverhill for a hundred years; it had never failed to give its testimony to Baptist doctrine; baptism before Communion seemed to it to be the New Testament order; unless I could see the matter in a different light, they must sorrowfully withdraw their invitation. So I left town not altogether displeased, for I had no great fancy for the place, yet certainly discomposed, because I knew that the same difficulty would bar the way to my acceptance of any other important pastorate in the Baptist denomination. I went home again to Rochester convinced that I must settle my denominational views at once. Rochester was a good place to study, and I began to study. But another disturbing complication arose. During the previous summer and soon after my return from Europe, I had made a visit to my aunt in Oberlin, Ohio, and I had, as I thought, fallen in love with Miss Julia Finney, daughter of President Finney of Oberlin College. I had proposed marriage, and she had accepted. We had had a little flurry of correspondence. Suddenly, without fault of mine and for reasons entirely personal to herself, she found that she could not marry me, and she broke off the engagement. I had many times in my sleeve laughed at Theodore Bacon, but I thought it no laughing matter when I came to be thrown overboard myself. Darkness seemed to be closing round me. I had wanted a city church, but the city church did not want me. A country church had wanted me, but I had not wanted the country church. A certain young lady of intelligence and refinement, of musical and social gifts, had seemed to suit me, but now I learned of insuperable obstacles which prevented all hope of securing her. I was at my father's house, pecuniarily dependent when I ought to be earning my own living and with the consciousness that I had already profited far too much by the paternal generosity. I began to be despondent, but I began anew to think and pray.

One evening in December, 1860, in great trouble of mind, I wandered out through East Avenue. I had no particular object in view—I only felt my great need of wisdom and strength. It was a bitterly cold night. The landscape was wrapped in snow, and a bright moon was shining. My own soul was as cold and desolate as the snowy fields. I went on and on as far as Brighton. In thought, I began to review my religious experience. I remembered the soft May evening when for the first time I looked from my college window up to the sky and felt assured that God was, and forever would be, my Father and my Friend. And then it occurred to me that as I had once in this way "hitched my wagon to a star," the same course was open to me still—in fact, no other course could give me any permanent stability or peace. The bright moon that shone so constantly and calmly in the heavens above seemed to me a new symbol of God's light and faithfulness. I saw that I had wandered from him, that I had been listening to the voices of pleasure and ambition, that I had brought only unrest, perplexity, and distress to my own soul. I said to myself, "This unfaithfulness and half-heartedness shall end. Whatever God bids me, I will do. I will follow where he leads, come life, come death!" And then my communion with God was restored. I looked up to the moon, and its steady shining was a promise of guidance and protection. In the very light of God I walked homeward, fully assured that he would show me the truth both as to doctrine and as to duty.

Very shortly after this I received an invitation to supply the pulpit of the North Baptist Church of Chicago, and I went to that city. It was an organization of less than fifty members, and they were so poor that for my three months' service they could not give me enough to pay my board bill, leaving me to defray the expense of travel to and fro. Yet they thought it strange when I declined their call to become pastor. They liked my preaching; yet they had no proper apprehension that he that labors in the gospel must live of the gospel. But although I did not remain permanently in Chicago, my stay there was very useful to me. I took up my abode at the house of Aunt Almira Spencer, who had just been widowed by the death of her husband, Rev. William H. Spencer, pastor of the Westminster Presbyterian Church. Aunt Almira was left with two young children and with almost no means of support. She took in boarders, of whom I was one. I think that had it not been for the cares of her household and the necessity of providing for her children, her grief and despondency would have crazed her. I learned that the most irksome and distressing routine may be a blessing in disguise—God's means of diverting and healing a wounded spirit. I think my presence was a comfort to my aunt, as her sorrow was a revelation to me of the almost boundless capacity of the human heart either for pain or pleasure.

In Chicago I preached but one sermon on the Sunday, and I consequently had time to make one fairly good sermon every week. I tried to do nothing else. My study and my visitation from house to house engrossed all my attention. I laid up a few sermons which constituted my stock in trade when I afterwards became a real pastor. So I went on, earnestly but quietly, until the first gun was fired at Fort Sumter and President Lincoln issued his first call for troops and the great Civil War broke out. The Sunday after the first overt act of rebellion was a day of unparalleled excitement. From morning to night recruiting officers with squads of volunteers were parading the streets with fife and drum. On the Monday following, the citizens of Chicago gathered in the vast auditorium in which the National Convention had nominated Abraham Lincoln to take the oath of allegiance to the government and to the Constitution. It was said that twenty thousand men stood under that single roof. They were of all classes and all parties, but it seemed to me that the Spirit of God had made them one. A justice of the Supreme Court of the United States stood forth and held aloft a Bible and called upon every man in that vast multitude to hold up his right hand and swear. With a voice that reached the remotest corners of the great enclosure he repeated the first words of the oath: "We do solemnly swear!" And like the sounding of the sea or the breaking of thunder from the sky, all that multitudinous host repeated after him: "We do solemnly swear!" "To support the Constitution of the United States!" And still they followed: "To support the Constitution of the United States!" And so the oath proceeded till the solemn close: "So help us, God!" For many a man the taking of that oath meant the giving up of property and life, but it was taken with an intense and even exultant enthusiasm, for the cause of the country was felt to be the cause of God. If there were traitors there that day, they made no sign. Rebellion hid itself in fear. On many occasions since then I have used that scene as an illustration of the greater gathering when the universe shall assemble to recognize the right of Holiness to reign and when the multitude that no man can number shall cry, as the voice of many waters and as the voice of mighty thunderings, saying, "Alleluia, for the Lord God Omnipotent reigneth!"

My sermons in Chicago were colored by the dangers through which the country was passing. One sermon in particular aimed to strengthen the hands of those who defended the Union. It was on the text "The street shall be built again, and the wall, even in troublous times." I came to feel the need of a strong government in the nation. But having charge now, though only temporarily, of a real church, I came also to feel the need of a strong government in the church. The members with whom I came in contact were well-meaning but uninstructed, warmhearted but undisciplined. I was tempted for a time to think that a less democratic church government might be better for them than our Baptist republicanism. But I soon found that self-government is an educating influence and that congregational polity is the best polity for good people. I saw the guarantee for stability in the precepts and precedents of the New Testament, and I saw the security for freedom in the duty of individual interpretation of Christ's will as it is expressed in his word. I began to put together my fragmentary ideas of the church as I had never done before. The relation of the two ordinances to each other began to dawn upon me—baptism, the entrance into the communion of Christ's death and resurrection; the Lord's Supper, the continual ratification and increase of that communion after it has once begun; baptism, the beginning of a new life; the Lord's Supper, the nourishment of that life unto life eternal; baptism, the symbol of the new birth or regeneration; the Lord's Supper, the symbol of Christian growth or sanctification. As birth must come before food, so it became clear to me that baptism, the ordinance that symbolizes birth, must come before the Lord's Supper, the ordinance that symbolizes nourishment, and that to reverse the order was to teach, pictorially and by object lesson, that man can be sanctified without regeneration. Moreover, I became convinced that the change of the ordinances could not have been left by Christ to individual willfulness or caprice but that the church must have been entrusted with their supervision and empowered to keep them as Christ first delivered them.

In this way I was unintentionally and unconsciously coming over to the Baptist position with regard to Communion, as I had already come over to the Baptist position with regard to baptism. I finally made up my mind that baptism was a New Testament prerequisite to the Lord's Supper and also that we could decline to admit a brother to *church* fellowship upon the ground that he was not baptized, while at the same time we could hold with him the most loving and hearty *Christian* fellowship. I found indeed in 2 Thessalonians 3:6 the model for our conduct in such a case, for that is an instance of exclusion from church fellowship and from the

Augustus Hopkins Strong in his middle years

Lord's Supper, its sign, while yet the offender is not excluded from Christian fellowship but is still counted "a brother." I saw my way to be a thoroughgoing Baptist—I could no longer be anything else. Though my worldly ambition and personal preference and college friendships and family relationships would have led me to be a Congregationalist or a Presbyterian, conscience and Scripture compelled me to be a Baptist. So I learned by practical experience my fourth lesson in doctrine, the doctrine of the church. And when I became ready to take my place in the Baptist ranks, Providence made a place in the Baptist ranks ready for me. Without any seeking or knowledge of mine, the same place that had been offered me six months before was now offered to me again. The church at Haverhill, Massachusetts, had found no one to take its pastorate, and they wrote again to me asking if I had not, after reflection, concluded that Baptist views of Communion were correct and if I would not now accept their call. I replied that I believed myself now to be a Baptist but that I could not determine until after further acquaintance whether it was my duty to become their pastor. The result was that I was invited to supply their pulpit for an indefinite time but with the hope that mutual acquaintance might sooner or later lead the church to extend a call and might lead me to accept it.

And as I bade farewell to the little North Church of Chicago, to which I had become much attached, and with about a dozen written sermons in my trunk, I made my way to Haverhill. I still had no love for the town. I went only because God sent me. When I set foot there for the second time, I wanted to flee like Jonah. I wanted a larger place, and I wanted a city church. But obeying God's call, I began work there. And I found after a little that the wisdom and plan of God were better than any wisdom and plan of mine. To all eternity I shall never cease to praise him that he did not permit me to have my own way but directed me instead to that little shoe-town in the northeastern corner of Massachusetts.

I found a church and a community very different from those I had just left. In Chicago, there had been extreme demonstrativeness but not an equal faithfulness, great promises but not so prompt and sure performance. People had crowded around me after the first sermon, inviting me to their houses and offering me their horses, but I could not get them to come to the prayer meeting or pay what they owed me. Haverhill was as lacking in demonstrativeness as Chicago was running over with it. Nobody came up to congratulate me upon my preaching—it was not the custom to talk in the house of God. It was two years before I knew whether the principal deacon was my friend or my foe—he did not regard it wise to flatter the young minister. But I learned after a time that he and dozens of others like him would stand by me through thick and thin—if they did not say many pleasant things to my face, they talked very well of me behind my back. It was worth much to me to get intimately acquainted with sterling New England Christians, who studied their Bibles and had regular family prayer and went to meeting three times on Sunday and once during the week. The meetinghouse was never called a church, for the only church was the body of believers. The Haverhill church had been wonderfully well trained, for Dr. Train had been its pastor. I learned from it more than it ever learned from me, and when I left it after four years of service, I took with me many ideas of church organization and order which I applied with excellent effect in my second pastorate.

The Haverhill community as well as the Haverhill church furnished me with ever new surprises. The first thing that impressed me was the fact that everybody was related to everybody else. All the leading families had married and intermarried until the network was inextricable. It was dangerous business to say a disparaging word of anybody, for the person *to* whom you spoke was sure to be first or second cousin to the person *of* whom you spoke. The second thing that impressed me was the fact that there were no young men in town. They had all gone West. So surely as a boy showed marked talent, he went either to Boston or to Chicago to seek his fortune. The result was that the town was overloaded with bright and fine girls who were left high and dry with not the ghost of a chance of ever getting married. The church was full of them, young women of education and good manners, many of them teachers in the day schools and in the Sunday School, but, as far as matrimony was concerned, wasting their sweetness on the desert air. It occurred to me that in the absence of young men these young women might do much to make the prayer meetings interesting. But alas, the former pastor had taken as applicable to all time Paul's injunction that women should keep silence in the churches. In fact, he had said that the speaking of women in social meetings of the church was as clearly forbidden in Scripture as murder or adultery. To the best women of the church a nameless horror attached itself to any participation on their part. Yet there was one exception. Each candidate for admission to the church, whether male or female, was required to relate to the church a Christian experience. For the women it was the first and the last speaking in meeting, and the difficulty of reconciling it with Paul's prohibition did not seem to occur to them.

The meetings for prayer and conference were very formal. Two or three deacons would pray for twenty minutes apiece after I had expounded the Scriptures, and then, unless Mr. Duncan or Deacon Keely made remarks, a long pause would follow, and the assembly would be dismissed. I endured this for a few weeks, and then I planned a revolution. I suggested a Young People's Meeting in order to train the younger members for service. But I was at once met with the objection that the church was one whole and one family, that its meetings should comprise all classes, that to have any single age or class meet by itself was to rend in sunder the body of Christ, that the young needed the supervision of the old. I succeeded in proving to my satisfaction that in the church, as in the school, the young learned some things better by themselves than in the company of their elders. At last, objections were overcome and, with two or three older brethren to watch and supervise, the Young People's Meeting was started. But still the young women were silent, and only two or three young men were to be found ready and capable of giving help. Then I preached a sermon on the text "Your sons and your daughters shall prophesy." I claimed that Paul's prohibition was only for the time and place for which he wrote. The principle of modesty and subordination was of perpetual obligation, but the method of showing this modesty and subordination varied from age to age. What was indecorous in apostolic times was now permissible and proper, and no woman should stifle her impulse to speak or pray in a social meeting of the church merely upon the ground of what Paul enjoined at Corinth.

My sermon was listened to in ominous silence. When I preached it, I took my life in my hand. But the members of the church had fortunately been taught to receive with reverence and humility all instruction from the sacred desk. They had a secret liking for the young preacher who dared to preach unpopular doctrine, and they bowed their heads in submission, either to Providence or to Fate. At the next prayer meeting everybody was agog to see the denouement. I had no sooner taken my seat after the introductory exercises than a voluble young woman who had come over to us from the Methodists, and had for months been aching for the chance, arose and poured forth an incoherent lot of sobs and protestations that made the judicious grieve and did the business for women's speaking for that evening and for many evenings after. But my sermon was not entirely without its fruit. Little by little, good women got courage to speak. The reform actually began, and when I went back to visit the church a few years ago, I found the old order entirely changed. It had given place to the new. The Haverhill church had become a church in which women as well as men freely expressed their love for Christ and their determination to serve him.

Two men in Haverhill must be mentioned with great respect and affection. The first was the Honorable James H. Duncan. He was a man of about sixty when I first knew him. Of Scotch-Irish descent and with a line of educated ancestors behind him, he united a fervid natural temperament with patrician elegance and refinement. He had been a classmate of Edward Everett at Harvard College, had practiced law for many years, and had served two terms as a member of Congress. After his political life was over, he settled down in Haverhill, occupied the family mansion, and cared for his farms and village property. His public life had given him a large circle of acquaintances; he was the friend of Daniel Webster and many other distinguished men; he loved to entertain, and his house always had visitors—in summer a constant succession of them. Mrs. Duncan was the kindest and most motherly of women; she had had thirteen children; some had died, but seven were often at home together. Into this household I had been introduced on my first flying visit to Haverhill, and when I came for the second time, as stated supply to the church, Mr. and Mrs. Duncan took me in again. For seven months I was a member of the family, treated as a son, and, more than this, honored because of my position as a preacher of the gospel. It was my first experience with a household conducted on the large plan. The merriment, the courtesy, the hospitality of it all struck a responsive chord in my heart. To see Mr. Duncan at the head of his princely board with Mrs. Duncan at the foot and a dozen children or guests sprinkled in between, all served with abundance and grace, was a large lesson in noble manners. The Christmas celebrations and the Associational gatherings, when the house was full of guests, were times of music and sprightly conversation that taught one something of the possible richness of human life.

Mr. Duncan was a man of moods, and it was important that you should see him at his best. Breakfast was his least engaging hour, for, till he had had his coffee, he was generally reserved and even frigid. Sometimes this mood continued through the morning, and then he was sometimes known to pass even his wife in the street without recognizing her. But he was a natural cavalier notwithstanding, and no one could ingratiate himself into a lady's affections better than Mr. Duncan. He was a devout man, an impressive reader of the Scripture, with a remarkable gift in prayer. The family devotions which he always conducted, and in which he poured forth his soul with an intensity and pathos all his own, could never afterward be forgotten by those who were privileged once to hear them. And when on a Sunday, after he had listened to a good sermon, he came to the evening meeting for prayer, he often spoke out the thoughts that had been suggested to him with a depth of feeling and an elegance of phrase which one would have called classic if they had not seemed almost angelic. His natural eloquence made him a prominent figure in our great denominational meetings. He was a man of the world at the same time that he was an earnest Christian. He thought well of dancing, but when the church reproved him for permitting it in his parlor, he submitted to the judgment of his brethren and permitted it no more. His children inherited from their mother consumptive tendencies, and one after another, James, Rose, Rebecca, George, and Lizzie succumbed to the disease, until now only four of those whom I then knew—Mary, Samuel, Caroline, and Margaret—still survive. But of the whole flock there was not one black sheep. All who died died in the faith, and those who live are living earnest Christian lives. To have known such a family was itself an education.

Of my lifelong connection with Samuel W. Duncan I must say one further word. When I went to Haverhill, he had just graduated from Brown University and was pondering the question what his profession in life should be. Sam was a young man of moods, like his father, and in the presence of his father he could neither speak nor pray, though he was an unusually earnest Christian. I think my influence and example did much to turn his thoughts to the ministry. But when he made up his mind to preach and made known his intention to his father, he met with opposition, all the more galling because it was unexpected. "Why, Sam! I want you to study law and succeed me in the care of my business and property! And besides, you know you have no gift in prayer!" Poor Sam was well aware that the words stuck in his throat when he tried to pray before his father. For a time he attempted to study law. But the plan did not work. His conscience would not let him rest. He broke away and spent a year at Newton in the theological seminary. Then he raised a company and went to the war. After his return he completed his theological course at Rochester. When I had become pastor at Cleveland, I secured for him the pastorate of the Erie Street, afterwards known as the Euclid Avenue, Baptist Church. When I came to Rochester, he came from Cincinnati to be pastor of our Second Baptist Church, and we were again together until he became foreign secretary of the American Baptist Missionary Union at Boston. Our long friendship has been one of the pleasant features of my life, and I have never ceased to be thankful that I ever had anything to do with getting him to preach the gospel. His noble lifework shows that fathers do not always know what is best for their children.

Deacon John Keely was one of the most godly men I have ever known. Grave and reticent, he was yet wise and true beyond any common standard. All his youth and early manhood he had lived a most moral and upright life; yet, though he was a regular attendant at church, he never called himself a Christian. In a time of revival, however, he was found to be engaged in urging others to attend the meetings and to seek their salvation. Members of the church told him that he ought to make a profession of religion. But he shrank from such a profession with fear and trembling. He was no Christian, he said, and he would be no hypocrite. But his efforts for others continued. At last he was persuaded to attend a meeting of the deacons and tell them the history of his life. It appeared that he had prayed from his mother's knee, had loved God and God's people for many years, desired to obey Christ and trust him, but, because he had had no rapturous experiences and knew so well his own unworthiness, he had never dared to hope that God had accepted him. The deacons advised him to follow Christ in baptism. He consented only on condition that they, and not he, should take the responsibility. So he came into the church and became one of its most useful members. Never elated but always in the place of duty, he proved one of the best advisers and most consistent examples that the church had ever had. He was a farmer, and he lived two miles from the village. But Deacon Keely was regularly at the prayer meeting, and his prayers were manifest communings with God. On one or two occasions, sickness in his household compelled him to be absent. He excused himself to me and added, "I wish you to know, Brother Strong, that when we are absent, my wife and I do not take the time from the Lord but spend the whole hour of the meeting in prayer together at home."

Such was the community and such the church in which I began my ministry. I went to Haverhill on trial, and the church put itself on trial as well. I found a depth of Christian experience and a genuineness of Christian character that drew out my love and admiration. I preached earnestly, and my sermons met with response. I began to feel that my prejudice against a country church was ill-founded and that Haverhill might, after all, be the place for me. In July the church, after consulting me, gave me a formal call; the society ratified it; they promised me twelve hundred dollars a year salary, payable monthly, and I accepted the call and began my labors. My ordination took place on the first day of August, 1861, Dr. Robinson preaching the sermon, Dr. Train making the ordaining prayer, and Dr. Mills giving the charge to the candidate. I had never attended an ordination service, and I had but little notion of what was expected of me. In my examination before the council, instead of giving a full statement of my views of doctrine, I summarized them much after the fashion of the Apostles' Creed and then invited the brethren to question me. It was a large and representative council, and when its members saw what was before them, they proceeded to examine me within an inch of my life.

Rochester was not popular in the neighborhood of Newton, and my inquisitors were all Newton men. For two hours they kept me on the rack. I fear I made a sorry exhibit of myself. And though they voted to ordain me, I resolved to warn every such candidate thereafter that he must occupy at least an hour with his own statement in order that the council might be too tired to torment him. I did not get over the humiliation of that trial until I received notice that I was elected a member of the famous Theological Circle of Boston, of which Doctors Alvah Hovey, Samuel L. Caldwell, and Herman Lincoln were members, and Dr. Caldwell informed me that I was the only Rochester man whom the Newton people thought of any account. Perhaps I did better on my examination than I myself thought at the time.

And now came an event of the utmost importance in my history, namely, my meeting with the young lady who afterwards became my wife. After my ordination, I took a month's vacation and spent the time in Rochester. I had been attracted during my college course by little Sallie Collins; after my return from Europe I was engaged for two or three months to Julia Finney; if it had not been that she was my cousin, I might have married Lillie Fowler; but now there rose before me a star that eclipsed them all. Mrs. Stillson, when I called upon her, told me she had found just the person for me and that her name was Miss Hattie Savage. One afternoon she brought us together at her house to tea. The house is still plain to see on East Avenue, corner of East Park, and the number is 134. Mrs. Henry Hartman and her family now occupy it. I think the young lady was ignorant of Mrs. Stillson's purpose, for she bore herself in a composed, if not an indifferent, manner. If she had been too engaging, I might have been suspicious. As it was, I came, I saw, and I was conquered. Her dark hair and bright eyes and clear complexion, together with an enchanting dress of green silk, took the fancy of the undersigned, from the first moment that he saw her. "Here is health and sincerity, character and self-respect, good looks and faithfulness, all combined"—this is what I said to myself, and I have never had occasion to think I was mistaken. Of course I had to see the said young lady home that evening; I requested permission to call; the courtship proceeded rapidly; within a week we were engaged, and within three months we were married. I would not advise any of my descendants to imitate the rapidity of this process unless they are sure they have found a treasure as great as mine.

This is the place to tell something of my dear wife's parents. Eleazer Savage was born in 1800, and so he was just as old as the century. He was a native of Middletown, Connecticut. He graduated from the Literary and Theological Institution at Hamilton, New York, in 1824 and became the first pastor of the First Baptist Church of Rochester in that same year. He was not tall, but he was a remarkably well-built and handsome man, endowed with robust health, unfailing spirits, and a very uncommon common sense. He had the aptness and quickness of expression which people call mother-wit. Always cheery and never dull, he was a welcome guest with young and old. His pastorate in Rochester lasted but a year or two, but he put the then weak and struggling church upon its foundations and then turned to the regions beyond. He conceived it to be his mission, not precisely to do pioneer work by starting new enterprises, but to rescue feeble churches that were ready to perish. A great economist, he had always something ahead, so that he was never absolutely dependent for his support upon the churches which he served. He would go to churches that had had no preaching for months, that were rent by quarrels, that were utterly discouraged, and would promise to set them upon their feet if they would only do what they could. Gathering the few faithful members together, he would inspire them to hope and pray, would reconcile enmities, bring back the neglectful, induce persistent rebels to ask for exclusion, or, in case they would not do this, secure their exclusion by the church, in spite of opposition on their part. Usually a great revival of religion would follow; large additions would be made to the membership; the spirit of liberality and self-support would be engendered. Then Mr. Savage would regard his work as done; he would find a permanent pastor for the church; he himself would move on and repeat the process with some other church that was just at the point to die.

So he resuscitated at least a dozen churches, giving to each of them from one to three years of labor, and everywhere winning for himself the name of an able, self-forgetful, and devoted minister of Christ. He was pastor at Oswego, Albion, Medina, Knowlesville, Kendall, York, Bath, Livonia, besides taking charge of the Rapids

Mission at Rochester and the Cottage Mission at Cleveland. For a time he was a traveling agent of the American Sunday School Union, and again he served as financial secretary of the New York Baptist Union for Ministerial Education. His keen observation and his large knowledge of the churches made him an expert in church government, and his little book on *Church Discipline, Formative and Corrective* is one of the most condensed, sensible, and scriptural treatises upon the subject that has ever been published. He was an incisive, piquant, scriptural preacher. He believed and he taught the old-fashioned gospel. Many hundreds were brought to Christ under his ministry, and those whom he baptized were shown the way of holiness and of service. His savings sufficed for his support in his old age, and he left something to his children and to benevolent institutions, but the best thing that he left was the memory of a noble life. He died at the Rapids at the age of eighty-six, honored by all who knew him.

Hattie's mother was a woman of excellent mind. She had patience and industry in larger measure than common. And indeed she needed to have them, for her husband's frequent absences and changes of location threw upon her the main burden of the family. The family was large—five sons and two daughters—the daughters, of whom Hattie was the elder, coming last in the order of succession. When I called at No. 6 Pleasant Street, Hattie's home, I saw more of the young lady than I did of her mother or her father. How they ever consented at such short notice to let me have the treasure of their house and the light of their eyes remains a mystery unto this day. It may be because I insisted that I could not do without her. Whatever be the explanation, I know there was a wedding on the morning of November 6, 1861. It was very private. My parents, sister Belle, and Mrs. Stillson were the only persons present outside of Hattie's family. Of course Mr. Savage married us. We had a wedding breakfast and a wedding cake, and then we took the train to Albany. The skies were clouded, but our hearts were peaceful. When we reached our room at the Delevan House and had had our supper, I am happy to say that the first thing we did was to kneel down together and commend ourselves and our whole future to God. I think the influence of that prayer has gone through our lives. Our union was begun, and it has continued, in Him who is the only source of truth and constancy, and so I believe it will be to the end.

Next day we went to New York, and there we had a blissful week at the Fifth Avenue Hotel, with rooms looking out over the Square, with a fine band of music playing in the evening, and with meals served in our own little parlor. Here Cousin Hop and his pretty wife came over from Brooklyn to call upon us, and my college classmate D. Stuart Dodge took us for a ride in the newly laid-out Central Park. We went to no theater or opera, but we heard Dr. Tyng preach. It was a strictly religious honeymoon from the beginning to the end. But it was quite as happy as if it had been a time of dissipation, for we meant it as a preparation for serving Christ. On the way to Boston we spent a day or two in Springfield, Massachusetts, and had a ride in a "one-hoss-shay" out into the country, which in its antique primness was unlike anything Hattie had ever seen before. At last we reached Haverhill and were welcomed by Mrs. Brown on Summer Street, with whom we were to board a year and ten months. She and her sister "Aunt Abby" were good women and members of our church. We lived in two rooms, a parlor below and a bedroom above, and we had wholesome but not extravagant fare. The people of the church, and Mr. Duncan's family in particular, were very kind to us, and yet they permitted us to begin our married life in quietness. I set to work with a will, though my zeal was somewhat without knowledge. I worked hard to prepare my first sermon after the marriage. The peculiarity of my subject never occurred to me until I saluted the curious and tittering congregation with the text "We all do fade as a leaf."

My church was very considerate. They appreciated and expected good preaching. They knew that the making of sermons required time. I had my study at the church. Only one deacon made me trouble. He knocked at my door mornings, set himself down, and expected me to entertain him for an hour. I gave notice from the pulpit that I would see visitors from twelve to one: from nine till twelve I must devote to work in preparation for the pulpit. The good deacon never came at the wrong hour again; yet he was not offended. My time in Haverhill was mostly spent upon the Bible. Determining to know nothing but Christ and him crucified, I unwisely cleared my library of many valuable books that seemed to me entirely secular. I sold my splendid sets of Goethe, Schiller, and Jean Paul, and bought Alford, Olshausen, and Delitzsch instead. I preached series of sermons on the "Law of God" and on "Sin, the Transgression of the Law." Henry Ward Beecher said once that after one had preached two successive sermons on hell and damnation, it was well to take another tack and preach some of the comforts of the gospel. I had not then learned wisdom, and I gave my people severe doctrine and plenty of it. I regarded this as simple faithfulness. I had a very lofty idea of what constituted a Christian—a legal idea, derived largely from Mr. Finney. I considered perhaps one-third of my church members to be genuine believers; one-third were pretty certainly hypocrites; and the remaining third were doubtful. I am thankful that this estimate was greatly changed by my experiences in Haverhill. Men whom I at first wished to exclude from the church proved in time of sorrow to be sustained by a Christian hope or in time of revival to be useful workers for others. One brother whose neglect of public worship puzzled me was found to have a half-insane wife at home, to whom he was obliged to give all the time he could spare from his business and whose sad condition he was trying to conceal. An old maiden lady, whom I had thought peculiarly offish, told me when I called that after praying twenty-three years for her former pastor she was distressed that she could not transfer her affections to me and pray for me as she had prayed for him and that she had set apart that day as a day of fasting and prayer that God would give her a better mind. Before I left the town after my four years' pastorate, I concluded that the hypocrites were very few and that in the judgment of charity at least nine-tenths of the members of the church were real disciples of Christ.

After about two years at hard study, in which I wrote my one elaborate sermon every week and preached another without notes, my cask seemed to run dry. Results were discouragingly few; some people rebelled against my minatory preaching and left the congregation. I found it hard to make sermons, and when I had made them, they came to naught. I lay awake Sunday nights thinking what a fool I had made of myself during the day, and I spent Monday mornings doubting whether I could ever make a sermon again. Many a time I walked out of the village and took refuge behind a great boulder in the open field, bowing my head in my hands and rocking it in vain for an idea. Fear took possession of me and trembling—at times it seemed as if I must give up preaching altogether. My knees smote together as I went up the pulpit steps; in the midst of my public prayers, I was sometimes seized with embarrassment, so that I doubted whether I could ever get through; at funerals I felt almost utterly devoid of sympathy, and my service seemed cold as ice; to call upon people in my flock and to pray with them sent shivers through me merely in the anticipation of it. In short, I felt deserted by God. I was set there to stand for him, and stand for him I would, till I died; but I felt that I was standing alone, with a whole universe of evil influences fighting against me; what was I, that I should be able to overcome the world and the flesh and the devil, all combined?

I now see that a part of my despondency was due to ill health. I took no regular exercise, and yet I ate hearty food. I was nervous and weak. Lassitude crept over me, and my brain would not work. But my physical state was connected with my spiritual state and had this in large part as its cause. I felt that I was far from God, that I somehow lacked the essence of a Christian experience, that my preaching was destitute of life and power. And yet at this very time I was exhausting myself with my efforts to do my duty. I worked, up to the last limit of my powers. I made pastoral calls till I was ready to drop with fatigue. I prayed, with an earnestness that amounted to agony. Strangely enough, at this very time of my greatest depression and hopelessness, a revival of religion began in Haverhill under the preaching of Rev. A. B. Earle. Our church, though conservative, participated to some extent in the meetings. A large number of persons were converted. I was called upon to preach to sinners and to direct inquirers. Yet though these were the very results I had been praying for, I took no pleasure in them. I could not feel any deep interest in those who were seeking their salvation. My exhortations seemed to be idle and perfunctory. My own dreadful state prevented me from rejoicing over the rescue of others. I began to fear that I had sinned away my day of grace and had committed the sin against the Holy Ghost.

Fortunately the summer vacation came on, and I made my way to Rochester. I was sick both in body and in mind. When I reached home, I made up my mind that whatever else those four weeks might or might not bring to me, they should at least reveal to me where I stood before God. I resolved that I would not look into a newspaper or read any book but the Bible until I knew whether I was a Christian or had any proper place in the ministry. Many days I lay on my bed, resting and praying. In some strange way—I know not how—I was led to contrast my state of mind with that of the early apostles. I read the book of the Acts—there I found no despondency and no gloom but rather an ebullient enthusiasm and an inspiring life. Courage and hope were their very breath, and every foe went down before them. Whence came all this, and what was the explanation of it? At last it occurred to me that it was due to the presence of Christ *in them;* the Savior who *began* both to do and to teach before his death was now doing and teaching in and through his apostles after his resurrection. But what reason had they for expecting this? I looked back to John's gospel, and there the secret was told me. I read the fourteenth, fifteenth, sixteenth, and seventeenth chapters of that gospel, and it seemed to me that I had never read them before—they were a new revelation. The apostles had experienced only what Jesus had promised long before. I read about the vine and the branches. I had never regarded this as more than an Oriental picture of a union of sympathy or friendship, a union of juxtaposition or moral likeness. Now I saw that it was a *union of life* which Christ was describing, a union in which the Spirit of Christ interpenetrates and energizes ours, a union in which he joins himself so indissolubly to us that neither life nor death, nor height nor depth, nor any other creature shall be able to separate us from him.

My great mistake and shortcoming was revealed to me in the light of Christ's own word. I had been content to be merely *in touch* with Christ; I had known him only as an external Savior, whose connection with me might be broken; as a matter of fact, I had come to think of him as severed from me by a distance as great as the distance of the cold North Star. Now I learned that he was "closer than breathing, nearer than hands or feet." He was "not so far as even to be near," for he was in my very mind and heart, and he had made himself to be a part of me forever. He had come to me at the time of my conversion, little as I then understood it, and had formed an indissoluble union with my poor weak soul. I had been ignorant of his presence within me; in my sinfulness and unbelief I had banished him to the remotest corner of the mean habitation; yet in his grace and mercy he had never deserted it but had still held on, waiting for the time when I should gladly open all the doors and the whole house should be filled with his light and love. And now the time had come to open the doors. I did open them, and my sorrow was turned to joy. The very glory of God overshadowed me. And this was not all. Christ within me was the hope of glory for all time to come. I knew that this union would never be dissolved, for all things were mine, whether the world or life or death or things present or things to come, because I was Christ's and Christ was God's.

So I learned by experience my fifth great lesson in doctrine—the great lesson of union with Christ. I have come to think, with Alexander, that it is the central truth of all theology and of all religion. From it radiate all the other doctrines of Christianity. With this lesson learned of a union of life with the Second Adam, which makes redeemed humanity partaker of his righteousness, I could also understand the prior union of life with the first Adam, which made fallen humanity partaker of his sin and guilt. Regeneration, conversion, justification, sanctification, perseverance, ecclesiology, and eschatology revealed themselves to me successively as mere correlates of this union of Christ with the believer. If I had never had this experience, I never could have taught theology. I do not mean to say that the theological implications of my experience were formulated at once. But the clue was given to me, and from this time the dark places of doctrine became increasingly light. The change in my practical life, however, was immediate, and even more marked than any change in my doctrinal views. Peace, joy, courage, and hope were infused into my soul. I looked forward to my work with irrepressible ardor. To preach such a Savior, to make known to Christians the unsearchable riches they possessed in him, to offer to sinners such life and power as the life and power of the Son of God—this seemed to me a work for angels, yet a work which *I* could do, with him in my heart to strengthen and inspire. Whereas, before, I had thought of myself as fighting single-handedly and alone against a universe of evil influences, any one of which could thwart and crush me, I now saw that with Christ in me I was virtually omnipotent; as soon as I put forth the least effort to perfect myself or to do good to others, Christ set all the wheels of the universe in motion to help me; all the forces of nature and all the agencies of history and all the powers of the Spirit of God were working together for my good.

I can describe the effect of all this upon my ministry only by saying that it was life from the dead. I went back to Haverhill in the fullness of the blessing of the gospel of Christ. I began to preach on Union with Christ, and on the Completeness of the Christian in Him. People were wonderfully touched and moved. The best of them said that very truly they had never heard the subject treated before but that it had been of unspeakable value to them. My fear and my despondency were gone; my physical health began to mend and has mended from that day to this, so that I can truly say that Christ healed my body as well as my soul. I preached with a joy and self-forgetfulness that I had never known before. Preparation of sermons became a delight. In five minutes, a passage would open before me, and a whole sermon would be virtually made that would have cost me a whole week's labor before. All this was connected with a new experience with regard to prayer. Up to this time prayer had been to me a struggle. I had tried to reach a God who was far away, and I fancied my success to be proportioned to the amount of effort which I put into my petitions. I had not then heard of the woman who was praying with great vociferation but greatly moderated her tone when a friend whispered in her ear, "Sister, if you will only get a little nearer to the Lord, you will not have to talk so loud!" The Lord had come near to me. He had become the soul of my soul and the life of my life. I did not need to weep or cry aloud. I learned that prayer was the breath of God in man, returning whence it came, and that when he inspired my soul to seek, he had an ear to hear. I well remember the day when I first prayed in simple faith and said to myself with childlike confidence, "My Father has heard, and he will surely answer. Blessed be God, who hath not turned away my prayer nor his mercy from me!" I not only prayed with a faith that I had never known before, but also I came to feel that the Lord desired me to ask great things and desired to accomplish great things by me. I took to myself the promise in Jeremiah: "Call unto me, and I will answer thee, and shew thee great and mighty things, which thou knowest not." A new spirit of hope and of holy ambition possessed me. Whereas, before this, life had seemed hardly worth the living and I pictured it to myself as a sort of railroad tunnel, with darkness all round and only a pinhole of light at the end, and the last day of my life seemed the only one I could call happy, I was now full of courage and of longing to live and to do great things for God.

I had many answers to prayer. My whole pastoral work took on a new aspect because I felt that Christ was with me in it. I would often kneel down in my study at two o'clock in the afternoon and ask his direction. I would go down the street expecting his guidance, and he would from moment to moment point out my duty. The sight of a business sign suggested the name of a man whom I ought to see; I turned in to the shop and found the man ready to receive my encouragement or my admonition. Jackson Swett was a portly, rich, and large-hearted man, about fifty years of age. There was no more popular man in the community than was he. He was genial, public-spirited, liberal to every good cause. His wife was a praying member of my church, and he was a regular attendant. But he was not a Christian man—indeed, he regarded himself as better than most of the Christian men he knew. I had felt it my duty to talk with him, but I had refrained from mere timidity. One afternoon I met him on a street corner. The Lord bade me speak and put words into my mouth: "Mr. Swett, I have wanted to talk with you, but I have been afraid. I respect you highly; yet I am concerned about you. I fear you have never yet surrendered yourself to Christ. Will you not do that?" It seemed to take his breath away. He answered gently but evasively, thanked me, and passed on. It was a little word, but the Lord had helped me to utter it, and I had delivered my soul. On the next Sunday morning, as I was about to enter my study at the church just before the service, Deacon Keely met me. "Pastor," he said, "Jackson Swett is converted, and he wants to come forward after the sermon and tell what the Lord has done for him!" So after the sermon I gave him the opportunity, and the great, generous, unwieldy man took his place before the pulpit amid breathless silence and began with faltering voice and with all the simplicity of a child to relate the story of a conversion like that of the apostle Paul. "My friends," he began, "I thought I was a very good man, but I have found out that I am a great sinner. Oh, how I have treated my Savior!"

He told us that on the preceding Saturday evening, after tea, he had parted from his wife in the hallway of his house and had gone down to his office to post some books. He opened his safe, took out his ledger, and was carrying it to his desk, when it flashed upon him that there was another account which he needed to settle first, namely, his account with God. And then he remembered nothing more, except that Christ himself appeared to him, in such glory that he fell to the floor and groveled in the dust. The sin of his heart and life seemed great enough to crush him down to hell, and he was in agony on account of it. But the mercy and love of Christ were greater than his sin, and, at the same instant that he was cast down, he was exalted and overwhelmed with the infinite generosity of Christ's free forgiveness. In fact, the love of God was so shed abroad in his heart that he burst out into floods of weeping. He rose from the floor, replaced his ledger in the safe, and took his way homeward. As he opened the door of his house, his wife met him in the hallway, saying, "Why, my dear, I thought you were going down to your office!" He had not been absent from the house, it seemed to her, more than ten minutes—indeed, her first impression was that he had not left the house at all. "Mary, can't you sing something?" was his first word. She did not understand what he meant till he drew her to the sofa and told her how Christ had appeared to him and had saved his soul. And this was the beginning of a humble and devoted Christian life. The church admitted him to its membership and afterwards made him one of its deacons. In that office he served faithfully till he died.

I felt moved in those days to make personal visitations upon all the men employed in the shoe factories. Their name was legion, and many of them were servants of the evil one. Whether it was wise to address successively a hundred men working side by side in gangs, when each man's work depended on the work of all the rest, is now a question to me. But I resolved to leave no stone unturned to show my interest in them and at least invite them to come and hear the gospel. William N. Long was one of these shoemakers. His wife was an earnest Christian, and she had long prayed for him, but he was bitter and scornful. As soon as he saw me approaching, he began to hammer upon his sole leather with new vigor in order to drown out my voice. I told him that I wanted him to be a Christian, but he made no reply except to hammer yet more angrily. When I gave up my effort and bade him good afternoon, he neither looked up nor responded. All the way home I accused myself of having played the fool and having gone on a wild-goose chase. But the next morning, as I was going down the hill toward my study in the church, I met Mrs. Long, coming up. "Oh, Mr. Strong," she said, "come and see my husband! He came home in the middle of the afternoon yesterday and said he was sick. But I found after a little that it was conviction of his sins. He could eat no supper; he could not sit still more than a minute at a time; and he has been walking the streets in his distress all night long. And now he wants to see you and has gone down to your study to meet you." And there I found him, ready to do anything or to be anything, if he might only have his sins forgiven. He told me that the moment I left him the day before, God so revealed to him the awfulness of his sin in insulting me when I had come out of sheer compassion for his soul that he could not eat or sleep or rest. He knelt down in my study and gave himself to Christ, and he rose up with the hope that the Lord had accepted him. He too was soon baptized, and he lived faithful to God and the church, even to the last.

Another case, little less remarkable, was that of Captain George Foster. He had a Christian mother, but he was very profligate and profane. He was at that time a seaman in the navy. He passed the forts with Farragut at Mobile. After that fearful day was over, it occurred to him that he had not uttered an oath during the whole day. Since he had previously sworn with every opening of his lips, he asked himself why he had so refrained. The only answer he could give was: "You were afraid! You knew that a shot might strike you at any moment and that you might be summoned to stand before God!" Then he called himself a coward for swearing when God was absent but abstaining when God was near, and he resolved that he would swear no more. He kept his vow. When the ship reached New Orleans, a furlough was given to the crew, and they all went ashore. Before he went, he said to himself, "Now you have never gone ashore up to this time without getting drunk. I wonder if you could for once get back sober?" He resolved that he would, and he kept this resolve also. All this proved afterwards to be prevenient grace and the working of God's Holy Spirit. It was not long before an evangelistic chaplain held a meeting on board and invited all the men who wanted to begin a new life to step forward from the ranks. The first who came was George Foster. He found Christ and was filled with joy and peace in believing. He became a continual witness for the Savior, instant in season and out of season, working day and night for the conversion of his shipmates. When he came home, he united with the church and told his story of the leadings of God before his conversion, a story very like that of John Bunyan.

My church was very conservative in receiving members. After candidates had approved themselves to the committee of the deacons, their names had to be presented to the church, and a month intervened before they were permitted to relate their experience or were actually received to membership. During this interval inquiry was made as to their conduct, and opportunity was given for objections to be made. The result was that few tares got mixed in with the wheat. Of all the hundred persons who united with the church during my pastorate of four years, I do not know of any who afterwards proved to be destitute of religious life. Baptisms were great and solemn occasions. No baptistry had ever been erected—it would have been regarded as a very doubtful innovation. A bend in the Merrimac River, where the bank sloped gradually down to the water, afforded a magnificent natural amphitheater, and on a summer's afternoon the stillness of the great throng that assembled there to witness the symbolic burial and resurrection with Christ of the those who had joined themselves for time and eternity to him was most impressive and affecting. The first persons that I baptized were Ellen Cogswell and Lucy Brown, both of them sweet and beautiful characters, whose whole after lives showed that they had been born again and that the life they lived was lived by the faith of the Son of God. I feel deeply grateful for all these experiences in connection with the dear old church in Haverhill. I tried to make full proof of my ministry, and I found that Christ was indeed the power and wisdom of God for men's salvation.

These were the times of our great Civil War. It is only for the sake of proper grouping that I have reserved until now the account of my relation to it. I was patriotic, and I did my part in strengthening the hands of the president and in nerving the people to give their money and their sons for the defense of the Union. I declared that "the powers that be are ordained of God" and that rebellion against just civil government is rebellion against God. I have always thought that as our Revolutionary War gave us liberty, so our Civil War gave us liberty regulated by law. I was ready to serve in the ranks, and when I was drafted, I would have gone to the front but for the fact that my church insisted that I could do better service to the cause by preaching at home and so raised $350 to procure a substitute. On a certain July afternoon in 1861 the news of the defeat at Bull Run came to Haverhill. Oh, how my heart sank! But then, too, how my heart rose, with the determination that that defeat should yet be changed into victory! The enlistments went on, and stirring meetings were held all along through my Haverhill pastorate. That pastorate covered a little more than the whole duration of the war, for while Lee surrendered on April 9, 1865, my work in Haverhill did not cease until August 1 in that year. On April 14 Abraham Lincoln was assassinated, and universal anguish swept through the land. I had been invited to preach as a candidate to the Strong Place Church in Brooklyn. The church did not call me, but during the week of my absence from home the remains of the dead president were taken through New York City on the way to their burial in Illinois. I stood upon a lofty elevation and looked up and down Broadway upon half a million of people gathered to pay their last tribute of respect to the memory of their murdered chief magistrate. The grand funeral cortege, guarded by regiment after regiment of artillery, cavalry, and infantry, passed slowly by. Muffled drums and mournful martial music filled the air with wailing. The stately car bearing the precious dust to its burial came and went and vanished at last from sight, and after hours of marching the representatives of the race which Abraham Lincoln's act had emancipated closed the great procession. It was the grandest spectacle America ever saw. No nation ever felt a deeper sorrow or shed more bitter tears over a ruler's grave. I have always thought that at the capital where he died, over against the Washington Monument, a second monument equally high ought to be erected to the memory of Lincoln.

I have spoken of the Theological Circle of Boston. Its monthly meetings were a source of stimulus and education. Drs. Hovey and

Stevens of Newton Theological Institution were members of it, and so were Drs. Caldwell and Lincoln of Providence, Dr. Lamson of Brookline, Dr. S. R. Mason of Cambridge, and A. J. Gordon, then just ordained at Jamaica Plain. We met at a hotel for dinner. After dinner each member gave a list of the books he had read during the month. As Caldwell and Lincoln were omnivorous readers, their accounts were almost awe-inspiring. Then came an essay from some member appointed beforehand, and after the essay the most frank and remorseless criticisms. Doctrine, style, and delivery were all subjected to searching examination. One of the fundamental maxims of the circle was that no reader was to be permitted to go away with any remaining feeling of self-complacency. There were often hot discussions. Dr. Hovey's candor and moderation usually succeeded in making peace. Gordon was then in the chrysallis state, timid and slow, yet giving occasional promise of wings and flight. Dr. Caldwell was my best friend. He was a gentleman and a scholar. He invited me to exchange with him, and so I became acquainted with Providence and the First Baptist Meetinghouse, with Brown University, its acting president Dr. Caswell, and its ex-president Dr. Wayland. I stayed at the house of Albert G. Greene, the friend of Holmes and Longfellow and Emerson, and the author of

> Old Grimes is dead, that good old man,
> We ne'er shall see him more,
>   He used to wear an old gray coat,
> All buttoned down before.

Mr. Greene was a great collector of books, a man of the finest literary taste, and a delightful conversationalist. His daughter Sarah was at that time engaged to Sam Duncan, whom she afterwards married. She took me to call on Dr. Francis Wayland. The old man had heard me preach the day before. He was brusque but kind. He gave me fatherly and pious counsel, such as Paul the aged might have given to young Timothy.

My mind and heart were expanding. But the birth of two children gave me a sense of dignity and responsibility that nothing else could have given. Charles was born at the same house on Summer Street to which I took Hattie as a bride. I was greatly disappointed when I first saw him because he had a snub nose. No one could have convinced me then that the nose would ever lengthen and straighten. Yet now I shall only be too well satisfied if Charles's theology gets to be as straight as his nose. He was a rather rampageous infant. We had to go into the attic, of nights, to escape his cries. But he has become a gentle and a generous man. He has been so good a son, as well as so fine a scholar and so acute a thinker, that I count it to have been a genuine omen that he was born on Thanksgiving Day, November 28, 1862. We named him Charles after Hattie's brother, who lost his life in the war. Charles Savage was a student in the senior class of the University of Rochester when he heard the call of the country to enlist in the army of her defenders. He was a good scholar and an affectionate son. He served as a soldier from April, 1861, to August, 1862, when, after having enjoyed one brief furlough and visit to his home, he rejoined his regiment, only to fall in the second battle of Bull Run. His body was never recovered, and he rests now in some forgotten grave. But his name is recorded upon a marble tablet in the chapel of the university, as one of those who died for their country.

Mary was born on August 29, 1864. We had remained with Mrs. Brown as boarders for a year and a half on Summer Street and then for three or four months in Bradford on the opposite side of the Merrimac River. The prospect of a second baby made it very desirable for us to set up housekeeping. Houses were difficult to rent. Several of our well-to-do members therefore bought a house and rented it to us for four dollars a week. It was beautifully situated on the very summit of a hill overlooking the river and on the edge of a deep ravine which prevented the further growth of the village in that direction, while it gave us a wide prospect of undulating meadowland beyond. From the piazza of our parsonage the view of the winding Merrimac and the open fields was often indescribably lovely. I made a garden behind my house, in which for the first and for the last time also I tried, and tried in vain, to raise beans and peas, corn and cabbage and tomatoes. The soil was sandy, and the water all ran away from it. I concluded to let other people thereafter do my horticulture for me. But here, amid these rural surroundings and in the depth of summer, little Mary Belle was born. No wonder she was then, and has ever continued to be, a peaceful child, sweet of spirit, patient and capable, a born manager, one whom everybody trusts and whom everybody loves. We named her after my sister Belle, and the two have proved to be very much alike. We are thankful that both of them ever were born.

When I went to Haverhill, the church offered me a salary of twelve hundred dollars. I thought that was all I was worth, and I gladly accepted it. My predecessor, Dr. Train, when he assisted me at my first Communion, compassionately told the people that he would do all he could to help the success of his young brother; he would abstain when in town from visiting the church members, and he would take care not to preach his best sermons. It speaks well for my humility that I really felt grateful to him for this announcement. I found, however, that twelve hundred dollars was a small allowance to live on, considering the fact that I was married and had for a number of years spent more than that sum as a single man. Truth is, I was originally intended for a millionaire. I have a natural taste for splendor. Largeness pleases me. I could easily spend twelve hundred a year for books. It can be readily seen that my father had to supplement my salary, even the first year, by three hundred dollars. By the time the second year had come round, the people began to think I could preach better than Dr. Train, and even his best sermons were no longer in request. The church increased my salary by three hundred dollars. But this only made up for what my father had given me the year before. The birth of children, the employment of nurses, the buying of furniture for a house—all these involved a larger expenditure than my salary could provide. I began to think that I must earn more money or must run heavily in debt.

I never would have left Haverhill for purely financial reasons. It was rather the conviction that I needed another and a larger field of labor. I wanted to branch out into new enterprises. The people of Haverhill were too conservative. The habits of the church were fixed, and it took too long to change them. Life was short, and I had but one life to live. Yet I would not take a new church unless God made it perfectly plain that this was his will. In July, 1865, I received a letter from Mr. James M. Hoyt, of Cleveland, Ohio, asking me to preach as a candidate for the vacant pulpit of the First Baptist Church of that city. I declined upon the ground that I had no desire to go West. In some way, however, that church got word a little later that my wife and I were intending to take an excursion in August to Lake Superior. They then invited us to visit Cleveland on the way and preach for a Sunday as mere supply. This invitation we accepted, and we found ourselves most graciously received, and most delightfully entertained, by Mr. and Mrs. Hoyt on Euclid Avenue. Here was another home of as great refinement and hospitality as that of Mr. Duncan in Haverhill. Wayland Hoyt had begun his pastorate in Pittsfield, Massachusetts, but he was the only absent member of the large family. The oldest daughter had married Mr. Farmer, but she and her husband were living with her parents. Colgate and James and Elton were all at home. Both father and mother were persons of the finest sensibility. There was a demonstrativeness and affection in all the family intercourse the like of which I had never seen in New England. Here were grace and goodness, but there was also freedom. No wonder that Hattie and I were from the first attracted and charmed.

I must say more about the Hoyts before I pass on. Their home was an elegant one, on one of the finest avenues in the world. A great smooth-shorn lawn of beautiful green sloped down toward the street. Mr. Hoyt was a passionate lover of trees and shrubs and flowers. His knowledge of arboriculture was accurate and extensive, and his chief recreation was the adorning of his grounds with every beautiful thing. He had been a lawyer, but he had given up his practice and had for some years dealt in real estate, cutting up tracts of ground in the suburbs and selling them on generous terms and long time to the poor. He had become rich. He kept horses, and he lived generously. He was a most courteous host as well as a most intelligent man. He was a great student of science and philosophy, a lay-preacher, and a leader in denominational affairs in the state of Ohio. He was for twenty-five years president of the Ohio Baptist State Convention. He was trustee of Denison University, and he gave at one time ten thousand dollars toward its endowment. He was a humble and faithful Christian man, always in his place and always taking part in the prayer meetings of the church, and with his great gifts of utterance and persuasion always diffusing around him the spirit of love and peace. No church ever had a better member, and no pastor ever had a better helper than Brother James M. Hoyt.

Mrs. Hoyt was an equally remarkable character. She was a woman of the most sensitive nervous organization. Everything touched her, roused her, inspired her. The enthusiastic, loving spirit, indeed, was too much for the frail physical organism, and "o'erinformed its tenement of clay." She would talk like an angel in the meetings of the church, but she could rarely do it without tears, and the reaction was prostrating. In the home, she was a model wife, mother, and friend. All the elocutionary and oratorical gifts of her children came by heredity from her. In their childhood she took them every Saturday and had them recite line by line, after her, passages from the most stirring poems, she putting her whole soul into the dramatic expression of the thought, and never resting until they had caught both thought and expression from her. They were taught to kneel down and ask God's blessing upon them before they started every morning for school. Yet conscientiousness and prayerfulness were consistent with a many-sided development. Society and art had their claims as well as church and school. It can be easily imagined that a week's visit in such a household, and with such entertainers, made a deep impression upon the two young friends who were somewhat afloat on the ocean of life and were seeking a fit place of abode.

We made our visit and took the steamboat for Detroit and the Sault. But before we went, we were induced to promise that we would stop on the way back. Then I preached for a second Sunday in the great meetinghouse on the corner of Euclid Avenue and Erie Street. Large audiences came to hear me, and the people seemed greatly pleased. The Committee of Seventeen, representing all shades of opinion in the church, unanimously recommended a call, and when I left Cleveland, I had promised to accept it. Hattie and the children remained in Rochester while I went on to Haverhill to resign my charge, pack my goods, and take my departure. To my church there it was a great surprise and sorrow, for they had had no previous warning. Indeed, in anticipation of our coming to begin a new year's work, the good women of the church had opened my house, stocked it with good things, and decorated it with flowers. But I resigned at the Thursday evening meeting, packed my books and furniture on Friday and Saturday, and preached my farewell sermon on Sunday evening. There was much weeping and some indignation. It was small comfort to me when the Reverend T. T. Munger, then pastor of the Central Congregational Church, who had given up his services to attend mine, told me that my service was so impressive that I ought to go around the country delivering farewell sermons.

I did not perceive at the time that the haste with which I broke the news of my decision and took myself out of town was unseemly, considering the ties of affection which bound me and the church together. Yet I meant it well. I never believed in cutting off a dog's tail by degrees. I had always found that when a disagreeable duty was to be performed, the sooner it was done the better. I knew that I could render the Haverhill church no more good service when my heart was in another place. And I feared to meet the multitude of friends whose laments I could not bear and whose questions I could not answer. My mistake was not so much in going quickly as in failing to give previous intimation that I might go. I have wondered ever since at the Christian way in which the church took the blow and the readiness with which they forgave me. The members of that church have during all subsequent years been warm friends of mine, and Haverhill has been a delightful place to visit. When I return, I feel as Jacob must have felt on returning to Bethel, for there I saw the heavenly ladder set up and the angels ascending and descending upon it. We may forget the scenes of our childhood, but we can never forget the spots where God was made manifest to our souls. Haverhill was the place where a change was wrought in my experience more striking than that at my conversion—the place where it pleased God to reveal his Son in me—and therefore Haverhill will always seem to me a veritable house of God and gate of heaven.

5

Second Pastorate

Cleveland, in the autumn of 1865, was a city of 60,000 inhabitants. Business of every sort had wonderfully prospered during the war, and everybody was hopeful for the future. Euclid Avenue was already one of the most beautiful streets in the world; fine residences were either built or being built; the lawns had no equal in this country, except in Newport. My church, on the corner of Euclid Avenue and Erie Street, was a large and fine auditorium, holding a thousand people, with expensive black walnut pews and wainscoting, but with an unfinished tower. I doubt whether anywhere in the land could be found a body of Baptist believers, six hundred in number, so intelligent, considerate, well-to-do, cultivated, and harmonious. They constituted a model church. The Reverend Seymour W. Adams, D.D., their former pastor, had served them nearly a quarter of a century, and his long pastorate witnessed to the worth both of the pastor and of the people. He was just the right man for me to follow. He had been a man of deep spiritual life, affectionate and modest, and he had gotten a great hold upon the hundreds whom he had baptized and trained. But he was also a born conservative, acquainted only with old methods, and neither brilliant nor especially able as a preacher. He was a man of God, and the impress of his sweet and peaceful nature was visible upon all the members of the church.

He had died, and the younger and more active portion of the church saw their opportunity. They wanted a vigorous and attractive preacher who would draw in the younger element of the community. They seemed to think that I could do this work. In some respects Providence had fitted me to do it. I was eager for a new field where I could employ new methods and where there was plastic material to work upon. I found such material in Cleveland. The people had a will to work, and they were ready to welcome new suggestions. It was not long before I had reformed the Sunday School and put new life into its management. I induced the church to adopt a new Covenant and Articles of Faith more definite and Calvinistic than they had had before. We revised our list of members and excluded those who needed discipline. We secured regular visitation of the members and introduced periodical social gatherings, which had been unknown before. We put in a new baptistry, stained-glass windows, and, in time, a great new organ. Best of all, we brought up the attendance at the prayer meetings to 250 or 300 and the attendance at the Sabbath services to 600 or 700, both morning and evening. Pew rentings had been dull affairs, and the pecuniary results had not been satisfactory. I prefaced the pew renting by a pastoral letter to each member, sent through the mail, and I followed the pew renting by accompanying the treasurer in a horse-and-buggy visit to every member who had failed to take a pew, with the result that every pew in the meetinghouse, except the last row in the dark under the gallery, was rented.

My Cleveland experience was an experience of practical administration, and no pastor ever had more willing helpers. The first prayer meeting that I attended convinced me that the church members were with me. It was the first Friday evening in October. Hattie and I, with two children and a nurse, were lodged at the American Hotel on Superior Street until we could find a house. The evening was chilly, and the trees had begun to put on their coats of many colors. To face a new people was trying. But the warmth of their greeting and the fervency of their prayers completely reassured me. I perceived that here was a noble set of Christian workers, rich in gifts of utterance, and waiting only to be led. The next Sunday morning I preached on the text "I am not ashamed of the gospel of Christ, for it is the power of God unto salvation," and the Communion season that followed seemed to cement the union that had already been formed. I can say truly that from that time my love for my people, and I can also humbly say their love for me, grew with every added week and year. Seven years followed of wonderfully happy service, in which the church never failed to follow my lead and to assure me in a thousand ways that they appreciated my work in the Lord.

After a week or so at the American Hotel Mr. and Mrs. W. W. Wright on Euclid Avenue took us to their house to board. The city was rapidly growing, and it was exceedingly difficult to rent a house of our own. By the middle of November, however, we secured a newly erected house in a block on Prospect Street, west of Erie, and here we remained until the next spring. But the premises were not suitable for our needs, and by May a house was bought for us and presented to us. It was on the south side of Prospect Street and east of Erie. Nine thousand dollars were paid for the place. Additions and improvements, including a wing of two stories with a beautiful library, cost three thousand dollars more, making the total cost twelve thousand dollars. Of this sum four thousand dollars were left as a mortgage on the property; three thousand were loaned without interest by Judge Jesse P. Bishop, Mr. R. P. Myers, and Mr. Hoyt, and five thousand were given, out and out, by Stillman Witt. The title to the place was made over to me. When I left Cleveland, it was sold for seventeen thousand dollars, having advanced in value five thousand dollars in seven years. The result was that after paying the mortgage of four thousand and the three thousand contributed by three of the brethren, I still had ten thousand dollars left. Of this sum I put one thousand into books and nine thousand into the house in Rochester on South Clinton Street. My salary when I went to Cleveland was three thousand dollars. It was raised successively to thirty-six hundred and then to four thousand. But as I had my house all this while rent free, or nearly so, it really amounted, before I left, to about five thousand dollars, without counting the ten thousand which I took away as the result of Mr. Witt's gift and of the rise in value of the house during the years I was there.

I have mentioned all this merely to show that I had in Cleveland a most generous people with which to deal. I had every motive to do my best. Large and intelligent congregations made it necessary to preach well. I cut myself loose from the fetters of tradition and branched out in new lines of thought and study. In Haverhill I had confined myself almost wholly to the study of the Bible. Now I began to see that I must be abreast of the times in matters of science, history, and philosophy if I was to be a proper interpreter of the Bible. The book of nature began to seem a part of God's revelation quite as much as the book of Scripture. A large part of this new impulse I attribute to a personal interview. At a class meeting in New Haven I met, about this time, my old classmate James W. Hubbell. He had made no particular mark in college, but to my surprise I found him unusually well informed; indeed, I was dismayed to perceive how much more he knew about science and literature than I did. I asked him how, with all the cares of a considerable pastorate, he had managed to acquire so much learning. He told me that he had taken up one by one the sciences he had studied in college, beginning by reviewing his old textbooks, then reading larger treatises, sticking to one subject till he felt that he knew something about it, and, only after he had gained a certain mastery of this, passing on to something else. I remembered Frederick W. Robertson and his studying chemistry until its principles entered like iron into his blood. I resolved that I would pursue the same course.

I began with geology, taking the manuscript notes which I had written down from Professor James D. Dana's dictations at Yale. I then bought his smaller handbook of geology and went through that. Then his larger handbook occupied me for a time. I found that I needed actual specimens of rocks, minerals, and fossils to make my knowledge concrete. Professor Henry A. Ward of Rochester helped me. I bought from him about three hundred typical specimens, gathered from all parts of the world. None of them were over three inches long; yet they illustrated all the main divisions of paleontology, and they make up even now the prettiest and completest little collection I have seen. I set to work to study the minerals. To classify them, I bought Professor Dana's small work on mineralogy and afterwards his great work on the same subject. I became so interested in minerals that I could well understand how a man might give his whole life to the study. It is to me a proof that God is in all things when I find the study of the most minute branching out into the Infinite. Mineralogy led me into microscopy. My geological collection cost me some two hundred dollars. A binocular microscope with varied apparatus and slides cost me two hundred dollars more. I began to put up my slides myself. I saw the movement of protoplasm in *Vallisneria* and of the *cilia* in *Volvox Globator*. I found a frog in the fountain that was playing before my door. I turned him to use by imprisoning his body and putting his webbed foot underneath my object glass. How wonderful it was to see the blood corpuscles tumbling over one another like round flat stones driven onward by a furious stream!

Then I studied botany with Professor Gray's books to guide me, chemistry with Professor Youmans and Professor Cooke. I dipped into some of the most recent works on meteorology and astronomy. Political economy absorbed me for the greater part of a year, and I read Adam Smith, Bowen, and John Stuart Mill; I even wrote a long essay on "The Relations Between Christianity and Political Economy" which I delivered at the anniversary of the theological seminary at Chicago.[1] Finally I got to studying metaphysics, for which I had natural liking but which I had neglected for five or six years. The philosophy of Comte was then threatening to sweep away the foundations of the faith. I greatly enjoyed the essays of James Martineau, and I read and reread the books of Porter and McCosh, putting my conclusions into the address on "Philosophy and Religion" which I delivered before the alumni of the Rochester Theological Seminary on May 20, 1868.[2] This last address as well as one which I gave at the commencement of the Cleveland Medical College in 1867 on "Science and Religion" gave me some reputation and perhaps made it possible for people to regard me as fitted for some place of instruction in college or

[1] *Philosophy and Religion,* pp. 443-460.
[2] *Ibid.,* pp. 1-18.

theological school.[3] I was indeed urged to take a professorship of philosophy at Brown University, with the idea that I might in time become president of that institution, and Dr. Castle came on, all the way from Crozer Theological Seminary, to induce me to accept a professorship there. But I was bent upon being a preacher, and I would have despised myself if I could have given up the pulpit for any ordinary chair.

In the account I have given of my scientific and philosophical reading, I must not be understood as intimating that this was more than my incidental work. Every morning I went into my library at nine o'clock, and the first hour, from nine to ten, I gave to the study of the Bible, one quarter of an hour to the Hebrew and three quarters of an hour to the Greek. I made notes in an interleaved English Bible. I went over a large part of both Testaments with the help of the most recent commentaries. Three hours of each morning, Tuesday, Wednesday, Thursday, and Friday, I devoted to the making of one sermon. This I wrote out in full, and I put into it all my power of thought and expression. I gradually acquired directness and force. My rhetoric became less bookish and more popular. For one whole year I memorized every sermon that I wrote, preaching one each week in this way and a second from a memorized skeleton. This led me to make my sermons shorter. I found that I had been putting too much matter into a sermon and delivering too rapidly what I had written. But I gave up the memorizing, after a good year's trial, simply because the nervous strain was too great. I had no remarkable verbal memory, and to spend two whole days merely getting my sermons into mind after they were written came to seem a waste of strength. But the best sermons I have ever preached have been prepared in this way. Occasionally I make this sort of preparation now. If I were to begin over again my life as a preacher, I would never take a manuscript into the pulpit.

One of the best preparations for my subsequent work as a teacher was the preaching of doctrinal sermons. With Mr. Duncan, who had come to be pastor of the Euclid Avenue, then the Erie Street, Church, I made a solemn compact that we would preach on

[3] *Ibid.,* pp. 19-30.

The chapel in Rockefeller Hall

the Articles of Faith of our respective churches on the second Sunday morning of each month. So we went over the doctrines of the existence of God, the Trinity, inspiration, sin, the person of Christ, the atonement, and all the main truths of theology. On Monday morning, after each sermon, we would meet in my study to read what we had written and to criticize each other's productions. We began the course as much for our own good as for the instruction of our congregations. But no long time passed before it appeared that people were interested in these sermons more than in any others; in fact, we tried to make them so full of illustration and so abounding in practical application that those who heard them forgot that they were doctrinal sermons at all. This, I think, is the true way to preach doctrine. I would make the exposition of truth level to the comprehension of a fifteen-year-old boy; I would make it thoroughly interesting by apt illustration, and I would by practical applications, at the close, send it home to the conscience and the heart. When I began to teach theology at Rochester, my main stock in trade was the series of doctrinal sermons I had preached in Cleveland.

A large part of my preaching was evangelistic. I aimed always to make the sermon a means of leading sinners to Christ. My predecessor had devoted himself to comforting and instructing the church. I felt that Christian work and the bringing of men to the Savior would comfort and instruct better than continual preaching of comforting and instructive sermons. When I went to Cleveland, there were many sons and daughters of members of the church and many unconverted persons in the congregation who were only waiting for a good opportunity to become Christians. I reached out after these persons, and I urged the church to labor and pray for their conversion. It was not long before a deep spirit of concern took possession of the church and the very people whom we most desired to influence began to attend, in considerable numbers, our meetings for prayer. Then came the necessity for private and personal labor with individuals. I saw that the church would never move unless I moved first; if I did not talk to sinners myself, my people would never do it. But to seek out men with whom I had little acquaintance and address them about their souls was always a trying work for me. This one thing, however, characterized my whole success in

Cleveland: I got the church to do its duty only as I set the example and led the way.

There was one man whom I greatly hated to approach. I got no rest until I conquered my unwillingness and set out to see him. It was a bitter winter's day, and his office was full of clerks, so that it was no place for a private interview. He had seemed to me a proud and rough man, and I was afraid of him. When I asked to speak a word with him in private, he took me outside the building, and I talked to him, with a strong wind blowing and the thermometer somewhere near zero. But I had hardly uttered a single sentence before it was plain that the Lord had gone before me and that the man was under strong conviction of sin and only anxious to be led to Christ. Then and there, in that icy atmosphere and under the lee of that great factory, he promised to surrender himself to the Savior. And his conversion was like the breaking down of a dam; it was followed by a flood, and a multitude of others came to Christ also.

I had some wonderful helpers, and it is time that I should describe them. I will begin with Father and Mother Rouse. Father Rouse was a man of seventy, somewhat crotchety, but full of emotion, and, when roused, he was a powerful speaker. He loved the service of song, and he could lead it well. Mother Rouse was an extraordinary woman. Small and wiry, she was somewhat younger than her husband and was possessed of an intellect, an insight, a judgment, a calmness, a decision to which he was a stranger. She had an administrative and executive ability of the very first order. She would have made a good president of a railway company, or she could have commanded a man-of-war. During our Civil War, Mrs. Rouse had been president of the Sanitary Commission for the state of Ohio and had organized the women of the state for the work of sending nurses and hospital supplies to the front. Her face is now perpetuated in bronze in the great monument erected in Cleveland to the heroes and heroines of the war. No one in the whole state did more for our Union soldiers than she. When the war was over and she no longer had the sick and wounded to care for, she gave her thoughts and energies once more to the church and the salvation of souls. She had a marvelous intensity of feeling and yet a marvelous self-control in the expression of it. When she rose to speak in a prayer meeting, there was breathless silence, for Mother Rouse would put more into five minutes than most people could put into an hour. Two months after I had begun my work, in a crowded evening meeting Mrs. Rouse arose. There was evidently a burden upon her heart. With burning words she told of a struggle and agony which she had been enduring in prayer. She spoke of her distress for the church and her anxiety for the unconverted in a way that seemed almost like a voice from another world. I could only think of the suffering of Christ in Gethsemane. But suddenly, in the very midst of this description of her spiritual anguish for sinners, her countenance lighted up; her voice changed; and she continued, "But I have never before come so near to Jesus, never yet have had such joy; my soul has been full to overflowing of the glory and peace of God." I have always had in this experience of Mother Rouse a proof that God is not impassible, that suffering on account of sin is not inconsistent with blessedness, that holy love necessarily renders God an atoning Savior.

A great revival followed in which more than a hundred persons were converted and brought into the church. Edwin C. Rouse and his wife, the son and daughter-in-law of Father and Mother Rouse, helped the work by their singing, though they were not otherwise active in the meetings. Benjamin F. Rouse, called for short "Frank Rouse," another son of the same parents, was a wonderful helper in the inquiry room and in prayer. He had once intended to preach the gospel, but ill health had prevented. He was superintendent of the Cottage Mission Sunday School, and in private Christian work he was more useful than is many a pastor in his pulpit. His magnificent bass voice, tremulous with emotion, and his unrivaled gifts of supplication and persuasion seemed to make him a power with men at the same time that he was a power with God. Though he was a man of moods and was not always at his best, he was on the whole an enthusiastic and faithful member of the church, while at his own mission school he infused such energy and devotion into his teachers that the whole body seemed fairly to throb and bound with his life. The conversions at the Cottage Chapel were many, and, as all the converts at first came to the church to relate their experiences in order for baptism, the mission was a constant stimulus to the religious life of the church.

Loren Prentiss married a sister of Edwin and Frank, a woman of warm sympathies and great practical ability, so that the Rouse family made up no small part of the working force of the church. Mr. Prentiss himself was superintendent of the Bethel Mission, an undenominational effort to reach the sailors on the lake craft in the harbor and the workmen on the wharves. Loren was the son of a Freewill Baptist minister and had been trained to Calvinophobia from his cradle. He was a sharp and successful lawyer, and how he ever succeeded in keeping down his resentment and putting up with my orthodox sermons is a mystery to this day. Perhaps he subconsciously recognized truth in my preaching which he could not formally square with his logic. At any rate he was always a strong friend and supporter of mine, and on one occasion at least he practically acknowledged that his Arminianism would not suffice and that the doctrine of divine decrees, if not true, certainly ought to be true if there is to be any comfort in time of bitter affliction. A sister of his had been living with her husband at New Orleans. The husband was stricken down with yellow fever. He had passed the crisis, and hope was entertained that he might recover, when in the middle of the night, the wife, worn out with watching and hardly knowing what she did, gave him the wrong potion, and before morning her husband was dead. She came north with his body, not only overcome with grief but almost insane with the thought that she was his murderer. Her brother Loren was entirely unable to quiet her, much less to console her. To her self-accusations he could only reply that she had done the best she knew how. He could not add that all that happened was in fulfillment of God's plan. At his wit's end, he called me in, with the hope that I might say something to help her. I began by asking her if she did not believe that God knew all this when she was born and when she was married. I asked if she did not think God could have prevented it if he had thought it best. Since he had permitted it to happen, with full previous knowledge and full power to prevent, ought she not to regard it as really *His* will rather than *her own?* Little by little the possibility and the certainty of a permissive decree of God dawned upon her, and though when I began my talk, I found her distracted and comfortless, I left her peaceful and resigned.

The family of Judge Jesse P. Bishop was an almost equally important factor in the church. The judge was a tall, energetic, warmhearted, demonstrative man. His friendships were unreasoning in their devotion; when he once gave his confidence, he gave it for good and all; he could see no defects in his friends. This was a fine thing for his pastor; whoever the pastor might be, he declared him to be the greatest preacher and noblest man alive. I always had the judge to blow my trumpet for me, not only in private but also upon the corner of the streets. No criticism or opposition ever dashed the judge; he had succeeded in his practice and in life by dint of labor and persistence; his method of reasoning reminded me of the average Englishman's way of answering objections, namely, to repeat what he had previously said, but in a louder tone of voice. Judge Bishop was very opinionated. What he knew, he knew, and argument was thrown away upon him. Sometimes he was wrong-headed, as when he insisted upon the removal of the Cottage Mission into the midst of an uninhabited part of the town and away from a densely populated region. A theory of future growth ran away with him. He was a born doctrinaire; if facts did not correspond with his theories, so much the worse for the facts. He was rigidly and fanatically orthodox. Though he never entered into the inner meaning of the symbols of the church, he was a great stickler for their outward form, as Drs. Behrends and Moxom ascertained when they attempted to preach new doctrine and swing off the church from its old moorings in the matter of Communion and inspiration.

Mrs. Bishop was the daughter of Deacon White, the patriarch of the church and one of the gentlest and sweetest old men I have ever known, a man who used to pour out his soul in his closet and in the gatherings of the saints as he prayed that God would "manifest his declarative glory in the church which he had redeemed with his precious blood." But the judge and his wife were generous and hospitable to a fault. They had a large family, and they kept almost an open house. They were constantly making tea parties for the weaker and poorer members of the church, and they were constantly sending presents to the pastor. Every peripatetic Baptist minister was sure to find entertainment at their house. With all their children around them, rollicking as they were, the Christian life seemed very attractive, and the home was a part of heaven below. But it was a heaven that was not intended to last, for suffering and death came to one member after another of the happy household until now the grandfather and both the parents have departed and only two of the children are left. But they were all Christians, and I have no doubt they will at last be all reunited in the true and lasting heaven the other side of the grave.

Deacon William T. Smith was a man of sunny temper, exquisite sensibility, and loving nature. He enjoyed nothing so much as the study and hearing of God's word. His countenance was so expressive; he was so alert and responsive to every thought of the preacher; he would so beam with joy and so melt with tenderness while you were preaching to him that I have sometimes had great difficulty in preventing myself from laughing aloud and then sympathetically crying as I have seen him smile and cry. He was the refuge and adviser of the poor, for he had a great stock of quick and homely sense at his disposal. He carried in his pockets peppermint drops for the children, and he was often surrounded by crowds of them. His large Bible class of young men was one of the best features of our Sunday School, and he taught at the mission as well. Scores of noble fellows in the course of years came from his classes into the church, and, once in the church, he never took his eye off them but looked after their mental, moral, religious, social, and business interests as if he had been their own father. Yet Deacon Smith and his excellent wife could not make all their own children Christians. The oldest son, George, tried his parents greatly by his rude skepticism and opposition to religious things. Charles and Frank, in like manner, were for years the objects of great anxiety, but both of them at last were soundly and wonderfully converted and became most active and useful workers for Christ. The daughter, Mrs. Sherwin, was always one of the brightest and best of women. Deacon Smith's family has been to me a vivid illustration of the fact that mere religious opportunities may harden and not save and that the Christian is "born not of blood, nor of the will of the flesh, nor of the will of man, but of God."

How shall I speak worthily of Stillman Witt? He was our richest man. He had been, with Amasa Stone, a builder of the Lake Shore Railroad, and he had accumulated a fortune of three million. He was emotional and impulsively generous. He could never be got to attend prayer meetings, but he was always in his pew on the Lord's Day, and he tried to make up by his giving for any shortcomings in other lines of duty. Large of frame and benign in aspect, he was an imposing figure in the meetinghouse. He was modest and never thought to control the action of the church, though he backed up munificently any enterprise in which the church was united. When I proposed a change of hymnbooks and urged the board of trustees to provide some four hundred of them for church service and prayer meeting, he said he had an engagement which would prevent him from staying to discuss the matter but that he favored it and would leave his contribution toward it. When he had departed, we found that he had left us a check for eight hundred dollars to pay the whole expense of the change. It was he who put in the stained-glass windows and paid a couple of thousand for them. He gave us our organ and paid six thousand for that. I have told of his contributing five thousand dollars toward my house and of his refusing to take back a cent of it when I resigned my pastorate. On my first Christmas he sent me a hundred dollars, and the hundred dollars came on every subsequent Christmas for all the seven years. On one occasion he gave two hundred dollars to take Hattie and me on a summer vacation to the seashore. Presents of flowers and of fruit were very frequent. He loved horticulture. He had an extensive conservatory, where he raised the Camelia Japonica and Hamburgh grapes. I asked him how much his grapes cost him, and he replied that when he made the last calculation, he found that they had cost him sixteen dollars a bunch.

He was largely a creature of impulse. He had a great love for sweets, and he indulged himself so immoderately that he brought on the gout. He liked nothing so much as maple sugar. He was accustomed to crumb bread into a bowl of syrup and eat it as he would have eaten bread and milk. I once heard that he was suffering excruciating pain in his feet. I called to see him and was shown to his bedroom. As I entered, he did not notice me. He was moaning piteously, and yet he seemed to be speaking. I waited for him to recognize me, and as I stood there, I heard him utter this most unique prayer: "O Lord! Let me off this time, and I will never touch another piece of maple sugar as long as I live!" With all his

generosity he was spasmodic in his gifts, and it was my constant
effort to educate him to give systematically, on principle, and in
proportion to his income. One day I took my life in my hand and
tried to tell him his duty. It was a hot summer's afternoon, and he
was sitting alone in the shade outside his house. I got him to talk
about missionary societies and educational institutions, and I told
him of my wish that he would contribute to them more largely and
regularly. He justified himself by saying that he had spent on
himself only thirteen thousand dollars the preceding year, while he
had given away twenty thousand. I knew that the interest on his
investments that same year had been three hundred thousand, and I
replied, "But, Mr. Witt, you know that twenty thousand dollars is
only a small portion of your income!" He colored deeply and said
somewhat angrily, "I suppose you think I am very mean." "No, Mr.
Witt," I answered. "I never thought you mean; I only want you to
take some of these great causes on your heart and do for them what
others cannot do." "Well," he replied, "I never have done it yet,
and I don't know that I ever shall." So my first tussle with a
millionaire resulted in failure. But it prepared me for other tussles
of the future which turned out more prosperously.

One day as I was walking on St. Clair Street, I saw the sign on a
Negro shanty which read as follows: "John Jones, Barber and
Hairdresser; also, Dealer in Old Clothes; also, Cures all Chronic
Diseases." John Jones was not a member of my church, but Dr.
Gibson was. He too advertised that he could cure all chronic
diseases, and as these diseases included many that are not
mentioned in polite society, his advertisements and placards were a
great offense to respectable people. I had a struggle with him which
quite threw into the shade my struggle with Mr. Witt. The doctor
was an impressive personage. He weighed at least 250 pounds, and
he had a massive forehead and overhanging eyebrows that would
have done credit to Daniel Webster. The peculiarity of his medical
practice was that he conducted it all by faith and prayer, which
seemed scandalous to many, because of the ugly cases with which he
had chiefly to do. He certainly knew a great deal of the Bible, and
occasionally he would speak in the prayer meeting with so much
thoughtfulness and sagacity that we could not doubt that he was a
Christian. But he was a mystic; he conceived that he had reached a

higher understanding of the truth than any of his brethren; he talked down to them from an elevation; he lectured them for their shortcomings like an Old Testament prophet. These airs became very offensive, and Dr. Gibson's addresses usually threw a chill over the meeting and made it almost impossible for anyone to follow him.

One evening Dr. Gibson made me a visit. He said that he had had difficulty in getting on with the former pastor, Dr. Adams, and he wished to have a thorough understanding with me. He therefore gave me the history of his life. He had begun his practice, he said, in the regular way. But God taught him after a time that he was leaning too much upon the wisdom of man and led him to trust wholly in the Lord. "A man comes to me with a case which other doctors have been unable to cure. Do I give him the remedies which the books prescribe for his disease? No! that would be leaning to my own understanding. What is my method? Why, I say to him, 'Let us pray!' I kneel down with him and ask the Lord what to give. And the Lord frequently tells me to give him precisely the opposite remedy from that which the books prescribe. And he gets well! I have scores of cases that I have cured in this way." As the doctor went on, I listened respectfully, but I mentally resolved that he should not be my family physician. "Yes," he continued, "the Lord tells me what to do, not only in my practice but in everything else. My daughters come to me and ask, 'Father, shall we take an umbrella today?' They know that the Lord very generally tells me when it is going to rain. Why, a few weeks ago, I went up the stairs to my office, and I saw a piece of crepe tied to the knob of the door. I said, 'Lord, what does this mean?' And the Lord told me, 'Your wife is going to die!' And you know, she *did* die!" I could have no manner of doubt that he spoke the truth, for I had attended her funeral and had conducted the service.

I concluded to cross-question the doctor and learn in what way he made sure that God spoke to him and answered his prayers. I asked whether it was by simple faith in the general promise that God would answer prayer. "Oh no!" he replied. "That is what everybody does. My answers are something special and peculiar." I inquired if there was any physical sign that God gave him. He said there was something of that nature. Then I saw the possibility of pinning him down, and I asked further in what particular portion of the body he received this intimation from God. Strange as it may seem, the doctor immediately and confidently pointed to the region of his own stomach and solemnly disclosed to me the fact that when God answered his prayers, he always had a peculiar sensation just there. When I told this story to Dr. King of Providence, he exclaimed, "That was a voice from the pit!" So, when poor Dr. Gibson felt a movement in the pit of his stomach, he was dead sure that the Lord had answered him.

The doctor had hope that I would come over to his side and defend him from his enemies. But he became a troubler of Israel. After a denunciatory speech which he made in one of the prayer meetings, I said to him, "Dr. Gibson, I cannot permit you to talk in this way. If you will tell your experience or interpret Scripture in a modest way, we shall be glad to hear you. But if you speak again in this dictatorial and censorious manner, I shall be obliged to call you to take your seat." The doctor drew himself up very majestically and replied, "Who are you, sir, to talk to me in this way?" "I am the pastor of this church, Doctor, and I am put in charge of these meetings, and I shall do just what I say." "Do you suppose," he responded, "that I come here on my own motion? No, sir! I come only because God sends me, and I speak only the message which he has commanded me to bring." "But, my dear Doctor," I replied, "are you sure that it is a message from God? Many of your brethren doubt that." To which he answered, "I never have been so insulted in my life!" "What?" I replied. "How have I insulted you?" "Why, I told you that the Lord sent me to speak for him, and you have virtually told me that I lie," he replied. "Oh, Doctor!" I responded, "I have only intimated that you are not infallible and that you may possibly be mistaken. I have no idea that you have any intention to deceive." But I could not persuade him that I had not insulted him, and he went away in great indignation. Soon after this the Lord, as he said, revealed to him that it was not his duty any longer to come to hear me preach. He began to attend other churches and to forsake our own. At last, after long laboring with him, the church excluded him for neglect of his covenant obligations. He became a wanderer. He disturbed one church after another in the same way. When driven out of one he would flee to another till at last he died and went to a world of peace. I have no doubt he was a Christian, but he was a striking illustration of the fact that the mystic, whose new communications from God render him independent of the Bible and the church, has a hard time himself and makes a hard time for others.

The Reverend Frederick Tolhurst had also something of the crank in him, but he was a very helpful man notwithstanding. He was English by birth. He had been pastor of little churches in the neighborhood of Cleveland. His great gift was that of prayer. He was not much of a preacher, but he was a most watchful and faithful carer for souls, a curate in the best sense. When I came to the city, he was employed by my church as assistant pastor and as preacher at the Cottage Mission. He was an indefatigable visitor, and he was everywhere welcome. He was rather lachrymose in manner, but that was largely due to his unfortunate domestic circumstances. He had taken a Seventh-Day Baptist for a wife, and the wife persecuted him as if he had been a heathen. When he was a pastor, she kept the seventh day so rigorously that no food could be cooked or work of any sort performed. The result was that on Saturday, when her husband needed a nourishing diet to enable him to prepare his sermons, she furnished nothing to eat but cold bread and butter while the Sunday was kept for her washing day, and the eyes of the members, as they passed her house on their way to church, were saluted by her ostentatious hanging out of clothes. Yet he was a very affectionate man. He used to call himself a shepherd's dog, and he aided me, the shepherd, by keeping the flock together. Wherever he went, he prayed. He never came to my study without proposing that we join in prayer; and after we had risen from our knees, he at first always tried to clasp me in his arms and give me a holy kiss. I soon let him know that this was distasteful to me, and I never heard of his trying this Christian salutation upon any of the sisters of the church. He was a godly, humble Christian man, and he won many to Christ. The Lord at last rewarded him by taking him away from his wife to a better world.

While I am speaking of the curious characters with whom I came in contact in Cleveland, I must not omit to mention John Givens. John's mental makeup had been determined before his birth. His father and six older brothers and sisters had all perished in a foundering ship upon the Atlantic. His mother, thus suddenly deprived of her whole family, was three or four months afterwards delivered of twins, and the marks of her grief were left upon her offspring. One of the twins came to an early death; the other was John. He was about thirty years of age when I first became acquainted with him. He was kindhearted, forth-putting, and a good Methodist. But he belonged to the universal church more than to any particular church. He was only half-witted, but he was entirely harmless. He had two peculiarities. The first was his ardent love for funerals. Attending funerals was his main business in life. He was hand in glove with the undertakers of the town, and wherever there was mourning, there was John Givens. Dirges and crepe were his especial delight. He usually succeeded in getting possession of the crepe attached to the knob of the doorbell, and it was said that he had trunks full of the accumulated gatherings of years. His second peculiarity was his presence at every great public function. He welcomed the coming, as he sped the parting, guest. If George William Curtis lectured in town, the first person to step forward and welcome him to the city after the lecture was John Givens. As I came down from the pulpit after my first sermon as pastor in Cleveland, John Givens was duly on hand and was the first to greet me.

After a year or two, Dr. and Mrs. Palmer, the Methodist revivalists, came to Cleveland and inaugurated a campaign. They were holiness people. Entire sanctification was commanded—it was therefore attainable, and attainable now. I attended an afternoon meeting of theirs. Mrs. Palmer was the chief speaker, Dr. Palmer helping out mainly by prayer. Mrs. Palmer spoke of the sin of Israel in not entering at the first into Canaan. God offered us the promised land of holiness and peace. It was a sin for us not to obey God's call. It was our duty to go up at once to possess it. She closed her remarks by inviting all who desired then and there to secure the blessing of entire sanctification to come forward to the front seats. There was a slight pause, and no one moved. But then there was a stir in the audience, and the first to move to the seats before the pulpit was John Givens. All who came forward were then invited to kneel in prayer while Dr. Palmer vociferously prayed. While all were yet upon their knees, Mrs. Palmer said that it was always a duty to confess what the Lord had done for us. If any of those who knelt were conscious that they had received the gift of entire sanctification in answer to their prayer, they should rise and acknowledge it. And the first to rise and acknowledge it was John Givens.

Before my time there had been jealousy between the Baptist churches of the city and very little of mission enterprise except at the Cottage. I established a ministers' meeting at my study every Monday morning and so drew the brethren together. We then instituted a City Mission Union and set ourselves to seize upon the strategic points for evangelical work. This Union became a mother of churches as well as of missions. The Cottage became an independent church during my pastorate. Other churches were formed, and the Union has resulted in multiplying the number from four in 1865 to sixteen in 1895. With all this increase there went also a growth in denominational love and pride. The spirit of fellowship came to prevail. The Cleveland Association came to be a strong and noble body, and its meetings were models of fraternal affection and spiritual power. Baptist polity was found extraordinarily favorable to denominational enlargement and the capture of unoccupied fields. At the same time that this work was going on in Cleveland, I became interested in the college at Granville. I was made a trustee of Denison University. Dr. Samson Talbot was then its president, a man whose unobtrusive patience blinded the world to the greatness of his powers and whose cruel overwork deprived the world too early of the services of a noble mind and heart. In the meetings of the board of trustees at Granville I became acquainted with Father Thresher and Father Barney, two wise and able counselors to whom our cause in Ohio owes more than can ever be told. The Ministers' Institutes held yearly at Granville interested me even more, for in them I was called to take some part in the way of instruction. Here I first began to think that I might have gifts for teaching and might enjoy that sort of life.

As I try to sum up my intellectual and spiritual gains in Cleveland, it seems to me that my life became objective, whereas before it had been largely subjective. I had been introspective; there I began to look out upon the world. My former experience had been needed to show me my entire dependence upon Christ, but when I had found him as an indwelling and omnipotent Savior, God gave me in Cleveland a wider view of the universe and prepared me to see the larger relations of Christ to the world he had made. Christ's creatorship was my sixth great lesson in doctrine. The immanence of Christ did not then impress itself upon me as it did afterwards in Rochester. But I was gathering material for broader conceptions. My studies of science gave me inspiring ideas of the wisdom and power of God. I drew from science a multitude of illustrations in preaching that I never should have thought of in Haverhill. So my sermons at once became more healthy and more interesting. From being somewhat abnormal and self-involved, they took a wider range and dealt with more universal interests. I took a more generous view of the gospel and the preaching of the gospel. I began to see that the preacher's business was to apply Christian principles to all the relations of life. Everything in heaven and earth and under the earth might furnish him with subject for treatment. History, art, literature, and society, as well as science and philosophy, might have a place in his preaching. But the center must be Christ; all treasures must be laid at his feet; he must be crowned Lord of all.

There was a danger in all this, and I did not wholly escape it. It was partly a doctrinal danger and partly a danger of experience. With the study of laws of nature, there was danger of regarding Christianity itself as a mere matter of law. This I think was the error of Dr. E. G. Robinson. He conceived of religion from the scientific point of view, and to his mind the scientific point of view was the point of view of physical science. He was a determinist, a believer in cause and effect. Personality, love, and miracle never impressed him as did the regular successions of nature. He had greatly influenced my ways of thinking, and I found these ways of thinking considerably confirmed by my studies of natural science. Reducing theology to scientific form involves the putting of great emotions into terms of mere intellect. You run the risk of purchasing clearness by the sacrifice of real power. During my later years in Cleveland I preached some sermons which tended in the direction of naturalism. I could not have done this if my Christian experience had not somewhat deteriorated. Management of externals withdrew my mind at times from that intimate communion with the Savior which was needed to keep my doctrine correct and my preaching effective. Fortunately I had a standard to judge myself by: the days of joy and power I had experienced in Haverhill. I had always possessed one gift for preaching. I mean fervency, warmth, and emotional energy. When I grew cold in heart, this flow of the emotions ceased; language failed me; the words were labored and constrained. Public prayer became a duty, whereas it had been a delight. I saw that my locks had been shorn, that my strength was gone. Then I returned to the Lord, and he had mercy upon me. The joy of his salvation was restored, and I began my work afresh, resolved never to wander more.

On the whole therefore I regard my Cleveland life as adding to my Haverhill experience the healthy objective element that was previously lacking. My religion and my preaching, while not losing the emotional fervor that had characterized them, took on a new freshness and breadth which were gained from larger knowledge of science and freer contact with the world. I was particularly encouraged by the results of some of my doctrinal sermons. After a sermon on the decrees of God, from the text "Who worketh all things after the counsel of his will," a young man came to me in great distress to ask what he should do to be saved. His name was Cole. He was the son of a widow who belonged to the church. He had been for some years in California but had now returned to his home. He said to me that he had attended the Methodist church during his absence. Arminian preaching had persuaded him that salvation was wholly a matter of the will, that the will was perfectly free, that he could become a Christian at any time, that there was no harm in delay. My sermon on the decrees of God showed him for the first time that he was dependent upon God, that his will might become hardened in impenitence, that only God could change it and save his soul, that he must seek God at once if he would not be lost. He did seek God, and he found God ready to forgive. He united with the church, became a consistent and useful member, took a letter to the church in Scoville Avenue, was made a deacon there, and when I last heard of him, was regarded by all as an exemplary and influential Christian.

Another man who finally became a deacon was Mr. Skinner. He lived in the neighborhood of the Cottage Mission. He was forty-five or fifty years of age. He had been editor of a newspaper and had had much contact with the world. His air was that of thoughtfulness, accompanied by a sort of rough vigor. One evening he appeared at my Inquiry Meeting. He was greatly depressed. The moment I gave him opportunity, he broke out, "I am a great sinner!" Seeing that he was a man of intelligence, it did not occur to me that he needed the alphabet of the gospel; so I replied, "Yes, but you can be made all over again. God can change your whole heart and life." And then he turned to me almost fiercely and said, "That is not what I want! I've a debt to pay first!" Ah, what a lesson that taught me! I had forgotten that before renewal and sanctification there must come reparation and atonement, and this soul, convicted by the Holy Spirit, instructed me in the first principles of the oracles of God. I changed my tactics and told him that God had anticipated his need, had paid his debt, and was willing to give him acquittance if he would only take Christ for his substitute and Savior. He listened as one dazed. He had listened all his life to preaching. All that I told him was familiar, but the meaning of it had never dawned upon him before. Indeed, he could not take it in then. He went away lost in reflection. I hardly expected to see him again. But a week from that evening he came once more, so changed that I hardly knew him. His countenance was lit up; he was rejoicing in a newfound hope; he cried, "Now I see it! Jesus has paid my debt! I have given myself to him!" He too joined the church, took a letter to the Cottage, was there made a deacon, and became a most active and useful Christian. His case has always been an illustration to me of the way in which the unsophisticated conscience, enlightened by the Spirit of God, witnesses to men's need of the atonement of Christ and of its power to give pardon and peace.

An illustration of justification occurs to me. During my Cleveland pastorate a man was sentenced to the penitentiary for grand larceny. He came down the courthouse steps in charge of the constable and entered a vehicle called "The Black Maria" which was to convey him to prison. There was no window to the vehicle, only a few horizontal slats near the roof. Just as he was about to be driven away, he stood up and looked through the slats to get a last view of the world from which he was so soon to be shut out. As Providence would have it, he caught sight of a placard which read "Friendly Inn. Strangers welcome. Good food. Prayer meeting at eight o'clock." "There!" he said to himself. "It is one of those Christian shops. It is all hypocrisy. I do not believe in their welcome. When I get out, I'll learn whether there is anything in it. I'll prove that it is a fraud!" He served out his term in the penitentiary. He did not forget. No sooner was he discharged than he made his way to the Friendly Inn. A kind Christian woman met him at the door. He told her his story. "Why, you are just the man we are looking for," she said. So she gave him a good supper, won his heart by her sympathy, asked him to stay for the prayer meeting at eight o'clock. Then and there he gave his heart to Christ. And he made the resolve to do to others as had been done to him. From that day it was his lifework to ascertain from the warden of the prison the exact date of each prisoner's discharge. As each man emerged from confinement, side by side with the human sharks who were waiting to lead him again into drink and crime, there was always one to take him by the hand, provide food and shelter and employment for him, and above all talk to him about Christ and a new life. Many were in this way saved from evil ways and made good men and good Christians. So when God justifies the sinner, he does not simply declare that his penalty has been borne and that he is now permitted to go free. God also admits him to favor, adopts him into his family, bestows upon him all needed helps to a holy life. And this generosity of God overwhelms him, melts his heart, draws forth his love and gratitude, so that he cannot any longer sin against so gracious a Lord and Savior.

I passed through certain dangers in Cleveland from contact with the female portion of my congregation. There were women who, either from imperfect training or too great warmth of temperament, were prone to demonstrate their liking for the pastor in unpleasant ways. More than once the grasp of the hand seemed too affectionate, and I was compelled to draw back with a dignity which had in it something of rebuke. I learned just enough to pity the young pastor who comes up from obscure surroundings, has been accustomed in his youth to plays in which kissing forms the great attraction, and thinks nothing of freedoms which to polite and educated people seem only rude and vulgar. An instinctive repugnance to such things belonged to me from childhood, and it often protected me when I was in danger. I owed much also to a resolve I formed when I first went to Cleveland that my first words to any new person whom I met should be words connected with my spiritual vocation. I had learned the danger of procrastination. If I delayed to speak of the concerns of the soul, it became harder every moment to do my duty. Therefore I determined to be instant in season and out of season and to blurt out my errand at the very first. I am sure that this habit saved me a great deal of trouble. People came to expect some kind word about their religious interests. And when they met me with this expectation, the greetings and the conversation could not easily take on a purely worldly, much less an amatory, character. I made a great many friends, but they were friends in Christ. I visited the poor much more than I visited the rich. I knew that the rich had plenty of friends, while many a poor member of the church had none but me to whom to tell the sorrows or the joys of the soul. When I left Cleveland, it cost me a greater pang to leave some of these weak and friendless ones than all the rest of the church.

My pastoral work was very taxing. To visit six hundred members every year was enough to employ all the afternoons from September to July. One year Hattie accompanied me (she could walk then, though she cannot now). I had numberless committee meetings to attend. After a time, I became a sort of Baptist bishop for Cuyahoga County and northern Ohio. I was invited to attend Associations and to preach sermons of ordination. The general affairs of the denomination took much time and required a large correspondence—all this while my conception of what constituted a good sermon was constantly growing, so that the preparation for my pulpit, instead of taking less of my time, took more and more. The conflict between pastoral work and preaching became very serious. I felt that I could do either one of these with great comfort and success but that to do both was an impossibility. The assistance of Mr. Tolhurst was valuable, but after a time he felt that he must be a pastor of a church of his own, and he was compelled to leave me. Mr. Savage took his place, but his work was confined to the Cottage Mission, and the burden of the home church still rested upon me. The death of Mrs. Savage broke up even this arrangement, and Hattie's father returned to Rochester. The Cottage became an independent church under the pastorate of Mr. Edwin A. Taft, a graduate of Rochester. But the home church, even after it had dismissed so many members, was very large, and it continued to grow. For some months I would give my mind mainly to pastoral visitation, and then my preaching suffered. My conscience would begin to reproach me for this, and for the next few months I would devote myself mainly to my sermons, with the result that I saw my pastoral work going to ruin. There was no way of reconciling these conflicting claims. I could not cut myself in two with a hatchet, and I could not multiply myself by two. The scattering sort of work I was compelled to do increasingly distressed me. I put away on Sunday night sermons that with another week's work might have been made good, but there was no time to make them good; so they went into the drawer. I longed for the opportunity to work continuously at a subject until I had exhausted it, or at least had done upon it all that I was capable of. I began to entertain very seriously the thought of either taking another parish or else leaving altogether the active ministry and entering upon the work of teaching.

The chance to take another church came to me in very attractive form. I had always had a love for New York City. To be in the center of the metropolis, with all its intellectual, social, and political life around me, had seemed the summit of earthly ambition. To be a preacher there, with a great congregation hanging upon my words, was a sort of heaven below. One Sunday morning I became aware that several intelligent strangers were in my audience. They appeared again in the evening. Fortunately I preached very well that day, and after the evening service these same strangers came to my study and held a long conversation with me. They were a committee from the Madison Avenue Church of New York City, and they asked me whether I would consider a call from that church, at six thousand dollars salary. I told them that I should prefer first to visit the church and preach for it. The result was such a visit. I was most heartily received, and a unanimous call was extended. But I perceived, as I thought, that the church was dying of indolence, that nothing but mission work would save it. I had before me the precedent of Cleveland and the growth of our denomination there. I was not willing to go to New York unless I had the means of carrying out a similar plan in the metropolis. I told the church in New York that I would accept their call, provided they would pledge themselves to erect and support a mission chapel. They replied that they would prefer to let this matter wait until I had accepted the call and had begun my work, although they thought it highly probable that they would undertake it under my leadership. This assurance was not enough for me. I wanted no peradventure in the matter. After a long correspondence and delay, lasting for at least two months, I telegraphed to them my declination of their call. I am convinced now that it was an instance of God's preventive providence. In spite of my liking for New York and ambition to preach there, I believe that I should have found myself physically unequal to the work of a pastor there and that God reserved me for another work to which I was much better adapted.

In this same year of 1869, I preached the Anniversary Sermon before the Judson Missionary Society of Brown University. I had just spent six weeks in the Adirondacks. I was in fine health and spirits. I had cut off my beard and taken to a simple moustache. I had a good sermon, and I delivered it well. Dr. Caldwell entertained me nobly. I returned to Cleveland, not thinking of any special results to follow the sermon. But at the next commencement of Brown University, in 1870, I received the degree of Doctor of Divinity. As I was not a graduate of Brown and was only thirty-four years of age, this was a great, and an unexpected, honor. I suppose that it had its influence in turning attention to me as a possible candidate for teacher of theology at Rochester when Dr. Robinson in 1872 resigned his presidency of the seminary to go to Brown. There had been some criticism of his theological position and influence. He was restive under it. His health was not good at Rochester. He thought there was malaria in the climate. Though he regarded the presidency of Brown University as a lower place than the presidency of the Rochester Theological Seminary, he at last made up his mind to exchange the latter for the former. I was in Rochester when the board of trustees of the seminary held its meeting. I was asked to accept the professorship of theology without the presidency. I declined, upon the ground that I could not work easily unless I had affairs in my own hands. They thereupon elected me both professor and president, and I accepted the election before I returned to Cleveland.

When I offered my resignation to the church I had served so happily for seven prosperous years, there was much sorrow. The church had treated me so well that my resignation seemed ungrateful. Mr. Witt, particularly, took it hardly. He had become much attached to me, as I had to him. It grieved me to wound his feelings, but I was compelled to do this. I felt the more sure that I was right and that he was wrong when he declared to me that if I went, he would never give me another cent. I knew that I ought not to stay for mere money. I did not at that time know how much I should need money for the institution of which I was about to take charge. Mr. Witt kept his vow. He never did contribute to the seminary, though his widow some years after sent me fifteen thousand dollars to found scholarships in his honor. But Mr. Witt never ceased to love me. On my first visit to Cleveland after I had begun my work at Rochester, I preached in my old church to a great congregation. When the sermon was over, my friends began to throng the spaces before the pulpit to grasp my hand and speak with me. I was much moved by their affectionate greetings, and when one poor member of the church burst out into weeping, I could not keep from tears myself. The thing became contagious, and the greatest scene of my life was there witnessed—a hundred people all in tears together. After all was over I made my way to the door, when, in one of the back seats, I found dear old Mr. Witt, the tears rolling down his cheeks while he fairly quivered with emotion, and he wrung my hand and said, "You don't deserve it! You don't deserve it!" Then he invited me to go home with him to dinner, and he was very friendly. But he never gave me any more money, notwithstanding.

And now about the children. John was born in the house on Prospect Street, on December 7, 1866. We named him Henry after my brother, and John after the beloved disciple, and this name has been prophetic, for he has been from his childhood an affectionate and blameless son. We have had only comfort in him; and as his mind and heart have developed together, we have come to believe that God has some great purpose of good in his life and work. At one time I thought that his intellectual gifts were not equal to those of Charles, but of late I begin to find in him an insight into philosophical and theological problems which is most gratifying, together with an emotional gift which itself is a great help in the investigation into truth. He has imagination as well as logic, sympathy as well as acumen, and it would not surprise me if he ultimately became, not simply a fine preacher for the crowd, but a fine teacher for trained students. And in that same house, 136 Prospect Street, on February 10, 1870, were born to us twins: Cora and Kate, both of them dear to us, and both of them gifted, in different ways: Cora in the way of art and Kate in the way of management. What we should do without Katy's intelligent and loving care is more than I can say.

When the twins were born, it became a serious problem how to name them. If they had been boy and girl, Jay and Fay would have been appropriate. I had not then attended the New York dog show, or I might have been helped by the names of the offspring of a Scotch terrier which I afterwards saw there: they were Kate, Duplicate, Certificate, and Syndicate. I rummaged through the Scriptures in hope of finding what I needed. If the twins had both been boys, I should have had no difficulty, for there were Jacob and Esau. But strangely enough the Bible makes no provision for female twins—at least, that was my first impression. One morning, however, at family prayers I read, "Salute Tryphena and Tryphosa." At once I said to myself, "There it is!" Doubts were suggested by certain members of the family. How could we be sure that Tryphena and Tryphosa were twins? To settle the matter, I wrote to President Samson Talbot of Denison University. I told him that I supposed universities were established for the purpose of solving questions for which the average man was incompetent, and I requested him to bring this matter before the faculty of the institution and give me their answer. After some weeks I received his reply. He said he had proposed the inquiry at the close of one of his faculty meetings, and a debate had ensued. The first opinions propounded seemed to be favorable to the conclusion that Tryphena and Tryphosa were twins. At last, however, the president himself suggested that this view was negatived by the etymology of the names. Tryphena and Tryphosa were evidently compounds of the syllable *tri, tris,* and suggested triplicity instead of duality. Tryphena and Tryphosa were triplets and not twins. There had probably been a brother who had died young, so that his name was not mentioned. It would never do to name my children Tryphena and Tryphosa. The whole faculty assented to the view of the president; I was compelled reluctantly to accept their decision. The result was that we looked about among our own relatives. My dear mother had no one in my family to perpetuate her name. We gave the name "Kate" to the younger. The name "Cora" had some similarity of sound. The children have rejoiced in the names "Kate" and "Cora" to this day. But further details with regard to the growth and education of the children must be postponed until the last of the number is added to the list fifteen years later.

I preached to my church until the first of June, 1872, when my pastorate in Cleveland ended. I felt the need of change and recreation before I began my new and arduous work in Rochester, and I therefore determined upon a tour of three months in Europe. I organized a party of seven, consisting of Colgate Hoyt and Henry C. Rouse, sons of James M. Hoyt and of Edwin C. Rouse respectively; Dr. Henry E. Robins, then pastor of the First Baptist Church of Rochester; Rev. C. E. Barrows, pastor of the First Baptist Church of Newport, R.I.; James D. Reid, the newly elected secretary of the New York Baptist Union for Ministerial Education, which had under its charge and management the Rochester Theological Seminary; and finally Rev. S. W. Duncan, then pastor of the Euclid Avenue Baptist Church of Cleveland, and my friend for many years. The party was a very heterogeneous one, and I should never again try to keep such a set together. I had invited Dr. Robins, Mr. Barrows, and Mr. Reid to join the rest without giving these others a chance to say yes or no. Dr. Robins and Mr. Barrows were men of the solemn sort, while Mr. Reid and the two boys were eager for all sorts of nonsense. Sam Duncan, who ought to have stood by me and who could have made matters pleasant, conceived a great dislike for Dr. Robins and communicated this to the others. I was the only bond of union. I had the advantage of them all in knowing a little French and German as they did not, in holding the purse strings, and paying the bills as conductor of the party, and, above all, in having some experience gained from going over the ground twelve years before. Though some infelicities attended our journey, it was on the whole an inspiring one and a great benefit to the health of all concerned. Dr. Robins was always ready for serious talk, and I learned much from him. The younger members of the party were always ready for fun, and they stirred me up in another and no less valuable way.

Our *terminus ad quem* was Switzerland, and our scheme was that of a pedestrian tour. We rushed from Liverpool to London, Brussels, and Cologne, and thence up the Rhine to Basel and Zürich. The ride up the Rhine on the deck of a steamer was the most charming I have ever taken. The sky was slightly overclouded, while yet the temperature was delightful, and the air was clear. A fine orchestra was playing all the while; we took our dinner in full view of the castled crags, and the day became one of the memorable days of my life. A company of German students came on board with the inevitable accompaniment of a keg of beer. They became very hilarious. One of them at last refused to drink more, saying, *"Ich habe schon genug."* The reply was characteristic: *"Man kann nie genug haben, nur zu viel!"* Which reminds me of the callow American who shrank from the immense schooner of beer which the waiting-maid brought him at Munich and begged for something smaller. The maid simply replied, *"Dies ist kein Platz für Kinder!"* My two boys had, I believe, never tasted either beer or wine, and I was bound that I would set them a good example of abstinence. What was my surprise to find that Dr. Robins, whom we thought so sober, was inclined to do in Rome as the Romans did and ordered a bottle of Rhine wine for our whole party. Even then I declined to partake. But little by little I perceived that there was no use of stemming the tide. We soon got to drinking wine every day with our dinner, and I think it did us good. I drink wine abroad, but not at home. I once told Theodore Bacon that I had to draw the line somewhere, and I drew mine in the middle of the Atlantic Ocean. Whereupon he remarked that that explained to him for the first time the meaning of the phrase "half-seas-over."

We reached Zürich on Saturday night. The great *Schützenfest* for all Switzerland was just at that time in full swing, and it was very difficult to find rooms at any of the hotels. But the spectacle of seven gentlemen, all Americans and all presumably rich, was too much for one hotel-keeper, and he not only let us in but also treated us sumptuously. Our numbers indeed ensured admirable accommodations wherever we went. We spent that Saturday evening on the banks of the famous lake, looking off upon the moonlit waters and the distant snowy range beyond. Next day was Sunday, but it was the great day of the marksmen. The report of the rifles was incessant. Mr. Reid tried to vary the monotony by going to the swimming bath. He hung up his clothes in the little compartment that looked out upon the tank and then plunged in. He dressed and came home to the hotel. Next morning he found that his pocketbook, with a hundred pounds in Bank of England notes, was missing. It was his whole reliance for the tour just before us. He discovered the loss just as we were starting for the train to Zug. The only reasonable conclusion was that some thief had entered his compartment the day before at the bath and had abstracted his money. I stayed with him for several hours in Zürich to inform the police. But to hunt up the thief was like looking for a needle in a haymow. We had to give up the search in despair. Mr. Reid had to borrow money of Colgate Hoyt to continue his tour. Who robbed Mr. Reid no man knoweth unto this day.

We walked up and down the Rigi, over the Furca Pass and past the Rhone glacier, ascended the Little Sidelhorn from which we got a magnificent view of the vast ice fields of the Bernese Oberland, and crossed the Wengern Alp to Lauterbrunnen. Here the party divided for a few days. Some of us were eager to try one of the more difficult passes, but others thought themselves unequal to such work. Duncan, Hoyt, and I undertook to cross the Kander glacier to Kandersteg while the rest went round to the same place by way of Interlaken and the Lake of Thun. First we made our way to Mürren, where we spent the night. Then we penetrated by a steep path into a remote Alpine valley, with the hope that after lodging at a little inn at the foot of the pass we might start for Kandersteg by three the next morning. We got in sight of the inn late in the afternoon when a fearful storm came on. The sky darkened and a hurricane of wind and rain swept down from the glaciers. The roaring of the mountain torrents and the crashing of the storm seemed almost to betoken the breaking up of the foundations of the world. It was as if night had suddenly set in and as if we, wrapped in clouds and darkness, were being seized and hurried away from a dissolving universe. Then just as I was about to despair of safety, the dense black veil of driving cloud and storm parted in an instant, and through the rift there shone down upon me the vision of a dazzling mountain peak of snow, serene in sunshine against a sky of cloudless blue; around, the furious hellish rush of dark and blinding and contending elements; above, the majesty of a spotless purity and the beauty of an ineffable calm. I have often used this experience to illustrate the sudden revelations of God's power to those who seek his glory through the dark path of self-sacrificing devotion to the fallen and the lost. So the sign of the Son of man shall at last appear to those who await His coming.

We reached the inn almost drenched with the rain. And what a scene met our eyes in that desolate spot! With the torrents raging around the house so that we could hardly hear each other talk, we learned that the keeper of the inn, an Alpine guide, had a few days before lost his life on the glacier. A company of mountaineers had been searching for his body and that very morning had brought it home to his family. The corpse was lying in the house awaiting its burial. The widow and her five children were the only persons to care for us. They got our dinner for us and waited at the table. It was a mournful time. We went early to bed, expecting to rise early. But at three in the morning our guide knocked at our door with the news that it was still raining, that higher up on the glacier the rain was undoubtedly snow, and that it would be useless to begin our journey in such weather. In fact it appeared impracticable to begin it for some days to come. We slept late, held a council of war, determined to retrace our steps. When the rain ceased in the middle of the morning, we started down the valley again to Mürren, Lauterbrunnen, Interlaken, and at last after two days we followed the rest of our party to Kandersteg by way of the Lake of Thun. It seemed too humiliating to confess our failure. We therefore went to a different hotel from that where our friends were awaiting us and met them in the streets of the village, as if by accident. We agreed together to keep from the rest just as long as possible the fact that we had come to Kandersteg by the same route as they. We would tell no lies but would see how long we could avoid telling the truth. So with every question as to our experiences, we retailed to the company descriptions from the guidebook of the glacier route and its dangers, the terrible ledge along the precipice with an abyss of a thousand feet beneath and rocks hurtling down upon the traveler from above, the ropes that tied him to his guide in order to hold him up when he slipped into a crevasse, and the tremendous fatigue of an eighteen hours' pull over the glacier. Our friends swallowed it all down and admired our bravery, while they thanked their stars that they had not been fools enough to attempt it. Yet we never said we had done it, and when at last they discovered the joke that had been played upon them, they were not able to accuse us of any sort of misrepresentation.

We all walked together over the Gemmi Pass to the Baths of Leuk on the way to the Rhone Valley. Another storm came on as we were plunging down the steep zigzags on the southern side. This time we were exposed to heavy rain for at least two hours, and we reached our hotel thoroughly soaked. There was nothing for it but to go to bed until dinner time while our clothes were dried in the kitchen before the fire. All of us appeared at the *table d'hôte* but Dr. Robins. We knew that he must be ravenously hungry like us, but we made no further inquiry until we had finished our dinner. Then we found him still in bed. It appeared that he had been unable to get his clothes from the kitchen. He had rung his bell, had opened his door in answer to a knock, had been scandalized by the maid's coming into his bedroom, had indignantly driven her out, and had then tried to hold communication with the door between them. As he knew no German and she knew no English, she could not tell what he wanted and went away in despair; he thought her perverse and in equal despair took to his bed once more, until we came to release him. We ordered up his clothes, had some sort of dinner served in his room, and tried to entertain him while he ate. But the picture of the grave doctor, so slightly clad, trying in vain to converse through the door with the maidservant, and then going supperless to bed, will never cease to provoke my laughter. Through all the remainder of our journey, indeed, it was common to hear some member of the party burst out suddenly into what seemed to be causeless and uncontrollable merriment. We never dared to ask what was the matter, nor did we need to ask—it was generally understood to be the recollection of Doctor Robins and the German maid.

From Leuk we went to Geneva and Chamonix. The *diligence* ride through Sallenches, with the great white mass of Mont Blanc in full view, lit up by the sun, abides in my memory still, and when I think of it, I repeat the lines of Lord Byron:

> Mount Blanc is the monarch of mountains;
>   They crowned him long ago,
> On a throne of rocks, in a robe of clouds,
>   With a diadem of snow.[4]

We saw the mountain from both sides, for after we had ascended the Brévent on the west, we made the Tour du Mont Blanc, by way of Saint Gervais, the Col du Bonhomme, Motet, and the Allée Blanche, to Courmayeur. It was a wonderful afternoon, that one in the Allée Blanche, for on the eastern side the great mountain chain is precipitous and seems twice as high as from Chamonix. The glittering snowfields contrasted gloriously with the azure heavens above and beyond them. From Courmayeur we went to Aosta and over the Saint Théodule Pass to Zermatt, and once more to Geneva. Saint Théodule, taken the second time from south to north, was not nearly as impressive as when I took it on my first tour as the way from Switzerland to Italy. At Geneva our party again divided. Colgate Hoyt and Henry Rouse stayed a little longer than the rest, in order to see Paris and London. The others accompanied me straight to Liverpool, and so to New York.

A chance conversation with an English fellow-traveler deserves to be mentioned. It was with regard to the liturgy of the Established Church. I told him frankly that it impressed me most when I first heard it; as it became familiar, it lost its charm. He cited its advantages as a medium of worship where great congregations were assembled and the single voice of the clergyman was well-nigh lost; in such cases the book held the people together and gave an intelligible bond between them. But then he urged as his chief argument the fact that it gave the people good prayers whatever the mood or the spirit of the officiating clergyman might be. "Good heavens!" he cried, "would you put us at the mercy of men who haven't a religious idea in their heads?" I replied that none of God's children were born dumb and inability to pray in public was the best deterrent for those who had no right to be in the ministry, whereas a printed form of prayer was the very means of concealing the

<hr>

[4]Lord Byron, *Manfred*, I, i. lines 60-63.

minister's unfitness both from himself and from others. My English friend emphasized the value of a liturgy where all knew what was to come; I declared that such a liturgy made no provision for special times of sorrow or the great occasions when sudden events demanded entirely new expression of the heart to God. He spoke of the worship of the heavenly host in the Apocalypse as evidently liturgical; I replied that however it might be in heaven, we had no New Testament injunction or example of liturgical prayer on earth. And I may add that forms of prayer have attraction for me only when I am dull and unspiritual; when my spirit is aglow, then nothing is so natural, nothing so glorious, as the free outpouring of the soul to God, as the Holy Spirit moves, and in words which the moment brings.

On the steamer by which we returned, I found among the second-class passengers my old companion and friend in Dr. Benedict's Academy, Henry A. Ward. He was a born naturalist and a born rover. He had before his mind's eye the ideal of a teaching museum, in which rocks, minerals, and fossils should be proportionately represented, and by the best specimens. He had the art of collecting. He went to the quarry and bought valuable material in quantity, and for a song. By exchanges with other collectors, he filled out the gaps. He has had extensive dealings with the British Museum and all the largest museums of the world. The collections of Vassar College, the University of Rochester, and the Field Museum at Chicago are monuments to his learning and skill. To gather them, he has traveled all over the globe. The stories of his adventures in Iceland, Australia, Arabia, Brazil, Egypt, and Alaska are so enchanting that he might make his fortune if he would only tell them in public as he tells them to our Pundit Club. I had not seen Professor Ward for ten or twelve years, and our talks on the deck of the homecoming steamer did much to shorten the voyage. Three or four of his narratives seem too good to be forgotten. Hence I set myself, though very imperfectly, to reproduce them.

At Algiers he met a woebegone set of Arabs on their way to Mecca. They were eight in number. They had nothing but rags to cover them and were half starved. Professor Ward, out of the kindness of his heart, drew from his pocket some copper coins worth no more than half a cent apiece and gave one to each Arab. One by one they bent before him and kissed the dust for gratitude. After they had risen, the professor remarked to the man who seemed to be their chief that he was glad to serve them; they were all children of one common Father; they were followers of the prophet, and he himself was a Christian, but that did not prevent him from trying to do them good. But no sooner had they heard the word "Christian" than the chief drew out from his rags the farthing that had been given him, spat upon it, and threw it upon the ground with hatred and contempt. One after another in solemn succession the others repeated the action of their leader, and then the whole band, transformed to cutthroats and cursing the infidel, turned their backs upon their benefactor. It was an illustration of the religious fanaticism of the Orient.

At the mouth of the Niger he learned what Christianity could do. He had been seized with the African fever, and on shipboard the captain, seeing that he could not live through another day, determined as the only chance of saving his life to take him ashore and leave him upon the beach. He was left alone in this dying condition upon a little island. The vessel sailed away. But Providence so ordered it that a poor black woman came down to the beach and took compassion upon him. She carried him in her arms to her hut, nursed him tenderly for four months, made friends for him among her people. She wept inconsolably when he got well enough to hail a passing ship and leave her. She was a convert to Christianity from some mission on the mainland, the only disciple of Christ upon the island. She saw in him a man of the same white race that had brought her the gospel. As she had freely received, she freely gave.

Professor Ward wrote me a letter from the southernmost port in the world, Punta Arenas, or Sandy Point, which is located at the end of the South American continent and looks across Magellan's Strait to Tierra del Fuego. His letter was written in June, but June was winter on that side of the equator. It described his voyage southward along the western coast of Patagonia. He was standing on deck with his heaviest overcoat, and the ladies were protected by their furs. A light rain was falling, which at length changed to snow. A long canoe was observed, putting out from shore. It drew near and proved to contain about thirty savages: men, women, and children. Not one of them had upon the body a single rag of clothing, though some of the men had a long piece of skin hanging down the back, from a thong tied round the neck, apparently intended for ornament rather than warmth. A naked woman was holding a naked baby, which vexed her by its crying. After ineffectually spanking it, she took it by one of its feet, held it up head downwards, and then plunged it several times into the briny deep. This had the proper effect of stilling its cries. She threw the sputtering infant into the bottom of the canoe, and there, with the snow falling upon its naked body, it curled itself up and went peacefully to sleep.

My friend, as I have intimated, was a prince of collectors. He knew that a bird in the hand is worth two in the bush, and he secured what he wanted wherever and whenever he found it. Observing a little stuffed monkey of an unusual kind in the window of a Parisian shop, he immediately went in and purchased it. It was done up in brown paper; the professor tucked it under his arm and proceeded toward his lodgings. By accident the string got untied; the envelope over the monkey's head fell off; and Professor Ward presented the unusual spectacle of a man with a captive ape grinning from under his arm upon all who followed him. And there were enough to follow him. The gamins of Paris got upon the scent, and while the professor was all unconsciously wending his way homewards, a long procession of jeering boys accompanied him. Only when he got to the end of his journey did he realize what an exhibition he had been making of himself.

He was accustomed to visit Fulton Market in New York. There he found a new and lovely specimen of eels. He bought a dozen specimens. They were small, and yet the question as to how he should carry them to his hotel was a delicate one. He concluded at last to drop them into the inside of his umbrella and then tie them in by the thread around the ferules. So he walked away, holding his umbrella by the handle, until he reached Broadway and got into a Broadway stage. The omnibus was full of ladies. Professor Ward is an admirer of female beauty, as well as a very absent-minded man. He looked at the ladies, and he forgot all about the eels. Suddenly he was horrified to find that his umbrella had fallen upon the floor of the bus and one of the eels had escaped. He foresaw an explosion, and, deeming discretion the better part of valor, he seized the handle of his umbrella, pulled the strap of the stage, and made his way to the sidewalk. But he knew that for the inmates of that vehicle trouble was coming. He therefore innocently followed along the walk. A few moments sufficed. A terrific shriek rent the air. Cries of "snakes" sounded out from the interior. A dozen women pulled the strap at once. They fairly piled over one another in their struggle to get out. And all the while the unsuspected author of the mischief looked on and laughed. Professor Ward has had so many adventures that he is a most entertaining storyteller. It was a great mistake that Mr. Rockefeller did not buy his World's Fair Collection for the University of Chicago as I urged him to do, instead of letting it go into the hands of Marshall Field. I am glad that by his recent fortunate marriage, the professor is now lifted above the mere quest for bread and butter and can at length devote himself to pure science.

6

Seminary Presidency

When I reached Rochester again, at the beginning of September, 1872, the seminary term was just about to open. A new and trying work loomed up before me. My sister Belle and her husband, Dr. Miller, were then living with Father and Mother at the mansion on Clinton Street and keeping house for them. We ourselves took a little wooden house on East Avenue just west of the seminary. It was a diminutive habitation compared with that which I had occupied in Cleveland, and it was ill adapted to the entertaining of professors and students which I was compelled to do. But it was the best place obtainable at the time, and I was willing to make a humble beginning. Though I had let my board of trustees know that I could do little good work without having seminary matters under control and though for that reason they had made me president, I still accepted a considerably smaller salary than my predecessor had received, and my house was not furnished me by the institution. The truth is, I felt myself a smaller and less promising man than Dr. Robinson, and I did not expect any great favors until I had proved my ability to manage and to teach. It was a

217

great satisfaction to me that the seniors had finished their theology during the previous year and that I had therefore only the middle class to instruct. I was also glad that the class was small—it numbered only seventeen—and that it was considerate.

I wrote out the matter of my first lecture on the morning of the day on which it was delivered, and so I continued to do for two years, until I had once gone over the whole system of theology. I gave my lecture in the afternoon. I dictated a synopsis and then filled up the remainder of the two-hour session with discussion. I was obliged to take important positions with very slight opportunity of investigation and with the certainty that errors at the beginning would multiply themselves greatly as I went on. I did my work with fear and trembling, but I also did it in dependence upon God. I was wonderfully led. Few of the points I made have I been obliged afterwards to retract. I have rather found that my early teaching was the germ and seed of all that followed. The French proverb is "When you are right, you are a great deal more right than you think you are." And God gave me boldness also. I had not long taught before I discovered that the books of theology, like the commentary Dr. Kendrick spoke of, were very good books, except upon the difficult passages. When I came up to a real problem, I generally had to work it out myself. After a little, I made up my mind that I would throw modesty and fear to the winds, that I would trust my own judgment, under the guidance of the Holy Spirit, that when I had come to a conclusion after investigation, I would believe my opinion as good as any other man's, that I would advocate and defend it boldly, whether men would hear or forbear. It was a great day when I made up my mind that my soul was my own. Without some measure of self-confidence I never could have succeeded as a teacher. In fact, I have come to regard the spirit of the propagandist as a more valuable element in the teacher's success than either learning or gifts of expression.

Up to this time my theology had been largely determined by my recollections of Dr. Robinson's instructions thirteen or fourteen years before. His deterministic view of the will and his conception of law as the transcript of God's nature had made a strong impression upon me. I could not well free myself from this influence. And yet I knew that to repeat Dr. Robinson's teaching would be fatal to all freshness or independence. He had been printing his revised and corrected notes, and I think he expected me to use them in my instruction. I have no doubt it was a trial to him that I preferred to blaze out a new path for myself. The truth is, I not only wished to be independent, but I had also begun to suspect that Dr. Robinson was wrong in some important points. A year or so before I left Cleveland, I went to Rochester almost expressly to learn his views about the person of Christ. After a two hours' interview, I concluded that either I was a fool or Dr. Robinson intended to mystify me. I was sure that I could neither accept nor comprehend his doctrine, and he sent me away with the air of one who could not furnish both ideas and brains to understand them. Some suspicion as to his teaching had arisen in other quarters, a suspicion justified, as I now think, by the inconsistencies of his system. In my essay on Dr. Robinson as a theologian, which forms a part of the memorial volume edited by Dr. Elias H. Johnson of Crozer Theological Seminary, I have shown what these inconsistencies were.[1] I believe it was his inability to reconcile these inconsistencies which really led him to suspend the work of printing his *Theology*, when it was two-thirds completed. Be this as it may, it is certain that the growing suspicion with which his work was regarded made it easier for him to leave Rochester. He naturally felt none too cordial toward a successor who was expected to revolutionize the Rochester theology. At the anniversary when I was elected, he abstained from any word of welcome or praise of his successor. But my course was plain. I boxed up the sheets of his printed notes instead of making them a textbook for my students, and they lay for twenty years unused, until Professor True after Dr. Robinson's death completed the printing, from notes copied at his dictation before I came, and at last published the doctor's *Christian Theology*. I wrote out and printed my own *Theology* without ever once looking at his, and I really learned what his final teachings were only when I made an exhaustive examination of his writings in 1894 for the purpose of furnishing my contribution to his memorial.

In the preparation of my lectures I depended more upon the German writers, and especially upon the orthodox Lutherans, than

---

[1] *Miscellanies* (Philadelphia: The Griffith and Rowland Press, 1912), vol. 2, pp. 58-109.

Dr. Robinson had done. Dorner, Thomasius, and Philippi were then modern theologians, and I read them with avidity. English and American theologians often evade or ignore difficulties and leave the reader unconscious of their existence. It provoked me to find that the critical point in my inquiries had not been touched. But German writers aim to cover the whole subject. When they come to a question they cannot answer, they at least recognize it, suggest a tentative answer, or declare it to be for the present unanswerable. A second edition corrects frankly the mistakes of the first; no pride of consistency leads a man to stick to an antiquated view. I learned from the Germans to be candid, to give up all pretense of omniscience, to strike a balance between opinions, to hold some things in suspense. I also learned to collect material for future use, to make notes on all my reading, to value every illustration that would throw light upon my subject. There is an old maxim to the effect that it is an ill mason that refuses any stone. I began to gather references. My system of theology grew like the seed in the parable, I knew not how. Before I was aware, I had a brief Compendium which, in 1876, I printed for the use of my students.[2] In 1886, I added the manifold notes and illustrations which had accumulated as the basis of my extemporaneous talks, and the result was my *Systematic Theology*. This has now passed to its fifth edition, and already nearly five thousand copies are in circulation. My aim in this book is to rescue theology from the realm of mere abstractions and to show its connections with literature and life. I wish to help the student and the preacher, the former by showing him where he may find new material and the latter by suggesting ways in which he may make doctrine practically effective.

This leads me to say that I began my teaching with the determination to make it not only an independent and original statement of the truth but also to infuse into it something of the persuasiveness and love of the gospel. Dr. Robinson had seemed to me cold and even harsh. His critical faculty mastered him. He had few words of praise for authors or for students. He stirred his students, but he also chilled them. I was convinced as the result of my pastoral experience that the critical spirit is of little use in

[2]*Lectures on Theology. Printed for the Use of Students in the Rochester Theological Seminary* (Rochester: E. R. Andrews, 1876).

preaching. The constructive mind is of a higher order than the destructive. The proclamation of positive truth wins converts, where the denunciation of errror attracts only transient attention. Wordsworth said well that "we live by admiration, hope, and love." I determined to mark out for myself a new course as a teacher. I set out to be a man of faith, to be a great believer, to hold the truth in love, and to make love my helper in all my intercourse with students. I was gifted with a fellow-feeling for the young. I put myself side by side with my scholars, assumed no dignity, insisted on no technical rights or prerogatives, made my instruction familiar and interesting, and, above all, infused it with all manner of practical religious suggestion and stimulus to faith and prayer. I have always rejoiced to teach theology because I could talk about everything in heaven and earth and under the earth and could make all things illustrate the greatness of Christ and the power of his gospel. I have made a pulpit out of a professor's chair and have tried to be a pastor to my pupils. Many of them have told me of new Christian experiences to which they were led by their studies of doctrine, and many have said that the impulses to a holy life which they have received from my teaching were even more valuable than the training they had obtained in systematic theology. In fact, I have never understood that my calling was to make simple theologians; I have understood my mission to be the making of Christian preachers. I have aimed to give my students something to preach but also to convince them that without love truth cannot be rightly seen and without God truth is an abstraction and not a power.

One of the best things I ever did for the seminary was the establishment of the daily noon prayer meeting. This occurred in the first years of my administration. I felt the need of some common ground upon which all the professors and students could meet together. I wanted each day's scholastic work to be mixed with prayer. The students needed to be taught the true method of conducting prayer meetings as they only could by taking part themselves. So we began at twelve o'clock one day with no leader and no fixed order of service. Someone gave out a hymn. Three verses were sung. Several prayed. A few remarks were made. When there were no more to speak, the meeting broke up by a common impulse, having lasted only fifteen, or at the most twenty, minutes. I had good help in establishing the meeting from Professor Wilkinson. It soon became a custom and a tradition. It affords an easy opportunity for saying anything that is needed in the way of encouragement or admonition. It gives excellent discipline in the art of brief and pointed address. But its chief use is to keep up the religious and missionary tone of the seminary, to cultivate fellowship between professors and students, and to draw our minds and hearts to God. Sometimes the feeling has been so deep and strong that it was difficult to close the meeting, even though it was protracted to a half hour. Twenty or more persons have spoken or prayed in a single meeting, each taking only a minute or two. When this is the case, I hear the sound of a going in the tops of the mulberry trees. The Spirit of God seems to be moving upon the body of students. I count it a revival of religion in the seminary. Such a revival means more than a revival in any single church. It means that many leaders of many churches are having their hearts kindled, so that they can carry the sacred fire to the congregations to which they minister. I regard the seminary prayer meeting as quite as valuable an adjunct to our work as is any single department of instruction. I discourage professors from beginning the meeting or in any way monopolizing it. The responsibility must rest with the students, and the professors must sit with them on a footing of perfect equality. Wednesday noon is always devoted to missions. When the prayer meeting languishes, I begin to feel that our work is vain.

By dint of courtesy, good nature, and sympathy, I have always got on well with both students and professors. I sometimes wonder which body is most difficult to deal with. Students are the more shortsighted and subject to panics. Before we entered upon our new regime and while we had many ill-prepared men in the seminary, government was sometimes attended with danger. But since we have had only college graduates in the student body, or those who had training equivalent with college graduates, administration has been increasingly easy. After a little time, the student becomes convinced that the faculty are his friends and that all his reasonable demands will be met. But traditions of this sort are of slow growth. I feel thankful that the early years of my presidency were so free from disturbance. Dr. Martin B. Anderson of the university used to say that a college president lived on a sleeping volcano—he never knew when an eruption would occur. I have always thought that there must be a future life for canal horses, washerwomen, and college presidents; since they do not get their deserts in this life, there must be another life, to justify the ways of God. If I had been president of a college, I do not know what would have become of me. In the seminary, the students have, as a body, been men of principle; they have settled their plan of life; they are intent upon gaining preparation for their future work; they have left the follies of boyhood behind them. To manage such men is comparatively easy, particularly if you have their respect and affection.

The faculty of the seminary has from the beginning been extremely heterogeneous, and it has required much patience and wisdom to keep its members at peace with the students and with one another. When I came to Rochester to teach, Dr. Horatio B. Hackett was the senior professor. He had a brilliant reputation as a scholar and was one of the best of teachers. In my book entitled *Philosophy and Religion* I have so fully described him that I must not enlarge upon his characteristics here.[3] But I can speak of some personal peculiarities. He was a recluse, sensitive in the extreme, shrinking from publicity, extraordinarily exact in all his utterances, nervous when his rights or his rest were invaded. He was affectionate as a father in all his dealings with me, and I sought to spare him every needless labor or trial. When I went abroad in 1874, he invoked God's blessing upon my journey, as the aged Jacob might have done for Joseph. He was very unwilling to express opinions on matters which he had not recently and thoroughly studied. I tried to draw from him some information about the Apocalypse, but it was difficult to gather from his answers that he had ever read that part of the New Testament. He walked out upon Monroe Avenue in the early spring. He reached the end of the plank sidewalk and hesitated about going farther. A countryman approached, driving a load of truck. Dr. Hackett most courteously addressed him: "Will you kindly inform me, sir, what the condition of the roads is yonder?" The countryman looked down upon the doctor and replied: "Wall, I should say that they was decidedly

---

[3]*Philosophy and Religion,* pp. 330-336.

The combined faculty of Rochester Theological Seminary in 1907: Back row—Professor Mason, Professor Woelfkin, Professor J. H. Strong, Professor Rauschenbusch, Professor Silvernail, Professor Kaiser; Front row—Professor Ramaker, Professor Stevens, President Strong, Professor Gubelmann, Dean Stewart, Professor Betteridge bilious!'' The countryman passed by, but the doctor remained standing for several minutes. He was lost in contemplation. He had read extensively the literature of the Hebrews, the Greeks, the Latins, the Germans, and the English, but he had never in all his reading met with such a use of the term "bilious." It remained a puzzle for him to his dying day. When he did die, we gave him a great funeral. Our students acted as a guard of honor and accompanied the remains to the cemetery. The palm leaves upon the coffin were never more truly symbolical, for Dr. Hackett was a great scholar, a great teacher, and in many respects a great man.

Of Dr. R.J.W. Buckland also, our professor of church history, I have given a full account in the same book, *Philosophy and Religion*.[4] The doctor was one of the most gracious men I ever met. Everlastingly obliging, he was a great help to me in every way. His taste for science inspired me to continue my own studies in that line. In history he was wonderfully well informed. He brought his subject down to date, and that meant to twelve o'clock at noon on the day of his lecture. I once told him that if a man were to teach history, the less he had to do with facts, the better. I intended to set him at grouping his material and giving attention to principles rather than details. He had great volubility, and he was an interesting lecturer. Some of his students said he could extemporize history most admirably. But this was a jest. When the student asked for authorities, the doctor could always direct him to them. Dr. Buckland was a most indefatigable worker. All day and away on past midnight he delved at his books. I fear that the stimulus came largely from tobacco. I once asked him how many cigars he smoked. He replied that he was now very moderate; he had once smoked twenty-five a day, now he smoked only fifteen. I told him I was afraid he could not stand it. He answered that I need have no fear; he had done it for years, and he could work more hours in the day and more days in the week and more weeks in the year than any man he knew. But his boasting was short-lived. Not long after, he came to me complaining of pain in his side. A little later he gave up work and took to his bed. He was afflicted with enlargement of the spleen, an organ which serves, I believe, as a sort of sponge to take

[4]*Ibid.,* pp. 337-343.

up temporarily the blood driven in from the surface of the body by sudden chills and which would otherwise produce fatal congestion of the lungs or the heart. The so-called "ague-cake" of malarial regions is nothing but a chronic enlargement of the spleen. Dr. Buckland suffered intolerable pain, and it soon became evident that his tenure on life was but short. Dr. E. M. Moore was his physician. When Professor Buckland became very weak, Dr. Moore proposed to prolong his life by transfusion of blood. A student of the seminary, a great healthy specimen of a man, consented to furnish the vital fluid to his beloved instructor. The apparatus was made ready; the student's arm was stripped; the incision was made; but behold, the blood would not flow! The student had fainted and had fallen to the floor. He was revived; preparations were made again, and again he fainted. This time, when he came to himself, he was so ashamed of himself that he screwed his courage to the sticking point. The transfusion was successfully accomplished. Dr. Buckland was benefited. For a few days there was hope. But soon he declined even more rapidly than before, and after a few days of pain he died, as I firmly believe, a victim to the poison of tobacco.

We had at that time a professor of Hebrew who was the youngest of our faculty, George H. Whittemore by name. He was a graduate of Harvard, a painstaking scholar, and a real gentleman. He had taken his theological course at Newton before Dr. Hackett left there to begin his work at Rochester. The doctor had recommended him for the chair of Hebrew in our seminary, and he had already been teaching for four years when I came. But he was never more than acting professor. As he went on, it appeared that there were defects in his mental makeup which prevented the highest usefulness. While he was industrious and careful, he was incapable of a broad view, and he never seemed to have any mind of his own. He could tell you the opinions of all the commentators, but he could never decide between them. When asked the meaning of a certain word in a certain connection, he would reply, "Meyer says this, and Ellicott says that." "But, Professor, what do you think yourself?" The answer was likely to be, "When so great authorities differ, it would not become me to express an opinion." The result was that he inspired little respect, in spite of his learning, his gentlemanliness, and his blameless life. When Dr. Robinson was asked how Professor Whittemore was getting on, he replied, "His boots are always well blacked." "But, Doctor, what sort of a teacher is he?" "He takes care to wear a clean shirt-collar." And so, when Dr. Hackett and Dr. Buckland both left us, it seemed necessary to strengthen our Hebrew department by putting in an older and more decided man. Dr. Howard Osgood came into our faculty and has remained with us ever since, and Professor Whittemore was told that we should no longer need his services.

(About Professor William C. Wilkinson I wrote when I was describing the members of my own seminary class.) Dr. Howard Osgood has been so faithful a friend and so excellent a teacher that I must say a word about him. He was born a gentleman, and his early social surroundings were of the best. His father was the owner of a large plantation in Louisiana. He studied at Harvard, went south after his graduation, was soundly converted, from being an Episcopalian became a Baptist, studied Hebrew with a rabbi whom he took into his house, went to Heidelberg for several years, became pastor at Flushing on Long Island and then in New York City, was chosen professor of Hebrew at Crozer Theological Seminary, lost his position there on account of some personal difficulty with the founder, was made member of the Old Testament company for revising the Scriptures, and finally in 1876 became our professor of Hebrew in the Rochester Theological Seminary. The doctor has many of the southern characteristics. He is wonderfully winning, vivacious, conversable. He has strong prejudices, and his orthodoxy is of the cast-iron sort. He loves and he hates, like the apostle John. He reminds me of a southerner of whom he himself told me: if he liked you, he would give his life for you; but if he hated you, he would kill you. Grace has done much for Dr. Osgood, but it has never yet taught him how to get on day by day with his enemies. The doctor's plan is to go nowhere near them, to avoid them, to let them serenely alone. But he is a most lovable as well as a most learned man. As a librarian he is unsurpassed. Though he has never been in Palestine or Egypt, he knows both of those countries better than those who have lived there for years. His writings and his social gifts have brought honor to himself and to the seminary.

At this present writing (1897) Professor William Arnold Stevens has been with us precisely twenty years. It was a great day when we induced him to leave the teaching of classical Greek at Denison University in Ohio and begin teaching New Testament Greek at Rochester. I regard him as a very thorough scholar and a very wise Christian man. His candor and caution have made a deep impression upon his students. I first met him at Granville. Then I saw him again when he made a visit to Cleveland during my pastorate. For a year or two he was acting president of Denison. His teaching of intellectual and moral philosophy gave him interest in all sorts of metaphysical inquiry. He has been, with the exception of Dr. Henry E. Robins, the only one with whom I could discuss the deeper speculative questions of theology. He has done great service to twenty successive classes of students by teaching them that interpretation is not a matter of guesswork but of science, that Christianity is a historical religion whose foundation facts can be proved by evidence as convincing as is ever adduced in any court of justice. His temperament is calmer than that of Dr. Osgood; he is less emotional, but his Christian life, equally with Dr. Osgood's, has been a power for good. Both have stood for the Bible as the Word of God. While Dr. Osgood has emphasized the external evidence, Dr. Stevens has laid stress upon the internal. *Par nobile fratrum,* the entire confidence I have been able to put in them has done much to make my life happy.

Many people are surprised to find that Mrs. Stevens is much older than her husband. It is said to have happened in this way: the professor lost his mother when he was a child. A young lady took interest in the motherless boy, wrote him letters, gave him advice. Time passed, the boy profited by her care, graduated from college, studied in Europe, became professor of Greek at Granville. He wondered why he could not become interested in young ladies. At last it occurred to him that it might be because he was so deeply interested in the one particular young lady who for so many years had been a mother to him. He found that he could not get along without her. She had not married. She was devoted to him. So they concluded to live the remainder of their lives together. It has proved a most happy union, for both are excellent people. And it has not been any the less happy for the portion of this world's goods that the professor got with his wife. Their home, like Dr. Osgood's, has been an object lesson to all our students in the matter of hospitality and of taste. So many theologians come from obscure surroundings that a well-ordered household affords them a piece of education. For this reason I have thought it a part of my duty to my classes from the beginning to entertain them at my own house at least once a year. Dr. Osgood and Professor Stevens have been excellent helpers in this matter of the social culture of our students.

I had hardly begun my work in the seminary when one day I heard a knocking on the outside door of Trevor Hall. As no one answered the knocks, I went to the door myself. There stood a gaunt, travel-stained young man in a linen duster. He inquired if this was the Rochester Theological Seminary. When I assured him that it was, he disclosed the fact that he had come from Georgia to enroll himself among our students. He seemed to me a somewhat rough customer. But I soon found that he had an unlimited industry which amounted to genius. His name was Albert H. Newman. He was a natural linguist. We have never had a student to whom the rapid reading of the Greek and Latin Fathers was so easy. He graduated with great honor. After a couple of years of experience in teaching at the South, we called him to take the place of professor of church history which Dr. Buckland had filled. He remained with us from 1877 to 1881. But his teaching ability was not equal to his learning. He could not command his classes. They rebelled against his instruction as minute and dull. Generalization was not natural to him, or he had not yet sufficient confidence to generalize. The same wave of discontent among students which swept Professor Wilkinson from his professorship of homiletics dislodged Professor Newman from his professorship of church history. But he was immediately chosen to a similar position in McMaster University, and he has since done royal work in publishing his *History of the Anabaptists* and his *History of Antipedobaptism.*

When Wilkinson and Newman left us, it seemed doubtful whether we could ever fill their places. But in the autumn of 1881, Dr. T. Harwood Pattison and Dr. Benjamin O. True began their work, and they have continued with us ever since. Dr. Pattison is one of the most versatile and interesting of men. Of English birth, he has much of the English quickness and irritability, yet much of the English sturdiness and courage also. When I asked Judge Frank Wayland about him, he told me that Dr. Pattison would make a model teacher of homiletics, but he also called him a rolling stone and predicted that we would keep him no more than two years. As we have now had him for sixteen years, I have no great regard for Judge Wayland's gifts as a prophet. We took him from the Immanuel Church at Albany, where he received a greater salary than we could give him. But during these sixteen years he has preached almost continuously. Presbyterian and Baptist churches have vied with each other in securing his services. The variety of audiences has seemed to please him, and the long summer vacations have given him a chance for recreation and travel which the pastorate would not afford. That a man so sociable and witty should also be so industrious and so careful in his preparations for every public exercise is itself a wonder. Temper and a certain ugly way of blurting out sharp speeches have cost him dearly at times, as when his criticism of Professor Morey resulted in defeating the effort made to elect him to the Pundit Club. But though occasionally wrong-headed and arbitrary, he is chivalrous and stands by his friends. His preaching has given him a wide popularity, and his newspaper letters are always entertaining. Like most impulsive and bright men, he is inclined to undervalue the slow and careful work of the scholar. But it has been a good thing for the seminary that it had one brilliant man, even though we have occasionally taken exception to some of his utterances.

Professor True is a manly man and a man who always asserts himself. Somewhat pessimistic and full of fine theories which cannot be reduced to practice, he is always impressive by reason of his enthusiasm and volubility. In this respect he makes a good teacher of church history. He can describe and expand with unequaled facility. Mere abstract statement does not move the average student. Professor True puts the facts in all sorts of light until they take hold of the memory. If he would write more and talk less, he would do well. His fault in preaching as in prayer is too great prolixity. There is a tendency to repetition rather than to condensed statement, which has its drawbacks as well as its merits. It sometimes becomes wearisome. But no one can doubt his popularity with students. They respect the man and admire his energy. Long sermons have spoiled his reputation as a preacher, so that he is not sought for as Dr. Pattison is. But his historical synopses are good specimens of generalization. He is thoroughly master of his facts. I hope to see from him someday an excellent textbook of church history. He and I have always agreed upon one thing—free trade. In general, of late years we have acted with Democrats rather than with Republicans. We have supported Grover Cleveland and have been admirers of his policy, while all the other professors, so far as I know, have been Republicans.

And now let me speak briefly of the German professors. When I came to Rochester, there were but two, Professors Augustus Rauschenbusch and Herman M. Schäffer, and the latter began his work when I began mine. During all the years before, Professor Rauschenbusch had been the only professor, though subordinate teachers had one by one been employed. He was a graduate of the University of Berlin and a favorite pupil of Neander. The son of a Lutheran minister, he became a Baptist. After coming to this country he acted for some time as translator for the American Tract Society. He then began his work of instruction in the German Department of our seminary, or rather, he created and founded the German Department. When he came, there were only eight German Baptist churches in the country. Now there are over two hundred. To him more than to any other man belongs the honor of this remarkable progress. He was a very learned man in the biblical languages, church history, and physical science. He taught all these various branches for years. He was the type of a German pedagogue, absorbed in his work, exacting in his requirements, delighted with the success of his pupils. He could be eloquent and even humorous in his classes, but he could not tolerate the least inattention, and his students greatly offended him when they laughed at any stories but his own. He was greatly respected, though he ruled with a rod of iron. He ruled his family with equal rigor. Poor Mrs. Rauschenbusch learned early that absolute submission was for her the only way of peace. This submission was not natural to her. There grew up a shocking alienation between them. Their mutual recriminations were a great vexation to their friends. When the professor once asked Mrs. Rauschenbusch to go to a picnic and she inquired if he really meant it, the professor characterized this doubt of his sincerity as " fiendish." He wanted to give up his work and go to Europe mainly to get rest from living with her.

For many years he suffered from malaria, which he pronounced, according to its Italian derivation, "mal-ah-ria." He took large quantities of quinine to counteract the trouble. He became very nervous and despondent. One day a messenger summoned me to his house. Professor Rauschenbusch met me at the door, somewhat pale and haggard, yet with a good deal of life left in him. He drew me into the parlor, planted himself in a chair before me, and proceeded to make an address: "I have requested you to come, Brother Strong, to receive my last words. I have a few days to live. I wish to communicate to you my final requests." He looked at me with such intensity and spoke in so firm a tone of voice that I began to smile. "Do not smile, Brother Strong! I am sincere in what I say. I am a dying man." At this, I could not refrain from a slight laugh. The spectacle of one so vigorous and stalwart, contrasted so greatly with his representation of himself as on the edge of the grave, was too much for me. This only made the professor angry. He brought his hand down upon his thigh with a tremendous clap while he cried in a stentorian voice, "I tell you I am a dying man, Brother Strong!" I had great difficulty in composing myself and in composing him. I listened to his "dying requests," but I also went immediately to his physician. The doctor persuaded him to take a vacation at the Thousand Islands, and in a month the professor was back again at his post and doing his work as well as ever. With all his arbitrariness and hypochondria, he was a noble teacher, and he was certainly the father of German Baptist education in America.

Professor Herman M. Schäffer began his work in the German Department at the same time that I began mine in the English Department, and he taught from 1872 to 1897, just twenty-five years. His life constituted a Christian romance. He was born in Germany, but his childhood was spent in the slums of Boston. One day a lady espied him looking with wonder at the impossible pictures of a circus placard. "Come with me," she said, "and I will show you something handsomer than that!" So she took his dirty hand in hers and led him to the Sunday School. He became interested in the school, and his teachers became interested in him. He was so bright that they encouraged him to secure an education. With their help he pushed forward through a partial course in our university and a full course in the seminary. He was ordained pastor of the German Baptist Church in New York City. Here he showed unusual gifts both of preaching and organization. His zeal and success in the pastorate led his brethren to promote him to a position of instruction in the seminary. The students who have come from his teaching into our English Department are, in general, better Greek scholars than the majority of graduates from our American colleges. This proves him to be an accurate and painstaking scholar. But his chief gift has been hopefulness and enterprise. While Professor Rauschenbusch is something of a pessimist, optimism has been the breath of Professor Schäffer's life. Breezy, courageous, determined, he has done much to infuse energy and spirit into the German churches. Our German Students' Home could never have been built but for his indomitable perseverance. His watchword has always been "Never say die!" When he asks for money and is refused, Professor Schäffer always has taken "No" to mean "Yes," and he has speedily made a second application to the same man. Five times he asked Mr. Rockefeller to give toward the $100,000 endowment fund of the German Department, in spite of the fact that Mr. Rockefeller's courteous declination had been followed by thundering No's.

The last "No" almost broke Professor Schäffer's heart. He had raised $69,025 by heroic effort in times of great financial depression. The payment was conditional upon the raising of the whole $100,000. When the last string had been pulled and there were none left to apply to, our professor's strength gave way; for the first time he became the victim of despondency; diabetes set in, and he declared that he must die. But his actual death was a very sorrowful one. He was greatly oppressed for breath and asked to be carried to a window. He looked with pleasure at the green grass and blossoming trees. He asked his wife to bring his Greek Testament. She thought this a good sign and went to get it. When she returned, he was gone. She saw the open window and looked out. He lay on the ground below. He had probably tried to lift the window to get more air, in his weakness had lost his balance and fallen out; when his wife reached him, he had strength only to give her one last look, and then he died. The German endowment cost him his life. I have hoped that his death might touch Mr. Rockefeller's heart and bring the needed aid.

Professor Jacob S. Gubelmann is as utterly lacking in business tact and energy as Profesor Schäffer was highly endowed with them. When money is to be raised, he folds his hands despairingly, saying, "It is not in me!" Gentle and forbearing to a fault, the thought of discipline and vigorous administration is far from him. Yet he is a saint of the first class, a fervent and noble preacher, in English as well as German. He is beloved in all the churches and by all his students. It has been greatly to our advantage that the German Department could be represented in our English pulpits by so gracious and apostolic a man. He is a sound and conservative theologian, and he illustrates the motto of Neander: *"Pectus est quod theologum facit."* I do not think anyone ever made fun of him by calling him a pectoral theologian, as the students of Berlin did with Neander. The air of unworldliness which encompasses him is also an air of sweetness. It repels no one. His gift in prayer is the survival of an almost lost art; one feels as if he were familiar with the presence-chamber of the Almighty. No one who hears Professor Gubelmann pray can doubt the reality of religion. The hearer feels as did the hearers of Christ's prayers, and they long to learn the art themselves. I have myself been moved to repeat the words "Lord, teach us to pray, even as John also taught his disciples."

With such a faculty, it can be easily seen that differences might arise. Professor Gubelmann could never agree with Professor Schäffer about a question of discipline, and Professor Schäffer could never agree with Professor Gubelmann about a question of business. Dr. Osgood and Dr. Stevens could never abide Dr. Pattison's brusque English ways and his lack of regard for mere scholarship; Dr. Pattison could not stand the conservatism and slowness of the exegetical method. If I had not had the confidence of all parties and had not shut my eyes to many infirmities, I should have seen our faculty many times split into fragments. I have been able to keep them together in part because they have regarded me as a fair-minded arbiter of disputes but also in part because they knew that I was the only man who could raise money. The sinews of war are to be found in the exchequer. It has been my lot to have the responsibility of supplies laid almost wholly upon me. Never, I suppose, since the foundation of the world has anybody but the president succeeded in getting subscriptions for an institution. As my history at Rochester has been largely a history of efforts to meet deficiencies in income and to increase endowments, I must devote a few pages to a story of finance.

When I accepted the presidency of the Rochester Theological Seminary, I made the condition that I should not be expected for at least two years to concern myself with the raising of money. I knew that I needed those two years for unbroken study if I were ever to evolve an original scheme of theology. But I had hardly been settled in my chair for three months when I found that my salary was not paid. The treasurer could not with certainty inform me when it would be paid. All he could say was that income was not sufficient to meet expenses; my salary would be paid as soon as money came in. There was no one who could get money but me. I began to see that I must collect it or starve. Begging I hated almost as much as being hanged. But I concluded that I must make the effort. I started for New York. I had an interview with a gentleman who was worth several millions. He was president of a bank and a well-known Baptist. I set before him the needs of the seminary in a courteous, concise, and, as I thought, telling manner. At the close of my appeal, to which he had listened with apparent attention, he said, "I have just two things to say, Dr. Strong. One is that I have no money to throw away, and the other is that I do not believe in education anyhow."

I have tramped up and down the New York streets, calling upon one man of wealth after another and getting evasions and denials in place of money. At last in despair I have committed my case to God and put his promises to the test. Some of the plainest answers to prayer that I have ever received have been in connection with the raising of money. And yet the prayer that has seemingly brought results has not been the agonizing prayer of my earlier days. I have learned that there is no use working myself up into a physical or mental furor any more than in the case of a petition to an earthly father or friend. The fervent effectual prayer of a righteous man is rather the simple presentation of a rational request, with such continuity and earnestness as imply sincerity and trust. We are not heard for our much speaking, but we are heard for our interest in God's cause and our faith in his promises. I learned to pray without ceasing, to push on in spite of discouragements, to rely upon God's leading, to expect success not from my own planning but from God's power.

Prayer is an entering into the mind and will of Christ. This is the seventh great lesson of doctrine which I now learned by practical experience. My time for praying changed. I had been accustomed to set apart a special hour during the day, usually after I had studied my Bible in the morning. But I was frequently interrupted—I could not depend upon being alone. It occurred to me that the first hour and the best hour belonged to God. It was safest to look to him with the first waking breath. So I learned to prevent the dawning of the day. At least it is true that when any serious enterprise was on my mind and heart, I naturally woke early and spent my first thoughts in prayer. That God's will might be done, that I might personally know and do God's will was my first petition. Then came supplication that he would make me pure and faithful and true, loving and wise and believing. I brought before God all the members of my family and invoked God's blessing upon them. I asked help and strength for the special work of the day. I commended to God the particular enterprise in which I was engaged. And here came in the effort to raise money. I said over to myself a series of God's promises and encouraged my heart to think that these promises applied to me. Many a time I have taken comfort in Christ's words that "greater things than these shall ye do, because I go to the Father." I have believed myself admitted to intimacy of friendship with Christ, so that I could discern his plans and purposes with regard to me, and to a certain extent with regard to his cause. "I have not called you servants but friends, for the servant knoweth not what his Lord doeth." So I have felt within me at times the spirit of the prophet and have felt sure that what I asked, Christ would grant.

The first outward success was scored in Yonkers, when Mr. John B. Trevor, in an interview with Dr. Behrends and me, promised to do for the seminary under my administration all he had intended to do for it under that of Dr. Robinson. On a later visit of mine to Yonkers, he rejoiced my soul by saying that he purposed to concentrate his gifts upon the Rochester Theological Seminary. Still later I saw him at his office in New York. He took me upstairs to his private room. He asked what the greatest need of the seminary was. I told him it was the payment of our floating debt of $13,000. In an instant he said, "Well, I will pay that. Is there anything else that you need?" I replied that Trevor Hall furnished no proper accommodations in the way of lecture rooms. We needed to purchase additional ground and put up a building that might temporarily be used for lectures but might ultimately serve as a gymnasium. This would cost about $14,000. He at once told me that he would pay the expense of that. "Well, is there anything else you want?" he asked. I answered that our grounds had no fence and a good fence of stone and iron would cost $2,500. And he agreed to pay for that. Before I left him, he had promised altogether to give $31,000. And it was all done so simply, so curtly, that it hardly seemed to be benevolence but rather a matter of business. His noble deeds were deeds of principle. He disposed of them as quickly as possible. When he made a subscription, he seemed never to be at rest till it was paid. He wished no praise for what he did. He was a man of few words, but he was a fast friend. I consulted him with regard to every important matter. He took the seminary upon his conscience and his heart, and I looked to him in every time of need. For several years he paid our recurring deficits and so relieved our perplexities. But he got tired at last of "putting money into a hole in the ground"—this is the way he styled the paying of past debts. I saw that forward movement and permanent provision for our future was necessary in order to keep up his interest. And then came my efforts to get large subscriptions from others. In these efforts Mr. Trevor either led the way or took an active part. Several gifts of $25,000 each and several of $10,000 each came from him. The aggregate amount he gave to the seminary was $209,307. He is the greatest benefactor the institution has had. I expected when he died that he had provided for us largely in his will. To my immense surprise and disappointment he left us nothing. I have attributed much of this result to the influence of Mrs. Trevor, for he once told me that if she were only a Baptist he could do far more for us. I cannot think that he expected to die when he did or that his will represented the real man. Certain it is that Providence has given us no friend so able and faithful since he was taken away.

It was in 1879 that I bethought me of Mr. John D. Rockefeller and determined to do what I could to secure his help. I had known him while I was pastor in Cleveland. His little daughter had died. In the absence of his pastor, I was called to conduct the funeral service. This gave me a little hold upon the family. After I came to Rochester, I was called back to Cleveland to preach a sermon at the dedication of a new Baptist church. I called upon Mr. Rockefeller. I found him in his garden. I told him that I had wished to interest him in our seminary. He replied that he had great regard for my work and wished to support it. If I would come into the house with him, he would give me $500 at once. "Oh, Mr. Rockefeller," I replied, "you mistake my meaning. It was not any such sum that I had in mind but a great many times that. Give me the opportunity of setting before you our needs, and I shall hope that you will become such a friend as Mr. Trevor is." He was courteous, but he made no favorable response. He said afterwards that if Dr. Strong did not care to take what he was willing to give, he might get on without anything. But I knew that he was getting to be rich, and I felt a responsibility toward him. When Mr. Trevor began to intimate that he could no longer pay our debts, it occurred to me to ask Mr. Rockefeller to put up a permanent building for library, chapel, and recitation rooms, and to combine with this an effort to raise money for additional endowment. I had plans drawn for Rockefeller Hall, to cost $38,000. I went to Cleveland and laid them before Mr. Rockefeller. He received me graciously and promised to put up the building if I could secure from others $100,000 for the other needs of the seminary. So began a connection which has resulted in his giving to us an aggregate of $145,635. He introduced me to his brother William Rockefeller, who quickly subscribed $25,000 for our library, and to Charles Pratt, who gave $25,000 to endow a professorship of elocution. Mr. Trevor added $25,000 for the support of our secretary, and Joseph B. Hoyt gave $25,000 for the professorship of Hebrew. So the $100,000 was raised, and not only this but $17,000 besides, including $15,000 from Mr. J. A. Bostwick, so that the whole subscription, with Mr. Rockefeller's $38,000 for the building, amounted to $155,000.

It seemed a great triumph, and it marked an epoch in our seminary history. The raising of this money from the beginning to the end was a religious work. Every step was taken with prayer, and God led the way. I met with many rebuffs, and my faith was greatly tried. But I asked the money from God, for the sake of Jesus Christ his Son, and in order to spread the knowledge of him. The love of the Father for the Son was ever in my mind as my ground of hope, and my assurance and delight in thus carrying out God's plan to honor Christ was at times almost overwhelming. When Rockefeller Hall was dedicated, it seemed to me that the building was set apart from all secular and common uses for the service of God, just as definitely and solemnly as was Solomon's temple of old. Two years afterwards I made still another effort to raise $100,000 more of endowment, and this time again, with the help of Mr. Rockefeller and Mr. Trevor, each subscribing $25,000, I was successful. Mr. Deane, Mr. Milbank, Mr. Cauldwell, Mr. Preble, and Dr. Bishop all gave their help in varying amounts. Again in 1887 another effort was made to raise $100,000. Mr. Rockefeller subscribed $55,000. We increased this to $87,000 and could get no further, when all the subscribers consented to pay their subscriptions without insisting upon the raising of the remainder. Then hard times came on. Messrs. Deane, Wyckoff, and Preble became bankrupt. Messrs. Trevor, Hoyt, Milbank, Pratt, Cauldwell, and Bishop all died, and no one has risen to take their places. Mr. Rockefeller has become so interested in Chicago that he cannot now be depended upon to do any great thing for Rochester. The fact that my son Charles has married his daughter makes it impossible for me any longer to raise money, for everybody regards it as incredible that any man or institution even indirectly or remotely connected with Mr. Rockefeller can ever be in want. Perhaps it is his recognition of this fact that has led him of late to help us out on our current expenses. He has given $37,635 altogether for this object, and his total gifts to the seminary now, in April, 1897, amount to $145,635. But he no longer gives to our endowment. It is fortunate that I made hay while the sun shone. The seminary, with all its present needs, is upon a far better financial basis than when I came to it twenty-five years ago. Then it had only $113,750 of endowment, and its whole property amounted to less than $200,000. Now it has $604,000 of endowment and about $815,000 of property. During the same time the number of students has increased from 61 to 148, and the standard of scholarship has been greatly raised. Our history has been a marvel of divine leading. I have often said to our board of trustees that we have prospered by running into debt. The meaning of it is that we have lived by faith—the faith of the Son of God—and that he has justified the faith we have put in him.

Three men of our board of trustees have done much to make this success possible, and I wish most gratefully to acknowledge my personal obligation to them. Ezra R. Andrews has been for many years the chairman of our executive committee. By his uncommon common sense, his hopefulness of spirit, his industry and loyalty and honor, he has been my chief adviser and helper. Cyrus F. Paine has been for more than forty years the treasurer of the New York Baptist Union for Ministerial Education. At great cost of time and labor, he has taken charge of our finances. His anxieties have been great, and he has had only a nominal compensation. His faithfulness and patience have prevented loss on our investments and have kept our affairs in wonderful order. I doubt if the world can show more beautiful and thorough bookkeeping than his. Austin H. Cole has been, during the whole period of my connection with the seminary, the recording secretary of our board of trustees. No institution ever had a burden-bearer more versatile or more useful than he. He has been a model of regularity and of devotion to the cause for which the seminary was established. If these men had been crotchety or contentious, if they had not been so open-minded and generous, life might have been a burden to me. They have been hindered, but they have always helped. And so it has been with our whole board. I have never led without securing their following. Good men and true, they will not lack their reward.

The three whom I have just mentioned all belonged to the First Baptist Church of Rochester. When I came back to the city, I thought it my duty, and it was very natural, to unite myself again with the church into whose membership I had sixteen years before been baptized. There were certain infelicities attending the renewal of these associations. Some of the older members saluted me by my nickname "Gus," and others seemed to show a sort of proprietary interest in me by offering cartloads of advice. But, by cultivating the *suaviter in modo,* I finally subdued them all to both friendship and respect. I tried to make myself useful in the church. I remembered how often retired ministers were a thorn in the sides of their pastor, and I determined to show how true a subordinate a former captain could be. I tried to furnish an object lesson to the private members of the church. I have always made it my business to attend not only the public Sunday services but also the regular weekly meetings for conference and prayer, to do my full share in all benevolent contributions, in the visiting of the flock, and in the conduct of the business of the church. And I have found my account in this. I could never have taught well in the seminary if I had not kept in touch with the life of the church. The teaching of a Sunday Bible class has for all these years been a great help to the teaching of doctrine to the classes of the seminary and has served to make this last more truly biblical.

My pastors have been men whom I have loved and honored, though three men more variously endowed it would be hard to find. Dr. Henry E. Robins served for a year or two after I came, a godly, acute, able man, with a most intense personality, and an eloquence, when he was in health, that carried everything before it. His saintliness had a little touch of asceticism about it, but he had a mighty influence in moulding the thought and action of the church and making it a power for God and the truth. When I once asked him to contribute an article to a review, he replied almost fiercely, "Dr. Strong, when I came to this First Baptist Church, I vowed before God to bury myself here!" Many a lesson of prayer and faith and generous giving has he taught me. Take him for all and all, I regard him as the most spiritual and consecrated man I have known. I have found him my best confidant in my doctrinal perplexities, even though his philosophy is of the old ironclad realistic sort. When he told me he had been invited to the presidency of Colby University, though I was sorry to lose him, I did not dare advise him to decline. He made a noble record in Maine, and after ten years of service he came back to Rochester only because of failing health. We elected him to a professorship of ethics in the seminary, but he was not able to perform its duties, and for a long while his tenure has been merely nominal. But he has been of incalculable worth as a private member of the church. His example, his talks, and his prayers have given character to the church and its meetings. He and I together have always supported the pastor and tried to use our influence in such a way as to make for harmony and peace. Whether as the result of our efforts or not, the First Baptist Church of Rochester is a church home where Christian life is characterized by intelligence as well as sympathy, and the communion of the saints on earth is a symbol of the communion of the saints above.

Charles J. Baldwin succeeded Dr. Robins in the pastorate, and he brought us a most excellent spirit, great breadth of reading, and genuine cultivation of manner. He was a heroic soul. Though he had a chronic weakness contracted in his army life and this at times gave him much pain, he studiously concealed it and pushed on with his work as if nothing were the matter. He was a striking example of heredity. His father was a man of *bonhommie,* a born pastor, full of vivacity and sociality. This became the heritage of Charles's brother George. The mother was a woman of intellect, dignity, and coldness; Charles inherited her reticence, thoughtfulness, and reserve. He was no pastor, but he was a natural preacher. I have never sat under the ministry of any man who has given such a constant succession of bright and entertaining sermons. He brought into them so much information, so much fine feeling, so much genuine Christian experience that listening to him was almost a liberal education. I have always congratulated myself that my older children, during their susceptible years, were instructed from Sunday to Sunday by Mr. Baldwin. He was not a theologian, and he never took strong positions in doctrine, but he also never made serious errors in matters of faith. His preaching was both scriptural and edifying. When he left us, mainly on account of his health, we greatly regretted his loss.

Dr. J. W. A. Stewart came to us from Canada. With brother E. R. Andrews, I went on a prospecting tour to Hamilton, Ontario, and there heard our future pastor. We liked him so well that he was invited to visit us, and he preached in Rochester so well that our church immediately called him. His Canadian peculiarities were at first distasteful to some, and for several years it was an even chance whether he would be voted a success or a failure. But his industry, honesty, ability, and discretion finally won the day and conquered all opposition. The church has steadily grown under his administration although many of its members have been dismissed to form other bodies. In fact, our Baptist numbers have nearly doubled in ten years, in part by reason of the persistency and faithfulness of Dr. Stewart. He is very different from Mr. Baldwin, in that he is an organizer. He is, moreover, more of a theologian. When he came to us, he was inclined to be liberal and somewhat erratic. But acquaintance with such liberal leaders as Myron Adams soon convinced him that nothing but the old orthodoxy could keep a church together or save the souls of men. His preaching has grown continually more scriptural and more solid till now I think he could make a very good teacher of theology.

My relations with President Anderson of the university were not altogether satisfactory. Dr. Anderson had not a theological, nor even a logical, mind, and he was accustomed to depreciate theology and put ethics in its place. He was an old-fashioned Hamiltonian in his philosophical views, and these he hammered into his students in such a way that they never forgot the substance of his teaching, even though his methods were so dogmatic. His notes on scientific method, which his senior classes were compelled to learn by heart because there was no other way to learn them, were models of all that such notes ought not to be. They were diffuse, obscure, pointless. He lacked the power to think clearly or to express his thought in clear and concise form. His power lay, not at all in the realm of abstract thought, but in the application of principles to practical life. There he had genuine ability, and his exhortations to his students to "bring things to pass" were worth ten times as much as all the doctrine he taught them. He was vigorous and driving in his personality, but he was also a man of indirection, and he sometimes sought to accomplish his ends by the methods of the politician. If he came to make a call, you were soon led to suspect that he had some ulterior purpose which he did not disclose; indeed, before the call ended, the purpose often revealed itself. Dr. Anderson always thought there should be but one president in town. He desired to make the seminary a part of the university, or if this could not be, so to subordinate it that in public estimation it should seem to be only the tail to the university kite. He had not been able to subdue Dr. Robinson. I was young and inexperienced: he thought he could subdue me.

Our first difference occurred with regard to the time of our seminary anniversary. Dr. Robinson had severed this from the college commencement, because, when the two were held together, the university swallowed the seminary, and we got no due place or attention. A movement for reuniting the two was begun, and Dr.

Anderson was back of it. I opposed this movement. Dr. Morehouse was then our secretary, and he took the part of Dr. Anderson and opposed me. But I got together the opinions of Dr. Robinson and Mr. Trevor, both of them unfavorable to a change. Mr. Trevor especially won my lasting gratitude by standing by me most manfully. When it came to a vote, I routed the opposition—and incurred the dislike of Dr. Anderson. But it was the raising of our endowment that specially irritated him. He thought the older man ought to be first aided. When I raised $138,000, by one effort, the vexation of the doctor was hard to control. Mrs. Anderson openly reproached me when she met me in a bookstore, and the trustees of the university accused me of all manner of underhandedness and presumption. My conscience, however, was clear. The money I raised was gotten by prayer and faith and hard work. If Dr. Anderson did not reap a harvest, it was because he had not used the means. My success did stir him up to make an effort shortly after, and a considerable subscripton was made to the funds of the university. But the feeling of Dr. Anderson and of some of his trustees was not changed. Jealousy of the seminary became a ruling passion. Our work was depreciated. I have some reason to believe that it was Dr. Anderson's influence that partially chilled Mr. Trevor's interest in the seminary and led him to retract the provision he had made for us in his will.

When Dr. Anderson died and Dr. David J. Hill became president of the university, a comparatively small man succeeded a comparatively great one. I was eager from the very first to have the breach between the seminary and the university completely healed. I laid myself out to make things pleasant for Dr. Hill. I invited him frequently to my house, and I made parties for him so as to make him acquainted with the very best people of Rochester. At first all went pleasantly. But soon it became evident that Dr. Hill was under the influence of men who disliked the seminary. He was told that we desired to make the university a mere preparatory school for our institution, that we desired to give it a sectarian character, that I myself was ambitious to be its president. The truth was that Dr. Anderson had wanted me to be his successor, not so much because he liked me as because he thought this the best way to unite the two institutions and secure their endowment. He had through Dr.

Robins asked me if I would not accept the presidency of the university, but I had no idea of teaching undergraduates or living continually on a sleeping volcano, and I absolutely declined. But Dr. Hill became inoculated with the old jealousy of the seminary and fear of me. At the same time he was strongly influenced by a clique of non-Baptist university graduates living in Rochester who had persuaded themselves that the only way to prosperity was to make the university an undenominational institution and take it out of the hands of the Baptists altogether. At alumni dinners and in the public press continual intimations were given that the university must be freed from sectarian restrictions and that the seminary yoke especially must be thrown off.

All this naturally roused the Baptist element in our churches to resistance. It was feared that the trustees of the university might hand over the institution to those who opposed Baptist views. This fear was not unjustified, for a large number of the so-called Baptist trustees were only nominally Baptists, while the able, active, and energetic trustees were many of them inclined to favor the new movement. If Dr. Hill had been willing to do so, he could have removed these fears by declaring himself unalterably opposed to any change. But he did nothing of the kind; he rather played into the hands of the enemy. Mrs. Hill freely asserted that the institution could not prosper as long as it was under denominational control. Dr. Hill was reported to have said, to a member of his own faculty, that if Baptists would not support the institution, they had no reason to object if others took possession of it, that he had changed his whole board of trustees at Lewisburgh, and that he could do so here. And in public utterances he intimated that the seminary was trying to get undue influence over the university, that a syndicate had been formed to malign it, that there was a disposition to make it narrow and sectarian as it had never been in Dr. Anderson's days. All the while our desire was only to keep the university true to Dr. Anderson's ideas, to make it a Christian instead of a rationalistic college, and to retain a Baptist majority in its board of trustees.

If President Hill had been an active Christian man, and especially if he had interested himself in our Baptist churches, he would have done much to disarm criticism. Dr. Anderson, when he was well, never missed attending the prayer meeting of the Second

Baptist Church, and his place was always filled morning and evening at the Sunday services. But Dr. Hill attended our church prayer meeting only once or twice during his seven years in Rochester. When I urged him to come regularly, he replied that he lived at too great a distance, but he added, "To tell you the truth, I am not a prayer meeting man." He was a pleasure-loving man instead. He once said that he got more pleasure out of his cigar than he did out of prayer. Every other Sunday he attended the morning service of the church, but that was the limit of his interest in religious observances. A dinner party could always secure his presence but seldom a meeting for prayer. He affronted the religious sentiment of the town by permitting his college faculty meeting to be regularly held on Wednesday evening when the churches of all denominations held their prayer meetings, thus compelling the members of his faculty to absent themselves. Mr. O'Connor, the editor of the *Post Express,* said truly of Dr. Hill that he was a man of no moral earnestness. He not only practically disregarded many of the duties of a Christian life, but also he taught his students to disregard them. He turned the old meeting of prayer for colleges into an exclusively preaching service, upon the plea that the interest in the old method of conducting it had died out, forgetting that, when one has least interest in prayer, he most needs to pray. In his talks to his students he ridiculed the idea of bringing to God a bread basket with the expectation of having it filled. In his public addresses, moreover, he generally took occasion to speak disrespectfully and even jocosely of the old views of Scripture and the church; he specially decried the old-fashioned theology as pretending to omniscience upon matters where doubt was the only proper attitude of mind; he urged greater liberality of view if we wished to hold the young and active minds of our generation. All these things gave the impression that Dr. Hill was not much of a Baptist, and not much of a Christian.

I do not think he had settled in his mind the purpose to take the university out of the hands of our denomination. But I do think he was willing to do this if he could see such a course to be popular. He therefore spoke ambiguously, failed to declare himself against the undenominational movement, left it to be inferred that he secretly favored it. Two things brought matters to a crisis. Dr. Robins, in an article in the *Examiner,* denounced the tendency which was manifest in the management of the university. Dr. Hill replied with a bitter attack on the seminary. The seminary faculty and trustees published a statement in which they denied any knowledge of a purpose to get control of the university or change its methods of instruction. But Dr. Hill's attack on our trustees and professors deprived him of all our respect and sympathy. I tried to convince him that he was wrong and that his mistake was due to a misunderstanding of our whole Baptist aim and position. But he was prejudiced and hostile, and all my attempts at explanation and conciliation were a failure. The second thing that brought matters to a crisis was a declaration of the Genesee Baptist Ministers' Conference that it desired to keep the university true to the views of President Anderson, that the institution was founded by Baptists, belonged to Baptists, and should in honor be kept under the control of Baptists. This declaration was not as important for what it asserted as for what it implied. It showed that the whole Baptist brotherhood was solidly united in opposition to Dr. Hill. It is no wonder that it became too hot for Dr. Hill in Rochester. He shortly after resigned his position as president. I have no doubt he will be more comfortable as a diplomat at some foreign capital or a writer of essays on evolution than he ever could be in teaching psychology to the boys of the senior class or getting up early on winter mornings to attend college prayers. He has great literary and social gifts, but he is very lacking in the ethical conviction and sense of a mission that made Dr. Anderson a successful college president.

Now that I have spoken of the university, I might as well tell the story of the great university that was to be, but was not, in the city of New York. When I became well acquainted with Mr. Rockefeller, there dawned upon me the need of a true university in America. Such a university did not then exist. Post-graduate instruction was yet in its infancy. Young men who wished to fit themselves for positions as instructors were obliged to study in Germany. Johns Hopkins alone had a well-articulated system of post-graduate work, but even Johns Hopkins spoiled its university work by tacking on a college course, in order that the rich men of Baltimore might not be obliged to send their sons to college at Harvard or Yale. Columbia College had as yet no university features, no fellowships, and no schools of philosophy or political science. All this while Baptist institutions were of a comparatively low grade, and we had no means of supplying them with competent professors. As New York was our great commercial center and was destined soon to become the second greatest city of the world and, furthermore, as its three millions of contiguous population had within its boundaries not the first vestige of a Baptist institution of learning, it seemed to me that the greatest of opportunities presented itself for doing at once the noblest service to the cause of American education and New Testament truth as represented by our Baptist churches. I regarded the small influence of Baptists in the city of New York as due to the fact that they were destitute of proper educational facilities, and I desired to make them leaders, instead of followers, in the highest educational work.

It was certainly a lofty ideal, and since President Seth Low has carried out many of my views and has made of Columbia a genuine university, I am fully convinced that my scheme was not chimerical but that, if money had been forthcoming, it could have been executed. To secure the money, I began as early as 1880 to write and talk to Mr. Rockefeller. I knew that I was the only person who had access to him and who would tell him the whole truth. I felt specially sent by God upon this errand. It was a matter of prayer by day and by night. I kept the thing continually before him. I fear I made life a burden to him. He asked how much such a university would cost. I told him that the ultimate cost would be not less than twenty million dollars but that a beginning might be made with three million. He told a friend that he thought he could give somewhat largely but he doubted whether he could keep up with Dr. Strong. All the while, however, the idea was gaining upon him. I printed a pamphlet, at my own expense, unfolding my plan and urging the reasons for its adoption. I gave elaborate statistics with regard to universities abroad both in England and in Germany, their vast revenues, their wonderful growth and influence. I showed that the small institutions in country places were becoming smaller, while those in great centers like Berlin and Vienna numbered their students by the five thousand. This pamphlet was sent to all our Baptist educators of prominence as well as our principal ministers and laymen. A hundred of them sent me replies, most of them heartily approving the scheme. All these replies, together with the pamphlet which called them forth, I laid before Mr. Rockefeller.

I had no opportunity for fully expanding my views in private. Mr. Rockefeller was naturally shy, but at last he invited me to go to Europe with him and said that during our stay abroad he would give me a chance to say all that I desired. My son Charles was at this time engaged to Bessie Rockefeller, and he was to meet us at Southampton. My daughter Mary was of the party, and the whole Rockefeller family went with us. Under the circumstances one would have thought that the opportunity for the promised conversation would have speedily come. On the other hand, Mr. Rockefeller postponed it until we reached Paris on our way homeward, fully three months after we sailed. As the main object of my journey was to unburden my mind upon this great subject, the delay was tantalizing and painful in the extreme. But at last I told the whole story. It seemed to make little impression—at least I received no response. On the steamer which brought us to New York I concluded to speak some plain truth. I told him that the Lord had blessed him with financial prosperity greater than that of any other man upon the planet—he had made more money in a single lifetime than any other man who ever lived, and if he did not do more for God than any other man who ever lived, he could never stand in God's judgment. He turned red, and he looked very angry. But I had delivered my message, and I left the result with God. A few weeks later I received a letter from Mr. Rockefeller asking if the university could be started by his paying interest on three million dollars, provided he made the principal a lien upon his estate. I replied that he could choose his own way as long as the permanence of the enterprise was assured. But the matter lagged, and I became impatient. "The servant of the Lord must not strive." But I strove. I wrote another letter still more urgent and intimated that with all the light he had, he could not safely neglect his opportunity. He was offended and concluded that if he took hold of the enterprise at all, it must be with a lieutenant somewhat less dictatorial than Dr. Strong.

It was God's way of letting me out of a work which would have been too much for me and of giving a new direction and management to it. As I had previously introduced Dr. John A. Broadus to Mr. Rockefeller, so I now introduced Dr. William Rainey Harper. I told Mr. Rockefeller that Dr. Harper, then a professor at Yale, was our greatest Baptist organizer. I had a long interview with Dr. Harper in New York, and he promised to cooperate with me in the effort to induce Mr. Rockefeller to found a university in New York City. But soon after, the Chicago people, whether through Dr. Harper or not I have never learned, got wind of my plan and resolved to leave no stone unturned to secure the university for Chicago instead of New York. Here I must accuse Dr. Harper of unfaithfulness to his agreement. He no longer cooperated with me, but, without giving me notice and without explaining his action, he threw his influence with Mr. Rockefeller in favor of the Chicago project. I was surprised and disgusted one day by finding that Mr. Rockefeller had offered Chicago $600,000 upon condition that the University of Chicago was resuscitated, and the new University of Chicago has been established and endowed. After all I had done for fifteen years, my New York University was gobbled up and transferred to Chicago. Mr. Rockefeller has now given to it about seven million dollars, and it already has about ten million dollars of property. He has found that my estimate of the cost of a university was not too high. He thought it hard to keep up with Dr. Strong, but he has found it harder to keep up with Dr. Harper, for when Dr. Harper was recently asked how much it would take to complete the university, he replied that he had once thought that twenty million would be sufficient but that further reflection had convinced him that the amount ought to be stated as fifty million.

Of course it was a sore trial to me to have my work seemingly come to naught and to have others reap the benefit of the seed I had sown. It was harder still to know that a sort of alienation had sprung up between Mr. Rockefeller and me. I was no longer in his confidence—it seemed even as if he held a grudge against me and withheld his help from all enterprises in which I was engaged. Little by little, however, this feeling on both sides has worn off. I have gradually become reconciled to my disappointment, have congratulated myself that I have been spared the killing labors connected with the founding of a new institution, have watched with admiration the marvelous growth of the university under Dr. Harper, and have even concluded that the future expansion of the West may in the end make Chicago a more influential educational center than New York. I have learned a lesson with regard to God's answers to prayer. What I prayed for so long and earnestly, namely, the establishment of a great Baptist university, has come about, but in a different and perhaps a better way than I ever contemplated. And I had the satisfaction, in Philadelphia a while ago, of hearing Mr. Gates, as Mr. Rockefeller's representative, read the Report of the American Baptist Education Society and in that Report, on Mr. Rockefeller's authority, attribute to me the first plan and conception of a great Baptist university.

It was well that the administration of this university fell into other hands than mine, for I was thus left free to work out certain theological problems for which extensive executive duties would have given no time. My intellectual life in Rochester has been the gradual crystallization and unifying of views which had been previously grasped only in their isolation. The central point of crystallization and unification has been Jesus Christ. My whole religious experience has been a larger and larger knowledge of him. Difficulties have vanished as I have seen more of his greatness and power. My first doctrinal lesson, with regard to the depth and enormity of sin, was the result of contrasting myself with him. The second lesson I learned, that only God can regenerate, was really the lesson that only Christ can make man like himself. The third truth I attained to was the truth that Christ's atonement is the only ground of acceptance with God and the only effectual persuasive to faith. The doctrine of the church followed next in order, for the church is, in the fourth place, composed of only those who believe in Christ. This faith is not an external matter but a matter of life; those who believe are joined inwardly to the Savior; union with Christ was the fifth great principle which I apprehended. Then I began to see that this same Christ who had recreated believers had also created nature and that all science was the shining of his light. After this sixth point came a seventh: prayer is an entering into the mind and will of Christ, so that the believer becomes partaker of his knowledge and power. Thus far I had come in my doctrinal progress. The person of Christ was the clue that I followed; his deity and atonement were the two foci of the great ellipse.

But here came difficulty: how to reconcile these two, how to make deity and atonement comprehensible, *hoc opus, hic labor est.* My theological gains at Rochester have been mainly in the understanding of these two factors and their mutual relations. The two natures of Christ perplexed me until I saw that I must work at the problem from the side of the one person; every son of man has a single personality, though father and mother have each contributed to it something of their natures; Christ is a unit, though God was his Father and Mary his mother. I have adopted Dr. Robinson's realism in explaining the justification of the believer by virtue of his vital union with Christ and the condemnation of the race by virtue of the derivation of its life from Adam. How now was to be explained the imputation of the sin of the race to Christ? The only possible answer seemed to be that our sin was laid upon him because he had become one with us by his assumption of human nature in the womb of the Virgin; here, too, as in the other two cases, imputation resulted from a prior vital union. In this explanation I rested for a time, and I wrought it into my book on theology. If I have added anything to theological science, it is by my application of the realistic principle to the atonement, as it had previously been applied by Dr. Shedd to original sin and justification. I removed the imputation to Christ of the sin of the race from the region of arbitrariness and put it within the realm of reality and order. If Christ took our nature, he must have taken it with all its exposures and liabilities. Though the immaculate conception freed him from depravity, it still left him under the burden of guilt. For the nature which he had in common with us all he was bound to suffer and to die. Hence it must needs be that Christ should suffer; hence he pressed forward to the cross as the reparation due from humanity to the violated holiness of God. And this constituted my eighth forward step in theology, and perhaps my first new and original contribution to theological science, showing the nexus between the personal holiness of Christ and his justly bearing the sin of the race. It was not the explanation of Edward Irving, for he held that Christ inherited depravity. My explanation was that by the taking of our nature Christ inherited guilt. For guilt and depravity are not inseparable. As the Christian has depravity but not guilt, so Christ had guilt but not depravity. And thus he could through the eternal Spirit offer himself without spot to God.

I had printed this theory of the atonement and was waiting, though vainly, for opposing criticisms when it occurred to me that my theory did not go far enough. It showed how Christ could bear the common guilt of the race, that guilt which belongs to all as a consequence of Adam's sin, but it did not show how Christ could bear the subsequent sins of Adam and the multitudinous sins of Adam's posterity. Yet personal sins, as well as original sin, are atoned for. It was not enough to say that he bore the guilt of the root-sin from which all other sins have sprung: this would be to deny any remainder of freedom and reduce all human sins to the one first sin of the father of mankind. Christ then must sustain an even larger relation to the race than that into which he enters when he takes our humanity in the womb of the Virgin. And here there flashed upon me with new meaning the previously acknowledged fact of Christ's creatorship. Christ's union with the race in his incarnation is only the outward and visible expression of a prior union with the race which began when he created the race. As in him all things were created and as in him all things consist or hold together, it follows that he who is the life of humanity must, though personally pure, be involved in responsibility for all human sin, and so it was necessary that the Christ should suffer. This suffering was a reaction of the divine holiness against sin, and so was a bearing of penalty, but it was also the voluntary execution of a plan that antedated creation, and Christ's sacrifice in time showed what had been in the heart of God from eternity. The atonement then is not only possible but also necessary, because Christ is from the beginning the life of humanity. This was the ninth step in my doctrinal progress and the second new and original contribution which I have made to theology.

Christ, however, is the life of humanity only as he is the life of the whole universe. I quickly saw that I must take another and a final step and must see in Christ not only the life and light of men but also the omnipresent and immanent God. The Son is the revealing God even as the Father is the God revealed. Christ is the principle of physical interaction as well as of mental interaction, the principle of logical induction, as well as of evolution and of moral unity. Nature is a continual manifestation of Christ. The hand that was nailed to the cross sustains the fabric of the worlds and guides the stars in their courses. And this great Being it is who has offered himself in our behalf. His historical atonement is but a manifestation to sense of what, as preincarnate Logos, he has been doing ever since man's first sin. The incarnation and death of Christ are only the outward and temporal exhibition of an eternal fact in the being of God and of a suffering for sin endured by the Son of God ever since the Fall. God's holiness necessarily visits sin with penalty. There is a wrath-principle in God. He who is the life of the race must undergo the reaction of God's holiness against the sin which is its antagonist and would-be destroyer. But love makes this bearing of penalty inure to the advantage of the sinner. Christ has redeemed us from the curse of the law by being made a curse for us, and by his stripes we are healed. This general doctrine of Christ's identification with the race because he is the Creator, Upholder, and Life of the universe, I called ethical monism. It regards the universe as a finite, partial, and graded manifestation of the divine life; matter being God's self-limitation under the law of necessity, humanity being God's self-limitation under the law of freedom, incarnation and atonement being God's self-limitations under the law of grace. Metaphysical monism, or the doctrine of one substance, principle, or ground of being, I maintained to be entirely consistent with psychological dualism, or the doctrine that soul is personally distinct from matter, on the one hand, and from God, on the other. And this ethical monism is the last, and the most important, addition which I have made to theology. It is the tenth distinct advance step in my doctrinal thinking.

Indeed, it was so radical and novel an advance that I hesitated long before I ventured to publish it to the world. I first delivered an essay on "Christ in Creation" at our Annual Theological Conference.[5] Then I waited for two years, trembling on the brink. At last I concluded that intellectual honesty required me to disclose my views even if they cost me my position as theological teacher. I felt that I could make no further progress without printing the conclusions I had already reached. The essay on ethical monism appeared in the *Examiner*. I tried to show that the drift of modern science, philosophy, literature, and theology was all in the direction of monism and that theology must make use of the new light or lose

---

[5] *Christ in Creation and Ethical Monism* (Philadelphia: The Roger Williams Press, 1899), pp. 1-15. Hereafter abbreviated *Christ in Creation*.

her hold upon thinking minds. It was only ethical monism, however, that in my judgment had promise of the future, and by ethical monism I meant a monism that held to freedom in man and transcendence in God. I maintained that such monism as this was but an interpretation of Paul and John when they say that Christ is all and in all and that in him we live and move and are. I claimed to be simply digging out the debris from the old wells of salvation and letting the waters flow forth that had been long choked back. But my protestations were not sufficient to prevent hostile criticism. While there was much favorable notice of my work and I received scores of letters assuring me that it was almost a new revelation, there were many ignorant denunciations of it, and I was called a pantheist and a Buddhist. It was the severest ordeal through which I ever passed. Dr. Elias H. Johnson of Crozer Theological Seminary wrote a reply, and I replied to him in a second series of articles, printed a year after the first, namely, in October, 1895. In these articles I gathered up all the criticisms that had been made upon me and answered them impersonally. I succeeded in doing it gently, though I must confess that I sometimes felt as Nero did when he wished that the inhabitants of Rome had but one head that he might cut it off at a single blow. I made clear the fact that I believed in freedom and transcendence, that my ethical monism held to Trinity and excluded pantheism, and that it had originated, not in philosophical speculation but, as I have tried in this history to show, in Scripture and in the logical necessities of a scriptural theology. The storm after a time blew over. The battle ceased, and I was left master of the field. Ethical monism is now confessed to be at least a permissible belief, while many regard it as affording the last and best key to the greatest mysteries of Christian doctrine.

In May, 1897, I completed the twenty-fifth year of my service as president and professor of biblical theology in the Rochester Theological Seminary. The anniversary was noted for sending out the largest class we ever graduated, as the incoming class of the succeeding autumn promised to be the largest that ever entered. There were many congratulations. At the alumni dinner I spoke upon "The Offence of the Cross" and gave thanks that I had been permitted for a quarter of a century to keep the faith, especially with regard to the deity and atonement of our Lord.[6] I summed up my personal experience by saying that I was a great sinner and that Christ was a great Savior. I felt no self-complacency in view of the past, but I did feel gratitude to the Savior that he had permitted me to live and to any extent to witness to his saving grace. At Pittsburgh, a little after, I addressed a meeting of Rochester men at our national anniversaries, and there I made mention of four things which I had learned, and with the repetition of these I will close this chapter of my autobiography. The first was hospitality to new ideas. When I began to teach, I felt inclined to challenge new truth rather than to welcome it. I have learned that all truth is of God and that it is my duty to bring forth out of my treasure things new as well as old. The second thing I have learned is that truth is not made to be error merely because it has been taught by heretics and wicked men. I have come to believe that Christ has shot some rays of his light even into the minds of Spinoza and Huxley. The third thing I have learned is that new truth does not exclude or supersede the old but rather elucidates and confirms it. I try to interpret the old in terms of the new philosophy and science, but I do not regard any of the old doctrines of theology as antiquated or outworn. And the fourth and final thing I have learned is that the truth to which I have arrived must be trusted by me and proclaimed by me, even though others may not yet accept or even understand it. There is no use of arguing about daylight with the night-bound antipodes. Assert the truth and the world will in time come round to see it. And though "my gospel" may not be the whole or the perfect gospel, God will take the weak things of the world to confound the mighty and will make it his wisdom and his power to men's salvation.

[6] The substance of the address is found in *Miscellanies,* vol. 1 (Philadelphia: The Griffith & Rowland Press, 1912), pp. 460-471.

7

Children
and Travel

History must be distinguished from annals. In all history there is grouping. The writer follows a person or principle to the end and then takes up another. In this sense the present composition is a history. I must now present my children in a family group. Here are the dates of their births, their names, and their nicknames:

November 28, 1862,	Charles Augustus Strong, Chickedido.
August 29, 1864,	Mary Belle Strong, Pinkywinky.
December 7, 1866,	John Henry Strong, Tickleumtan.
February 10, 1870,	Cora Harriet Strong, Mollychumkamug.
February 10, 1870,	Katherine Louise Strong, Sissiladobsis.
June 19, 1884,	Laura Rockefeller Strong, Flibbertigibbet.

Charles has a sharp, analytical mind. Precision and clearness are characteristic of him. He catches the pronunciation of a foreign language; grammatical solecisms and incompleteness disturb him; he cannot endure the vague. But accurate and logical as he is, he lacks one instrument for the attainment of truth—that which consists in imagination and the emotions. He is not a poet. He is afraid of enthusiasm. He depreciates insight. He is critical rather than constructive. He does not see that imagination is only creative reason, that it penetrates into the meaning of the world as mathematics cannot. He will believe only what is demonstrated to him; he doubts the conclusions of mere intuition or affection. Yet he trusts his friends. He has a warm filial spirit. He is earnest, loyal, conscientious, though these traits presuppose every one of them a sort of faith that can never be verified.

Charles was twelve years old when he united with the church. He followed his good impulses and committed himself to the service of Christ. I believe that the Holy Spirit quickened his conscience and made him clearly see his duty. Yet his faith was largely traditional and needed to be made more intelligent. It was the faith of a boy: it only needed to become the faith of a man. One Saturday he was gone from home all day long. At night he came in, the very picture of disconsolateness. He seemed very near to crying. I took him upon my knee and asked him the reason for his trouble. It went to my heart when he replied, "I have been fishing on a stone in the river. I prayed God this morning to give me a fish. But I have fished all day and have not caught one—boo-hoo!" To me there was nothing amusing in this—it was only pathetic. The whole problem of prayer was suggested. I tried to quiet the dear boy and yet to inspire faith; to show that God's promises were true, yet to point out the proper limitations. Prayer must be not for our sakes but for God's sake; God knows best what we need; we must ask in submission to his will. When the child asks the father's razor to whittle with, the father will not grant the request. I honored and loved Charley's simple and childlike faith. I tried to show him that the trial of his faith was for some good purpose which God knew, if he did not. It was a day of great joy when Charles and Mary were baptized together, and I myself had the privilege of baptizing them.

My eldest son was a natural grammarian, but he had also the great advantage of being under the instruction of a good teacher of grammar, Mr. Parshall, of District Number Twelve. Both he and Mary completed the grammar school course in the public schools and were better off than they would have been in any private school. My own unfortunate experience in preparing for college at Rochester determined me to send Charles to Phillips Exeter

Academy. I secured room and board for him in a good Baptist family, and he began his preparation under very favorable circumstances. As he stood second or third in his class, I did not inquire minutely about his methods of study. One vacation, however, I asked him how much time he spent over his Latin lesson before going into the recitation. To my surprise he answered that he spent no time at all. "And how are you able to recite?" I asked. "Why, I read on ahead while the boy before me is reciting," he replied. I was horrified and gave my son a long lecture. I told him that the aim of a student should not be simply to meet the demand of his teacher but to inform himself as perfectly as possible with regard to the subject. This seemed an entirely novel view to Charles. I believe he changed his methods somewhat, and my impression is that he took a higher standing than before. The incident showed at any rate that he had a quick mind.

He had a good deal of superfluous energy which the studies of the school did not enable him to work off. It was a good thing for him that he was elected editor of *The Exonian,* the paper published by the Exeter students. He reported ball games and learned the art of rapid writing. His powers of observation were cultivated. He was brought into social contact with his fellows. His preparatory course was one of mental and, I think, spiritual progress. He wished to go with many of his classmates immediately to Harvard. But I felt under some obligation to the University of Rochester and persuaded him to take his college course there by assuring him that he might afterwards have a year of study at Cambridge. So he went through the freshman year at home. I then examined him in his Latin. He had read the *Eclogues* of Virgil. I was disappointed to find that his Exeter training had given him no great love for poetry and that he had not even heard of Virgil's prophecy of a coming deliverer and of a golden age. It seemed to me that it was useless to go further until those defects were remedied. I resolved to send him to a German Gymnasium, where the Latin and Greek would be ground into him and he would be trained within an inch of his life.

So Charles went abroad. Before he went, I asked him to make up his mind what course he would pursue with regard to beer, wine, and tobacco. He reflected for a couple of weeks upon the problem and finally announced his determination to abstain from all of them during the whole period of his absence from home. Curiously enough, he added coffee to the list, upon the ground that he felt better without it. He spent a couple of months in Hamburg with a good German teacher. Then he entered the Gymnasium at Gütersloh in Westphalia. It numbered five hundred boys. There were six recitations a day. All the work was done, of course, in German, of which Charles had known almost nothing until that summer. At the end of the first year, he stood eighth in his class of fifty, and at the end of the second year he stood second. I felt proud of his success as a scholar, but I felt more proud that he carried out his resolve with regard to beer, wine, tobacco, and coffee. On a holiday when the whole body of students gathered at the athletic grounds outside the town and every other boy smoked tobacco and drank beer, Charles and his friend Walter Rauschenbusch were the only abstainers. And when my son was invited to spend Christmas with a classmate in Bremen and the father proposed the health of his son in champagne, Charles drank the toast with a glass of water and boldly though courteously pleaded the obligations of his vow.

My dear old father provided three hundred dollars a year for Charles's expenses abroad, and I added a matter of two hundred more. It was a rather slim provision, but it was all I could at the time afford. Yet with this little income my son managed not only to pay his school expenses but also to spend his vacations in travel, which was largely pedestrian. He had learned French as well as German, and before he came back to America he had seen Paris and London. He had become a good deal of a cosmopolitan. Returning to Rochester, he entered his old class in the university, though he had to study hard to make up some of the studies he had lost. He graduated with great honor, taking the prize for the essay in political economy. Then, as had been long before agreed upon, he took a year at Harvard, entering the senior class and taking the Harvard degree of B.A. in addition to the same degree he had received at Rochester.

Charles's work at Cambridge was almost wholly in philosophy. He took six courses at once. James, Goodwin, Palmer, and Royce were his teachers. The Harvard atmosphere was very liberal, and I soon found that my son was beginning to question the faith in which he had been brought up. At that time I was myself less open to modern ideas than I have been since. The natural realism which I had imbibed under Professor Noah Porter still seemed to me the ultimate philosophy. I became alarmed at Charles's tendencies. Instead of trusting that his honesty of purpose would lead him into the light, I feared that he would become an apostate from Christianity. I wrote to him of my fears and worried him by them. It was all a mistake on my part, and I now greatly regret that I did not leave him to himself and to the teaching of the Spirit of truth. He was desperately hard at work, and my anxieties only made life the harder for him. He spent too many hours in study. I am afraid that he injured his health. But he was wonderfully successful in making friends and in taking the highest rank in his class. He graduated *summa cum laude,* in a class of about two hundred.

Unfortunately we cannot undo the past. I was conscientious, and I thought I was doing God service. Charles manifested the most filial regard for my wishes even though he could not agree with my views. During his senior year at Rochester he had given me great joy by declaring his purpose to study for the ministry and to preach the gospel. Though his course at Harvard changed his beliefs to some extent, he still concluded to enter our seminary and to give a thorough examination to Christian doctrine. During the vacation that intervened between his Harvard and his seminary courses he preached for a couple of months at Salem, Ohio, and also made a visit at Mr. Rockefeller's at Forest Hill in Cleveland. That visit resulted in an engagement of marriage between him and Bessie Rockefeller.

His seminary course was very unsatisfactory both to him and to me. I am doubtful now whether, with his disposition to question the old statements of doctrine, it was not an error of judgment on the part of both of us for him to enter the seminary at all. A mind skeptically inclined cannot throw itself into the life of a theological school, and he felt a difficulty in preaching the gospel until he was more sure of his ground. Thus he lacked some of the practical associations which help right thinking. Yet I must praise the faithfulness with which he taught his Sunday School classes at the church and at the Bronson Avenue Mission. He tried to do his duty in the prayer meetings. When revival interest sprang up in the church, he did his best to help on the work. I hoped that all this, together with the seminary studies, would correct his erroneous views and lead him into a deeper Christian experience. But the result seemed to be precisely the opposite. When the International Seminary Alliance met in Rochester, instead of giving himself to missionary work as I had hoped he would do, he seemed to set himself against it. When I told him that he who did not yield to Christ would find that stone grinding him to powder, he replied that he would not yield to one whom he could not see to be God. He sold his Hebrew Bible and his theological books, as if to burn his ships and to put the ministry of Christ forever behind him.

It was the greatest disappointment and sorrow of my life. I had desired above all things that my eldest son should be a witness for Christ and a preacher of his truth. It now seemed to me that he was bound to be an opposer of the truth and a means of leading men astray. I confess that I myself showed lack of faith in my very anxiety about him. Irritated as he was, and rebelling against what seemed to him the arbitrariness of Christian doctrine, I am still compelled to acknowledge that there was no conscious dishonesty or unconscientiousness. I ought to have believed in Christ's power to lead him out of darkness into light. But I almost despaired, and when he replied to a letter of the church and declared his inability to remain in their faith and fellowship, I myself thought it my duty to the church to make the motion to exclude him. I must leave to God and to the judgment day the decision of the question whether I did right.

He wrote a thesis which secured him a Harvard fellowship. He went abroad again for study in the University of Berlin, and in Freiburg in Breisgau. Here he became acquainted with Münsterburg, the psychologist. In the summer of 1887 the whole Rockefeller family, with my daughter Mary and me, traveled with him, and he returned to take the position of instructor in Cornell University. Two years after, he was married in New York, and with his wife he sailed again for Europe. After a few months of travel he settled again for the winter in Berlin. Here he studied the physiological side of psychology. After coming back to America he became, first, docent at Worcester, Massachusetts; then, after an interval, professor of psychology in the new University of Chicago; afterwards, when Bessie's health could not endure the Chicago climate, he accepted a position of instruction in Columbia College

The Strong Family at Cook's Point, Canandaigua Lake, New York, August 4, 1886. Top row: Mrs. A. H. Strong (Harriet L. Savage), Mrs. George Cook (Caroline Bull); Middle row: Sarah Elmendorf (Mrs. Edward Shove), Mary Belle Strong (Mrs. Robert G. Cook), Emma Flagler, Meda Carter; Bottom row: Dr. A. H. Strong, holding Laura Strong (Mrs. Edmund H. Lewis), Kate Strong (Mrs. C. G. Sewall), Cora Strong, unknown in New York City. Very few young men have had so varied or so liberal a training. But to whom much has been given much shall be required. When I think of his great abilities, opportunities, and responsibilities and then think of the many prayers that have followed him from his birth until now, I still believe that these prayers will be answered and that he will be brought to the glad acknowledgment of the deity and atonement of Jesus Christ. I shall not be satisfied, indeed, unless he becomes, though late, an advocate and defender of the truth once for all delivered to the saints.

On this last eleventh of June, 1897, an event occurred which may possibly hasten the consummation which I desire. On that day a daughter was born to Charles and Bessie, and of course a granddaughter to me. An organic weakness of the heart in Bessie's case had made us doubt whether she could ever safely bear a child. For this reason her skilled physician hastened the birth by a whole month, and Margaret is an eight months' child. But all went well, and it was with great rejoicing that her advent was welcomed by her family and by a large circle of friends. The delight of Charles in receiving this little one committed through such hazards to his care has been very pleasing to us all. I greatly hope that the new outlet to his affections will be of great service to his religious life. Shut up to intellectual work, the emotional side of his nature has never had sufficient development. He has been individualistic. The sense of community has been partially wanting. A little child upon his knee, pleading with him, asserting her will against his, putting the utmost faith in him, looking to him for instruction with regard to God and duty, will teach him more of religion than all his researches into psychology. I trust it will lead him to the Savior for counsel and help and that he will in turn lead Margaret to the Lamb of God who taketh away the sins of the world.

Mary Belle was a good baby, as her mother declares. I can testify that she was a good girl and has become a good wife and a good mother. She is fortunate in the endowment of a placid temper. But calmness is accompanied with industry. Mary's mind is not the literary or the philosophical. Abstract questions do not trouble her. But she has a genius for practical affairs. She is a natural housekeeper and manager. She comprehends a situation and is full of plans to meet it. She can use money to the best advantage. She has will and skill in influencing her husband and in training her children. But with all this she is not of the humdrum sort. She loves society and is universally popular. She could be a social leader. She loves art and could make her living, if need be, by artistic decoration, embroidery, millinery, or dressmaking. Mary was a good scholar in school. She had a taste for political economy. She wrote some well-considered essays. But her gifts are mainly social, artistic, and practical.

Like Charles and John, she completed her grammar school course at District Number Twelve. Then for three years she attended the Granger Place School in Canandaigua. As Canandaigua mingles more or less with my history, I must explain the beginnings of my interest in the place. My father and mother had spent one or two summers at Seneca Point on Canandaigua Lake. During our summer vacations Hattie and I had gone out with them. We came to like the wooded hills at the southern end of the lake and the people who gathered at Cook's Point. After Rochester became my permanent home and my family grew to number six children, Cook's Point was the most accessible and the least expensive summer resort that we could easily find. "He that hath wife and children hath given hostages to fortune," says Lord Bacon. I found that I could not take the whole family very far away.

Acquaintance with the pleasant and cultivated people from Canandaigua who summered at Cook's Point led naturally to my preaching as supply for the Congregational Church of Canandaigua. One Sunday when I preached on the text "If any man will do my will, he shall know of the doctrine," Miss Slocum, one of the principal teachers of the Granger Place School, was present and was so greatly affected by the truth that she soon after made public confession of Christ by uniting with the Congregational Church. Another of the teachers in the same school, Miss Sihler by name, was at the same time similarly impressed, and from that day dated the beginning of a Christian experience. The copy of Dante's *La Divina Commedia* in miniature, a real Italic edition of 1629, is a present to me from Miss Sihler, given as a memento of that day. Miss Slocum's gratitude was testified by her receiving my daughter Mary as a pupil and boarder in the school at the cost of only two hundred dollars a year in place of the customary four hundred.

Mary made valuable acquaintances during her three years' absence from home. But the chief advantage of her schooling was a larger outlook. I think she might have gone on to prepare for college, but the illness of her mother at that time made it needful for her to come home and superintend the household. After a year of this work, ambition to take a college course had somewhat waned; she had become enamored of society; and we still needed her at home. Money, moreover, in those days was not abundant. Charles and John were both drawing heavily upon the family purse. Mary was permitted to leave school life behind her. It was just as well, for she gained wonderfully from the responsibilities that were thrown upon her. In her mother's stead she entertained all my company, managed all the finances, dressed the children as well as her mother and herself, and made her way at the same time to a high place in Rochester society. In fine, she showed herself a person of faculty. I think, if it were necessary, she could preside over a railroad or command a man-of-war.

Indirectly, the Canandaigua experiences prepared the way for her marriage. Mrs. Cook, who occupied the Lodge at the Point, was a woman of remarkable quickness of mind and of unusual literary taste. We learned to admire and to love her for herself. But she had two children whom it was a pleasure to know also. Nettie was bright and vivacious, and she married Mr. Thomas Hawks. Robert was quiet and somewhat reserved, but all who knew him felt that underneath that undemonstrative exterior there were the hidings of power. He was a Harvard student and after his graduation a student at the College of Physicians and Surgeons. He spent part of every summer on Canandaigua Lake. As our family was at Canadaigua Lake also, there grew up an intimacy between the young people on both sides. And yet it was almost as much of a surprise as of a joy to us, when, after waiting till his preparatory studies were over and he had secured a position in the State Hospital at Ogdensburg, Robert came to Rochester and proposed to make Mary his wife. It did not take her long to consent, nor did it take her parents long to sanction the arrangement. Mary's faithfulness and success in every trust previously committed to her gave good augury that she would not fail in her duties as a married woman. She has shown a world of patience and cheerfulness while Robert has been building up a practice in Rochester. The wedding must have been made in heaven, but it took place on earth June 2, 1892.

The children, Robert Strong and Alan Augustus, have brought brightness into the lives of the grandparents as well as the parents. Alan's sympathetic and gentle nature seems the complement of Robert's quickness and vivacity. I do not doubt that they will lead both the father and the mother to feel the need of heavenly wisdom. If my dear Mary has any defect or danger, it is that of absorbing herself too much in the things of this present world. The joy of living, the desire to shine, the intercourse with friends, the hope of worldly success—these influence her strongly. They ought to have proper weight, but there is a disproportionate place which they may occupy. I would have my daughter to be alive to all these things; yet I would have her seek first the kingdom of God and his righteousness. I want to see Robert an open follower of his Lord. And I want to see their children and their children's children ranged on the side of Christ and witnessing for him. Mary has held to her Christian faith, and she is training her two boys to pray. So much rests upon her, in a family where she is the only professing Christian, that I daily ask for her a double portion of God's Spirit. I feel confident that every other kind of success will reward the efforts of her and of her husband. I cannot be satisfied until they are united in the service of Christ. Mary has gratified us more and more of late by the sympathy and interest she has taken in her parents. Her own cares have taught her what her mother and father have been through before her. She has a generous soul. There is not a mean thing in her. If she will remember to deal as kindly and truly with her heavenly Father as she has with her earthly father, I will be content and more than content. And as for Robert, I am proud of the patience and steadfastness he has shown in the hard fight for success. I do not doubt that he will find his reward. He has the affection and respect of all who know him. May he also have that eternal life which consists in knowing the true God and Jesus Christ whom he has sent!

When I come to write of John, my heart goes out to the dear boy. He has always been so gentle, affectionate, and tender toward his parents that his presence has been a joy in the household. When he was about ten years of age, he was terribly ill with typhoid fever. He just escaped with his life. The fever left him with a tendency of blood to his head and a slight deficiency of physical vigor. He has done much to build himself up. In athletics he has gone ahead of Charles. He was champion in the tennis tournament for one year, and the silver cup was for months the ornament of our parlor. He is adept at the bicycle and has made prolonged tours upon that vehicle. Everybody likes John, and his winning ways are a great help in influencing others. But for a long time I wondered whether he would develop robustness of body or mind. His modesty and quietness prevented us from recognizing his real strength. I now see that behind his undemonstrative manner there lies a clearness and penetration of intelligence which very few possess. Imagination and affection are with him great aids to the attainment of truth.

I was of the opinion that the critical time in a boy's education was the time when he began to learn Latin. Let him be thoroughly drilled then, and he may possibly make a scholar. Let his training at that time be imperfect, and the defect can never afterward be made up for. Will Witter was a distant relative of ours and lived in La Grange, Genesee County. He was a graduate of the University of Rochester and a student for the ministry in our seminary. I committed John to his care during a summer vacation. One task was imposed upon them. Will was to teach and John was to learn the paradigms of the Latin Grammar, so that they could be recited backwards, forwards, or even crossways. Afternoons could be devoted to hunting and evenings to visiting, but mornings were to be given to Latin nouns, pronouns, adjectives, and verbs. I wanted John to have the forms so ground into him that he could never forget them. The scheme was very successful. The boy enjoyed his summer. In the autumn he began a three years' course of preparation for college at the Phillips Andover Academy.

The large life of the preparatory school was a great advantage to John. He took interest in the baseball games between Exeter and Andover. From some of the students in the theological seminary he got instruction in elocution. He had a good home in the family of Professor Comstock, the teacher of Latin. Proximity to Boston gave him some acquaintance with the hub of the universe. He made an occasional visit to Haverhill, the scene of my first pastorate, and there were always kind friends at the Duncans' and elsewhere to give him welcome. He always did credit to the Strong family both in society and in scholarship. Through all his years of preparation, he never gave me cause for a moment's anxiety.

Two years of Charles's college course were taken in Europe. I did not think John's health quite strong enough to justify a similar procedure in his case. He spent all his four years at Rochester, but he made good use of his time. He took the first prize for sophomore declamation; and when he graduated, he took the first prize for the matter and manner of his commencement oration. Then I sent him to Yale to take his senior year over again. Ryland Kendrick went with him. The two friends and classmates roomed together. John's studies were mainly in philosophy and Greek. Entering so late, it was impossible that he should be a member of a senior society or become thoroughly acquainted with all the ins and outs of college life. But he did valuable work under ex-President Porter and Professor Seymour. He was popular with his classmates. It will always be a matter of pride and gratitude with me that he showed his colors and stood for Christ at Yale. With Ryland Kendrick and a few others, he instituted a plan of personal religious conversation and influence for the benefit of the unconverted members of his class. Some striking reformations were the result. He showed that he had the courage and piety to lead an aggressive Christian life in college. His gentle and gentlemanly way of introducing the subject of religion in private talk and urging his fellows to begin the service of God gave him an enviable reputation and induced President Dwight to offer him the position of secretary of the Young Men's Christian Association and superintendent of Dwight Hall for the year next following.

John took his A.B. degree from Yale just as Charles had taken his from Harvard, although both of them had previously taken the same degree from the University of Rochester. John has always declared that his proper designation is John H. Strong, 2 A.B. In the case of both boys I regard the doubling of the senior year and the taking of its broadening studies under two sets of instructors as one of the best features of their education. If John had remained at New Haven still another year and taken charge of the religious work among the students, I do not doubt that he would have gotten much additional good. He would have been called on to deliver many public addresses at Yale and other colleges, and he would have made a large circle of valuable acquaintances. But I felt that John's resolve to enter the regular ministry needed to be strengthened. Both experience and observation taught me that delays are dangerous in the matter of preparation to preach. It seemed to me that he would make more by pushing on with his theological course. At my advice therefore he declined Dr. Timothy Dwight's flattering invitation and set himself to study theology at Rochester—not, however, till he had taken a little vacation in Europe.

Before the commencement at Yale was fairly over, John was on the Atlantic. His tour abroad was not an extensive one. He went to Freiburg where Charles was studying, Bessie being with him, and there John devoted himself for some weeks to German, winding up his time with a little turn in Switzerland and a little visit to Paris and London. The most momentous part of that European tour, however, was the return on the ocean steamer. There a handsome young lady met John's gaze. In an artful way the young man succeeded in making her acquaintance. For some reason she did not insist upon a formal introduction. When John returned to his Rochester home, he was full of praises of Miss Eliza Livingston McCreery.

The seminary term opened pleasantly. John was happily engaged in his theological studies when delegates were appointed to the Inter-Seminary Missionary Alliance to be held at Pittsburgh. John was appointed a delegate. Curiously enough, Pittsburgh was the residence of Miss Eliza Livingston McCreery. Still more curiously, an invitation came to John to make Mrs. McCreery's house his home during his stay at the Alliance. I do not know how much John attended the meetings. I have some reason to believe that there were other meetings which he preferred to those. During the following summer Mary and he spent some time in Canada. Mrs. McCreery and her daughters were there. After a while we heard that John Henry Strong and Eliza Livingston McCreery [Lide] were engaged to be married.

In this case true love ran smoothly. We were happy in John's happiness. John was idealistic. He had his head in the clouds. Lide brought to him the practical element, knowledge of affairs, health and courage, and social gifts. From the very beginning we have always thought it a good Providence that the two were so fitted to each other. John's studies were not hindered but helped by his engagement. He did thoroughly well in his seminary course. He showed fine scholarship, but he developed what was still better—a doctrinal insight, a sense of the connections of truth. I began to think that he had in him the making of a theologian, and I began to cherish the hope that he might ultimately make his way into some professorship of the theological seminary and perhaps might even fill the place which I myself now occupy.

The three years of his theological study soon passed. On the very night of his graduation he took the train for New York, and the next day he sailed for Europe. Miss McCreery, together with her mother and sister, had been abroad for nearly a year, and John was most eager to see her. He needed rest and recreation, for his health had given out near the close of his course in the seminary, and it was only by the hardest effort that he had been able to pass his examinations and make his graduating address. That address on "Union with Christ" was regarded by all as the most promising address of the occasion. John's health was not immediately restored. Travel and excitement were upon him. It was not till he went to Munich and submitted to regular treatment that he began permanently to improve. But there, with baths and exercise, he did get back his health. And the constant talking and reading of German gave him a new and invaluable piece of education. I am inclined to believe that the discipline of ill health at the very threshold of his career was also made by God the means of teaching him important spiritual lessons. He learned his dependence upon divine power and the necessity of faith.

It had been a matter of constant prayer with us at home that John might find a church where he might begin his ministry without undue friction. A quarrelsome or unsympathetic people might have ruined his ministry. God was very good to him in ordering it that he should have his first pastorate at Mount Auburn, Cincinnati. The opportunity came unsought. Dr. Sage, a retired pastor who had held important positions in our Baptist denomination, was a leading member of the Mount Auburn Church, and Deacon Holden, a lovely old man, was its chief financial supporter. They both conceived a warm affection for my son and treated him almost as if he were a son of their own. It was one of the happiest days of my life when I attended his ordination. He gave a statement of his Christian experience, call to the ministry, and views of doctrine such as would have done credit to the oldest and wisest. The spiritual elevation of it all, combined with its intellectual grasp and judgment, made a profound impression upon all who heard. I myself preached the sermon on the subject "Saving Faith," and the aged Dr. Robinson, who at that time was visiting Deacon Holden, made one of the very last addresses of his life as he gave the charge to the candidate. He spoke of hearing my own confession of Christ thirty or so years before in the First Baptist Church of Rochester and of his gratification in now hearing John's account of his Christian experience. As the tall man with white hair stood upon the platform facing the tall young man with dark locks and congratulated him that he was now entering upon his great work while he himself was just about to step down into his grave, there was a world of sadness in the scene, and yet it was a fulfillment of the prophet's word: "Instead of the fathers shall be the children."

John's ministry in Mount Auburn lasted just two years. He grew as a preacher and as a man. He began to think for himself. In his desire to be true to his convictions and to act upon the maxim *Nullius addictus jurare in verba magistri,* I think he has swung off too far from the old orthodox views of the atonement and has been inclined to merge the divine work of regeneration in the human work of conversion. But I have learned something, I trust, from my experience with Charles. I believe that the Holy Spirit will lead him into the whole truth, though the process may take time. The portions of truth which he emphasizes are in themselves important, possibly more important than I have imagined. And all truth is a connected whole, because it is the wisdom of the living Christ. He who teaches one portion of the truth will in due season teach the rest. I commend John to that Spirit of Christ which did not leave the world when our Savior ascended but according to promise taught the apostles after him and left in the completed New Testament his infallible testimony to the world. There would have been no offense of the cross if Jesus had been merely a heroic example, a martyr to truth, a stimulus to moral effort. Only because he offered himself through the eternal Spirit without spot to God and by his blood removed an obstacle in the divine mind to the pardon of the sinner was Christ crucified a stumbling block to the Jew and foolishness to the Greek. But for that very reason also is his cross the very power and wisdom of God for man's salvation.

John's wedding followed almost at once upon his ordination. He spent two happy years in Cincinnati. But then the depressing climate began to tell upon his health, and in April, 1896, he was compelled to resign his charge. Mr. Rockefeller's kindness enabled him and Lide to take a foreign tour with John and Alta Rockefeller. They went together to St. Petersburg and Moscow, to the North Cape and Spitzbergen, to the Rhine and the Netherlands, these last upon the bicycle. After five or six months they came home, and for a winter they lodged with us in Rochester, to our great delight. Then, through the kindness of Professor True, an opening for John occurred at New Britain, Connecticut. There, in a solid New England manufacturing community, with a united church of from four to five hundred members, and a climate more bracing than that of Mount Auburn, I trust he will have a long and successful pastorate. He has a pleasant parsonage, decorated by Lide's taste and genius, a sufficient number of intelligent hearers, a people more heterogeneous than that in Cincinnati, a chance to reach the outlying masses of population. Mount Auburn had one great defect for a Christian church—there was almost no poverty in it. In New Britain John will be brought into contact with the wants and woes of humanity. I anticipate for him a constantly growing influence. I rejoice that God ever led him to devote himself to the service of Jesus Christ, and my great desire is that he may make full proof of his ministry.

As I come to speak of Cora, I am reminded of a good woman who had much to do with the early history of both the twins. Mrs. Martha George had been in her young married life a member of the church in Holley which Father Savage served as pastor. She helped support her family by millinery. She was a singer and an active Christian. But her name "Martha" was significant—she was "cumbered with much serving." Faithful and devoted as she was to her friends and the church, she was at times melancholy and depressed. Before Cora and Kate were born, she came to us in

Cleveland, said that her husband was dead and her children did not need her, and offered for small compensation to be a helper in our household. So for four months she stayed with us until the babies came into the world, and after their birth she was for two years and four months more their nurse. She bore the brunt of their care as long as we lived in Cleveland. Hattie was saved from worry and sleeplessness by her vigilance. When we came to Rochester in 1872, she kept the twins in Cleveland until our Rochester house was ready, and then she brought them to us. Then she made a two weeks' visit to her old home in Holley before she left us finally to return to Cleveland. After the two weeks, Katy had forgotten her and refused to go to her from her mother. But Cora remembered her and went. It almost broke Mrs. George's heart that she had lost her hold upon Katy. Her life soon after came to a mournful end. In the dreadful Ashtabula railway accident, when so many people in winter and at dead of night were precipitated into a yawning chasm and burned beyond recognition, she was a victim. Though she was not burned to death, she was mortally injured. After great suffering, she died, and her funeral was held in Cleveland. Cora and Kate cannot remember her now, but they owe much to her affectionate care in their childhood. I think she devoted herself to them very disinterestedly, and I do not doubt that she has entered into an exceeding great reward.

It was always a puzzle to us how twins could differ as much as Cora and Kate. Hall Caine, in his novel called *The Manxman,* says that the Deemster, the governor and judge of the Isle of Man, had two sons who were as totally unlike yet as perfect complements of each other as the inside and the outside of a bowl, but he adds that in this case the bowl was the old Deemster himself. I suppose all of Cora's and Katy's traits might possibly be found in their parents or somewhere in their ancestry. But we have never yet succeeded in tracing out their origin. Cora has her peculiar gifts. She has considerable accuracy and skill in her use of language, and she writes an interesting letter. Her sense of beauty in the matter of form and color is quite acute. She quickly catches a melody, and improvisation on the piano is one of her amusements. She has a good deal of determination when she gets interested in a subject or project. She has a mind of her own and a desire to accomplish something in the world by making a real contribution.

At the age of ten or eleven, on account of Katy's sickness, both the twins were taken out of Grammar School Number Twelve, where the older children had all their preliminary training, and were sent to Miss Cruttenden's private school, where it was expected that their health would be better cared for. I have always regretted this as involving some misfortune. Changing teachers and breaking up routine have their disadvantages. If Cora had continued in Number Twelve till she finished the grammar school course, she might have had a certain discipline which the private school did not give her. A tendency to reverie might have been more perfectly controlled. She might have learned more thoroughly the art of concentrating her powers and working persistently to a definite end. As it was, she did not take kindly to the idea of a college education, and though she spent a year at Granger Place School, Canandaigua, the experiment was not entirely satisfactory. Domestic life suits her better than schoolwork. Of late she has attended the Mechanics' Institute and has studied designing. The coming winter she purposes to learn the art of cooking and so to prepare herself for practical life.

With Katy, Cora was baptized by the Reverend Mr. Charles J. Baldwin and united with our First Baptist Church in 1883. I was touched with the simplicity and sincerity of her early religious experience. She sought to influence others, both by speaking in the prayer meetings and by writing letters to those who might be benefited. Of late years she has occasionally thought it her duty and privilege to print little essays on "Forethought" and "Persistence" for private circulation among her friends. I did not discourage this because I knew that her own cultivation of these qualities would be promoted by writing upon them and that any effort to do good would lead her out into new fields of thought and usefulness. Cora has powers of her own. Let her only remember that she is responsible for using these, instead of idly wishing that she had the gifts of others. Let her cease to dream of larger spheres of activity and content herself with filling the sphere in which she now is. Let her strive day by day to gain some new knowledge of the Bible and to do some humble work for Christ in the household and in the church, and she will be happy and make others happy. Introspection and theorizing are her dangers.

Getting out of herself and finding her joy in service will enable her to fulfill the plan of God in her existence.

When Cora went to Granger Place School, Katy went to Vassar College. This was in 1887, and she graduated in 1891. Her preparation for college was made at Miss Cruttenden's, afterwards called Professor Kingsley's, school. I now wish that we had kept Katy at home for a year longer before sending her to college. It would have saved her a long and needless tug with the Greek after she entered. But she took hold of her work with a docility and faithfulness worthy of all praise. I urged her when she left home to be a model of religious living and, instead of trying continually to *get* a blessing, make it her endeavor to *be* a blessing. I have good reason to know that she obeyed my injunctions. I have been told that she was universally beloved. Her unfortunate deficiency in Greek preparation lowered her standing in her freshman year and so prevented her from obtaining honors in scholarship. But she was continually advancing her rank, and in some departments, especially in history, she had no superior in her class. Miss Lucy Salmon, her professor in that department, has repeatedly spoken with enthusiasm of her power of analyzing a historical movement and presenting the results in a lucid and organic way.

It was through Professor Salmon that there came to her in 1893, two years after her graduation from Vassar, the opportunity to spend a year in Greece. Professor Richardson of Dartmouth had been appointed for a second time the director of the American School at Athens, and he desired to take into his family some college-bred young woman, partly as a student and partly as a companion. Miss Salmon kindly named Katy to him, as possessing all the necessary qualifications. So we fitted her out in a modest way, and she sailed on a North German Lloyd steamer for Gibraltar, Genoa, Naples, Palermo, and Athens. Professor White of Cambridge and his family were on the same steamer, as well as Professor Richardson with his wife and daughters. As they were all seasick and Katy was entirely well, she was able to minister to them and to win their affections. They passed Stromboli and saw in the night its active volcano. They endured quarantine in the Gulf of Athens. At last they landed in classic Greece. As an inmate of Professor Richardson's family, Katy saw much distinguished society. At one dinner given at the American School, Dr. Dörpfeld of the German School, Dr. Waldstein of Cambridge in England, and Dr. White of Cambridge in America were present. She was invited to Madame Schliemann's and was even presented at court. And yet her head was not turned, and she came back the same sweet and affectionate little girl that she went.

It was a great thing for Katy that she had the Vassar training and then the experience abroad. She gained confidence in herself. She found that she had executive ability. She learned to appear in public and to manage enterprises of importance. She brought from Greece a noble collection of pictures of the country and the people. These were transferred to glass and used to illustrate a series of lectures. I was proud of my daughter when I heard her go through such a thoughtful and interesting course without a manuscript and without hesitation. But she did not give up her work in the household. She became housekeeper. Through her mother's long and trying sickness, she was an angel of mercy. I doubt whether Mamma's life or reason would have survived if it had not been for Katy's unwearying patience and encouragement. All our entertaining now depends upon her. She receives the company and amuses them. Everybody likes her because she forgets herself in caring for others. Blessed little girl! Her father and mother love her, and they will weep if she ever leaves them.

Yet Katy is made for larger things than the mere management of her parents' house or caring for them as their old age comes on. We want her to have a home of her own. She has conducted the affairs of Vassar Aid Societies and has made it possible for many a poor girl to take a college course. She has helped distressed and worthy people who had no one else to sympathize with them. She has taught a Sunday School class and has made it a means of leading its members out into appreciation of literature and art. But she has not yet married.

Here I am reminded of Miss Cushing, a most cultivated and charming single woman, a graduate of Vassar, and a trustee of that college awhile ago.[1] I sat with her one evening at the college

[1]Strong was a trustee of Vassar College from 1884 to 1918, serving as chairman of the board of trustees from 1906 to 1911.

prayers. It was a soothing and delightful service. We rose and passed together down the aisle. Miss Cushing is a Unitarian, but she said to me, "Dr. Strong, this chapel service always impresses me deeply. I keep the memory of it. I can never forget the prayers of my college days." "Yes," I replied, "it is beautiful. But are you not afraid that college life will unfit young women for being wives and mothers? They get such lofty ideas that they will not look at any ordinary young man. Are we not bringing about a state of things in which there will be no more marrying and giving in marriage?" "Do not let that be a burden to your mind," she answered. "Your fears are like my own when I visited my Uncle Ezekiel. He is a great chair manufacturer near Boston. He took me through his ware-rooms and I saw them piled full of chairs to the very ceiling. I began to be alarmed. I cried out at last, 'Why, Uncle Zeke, you never can sell all these chairs!' 'Don't worry, Mary Jane,' he said; 'settin' down ain't a goin' out o' fashion jest yit!' "

I have sometimes wondered whether Kate's very education might not have given her a critical bent which would make it difficult for her to fancy any but an ideal man. She permits the outward form of a sermon or one's manner in conversation to influence her judgment more than it ought. Delicate and sensitive as she is, she needs to remember that men are not always able to express themselves, that the substance is often better than the show, that they must be judged by what they may become almost as much as what they now are. It is a worthy thing for a young woman, when she knows that a young man's aims are high, to help him struggle toward his ideal even though he is now far from attaining it. Marriage is always a matter of faith. Upon the basis of the imperfect good we know, we give ourselves to develop the perfect good that yet lies in the distance. After all, imperfection clings to us as well as to others, and they must bear with us in turn. But I leave my dear Katy to God, knowing that if any man succeeds in winning her, he will win one of the greatest of matrimonial prizes, and if the right man never comes, she will have her career and will be a blessing anyhow.

Fourteen years passed after Katy's birth, and the quiet of the household was not disturbed by any child's cries or laughter. We had settled down to the ways of elderly people when suddenly, like a clap of thunder from a clear sky, as it were, Laura was born. Perhaps

I ought to say that outsiders were startled more than the parents were, but it remains true that the parents were startled also. I had thought it would be well to even up matters. As we had three daughters and only two sons, what was more natural than to wish for one additional boy and, in fact, to expect one? Visions of good that boy might accomplish in the kingdom of God passed before me. I prayed much about the matter. Providence answered my prayers very differently from my intent. The eventful day came around, and the boy was a girl! I have always thought Laura was bound to be of greater use in the world than any man could be, simply because that would be the only known method of reconciling the ways of God to men.

The child made a great sensation in the world for a thing so small. We came to love her very much and to take great interest in her development. Mamma said that I gave more attention to that baby than I had given to all the other five put together. Perhaps it was because my own thinking powers had become more fully developed. I was immensely interested in the psychological problems involved. When does a baby first smile? How far back in human experience does memory extend? Can we ever remember what we have not put into language? Do we have ideas without words? Are there selfish and depraved tendencies in little children? When should the process of education begin? What is the proper order of development in the human powers? All these questions could now be settled, and I gave much time to settling them. If I did not succeed in evolving a philosophy of childhood, I certainly got a great deal of fun out of it. People looked on and said I had all the comfort of a father and a grandfather at the same time. It was a great delight to make Laura acquainted with the world and the things that God has made. I tried to convince her that spiders were not to be feared and that little pigs were beautiful. I illustrated the story of the three Hebrew children by offering to throw her into the burning fiery furnace of the steamboat on Canandaigua Lake. Curiously enough she insisted on having ideas of her own about all these things. One of the pleasantest summers I ever spent was one at Cook's Point when the place constituted a great menagerie, with one peacock, two cows, three horses, four dogs, five cats, ten pigs, and innumerable chickens. I took Laura up a ladder and showed her a robin's nest with the scrawny little birds opening their big bills for worms and the mother bird coming to feed them. I put her on the backs of the horses and taught her to pat their cheeks. All this was an education for me as well as for her. I have often envied English children their training in a country home where there were plenty of horses and dogs and where one learned sympathy with God's dumb creatures.

She reached the age of six without any other literary acquisitions than the learning of the letters of the alphabet. I then concluded that it was time for her to learn to read. A progressive reader without pictures commended itself to me. I thought there should be no adventitious helps. The work should be solid and scientific. Laura could not spell "R-A-T" instead of "m-o-u-s-e," for she had no picture of a mouse to divert her from the sounds of the letters. So she made rapid progress, and what she did learn she learned thoroughly. In a similar manner somewhat later I gave her the first lessons in French, and I fancy that her French pronunciation shows the advantage of my instruction. Latin also was begun in much the same way when she was about ten years old, the lessons being given during the half hour immediately after breakfast, sometimes in my term-time and sometimes in my summer vacations. It often seemed hard to her to be subjected to rigid discipline and to be held to absolute exactness. But it was good for her to learn that a substantive in a certain case could have but one possible meaning and that by a little thought that meaning could be ascertained.

Laura seems to me to have a naturally accurate mind and to be capable of making a good scholar. I wanted her, however, to be something more than a mere student of textbooks. I wished to inspire the love of literature. For some years it was my custom to read to her directly after tea each evening. I went over *The Pilgrim's Progress, The Exiles of Siberia, The Vicar of Wakefield, Picciola, Vathek,* and *The Arabian Nights.* I read, in course, Walter Scott's *Ivanhoe* and *The Talisman.* Some poetry was added to the list, such as Tennyson's *Idylls of the King.* It has pleased me to find that with regard to some of this reading, she has a tenacious memory. She has learned to read for herself, rather too rapidly and too desultorily, I fear, yet in a way to give her a considerable fund of information. I trust that, by the time she enters college, she will have some literary resources to draw from when she comes to write her essays and compositions.

Laura has a decided mind of her own. I like her independence. But it has its dangers. She might easily become domineering and forgetful of other people's comfort and rights. Her own quickness might lead her to look down upon others who are not so quick as she. She cannot well be driven, but she listens to reason and is strongly influenced by affection. It has gratified me to see how sympathetic she has been in her mother's illnesses. At times she has shown a desire to lead a Christian life. She needs above all things the presence in her heart of an overmastering love for the Lord Jesus Christ. I shall not feel that she is safe from temptation and disaster until she has intelligently and fully submitted herself to the Savior's control. I long to hear her say that she has given herself for time and eternity to God. She has a good mind and a strong will. With Christ in her heart she can be very happy and very useful, while without Christ she will always be restless and exposed to danger. As her birth was preceded by prayer and as we have never ceased since then to seek God's blessing upon her, I confidently expect that He will soon, if he has not already, make her his child and show her his salvation.

In the case of each one of the children there was a struggle of the child's will with my will, but the child was subdued so early in its history that it never remembered the conflict. I owe much in this matter of family discipline to President Woolsey. Just before my class graduated from college, the president made to us some practical remarks. We all knew that he had a fiery temper, but we were hardly prepared to hear him allude to it. He told us never to permit a child of ours to grow up with an ungoverned will. That will would be a source of lifelong anxiety both to the child and the parent. It would be a great obstacle to the child's conversion to God to have a will that never had been taught to bow either to God or man. He urged us to take this matter in hand very early, before the habit of resistance had become inveterate. He intimated that the neglect of his own parents to compel obedience had made his subsequent life in many ways a burden to him.

One of his hearers took these remarks to heart and acted upon them. Each of my children passed through a crisis. It was usually at the age of two or three years. Charles, for example, when first permitted to sit at the table in a high chair, would put out his hand for things he ought not to have. Saying "No! No!" was not sufficient. The child proposed to test his ability. He was determined to have his own way. A rap on his little knuckles startled him. But he persisted. A harder rap followed. He cried, but he did not persevere. He had learned the lesson. He afterwards looked very much as if he would like to repeat the effort, but he had learned the meaning of signs; a slight movement of my hand caused him to give up the attempt. So without any further punishment Charles grew up a most obedient boy.

Strange to say, Mary, the calmest and least nervous of the whole lot, proved the most refractory. She was three years of age when one afternoon her mother asked her to pick up a spool from the carpet and bring it to her. Mary simply refused. Mamma tried to come a flank movement on her and asked her to bring other things. She consented most readily. "Now, bring me the spool." "No, No," Mary replied. After ten or fifteen minutes of vain coaxing, it became only too evident that she had set herself not to do that particular thing. Mamma came to me. She thought it time that Mary was taught to mind. I agreed. But to make her mind was quite another thing. I repeated the same old tactics at first, but entirely in vain. Then I punished her a little. This seemed to accomplish nothing. She cried, but she did not yield. Then came harder punishment and very loud crying, but still there was no yielding. The conflict went on for fully two hours. The little three-year-old seemed the picture of indomitable resolution. I was really alarmed and exhausted. But I knew that to give up then was to imperil the child's soul and future. I put her into a dark closet. This was a novelty to her. She was frightened, and she also had time to think. At first she screamed. Then she grew quiet. Finally she exclaimed, "I *will* be good! I *will* be good!" We brought her out with fear and trembling. But she picked up the spool, and we never were troubled by disobedience in her case afterwards.

The other children were managed in a similar way. Each one has a will, but each one has been taught that there is a power in heaven and earth superior to that will. Our family prayers have had much to do in teaching about the power in heaven. Ever since

Mamma and I were married, we have had daily reading of the Bible and prayer. I have always aimed to make the Scripture reading interesting and to make the prayer brief. We have united in saying the Lord's Prayer at the close. Sometimes we have followed the custom of Mr. Rockefeller's family and have all kissed each other when we rose. But even better than the regular daily prayers has been the little family prayer meeting on Sunday afternoon. After the dinner and the nap, the whole family gathered in the sitting room. I began with a little talk. Any particular merit I had discovered in one of the children during the preceding week was mentioned. Attention was gently called to any particular fault that was outcropping at that time. The nature of prayer was spoken of, and the three sorts of prayer were mentioned: thanksgiving, confession, supplication—we must thank, confess, ask. Then the children were encouraged to mention things for which we should thank God that week, things which we should confess, things which we needed to ask. After all this we kneeled down, and each child prayed aloud, beginning with the youngest and ending with the oldest, mother and father following the children. If the child was too young to find the words of prayer, I put the words into its mouth.

One of the most delightful experiences of my life has been to perceive the growing desire and ability of the very young child to pray. When prayer was no longer made a mystery but was treated as thanking, confessing, asking, and it was regarded needful to thank, confess, and ask only one thing, it was surprising how soon the child caught the art and even regarded it as a privilege to pray. These family prayer meetings have been opportunities of general religious instruction. I have given many little lectures on manners and morals in them, have answered many important questions which the moment suggested, and have in this way made the religious life seem less formidable. Now and then we have had guests on a Sunday, and we have invited them to participate. In one or two instances persons who had never been accustomed to family prayer have been deeply impressed by the scene. Praying in the family has made praying and speaking in meetings of the church more easy than it otherwise would have been. I have frequently told about my family prayer meeting, but I have never seen another except in the family of President L. Clark Seelye of Smith College. There they had the recitation of the Creed, and the whole exercise was somewhat more formal than my own, although my presence may have given it an air of stiffness that it did not ordinarily possess. I am persuaded that we need to have more family religion in our day. Parents cannot safely commit the religious instruction of their children entirely to Sunday School teachers. And the family prayer meeting utilizes a Sunday afternoon and makes it precious and memorable as nothing else can.

When Laura was about five years of age, I took her every morning after breakfast upstairs and tried to teach her how to pray. One day she offered a singular prayer. We had been to a dime museum on the previous afternoon. It was a mournful sort of performance. A man pretended to eat glass, wound a snake around his neck, exhibited a lot of cockatoos, and some monkeys in a cage. Laura got too near the cage, and suddenly a monkey thrust his paw through the bars and grabbed one of her curls. She screamed, but the monkey held her fast. I succeeded with difficulty in extricating the curl from the monkey's grasp. The child was greatly frightened but even more disgusted. Next morning, when the time came to present her thanksgiving to God, she began, "O Lord, I thank thee that I am not a snake, or a cockatoo, or a monkey!" And then she continued, "Make me a good little girl, and don't let that monkey catch me again!" We used to take walks together, she holding my hand and asking questions as we went. Peanuts and gumdrops were a very common acquisition from these excursions, and I am not sure that they were not valued more than the information which I communicated. I only aim to show that my government was humane and that both the discipline and the religious instruction were paternal and adapted to win the childish mind. Nobody who entered our family would have doubted that the children's motive to obedience was love rather than fear.

One of my fundamental principles of family education has been never to laugh at the children but to treat them as equals. The spirit of comradeship between parents and children is essential to the best development. The maxims that "children should be seen and not heard" and that they should be kept away from the family board until they are well grown seem to me very heartless and absurd. The child needs to hear the family talk. It is of itself an education, where the family is one of refinement and intelligence. The freedom to express one's mind is a great help to independent thinking. And the freedom will not degenerate into license where there are a number of brothers and sisters to criticize. I have tried to make my children partake of all my knowledge and experience. I have told them the story of my life, even as I am now telling it for the benefit of my children's children. I have taken them with me, so far as I could, on my journeys. Charles, Mary, and John will remember our excursions together to New York, Rice Lake, and Newport.

It has seemed to me desirable always to keep before the child something attractive in the way of a motive and reward. Obedience becomes monotonous unless there is something to inspirit. To hold out as an inducement to faithfulness the prospect of a book or journey or vacation helps the young mind wonderfully. We live by admiration, hope, and love, not so much by compulsion and dread. It has been a great gratification to me to know that the children when away from home kept up their correspondence with father and mother, weekly letters being the rule and the failures few and far between. We have tried to make home pleasant by providing good fare, and it is good to hear the children say that they get such good food nowhere else. Moreover, we have never had in our household that bitter wrangling and harsh criticism which turn many families into places quite the opposite to heaven. Our children have been kind to their parents and obliging to one another. Much of this has been due to the Spirit of Christ. Before Charles and Mary were converted, there was something of strife. When they made a profession of religion, their spirit seemed to change. They became unselfish. The household seemed like a little heaven below. It has been to me an illustration of the true uniting bond of the church of Christ. A quarreling church will become the home of peace after a revival of religion has drawn its members closer to Christ once more.

One of the features of my life has been my habit of taking regular vacations. Never since my first pastorate began have I worked a whole summer through. There has always been a midsummer rest, and that time of recreation has always been spent partly in travel. It has cost a great deal of money, but it has restored my strength and enabled us to do better work afterwards. I have given account of my first two journeys to Europe. I must now relate the story of the last two. In 1874 I took Hattie and made a tour of three months. I had been preaching continuously at the First Baptist Church of Rochester as supply during the interregnum between the pastorates of Dr. Robins and of Mr. Baldwin. I had laid by the proceeds, nearly a thousand dollars. Hattie had never been to Europe. It seemed to me that then was the time, or never. Mr. John B. Trevor added two hundred dollars as a special present to my wife, and with these resources we set sail. Our steamer was the *Atlas*, a small Cunarder, and we started for Europe about the middle of May.

Hattie was not much of a sailor. She was not ill in the ordinary way, but she was worse off than if she had been. Her troubles vanished, however, when we reached Cork. It was my first visit to Ireland. In America the spring was late, and the trees had hardly blossomed out. As we went up the channel from Queenstown to Cork, the vivid green of the shores sent a thrill through me such as I had not felt since engineering in the woods at the age of seventeen. Lawns and groves seemed to have an exuberance of loveliness. I understood now why Erin was called "the Emerald Isle." We had made the acquaintance of a few very pleasant people on the steamer, and quite a number of us kept together for a week after landing. There were Mr. and Mrs. Pemberton from Richmond, Virginia, whom we have visited and who have since visited us. There was a Mr. Abendroth and his daughter from New York. We all heard

> . . . the bells of Shandon
> That sound so grand on
> The pleasant waters of the river Lee.[2]

We made an excursion to Blarney Castle, and some of us kissed the Blarney Stone. Best of all, we went to the Lakes of Killarney, rode over the Pass of Glencoe, wandered through the ruins of Muckross Abbey. These lakes with their picturesque beauty have always been to me the type of the paradise into which man might turn this earth of ours. Mr. Herbert, the owner of the whole region, has emphasized every natural advantage of the landscape and softened

[2]Father Prout (Francis Sylvester Mahony), "The Bells of Shandon," lines 7-9.

Augustus Hopkins Strong in his later years

or removed everything ugly until his vast estate is like a bit of fairyland. The echoes were like "the horns of elfland faintly blowing," and the song of the uniformed boatmen who rowed us through the lakes kept time to the beat of their oars.

The long day's ride by rail to Dublin, through a desolate region of peat and hovel, showed us by way of contrast how wretched a country may become through oppression and neglect. At Dublin our large party of steamer passengers separated. We had a last dinner together, Mr. Abendroth furnishing the champagne. Mamma and I heard a sermon at the university on Sunday morning which was preached, as we understood, as one of the conditions of obtaining the degree of Doctor of Divinity. On Monday we crossed the channel to Holyhead and Bangor. Then I had my first view of Wales. We made a point of visiting the castles. Beaumaris, Carnarvon, and Conway, all vast, somber, intricate, ivy clad, seem like the worn-out abodes of giants. The banquet halls are deserted and crumbling to ruin.

> The Knight's bones are dust,
> And his good sword rust;—
> His soul is with the saints, I trust.[3]

A day's ride in a dogcart over the Pass of Llanberis to Bettws-y-Coed and in full view of Snowdon was something to be remembered. At last we came to Chester and put up at the Grosvenor Hotel, a hostelry built by the then Marquis of Westminster and strikingly congruous in its architecture with the medieval aspect of the town.

From Chester we went southward to Shrewsbury and to Ludlow where we spent the night. The old parish church interested us but chiefly Ludlow Castle, where Milton's *Comus* was first acted before the Lord President of Wales. Hereford was delightful for its cathedral, recently restored and bright as a new tin pan. Then to Ross and Monmouth, and from Monmouth by carriage down the valley of the Wye—a lovely ride, with Tintern Abbey by the way—to Chepstow, and thence by rail to Bristol. At Bristol I had

[3]Samuel Taylor Coleridge, "The Knight's Tomb," lines 9-11.

hoped to visit George Müller's orphan houses. But George Müller himself was absent on a missionary expedition. We reached Bristol on a Saturday night. Monday was cleaning day at the orphanage, and no visitors were admitted. Two things, however, made the Sunday memorable. The first was the worship of the Plymouth Brethren in the morning. The Plymouth Brethren dislike church organizations, for fear they will become machines; they dislike ordained ministers, for fear they will become bishops. I was curious to see how their service would be conducted. I found the great gallery filled by the children of the orphan houses. Two or three brethren seemed to monopolize the worship. Though no one man formally presided, the exercises proceeded as methodically as any church service of the Baptists. It became evident to me that they had plenty of organization in reality, if not in form. The second striking experience of that Sabbath day was our hearing the Reverend Mr. Gange preach in the afternoon. He filled the pulpit formerly occupied by Robert Hall. It was a packed and breathless congregation. The sermon was a masterpiece of fluency and unction, one of the best gospel sermons I have listened to in England. I talked with the preacher after the services. He declared that the sermon was a wholly *memoriter* discourse, written out word for word beforehand. He said he could preach in no other way. The only man I have heard who has seemed to have everything he writes at once impressed upon the tablets of his memory, so that he can read it off before an audience like the pages of a book, is Dr. John Hall of New York.

I will leave the account of our European tour long enough to tell of an experience with Dr. John Hall. Years ago I engaged him to give a series of four lectures before the seminary on the "Christian Law of Benevolent Giving." Two of these lectures were to be given each week, on Tuesday and on Thursday evenings. Dr. Hall reached Rochester at about ten o'clock on Tuesday morning. He stayed at the hotel, and I called upon him soon after his arrival. I invited him to dine with me at one o'clock. He replied that he could not, as he had yet to write his lecture for the evening. I told him that he would be obliged to get his dinner somewhere, that my house was not far from the hotel, that we would let him go as soon after dinner as he chose. He consented at length, and about two o'clock he returned to his hotel. At seven in the evening I called to conduct him to the First Baptist Church. When he came down the stairs to meet me, he had in his hand a lot of manuscript. The last sheet, he said, had been written only a minute or two before. The ink was not fairly dry. He gave me the manuscript then and there, saying that I might as well have it at once, since it was to be printed. He then went to the church, and before a large audience he gave his lecture of more than an hour without a moment's break or hesitation, a most elaborate and finished address. When I reached home, I read over the manuscript to see how completely he had followed it in actual delivery. So far as I could see, he had given it in public precisely as it was written, with the exception that at certain points he had interjected extemporaneous illustrations from his personal experience. Such feats of memory fill me with admiration and almost with envy. They also give me a sort of despair, for memorizing has always been to me a great effort of nerve and will. I can do it, but the process is so exhausting that I have ceased to think it a duty.

From Bristol, Hattie and I went to Wells. The cathedral, with its moat and drawbridge, seemed an extraordinary survival. Yet the close was beautiful—"a haunt of ancient peace." Then we visited Glastonbury Abbey, so famed in Tennyson's *Idylls of the King*. The "Vale of Avalon" charmed us. We reached Exeter, the southwesternmost limit of our travel in England. The Norman transept towers, the long unbroken roof, and the exceedingly rich west front of decorated Gothic are striking and almost unique features of its noble cathedral. I am almost ashamed to say that a certain dinner of salmon, chicken, gooseberry tart, and clotted cream, with Moselle Mousseux accompaniment, after a long day of riding and sight-seeing, lingers in my memory side by side with the Exeter Cathedral. Salisbury succeeded to Exeter, and there I bought the picture of Salisbury Cathedral, taken from the cloisters, which now adorns my study. The interior was in the process of restoration, so that we had little opportunity to judge its beauty. In fact, throughout England, it was the epoch of cathedral repairs. The nearly forty years that have now elapsed since my first visit to the old country have seen these great structures made over anew, and if we attribute the original building of them to the religious spirit, I do not know why we should not call the new beauty of these gorgeous fanes the result of a great religious revival. Money is not given in this way by the million unless there is something more than a commercial or even artistic motive. Much of it, to say the least, has been given to God with the simple purpose of promoting the worship of his Son and the spread of his gospel.

In London we stayed at the Langham Hotel. There we met Mr. and Mrs. George C. Buell and with them made a delightful day's excursion to Windsor. We saw the ordinary London sights, heard Adelina Patti at Covent Garden when her voice was still fresh and inexhaustible as a bird's, and attended a concert at the Royal Albert Hall where choral singing reached a perfection I had never imagined before. We visited Ely and Cambridge and Canterbury. Each of them had its own peculiar interest. The vaulting of the octagon at Ely, the magnificence of King's College Chapel at Cambridge, the raised chancel at Canterbury, so wonderfully adapted for scenic display, are all wonders of architecture. But the thing I remember with most interest is the kindness of a Cambridge don, a most gentle and courteous soul, who took me to his room, treated me like a prince, opened all the doors of the university to me, and made the impression upon me of the man of highest breeding and culture I had seen in England. Strange to say, I cannot now remember his name or his rank. But I shall never forget how gracious he was to an utter stranger. The statues of Sir Isaac Newton and Lord Macaulay in Trinity College deeply impressed me, and the refectories with the portraits of the great graduates looking down from the walls seemed fit places to nourish the elect youth of Britain.

The weather of the British Isles was damp and chilly, though the verdure was enchanting. I wore my overcoat every day for a month or six weeks after landing at Cork. At last we started for the Continent. But as we crossed the channel to Belgium, the weather changed, and we had a month of heat as great as I have ever known in America. We visited Ghent and Bruges and then made our way to Brussels. Here the Würtz Gallery was very curious, with its grotesque and startling surprises, the work of a painter who, like William Blake, was somewhat unbalanced in mind but had remarkable powers of invention. Antwerp kept us for a single day, and then we made a dash for Cologne. Here we attended a service in the great cathedral and heard congregational singing in the nave that surpassed all I had ever heard before. We had a lovely ride up the Rhine to Bingen, and from Bingen we took Mainz, Heidelberg, Baden Baden, and Strasbourg on our way to Basel and Lucerne. We went up the Rigi and spent a night on the summit, though the sunrise was not wholly satisfactory. When we descended to Lucerne, the heat became so oppressive that we concluded not to travel until the weather moderated. So we stayed for a week at the foot of the mountains when we might have escaped the heat by going higher up. Yet it was a good rest, after all—the only real rest we got during our three and one-half months abroad.

From Lucerne we went over the Brünig Pass by *diligence* to Meyringen and from there by rail and boat to Interlaken. From our hotel window at Interlaken we had magnificent views of the Jungfrau. But when we attempted closer intimacy with the young lady by a carriage ride to Grindelwald, she hid her face, sent down the rain upon us, and we were forced to return disconsolate. We consoled ourselves by making our way to Berne and Fribourg. In Fribourg we heard the organ. Then to Geneva, and thence by *diligence* through Sallenches to Chamonix. A glorious view of Mont Blanc rewarded us as we sat in the coupé and gazed upward and onward. From Chamonix we went to Martigny over the newly constructed Tête Noire road, and the way our driver swung our vehicle around the sudden turns on the edge of the precipices was appalling. But we reached Martigny in safety. In Geneva we bought some jewelry for Mamma and a watch for my brother Henry precisely like that which I had bought for myself two years before. The watches were minute repeaters. They cost three hundred dollars each. With a little expense for repairs, they have served us admirably well until now. My own seems as good today as it was twenty-five years ago.

At Neuchâtel, on the banks of the beautiful lake of the same name, we stayed a couple of days. I had business to do for my father with a manufacturer of knitting machines. I made my way to his workshops and collected the royalties that were due, in spite of my very imperfect command of colloquial French. But I was struck with the great difference between business methods in Europe and America. In Europe everything seemed to go on with infinite leisure. There was no rush and no anxiety. The banks were all closed for dinner and for rest in the middle of the day, and the manufacturers seemed to care little whether they had orders or not. They were bound to enjoy life even if they failed to make money. In Paris I had the same duty to perform for my father, and I received the same impressions. We enjoyed the beauty and lightness of Paris. My classmate Rev. Edward W. Hitchcock was pastor of the American Chapel, and he entertained us beautifully. He gave a dinner in our honor and afterwards held an evening reception.

My friend's lodgings were on the fourth floor of a fine house near the Arc de Triomphe. As the sun set, the light was reflected from myriads of windows in the city below, and the effect was that of a universal illumination. At dinner I sat next to a very interesting American clergyman. He had been in Paris for two years. I asked him what his object was in living abroad. He replied that he had discovered the clue to the book of Revelation and was getting material in the National Library for a book on the subject. I was reminded of Lord Brougham's remark that the study of prophecy either found a man crazy or it left him so.

The sights and the restaurants of Paris having been exhausted, we started for Amiens. The lofty nave of the superb cathedral seemed to me in some respects the most beautiful in existence. One could only regret that no one of the French cathedrals is more than a fragment. The builders began but were not able to finish. The designs at Salisbury and Cologne were not so daring, but what was planned was carried out. One is tempted to attribute the results to French dash on the one hand and English and German steadfastness on the other. On the trip across the English Channel from Calais to Dover I had my first experience of real seasickness. I had made five voyages across the Atlantic and had been fourteen days and nights on the Mediterranean, and I had never succumbed before. I deemed myself so proof against the malady that I stayed calmly on the deck of that channel steamer while I sent Mrs. Strong below to lie down. I was enjoying the tossing of the vessel when suddenly I began to feel weak. I did not suspect what was the matter. But I soon knew, and for a couple of hours I was as wretched as one could well be. It took me a whole week to get over it. It cured me of self-complacency and of bragging. My experience reminds me of Dr. Dowling's story. A young man was crossing the ocean with his intended bride. At the close of the voyage he said admiringly, "I never knew before how much there was in that girl!"

But we reached London alive, and a few days afterwards we took passage for home in the steamship *Queen* from Liverpool. We found on board Dr. Kerfoot, afterwards pastor of Strong Place Church in Brooklyn, and professor of systematic theology in the Louisville Theological Seminary; Mr. Orange Judd, who had had extensive experience as a journalist and a diplomatist; and Mrs. Isabella Hooker of Hartford, a sister of Henry Ward Beecher. Hattie showed her usual tact and skill by getting acquainted with the whole ship's company and then introducing me to them. She was the life of the table and everybody liked her. But she did not like the sea, notwithstanding. In fact her suffering was great, in spite of the fact that she was not actually sick, and she declares to this day that nothing can ever induce her to cross the ocean again.

There was no drawback to my enjoyment of this third European tour except the giving out of my eyes. I had never worn glasses. I had done a great deal of evening work before I left home. My book on theology was going through the press, and there had been a great deal of proofreading. I was quite run down with preaching and this typographical labor. When I entered a picture gallery or a cathedral, a few minutes were enough to exhaust my vitality. After a little time I felt faint. I sat down, or I shut my eyes while Hattie led me around. It never occurred to me that my eyes might need the assistance of spectacles. I returned to this country rested and strengthened, and my work so absorbed me for a time that I forgot my eyes. But after a while the same old feelings that I had had in Europe came back in this country, and at last it was suggested to me that I should consult an oculist. He told me that I ought to have taken to the use of glasses five years before. With the glasses he gave me I recovered the use of my lost evenings, and life became twice as bright as it had been.

During our absence abroad, Charles and John had been sent out into the country. Mr. and Mrs. Fordyce of Scipio took the boys to board, and they had a taste of farm life. They behaved themselves well, and they learned something from their rural surroundings. Mary, Cora, and Katy were kindly cared for by my dear mother at home. Both Mother and Father were capable of endless sacrifice for their children and their children's children, and they often made their own interests in comparison of altogether too little account. They thought the little house on East Avenue which we occupied when we first came to town unfit, as indeed it was, to be the house of a president of the seminary. When Dr. Miller and sister Belle left them to set up housekeeping for themselves, Father and Mother invited us to come in and take them in lieu of rent as boarders with us. But Mother found that she needed greater quiet than a house full of children could give, and the result was that the house in the rear was newly fitted up for our parents, while the family mansion remained in our possession without any rent at all. It has always been a question to me since whether I should have permitted this, whether indeed I should not have insisted on Father and Mother taking their own house back and staying there to the end of their days. I do not know that they would ever have done this or whether Mother could have kept house again, but I am sorry I did not propose it. As it was, her health grew weaker; she went out less and less; consumption, which had for a long time had hold upon her, developed quite rapidly; on April 9, 1877, she died. Dear Mother! If I could only for a few hours have her back and tell her how much I love her and how much I repent that I did not do more while she lived to show her that I loved her, it would seem a great favor of God. I look forward to heaven as the place where I shall have the opportunity I cannot have here. Next to seeing my Savior, I think I shall put the joy of seeing her.

When Mother died, she was but sixty-eight years of age, having been born on June 9, 1808. She was a little older than Father, for he was born on July 18, 1809. But Father lived to be seventy-five. After Mother's death, he insisted upon dividing up his property among his children, so that he should have no care and we should have no disputes. He counted himself worth about fifty thousand dollars. As my quarter would amount only to about twelve thousand, what I received from my Cleveland house went to make up the difference between this sum and the value of the mansion on South Clinton Street. I paid over eight thousand dollars to the other children, and I became the proprietor of the house where I lived for the next twenty years. Henry in a somewhat similar way took the property on Court Street; Kate, the house and lot on Meigs Street; Belle, the house and lot on Fitzhugh Street. So we were all provided with houses, and these houses have done much to keep the children in Rochester and to keep them together. Indeed, one of Father's great desires was that brotherly and sisterly love might continue among us. I think his prayer has been answered. There has been no bitterness and no ill feeling among us as far as I know. We have rejoiced in each other's joys and sympathized with each other's sorrows, and as far as we could, we have lent a hand to help.

My father, after he distributed the main part of his property, had still a little income from invested funds, and on this he lived till he died. He boarded with sister Kate in her house on Meigs Street. This was help and company for her, as her husband had died long before, and her children required all she could do to support them. Fortunately they, like all the children of Henry and of Belle, came up well, proved themselves industrious and self-respecting, and were a comfort to their mother. Arthur's long and patient service for his employers has recently been rewarded by his securing a position where he may in time amass wealth, and Jessie has shown such Christian devotion and sacrifice that we all love her. Father lived long enough to see the promise, if not the consummation. He spent his last days most usefully in work for the church and seminary. Being without regular business engagements, he could do many things which otherwise would have been left undone. He was a great helper in the first years of my seminary administration. The care of the building fell on him, as far as supervision was concerned. In the church he was a constant attendant and a constant influence for good. His last feeble but trustful utterances in our prayer meetings showed his determination to be faithful to the very last. He could never be persuaded to take to his bed, even though he seemed exhausted. He declared that when he took to his bed, we might know he was going to die. He kept up in spite of illness. He went to Henry's house on Lake Avenue because he could be somewhat more comfortable there. When I made him my last visit, he was lying on a sofa in the sitting room. He kissed me good-bye. Soon after I had gone, he found that he could not keep up longer. He was helped to bed, and there very quickly he died. Henry was privileged to catch his last words and to give him the last care. His funeral, like Mother's, was very simple. At Mother's we sang the old tune

"China" with the words:

> Why do we mourn departing friends,
>   Or shake at death's alarms?
> 'Tis but the voice that Jesus sends
>   To call them to his arms.

And at Father's funeral the hymn was:

> Asleep in Jesus, blessed sleep!
>   From which none ever wakes to weep;
> A calm and undisturbed repose
>   Unbroken by the last of foes.

The day of Father's death was April 20, 1885. He had survived my mother a little more than eight years. He left behind him a most fragrant and precious memory. "Let me die the death of the righteous, and may my last end be like his!"

When I next went to Europe, I went at the invitation and expense of Mr. Rockefeller. Mary went with me, taking the place of her mother, who had been originally invited. Mr. Rockefeller's whole family accompanied him. Charles was then engaged to Bessie. He had been studying in Europe. He met us on our arrival at Southampton and traveled with us afterwards. Dr. and Mrs. Biggar from Cleveland were also of the party, Dr. Biggar being the physician, as I was the chaplain. Other persons, like Professor Nason of Troy, from time to time and for a little while joined us, but the regular company numbered thirteen persons, including Mrs. Rockefeller's maid and the courier. We went over and came back on the *Aller* of the North German Lloyd line, the most comfortable of all the steamers I have traveled on. We had every luxury. Ordinarily salon-cars were ready for us at the railway stations, private dining rooms and parlors at the hotels, tallyho coaches for our rides on country roads. It was 1887, the Jubilee year, the fiftieth anniversary of Queen Victoria's accession to the throne. We lodged at the Buckingham Palace Hotel, just opposite the royal residence, and some of her Majesty's guests who could not be accommodated at the palace overflowed into our hostelry. For the first time I saw full dress every evening at a regular hotel table. The town was crowded. Seats for viewing the Jubilee Procession commanded great prices. For two windows and balconies at Hatchard's Hotel in Piccadilly, which we held for about six hours and where we had a very simple cold luncheon, Mr. Rockefeller paid $187.

We were obliged to take our places three hours before the procession passed, for the reason that shortly after nine o'clock in the morning the streets were closed; long lines of soldiers guarded them from end to end; and the crowds behind the soldiers made them absolutely impassable. Where cross streets debouched into the main avenues, the exit was guarded by cavalry, the horses standing side by side close together with their haunches toward the crowd. From our windows we could observe the throng behind pressing those in front upon the horses' heels until the animals began to kick and there was a sudden squeeze backward. Now and then someone was carried out fainting. There was almost no drunkenness, but there were exhibitions of almost insane mischief, for though men were close to the horses' heels, they amused themselves occasionally by sticking pins into the beasts. I admired the behavior of the dragoons. Through all this deviltry they sat unmoved as statues; they were jeered at, but they did not resent it; they seemed absolutely to ignore the crowd behind them; they were there simply to keep their places, and they kept them. The procession, when it came, was magnificent. The guests were most of them in closed carriages, the royalty in open barouches, the chief among them on horseback. The short and dumpy Prince of Wales, in spite of his exquisite mount, looked very insignificant as he rode side by side with Frederick, the Crown Prince of Germany. "Unser Fritz" was the most splendid specimen of a man that I ever saw, a soldier in every fiber of his being, yet a gentleman, a scholar, and a prince as well. The after story of his accession to the throne of the empire, his trying illness, and his death before he had reigned even a single year is so sad a one that I have always gladly remembered that hour of his health and strength in London. The Queen, in her state carriage with four horses, was simply dressed in plain black bonnet and mantilla. There were no jewels and there was no crown. The little old lady seemed grateful for the reverence and love of her people, yet anxious lest loyalty might cause them harm. And she was right. To care for so vast a concourse and to prevent accident or riot requires almost superhuman generalship.

Fortunately, the Jubilee was a perfect success. And yet I did not care to repeat my visit ten years after, when her Majesty celebrated the sixtieth anniversary of her coronation. Perhaps it was because I was not invited, however. The first experience was nonetheless pleasant. One feature of it was the visit Mr. Rockefeller and I made to the Regent's Park College. I was eager to impress upon him the desirableness of giving to a university the best equipment and surroundings. The beautiful situation of this Baptist institution in national grounds, with the whole of Regent's Park for its campus, seemed to please him much. I was reminded of my first visit to the college years before when it was in session and Dr. Joseph Angus was presiding. He treated me with great cordiality and entertained me at the college dinner. The students were seated on the outside of three tables parallel to three sides of the room. At the center of the middle table sat Mrs. Angus. I was at her right, and Dr. Angus was at her left. Mrs. Angus carved for all those thirty or forty students, and the butler carried the portions from her to them. After the meat and the vegetables were served, that official, to my immense surprise, also distributed beer from a pewter pitcher. At the close of the dinner all rose. Dr. Angus made of me some inarticulate request. I was just about to be embarrassed by their all standing in silence. Fortunately it occurred to me just in time that this was grace after meat. I said my few words of thanks, and the trying exercise was over.

A visit to Mr. Spurgeon was even more memorable. I had written the great preacher a note saying that I wished to bring Mr. Rockefeller to see him. He replied very graciously that the outing for the students of his college was to take place at his house the following day and that he would be happy to see us on that occasion. So we took the train past the Crystal Palace at Sydenham and reached Norwood at about eleven o'clock in the morning. Mr. Spurgeon met us in a slouch hat and a yellow linen duster—an inappropriate and a rather ungainly attire for a festival occasion. But he was very cordial. He gathered his students in the lea of his large and beautiful house. Chairs were placed for all. He named a hymn and lined it out with a couplet at a time, the students singing with enthusiasm. Then he offered a fervent prayer. There should have followed the "Question and Answer Meeting," a peculiar exercise in which, on these outing days, he was accustomed to give his students opportunity to put to him the most varied inquiries about marriage, etiquette, politics, history, church discipline, or pulpit delivery. He rose, as I supposed, to begin this meeting, and I was expecting to be greatly entertained by it. But he remarked simply that they had with them a noted preacher and theological writer from America and that they would now be pleased to have an address from him. I was never in my life so taken aback. Without the slightest opportunity for thinking over what I should say, I was forced to rise and speak. Fortunately I bethought me of the address on "Zeal" which I had given to my own graduates a month or two before. The substance, though not the form of it, remained with me. I reproduced it as well as I could, and it seemed to meet the demand of the occasion. I was unspeakably thankful that I was not left to be confounded in the presence of Mr. Spurgeon and his college.

When I sat down, our host told his students that the "Question and Answer Meeting" would be postponed until the afternoon. In the meantime they were invited to play cricket or wander round the estate. He devoted the two hours' interval to Mr. Rockefeller and me. He took us through his house and library; showed us the albums in which were preserved the caricatures of his early ministry, one of them representing him as a donkey haranguing a crowd from a platform; introduced us to Mrs. Spurgeon, who sat in an invalid's chair; showed us through the grounds; finally conducted us to an arbor, and there told us the story of his acquisition of the place. We plied him with questions. He responded very freely and simply; warmed with the recital of his experiences in receiving answers to prayer, he showed us how childlike was his faith. We had from his own lips the account of the building of the Tabernacle and the giving of the sum required by a man whom he had never seen until the day he gave it. Little things as well as great he carried to God in prayer. His wife had once a desire for an emerald ring. He took the matter to the Lord, and next day a jeweler unexpectedly sent her for a present the very ring she had set her heart on. We concluded that the secret of Mr. Spurgeon's success was his piety and his faith. Above all things else he seemed to be a man of prayer. Afterwards with our whole party we visited the orphanage. It was a pretty sight when the three hundred orphans gathered round him as if he had been their father. Mr. Rockefeller made a nice little address to the children and left a donation for the school. We hardly thought, when we left him, that his career in the ministry would so soon be ended. But even then he was struggling with the disease which was destined to bring him to his grave.

It was the time of the Oxford Commemoration. As I had never attended that unique celebration, I wrote to the vice-chancellor for tickets, which were courteously sent me by return mail. Charles accompanied me on my visit. We found the Sheldonian Theatre crowded from floor to attic, the upper gallery filled with students, the lower gallery with ladies and visitors. On the floor there were no seats; everybody stood, and the space was packed except where an aisle was kept clear for the procession of dignitaries. Soon the dons came in with their varicolored gowns and hoods. Then the vice-chancellor from the pulpit began a Latin address. "Speak up louder, sir!" sang out an undergraduate from the upper gallery. The vice-chancellor was the most dignified official of the university, but he could not prevent a smile from stealing over his features. "Take off that Jubilee smile!" returned another voice from the gallery. So to the end of his speech the head of the great institution sailed through stormy seas, interrupted at almost every sentence by some bit of undergraduate impertinence. It was the one day of all the year when by common consent and tradition the student tongue was let loose and pandemonium reigned. The impudence of it all was unspeakable. It seemed to me to argue a nerve that was without limits. Occasionally there was something like wit, but for the most part it was broad horseplay, interesting only as an exhibition of unblushing effrontery.

When the Latin orator of the day began his oration, it did my soul good to find that he adhered to the English method of pronunciation. It was *Consul Romānus* and *Victoria Regīna,* as when I studied Latin of old. *Victoria Regīna* provoked an instant outburst of applause. The whole audience in the galleries rose to their feet and began singing the national anthem: "God save our Gracious Queen!" The great organ joined its thunders to the chorus, and the scene was thrilling. As it was the Jubilee year, the demonstration seemed spontaneous and sincere. Sarcastic remarks about the orator's Latin were interjected at nearly every pause. I thought that worthy must be grateful when his performance came to an end. When the candidates were presented for their degrees, the real fun of the occasion began. Every one of them was saluted with some quip from the students. The first was Arthur Wellesley Peel, Speaker of the House of Commons. As he came forward to receive his D.C.L., someone from the gallery began to sing:

> He's a jolly good fellow,
> He's a jolly good fellow,
> He's a jolly good fellow
> Is Arthur Wellesley Peel!

and the whole student body of a thousand or more joined in the chorus, the investiture being suspended until the chorus was concluded.

Mr. Bryce, professor of history and author of *The American Commonwealth,* presented the candidates to the vice-chancellor in brief Latin addresses which recited their various gifts and services. Maspere, the Egyptologist; Gray, the botanist; Story, the sculptor (the last two Americans) were among the men honored. Robert Browning was present in the procession, with his doctor's hood and gown, though the dignity had been conferred upon him some years before, a red cotton nightcap being let down upon his head from the gallery above in allusion to his poem of that name. When Tennyson received the degree, his unkempt hair provoked the salutation, "Did your mother call you too early this morning, Alfred, dear?" And Oliver Wendell Holmes was affectionately asked, "Did you come in a 'One Hoss Shay'?" In all the fun of Commemoration Day, I noticed no sign of ill feeling except when someone proposed three cheers for the "Grand Old Man." Instead of cheers, there followed a storm of hisses, which showed that at this particular time Mr. William Gladstone was far from popular at Oxford.

We made a hurried trip to Stratford-on-Avon, Kenilworth, and Warwick, and then to Chester, Hawarden, and Eton Hall. Hawarden was extremely interesting as the home of Mr. Gladstone, Eton Hall as the palace of the Duke of Westminster, the richest man in England. Since my first visit in 1859, Eton Hall had been wholly rebuilt, at a cost, it was said, of fifteen to twenty million dollars. As the family were absent, we were shown through it from end to end.

It seemed to me the most beautiful house in the world. The library, the drawing-room, the chapel, and the entrance hall were all wonderful in their way. Most of the palaces of Europe are oppressive in their stateliness; the marbles have a chilling effect; there is no air of comfort; they are the last places in the world where one would desire to live. But at Eton Hall the architect has evidently aimed to combine grandeur and homelikeness. There is warmth of color. There are no end of cozy nooks. Every room is made for actual habitation. A long corridor connecting two parts of the edifice was adorned on either side with stained-glass windows representing scenes by Millais from Tennyson's *Idylls of the King*. The library had not only a great array of books in many-colored bindings, but also it had desks and easy chairs, rugs and electric lights, to make study delightful. The chapel was a gem of Gothic architecture. The stables were models of horse keeping. The hothouses and gardens, the lawns and fountains were all beautiful in themselves and fitted to enhance the beauty of the great house to which they ministered. If the many mansions of the Father's house above are more beautiful than this one, they must be beautiful indeed.

We had some noble tallyho rides through the Lake Country of England and a charming visit to Grasmere and the church where Wordsworth is buried. We read a fine-print Testament by daylight at ten o'clock in the evening as we were entering Glasgow by rail. Our steamboat ride through Loch Lomond in the early morning and our carriage ride through the Trossachs were both memorable. Edinburgh detained us two or three days. The unexampled beauty of its situation impressed me more than at my first visit. It was manifestly the Castle Rock that first caused men to settle here. Like the Acropolis of Athens, it served an excellent purpose for defense, and the city grew up around it. Salisbury Crags and Arthur's Seat were now accessible by a fine carriage road. We drove to the top and then walked down. John Rockefeller, Jr., lingered behind. When we got to the bottom, we were alarmed at seeing him coming down the face of the cliff. As he made his way from ledge to ledge, getting into places of extreme danger and apparently ready at times to fall over the precipice, our hearts almost stood still within us, and when he landed among us safe and sound, a great sigh of relief was heard. Little John was daring, but that time he risked too much.

Abbotsford and Durham and York claimed our attention in turn. At last we reached London and started for the Continent. Brussels, Antwerp, Cologne, and the Rhine followed in quick succession. Then a resting spell at Wiesbaden, one of the loveliest of German watering places. The long line of visitors waiting for their warm draught at the spring before breakfast, while the orchestra discoursed fine music, was a novel sight to me. The baths sunk in the pavement and fed from the same hot spring were also new. Charming paths around the lake and under the trees invited one's feet. Art had done its utmost to make nature attractive. For a honeymoon, commend me to Wiesbaden. Eisenach and the Wartburg attracted us next, and neither of them had I seen before. The old medieval castle, now restored in even more than its original magnificence by the German government, presents a striking picture of the past. Luther's imprisonment here was overruled for the translation of the Bible as Paul's imprisonments were overruled for the writing of his great epistles. From Eisenach we went to Berlin. There, upon Dr. Biggar's invitation, I attended a clinic of the medical department of the university and saw one of the most wonderful operations of modern surgery. That the human body could be turned inside out, repaired, and put together again as good as new excited my astonishment and admiration. And the great university with its fifty-five hundred students seemed almost the greatest product of civilization.

Alas, that German civilization has not put woman in her proper place. In Berlin on a Sunday afternoon I saw a great building going up, and a woman was carrying a hod of mortar on her shoulder straight up a ladder to the third story. From the window of a railway carriage I saw women shoveling earth into wheelbarrows to make embankments and other women yoked with horses to the plow. Yet at this very time, women in England were taking the highest mathematical honors of Cambridge, and in some of our American states they were granted the right of suffrage. I confess that my views with regard to the position of women have changed during the last quarter of a century. I was once inclined to deny them the franchise. But I have come to see that in Christ there is neither male nor female. Woman is the natural equal of man. Christ lifts her out of the degradation to which sin has consigned her. She has a right to use all her powers of speech and of influence. If she can speak in public so as to win others to truth and righteousness, she has no right to hide her light under a bushel. I believe that women will not only vote, but I also believe that they will preach the gospel. The power of the ministry will be doubled when the women enter it. Let us call out the reserves in the battle with iniquity. Women can take part in the struggle with sin without losing the modesty or subordination which Paul enjoins. When the Holy Spirit takes possession of humanity, our sons and our daughters will alike prophesy.

After a visit to Potsdam and the simple home of the Emperor William, we took the train for Dresden and Vienna. Dresden I have spoken of before. Vienna had changed greatly. The old walls had been replaced by the Ringstrasse, a magnificent boulevard encircling the town, lined with edifices not excelled in Europe for nobility and beauty. We drove through the Prater, and visited Schönbrunn. The galleries of pictures, jewels, and armor were superb. But the most interesting incident of our stay in Vienna was our attendance upon the service of the poor, persecuted Baptists. It was hard to find the place. No steeple, bell, or placard of any sort was permitted. For every meeting permission had to be obtained from the police. We drove to a remote corner of the city, passed through a gateway and an inner court, and lifted an iron knocker which resounded far and wide. A timid person opened the door in a way to intimate suspicion. When we had explained who we were, we were conducted through a long corridor to the place of assemblage. There from fifty to a hundred people were gathered. They seemed alarmed at our entrance, as if they feared a visit from the police and possible arrest. But when they learned that we were Baptists from America, their joy was great. Representatives of the Baptist seminary at Hamburg had preached to them and had told them of America and the strength of their brethren there. They begged me to speak to them. I had never made a German speech in my life. But I got up on my feet and began. When I lacked a word, I appealed to my audience to supply it. Their sympathy helped me wonderfully. I did what I never would have thought possible—I spoke twenty minutes to them in German. It was such German as never was heard on this planet before. But it answered the purpose. My auditors were satisfied, and when Mr. Rockefeller left a generous contribution for their work, they were delighted. That afternoon's experience made me appreciate the blessings of religious freedom. Liberty to worship God according to the dictates of one's own conscience, without let or hindrance and with none to molest or make afraid, is found almost nowhere on earth but in the United States of America.

From Vienna we went to Switzerland by way of Salzburg and Innsbruck—places so picturesque that we wished to stay in them instead of leaving them. The Vorarlberg Railway, with its eight- or nine-mile tunnel, presented a constant succession of surprises in the way of splendid scenery. We spent a night on the Rigi and had a fine sunrise. Two guests increased our party to fifteen. We had all the front rooms on the first floor of the Rigikulm Hotel, including a beautiful salon where our dinner and breakfast were served. There were wax candles and flowers in plenty, though we were eight thousand feet above the sea. When we came to depart, the bill was about ninety dollars for supper, lodging, and breakfast. Mr. Rockefeller demurred and paid it under protest. I tried in vain to convince him that if he had had the same accommodations at the Grand Union Hotel at Saratoga Springs, he would have had to pay more. Private parlor, sumptuous dinner, wax candles, and flowers on the top of a mountain are not to be had for nothing. Six dollars apiece did not seem to me an exorbitant charge. But Mr. Rockefeller was on his guard against extortion. The innkeepers informed one another of his coming. The newspapers announced the arrival of the "Petroleum King." It is no wonder that he sometimes suspected a conspiracy against his pocketbook. When one of the Georges of England was charged a guinea apiece for eggs, he asked the innkeeper if eggs were so scarce. "No, your Majesty," was the reply, "but kings are!"

We took horses from Grindelwald and spent the night on the Wengern Alp. Long before sunrise I went out to look at the Jungfrau. Not a single cloud hid her face. She looked down upon me in chilly majesty. It was a solemn hour as I stood alone opposite those ramparts of eternal snow. I went back to my bed to get warm, but I was soon roused by the guide, who called me to an early breakfast. We rode down the breakneck path to Lauterbrunnen, wondering how our horses could possibly avoid stumbling and throwing us over their heads and down the precipices that were so close at hand. We went on to Berne, Freiburg, and Geneva, with an excursion to Chamonix in a beautiful tallyho coach, and an experience in the inside of a glacier. This last is worth describing, for it was something unique. A tunnel had been dug into the ice, and at the end of the tunnel a circular room had been constructed. It was illuminated by candles. The ice was pale green and transparent, but it was so thick that no light of the sun entered there. Chilly and dripping, it was a chamber of death. Though it had a beauty of its own, we were glad to leave it and put off the wraps we had encased ourselves in to protect us from the wet and the cold.

All the way back to Geneva, we had magnificent views. At Sallenaches especially, Mont Blanc unveiled himself completely for our benefit. We took a sleeping car from Geneva to Paris. It was a sleeping car of the French fashion—a combination of the compartment and the berth—more stuffy and inconvenient than tongue can tell. There was little sleep that night, and it took two or three days at the Continental Hotel in Paris to restore us. We attended the Baptist church in the Rue du Bac and the McAll Mission near the Madelaine. But we also attended the Café des Ambassadeurs, one of the most famous *cafés chantants* of the capital. We made a delightful tallyho excursion to Versailles. But to me the most important incident of my Parisian experience was the conversation I had with Mr. Rockefeller with regard to a university. My great object in going with him to Europe had been to secure an opportunity to talk with him upon this subject. He had promised me to listen to whatever I might wish to say. For the three months since we left home, I had been expecting him to give me the chance. But he seemed to postpone and to postpone, until my heart grew sick. I prayed day and night about the matter. I suppose my very anxiety hurt my cause. I ought to have thrown off care. I ought to have devoted myself to the amusement of the party. More faith would have made me more cheerful and would have made my message more agreeable when I delivered it.

It was only through Mrs. Rockefeller that I finally secured a hearing at all, and that not until we were about to leave Paris. Then Mr. Rockefeller appointed a morning and gave ear to my tale. He showed no signs of being impressed by it at the time. But Mr.

Chauncey Depew was at the hotel, and I made Mr. Rockefeller acquainted with him. So Mr. Depew was invited one evening to our salon. A discussion followed. I proved to Mr. Depew that there were more Yale graduates in the College of Physicians and Surgeons than in the Yale Medical School, more Yale graduates in the Columbia College Law School than in the Yale Law School, and more Yale graduates in the Union Theological Seminary than in the Yale Divinity School. I drew the inference that New York City and not New Haven was the place for a great university. Columbia College had not then become a university. A few millions could at that time establish a post-graduate institution superior to anything then existing in America. I knew more about the subject than Mr. Depew did, and I thought I gained an easy victory. But Mr. Rockefeller seemed convinced against his will. I thought it my duty to address him once more on the homebound steamer. I told him that God had laid this burden upon me and that I could not rest until I had laid it upon him. Still he seemed to listen unwillingly. It was not till I reached home that I received a letter from him asking if his paying the interest on three million dollars and making the principal a lien upon his estate would make the beginning of such a university possible. I replied, of course, in the affirmative. But the university was established in Chicago, not in New York. Columbia College now has possession of the very site which I urged Mr. Rockefeller to purchase, and it has taken the very steps toward post-graduate instruction which I urged Mr. Rockefeller to take. Baptists lost this one great opportunity to get a foothold and exert an influence in New York. The Greater New York, with its population of three million, the second largest city in the world, still has not the vestige of a Baptist institution of learning, and without such an institution, either university or theological seminary, it is difficult to see how we can ever reach a position such as the Presbyterians and Episcopalians now hold. But Chicago gained what New York lost. My prayers were answered, not in my way but in God's way. I still live in hope that the growing weakness of our cause in New York may convince Mr. Rockefeller of his duty to the metropolis in which he lives. He cannot lay his responsibility upon others nor transfer it to the next generation. I try to think that the day of New York's redemption will yet come and that it was not in vain that for so many years I carried on my heart a burden for that great city. Chicago, with all its success, is not the complete answer to my prayers, though the university there makes me glad that in Paris and on shipboard I set before Mr. Rockefeller his obligation to Christ and to the cause of education.

8

Habits
and
Associations

During all that tour of one hundred days I wrote every single day a letter to my wife at home. I have always had a certain facility in letter writing, and this has made my administrative work easier than it otherwise would have been. My habit for many years has been to answer letters, if possible, the instant they were received. Instead of letting them lie till no answer was needed, I have found it better to get them off my hands at once. In fact, my general principle has been always to do the hardest thing first, for the reason that postponement of duty makes duty all the harder to perform. I have gotten through much work by dint of resolutely setting at whatever I had on hand. Someone asked Dr. Samuel Johnson whether he should wait for the Muse or should begin at once to write. "Sit down, and write doggedly!" was his reply. I have found that the Muse favored when I did hard work. The first few pages of an essay or an address cost me much toil of brain and heart: when I once get to going, all is easy, and I wind up with a rush. Things grow, moreover, as they are pondered. My best productions are those which have been worked over many times. The first suggestion has often come to me on waking in the morning. I have put the thought into a brief prayer meeting talk, then into a sermon, finally, in expanded and elaborate form into an essay for publication.

In my earlier ministerial life I was physically weak and felt the need of some stimulant to give me strength. Coffee and tea played a considerable part in my plan of life. Later experience has changed my views. I have come to think that it is better to rely simply on my natural strength. Coffee and tea seem now to scatter my powers instead of increasing them; indeed, they often induce a premature excitement which exhausts and prevent me from being fully master of myself when the time of trial comes. There is another and a very important side to the matter—I mean the religious side. Trusting in adventitious aids is often renunciation of the aid of the Holy Spirit. Simple diet, regular and abundant sleep, and vigorous exercise are the best guarantees of a sound mind when these are accompanied by simple dependence upon God. I have derived great advantage from my summer vacations, even though I have accomplished in them work that could not be done at other times of the year. I have tried to foresee the claims that would be made upon me and to prepare beforehand the required addresses or essays. The results appear in part in my two books, *Philosophy and Religion,* dedicated to Mr. Rockefeller, and *The Great Poets and Their Theology,*[1] dedicated to my wife, as I had previously dedicated my *Systematic Theology* to Mr. Trevor. The book about poets represents the vacation work of thirteen consecutive years. I do not know that I should ever have been led to undertake it had it not been for the influence of the Browning Club. But before I speak of the Browning Club, I must speak of the "Pundit Club," so called, with which I have been longer connected.

So early as 1872, when I first assumed the charge of the seminary, I was asked to join "The Club"—for it has no other name, the title "Pundit Club" being simply a popular one given it by outsiders who hold *omne ignotum pro mirifico.* Theodore Bacon, of whom I have already spoken, conveyed to me the news of my election and said, when he urged me to accept, that nobody who was

---

[1] *The Great Poets and Their Theology* (Philadelphia: American Baptist Publication Society, 1897). Hereafter abbreviated *Great Poets.*

invited ever declined. I did not decline, and The Club, next to the seminary and the church, has been my greatest source of profit and enjoyment in Rochester. When I first united with it, The Club had a notable and varied membership. President Anderson and Dr. Kendrick, with Professors Lattimore and Mixer, represented the university. Dr. Buckland, Dr. Wilkinson, and I represented the seminary. Drs. Moore and Dean stood for the medical fraternity, Drs. Ely and Stoddard being later additions. Judge Danforth and Messrs. Bacon, Whittlesey, and Durand were lawyers. Then there were E. Peshine Smith and Lewis H. Morgan, both of them, I believe, originally members of the legal profession, but in their later years given to scientific and literary work. Samuel D. Porter was a retired businessman and an amateur theologian. Professor Morey and Professor Dodge of the university are adepts in history and in biology, respectively. All of these men had views of their own and were not at all loath to express them. The collision of opinion was often very sharp, but I do not know that there was ever a quarrel. Each man presented a yearly paper, generally in the line of his specialty. Each man entertained the club at his house during the year. The meetings were fortnightly from the beginning of November to the end of May. It can easily be imagined that intercourse with such men was stimulating and broadening.

For many years the only stimulant was the feast of reason and the flow of soul. Wine was rigorously excluded. Of late we have fallen from grace, and some members furnish wine. I hardly know what the result would have been if this had been done in the early days. Mr. E. Peshine Smith loved wine altogether too well. It was said of him that he read the Latin breviary as soon as he rose every morning and went to bed drunk every night. I need to correct what I have said. It was not wine but whiskey to which he was specially addicted. He was a unique compound of pure intellect and Bourbon whiskey. When someone in his presence used the phrase "bad whiskey," he seemed grieved and replied, "Don't apply any slighting epithets to whiskey. Whiskey has, I grant, various degrees of goodness. But there is no whiskey that is absolutely bad!" One of his friends died of drunkenness. E. Peshine simply remarked, "I told him so. He drank brandy. Why, if that man had only drunk whiskey, he would have lived forever!" Mr. Smith was a strong protectionist and wrote a *Political Economy* in the interest of protection. He was the right-hand man of William H. Seward in the State Department at Washington during our Civil War. He became legal adviser of the Japanese government after our war was over and for ten years lived in great style at Tokyo. Then he came home with the money he had saved and spent the last years of his life in Rochester.

Lewis H. Morgan was an original investigator in ethnology. Having property sufficient to support him, he early interested himself in the American Indians. He lived together with them for months, was adopted into a tribe, and received an Indian name. In Michigan he studied the habits of the beaver and wrote an exhaustive monograph upon the subject. His *League of the Iroquois* was followed by *Systems of Consanguinity and Affinity of the Human Family.* In this latter work, which was published by the Smithsonian Institution, he gave the results of most extensive correspondence with consuls and missionaries in the remotest parts of the globe, all tending to show, as he believed, that descent was originally and universally traced in the female line and that the family is a later development from primeval promiscuity. As this fell in with the Darwinian theory of man's derivation from the brute, it gave Mr. Morgan a high rank among scientific men. More recently, however, the drift has been in the other direction, and now Westermarck, in his *History of Human Marriage,* can say: "Marriage is rooted in the family rather than the family in marriage."[2] Westermarck concludes that there is no evidence that promiscuity was ever a stage in the social history of mankind. Thus the hypothesis of promiscuity has no real foundation. Mr. Morgan was a man of ardent temperament, a born fighter, and a most picturesque talker. He loved The Club and he built a library like Walter Scott's at Abbottsford in which to entertain The Club. Only one or two meetings were held there, one of them, as Mr. Whittlesey called it, "a lodge of sorrow" in commemoration of its twenty-fifth anniversary. It had not been intended to make it a mournful occasion, but inasmuch as mention was to be made of the

---

[2] Edward Westermarck, *The History of Human Marriage* (New York: The Allerton Book Company, 1922), vol. 1, p. 72.

deceased members, it was thought best to invite their widows to be present. The result was a most lachrymose and funereal meeting. This took place in 1879, and in 1881 Mr. Morgan himself died, so that the great library room has been since then almost unused.

It is not my purpose to speak of more than one other member of The Club, and that shall be Dr. Edward M. Moore. Dr. Moore was built upon a large pattern, both physically and mentally. He had calmness and sweetness of mind combined with unusual gifts of speech. He seemed naturally benevolent, as a man of Quaker ancestry should be. He was interested in every phase of science, but his specialty was surgery, and in this he had no superior in western New York. He lectured for years in the medical college at Buffalo, and his practice at home was very large. It is safe to say that no citizen of Rochester was better known or loved. He was a man of public spirit. On our board of health he rendered invaluable service. He rectified our whole system of sewers, helped greatly in introducing our waterworks, and practically superintended the laying out of our public parks. He was a lover of nature. I wish I could say that he was a Christian. This he was not, in the technical sense, for a materialistic and agnostic philosophy had captured him. But he was a lover of his kind and a worker for the welfare of man, as he conceived it. It has always been a problem to me where to classify Dr. Moore. I am inclined to say that he was one of those whom Christ taught, though he did not know it; that his opposition to dogmatic Christianity was the result of what the Romanists call "invincible ignorance"; that in his heart after all was hid a reverence for God and for truth. His noble nature was superior to petty hatreds; he advocated education and every true reform; he was candid and a lover of peace. In spite of his so-called infidelity, I hope to see him in the New Jerusalem.

For some years after coming to Rochester I devoted myself so exclusively to my proper work that I gave no time to society. About the year 1884, however, I was asked to join the Browning Club, a company of ladies and gentlemen who met at Mrs. George W. Fisher's on Troup Street every Friday afternoon from the beginning of Lent to the end of April. I had never read Browning to any considerable extent. Years before, I had tried *The Ring and the Book,* but its uncouthness had repelled me, and I had given it up in despair. Professor J. H. Gilmore's readings in the Browning Club first gave me a suspicion that I was wrong. I made another trial, beginning with *Saul* and some of the easier poems. Little by little I came to see that here was a new elemental force in literature. The roughness became an evidence of originality and vigor. Going to the Browning Club to scoff, I remained to pray. I read extensively and with increasing avidity. Before the end of the year I had concluded that Browning was one of the greatest teachers of our time, the representative of a new philosophy, the poet of optimism. I put the results of my reflection into an essay which I presented to both the Browning Club and the Pundit Club and delivered as a lecture at Canandaigua, Elmira, and Poughkeepsie. I have never changed my opinion since then. More than ten years after this first essay on Browning as a poet, I wrote a second on Browning as a philosophical and religious teacher, and the two together now form the chapter on "Browning, His Philosophy and His Theology" in my book on *The Great Poets*.[3]

In successive years the need of presenting an essay to the Browning Club led me to study other poets, always with a view to ascertaining their theological opinions. I made my summer vacations the time of preparatory work. At "The Lodge" at Cook's Point, quite a number of cultivated people gathered for an hour each morning, and I read to them from some great poet. One year we went through *The Divine Comedy* of Dante. The next year we took up the *Iliad* of Homer and the following year his *Odyssey*. Then came two years of Shakespeare, one year of Milton, one each devoted to Goethe, Wordsworth, and Tennyson. Each summer I wrote out an essay on the poet then under consideration. Next spring I read this essay to the Browning Club and to the Pundit Club as well. So gradually, without my intending it at the start, a book grew up upon my hands. I conceived the idea of printing it. It has now appeared from the press of our Publication Society; they gave me six hundred dollars for the manuscript and a royalty of twenty cents on each volume sold after the first thousand. After the lapse of thirteen years, it surprises me that I could ever have gone through with all the necessary work. I built better than I knew. Providence had more to do with it than I had.

[3] *Great Poets,* pp. 373-447.

Alvah Strong Hall, Rochester Theological Seminary, completed in 1907. It was mainly a dormitory and also contained some faculty offices, including Rauschenbusch's.

Even though no one else had benefited by it, the Browning Club has certainly been a great advantage to me. It has held me for all these years to the continuous study of the poets. I have become convinced that God has not left these great teachers of the world without the influence of his Spirit. They witness with wonderful unanimity to the great truths of natural religion, and they confirm the Christian faith. Some of the pleasantest social events of my life have been the discussions in the parlors of Mrs. G. W. Fisher. Dr. Kendrick, Mr. and Mrs. O'Connor, Dr. and Mrs. Millard, Mr. Peck, Mr. McElroy, Mrs. Hopkins, and Dr. Pattison have all added thought and brilliancy to the meetings. It has been a liberal education to the best women of the city. And through the Browning Club I have come to know some noble women whom perhaps I should otherwise have missed, such as Mrs. John H. Rochester, Mrs. Gilman H. Perkins, Mrs. Edward Meigs Smith, Mrs. Oothout, Mrs. Stoddard, Mrs. O'Hare, and Mrs. George Hollister. Some of these women have proved to be true friends, and acquaintance with them has added to the interest and enjoyment of life. Mrs. Fisher, the patron and hostess of the Browning Club, has won for herself a good degree by the persistence and devotion with which she has kept the club together through so many successive years and has provided at great cost to herself so excellent a series of studies in English literature.

Alph Chi—Christian Brothers—is a society, now half a dozen years old, of city ministers and professors, which meets once each month on Thursday afternoon for a paper and discussion on some philosophical or theological theme. After the paper and discussion comes dinner at the Powers Hotel. We are together from half-past-four to half-past-seven o'clock. Dr. Stewart and Mr. Anderson of the Baptist pastors, Drs. Millard, Stebbins, Taylor, and Hutton of the Presbyterians, Professors Forbes, Fairchild, and Burton from the university, and Professors Stevens, Pattison, and I from the seminary at present make up the membership. President Hill, Dr. Robins, Professor True, and Dr. Lattimore have been members, but they have now withdrawn. There is the utmost frankness and freedom in the expression of conviction. The tendency is in the direction of a liberal theology. But I have been grateful for the opportunity of learning the drift of thought in other denominations as well as for the opportunity of defending the old theology in the presence of men who are inclined to depreciate it. More and more I have become convinced that modern science and philosophy are raising up new buttresses for the Christian faith. Natural law shows the immutability of moral law; heredity is the modern proof of original sin; the derivation of all physical life from Adam makes probable the derivation of all spiritual life from Christ. In spite of the avowal of many doubts and the suggestion of many objections to current theology, the Alpha Chi has done much to confirm this faith of its members and to make their preaching more intelligent.

For several years I have been a member of the Rochester Historical Society, and for two years I was its president. The society was formed in the house of Mrs. Gilman H. Perkins, largely through her influence. She furnished simple refreshments at the close of each meeting and made the occasion genuinely social. Dr. E. M. Moore presided for the first two years. One old resident after another related stories of the past. My own recollection was quickened. A hundred things that I had forgotten revived. The burial places of memory gave up their dead. Many things narrated in the early part of this autobiography would probably never have been recorded if the Rochester Historical Society had not freshened my wits. During the two years of my presidency I exercised a large liberty with regard to my own participation in the meetings. I made them interesting, whether I stuck to history or not. The membership and the attendance increased; additions were made to the library and museum, and many facts of importance were rescued from oblivion. Such a society may contribute much to the public spirit of a city, may preserve relics of the past, may teach the new generation how much it owes to the industry, faith, and patience of the generations that sleep beneath the sod.

In 1892 I was elected president of the American Baptist Missionary Union, and I presided at the three meetings of the great organization at Denver, Colorado, in 1893, and at Saratoga Springs in 1894 and 1895. To prepare myself for this, I had to give new study to parliamentary law. For three years I taught the subject in the theological seminary. We had a Seminary Congress which met once a week. With all manner of mock propositions and dilatory motions, the task of the chairman was no easy one, but it gave me the practice I needed. At Saratoga the debates on the adoption of amendments to the constitution and of the report on education abroad required all my knowledge and all my tact. I made one or two mistakes, but I ruled the Union with a rod of iron, and no one appealed from the decisions of the chair. The business was put through with celerity. I felt that I had really served the missionary cause by wielding "that fierce democratie." In the spring of 1895 the Presbyterian General Assembly met in Saratoga at the same time with the Missionary Union. I was appointed to represent our denomination in conveying to the Presbyterians an expression of fraternal feeling. Dr. Hovey and Dr. Northrup accompanied me. It was a trying occasion. I was assured that my speech met the demands of the hour. When the Presbyterian deputation came to address us, I received them and introduced them to the Union. Though I greatly shrank from such publicity, I was helped from above.

The three elaborate addresses which I made in successive years in opening the sessions of the Union cost me much labor in preparation. As a president usually holds office for three years, by being twice reelected, I bethought me that the relations of the missionary cause to the persons of the Trinity furnished me with an appropriate theme. The subject of the first address was "The Decree of God the Great Encouragement to Missions." The second was entitled "The Love of Christ the Great Motive to Missions." The third: "The Holy Spirit the One and Only Power in Missions."[4] Ethical monism was beginning to take possession of my thoughts, and these three addresses were tinged with it. They provoked some criticism, but they also awakened enthusiasm. As with Paul's hearers at Rome, some believed and some disbelieved. I have always been glad that I attended a New England clambake, because I knew that I should never have to do that thing again. So I am glad that I have once been president of the American Baptist Missionary Union. Lightning never strikes twice in the same place, and that honor will never be mine again.

The degree of Doctor of Divinity was conferred upon me by Brown University in 1870, as I have already related. In 1891,

---

[4] These lectures appeared in *Christ in Creation*, pp. 268-283, 284-296, and 297-313.

Bucknell University gave me the degree of Doctor of Laws. My alma mater Yale, in 1892, made me a Doctor of Divinity over again, Dr. A. J. F. Behrends receiving the same honor at the same time. I valued quite highly this mark of appreciation from my own college, especially since my theology was so unlike that taught at the Yale Divinity School. I have thought it probably due to the affectionate regard of President Noah Porter though, at the time it was conferred, he had already demitted his office. But perhaps the greatest public honor I have received was the conferring of this same degree of Doctor of Divinity in 1896 by Princeton at her Sesquicentennial Anniversary, when she branched out from a college into a university. For some time I hesitated about going to receive it, lest it might seem to disparage my doctorate at Yale. I had, moreover, to purchase a gown, hood, and cap, which altogether cost sixty or eighty dollars. I smothered my scruples, however, and landed in Princeton on the morning of the ceremony armed and equipped as the law directed. Then I was glad I had come, for I found a great array of dignitaries. I stood up to receive the degree with Dr. George P. Fisher, my old teacher at Yale, Dr. Thayer of Harvard, Dr. Riddle of the Western Theological Seminary at Pittsburgh, Drs. W. R. Huntington and Morgan Dix of New York, Bishop Hurst of the Methodist Episcopal Church, Dr. Mead of Hartford, Dr. Caven of Toronto, and some others. Among those who received the degree of Doctor of Laws were Professors Newcomb, Remsen, Rowland, and President Gilman of Johns Hopkins; Professor Dörpfeld of Berlin; Professor Moissan, the maker of artificial diamonds, from the University of Paris; Professor Andrew Seth from Edinburgh; Professors Gibbs, Ladd, and Lounsbury from Yale; Professor James from Harvard; Hale from Chicago; Wheeler from Cornell; Dowden from Dublin; Goldwin Smith and Thomson from Oxford; Langley from the Smithsonian Institution in Washington; Le Conte from Stanford University in California; W. T. Harris, the Commissioner of Education; President Angell of Michigan; President Low of Columbia; Dudley Warner and R. H. Gilder of the literary fraternity; H. C. Lea and Weir Mitchell from Philadelphia; and Professor Young of Princeton.

The procession that moved to Alexander Hall was very impressive. All the candidates for degrees had been invested with hoods lined with the Princeton orange. They followed the president of the university, who had at his right Grover Cleveland, the president of the United States. The platform was reserved for these two presidents and for the fifty men more or less, who were to receive degrees. As the procession filed in, clad in cap and gown, the audience rose to honor the guests of the university. The ground floor was filled with other guests and former graduates, all attired in a similar way. An outer circle of rising seats was occupied by ladies, and the gallery above was crowded by more than a thousand students. The scene reminded me of the Oxford Commemoration, though it was more serious. President Patton, after conducting President Cleveland to a chair of haircloth and mahogany at his right hand, sat down upon a sort of alabaster throne which reminded me of Milton's description of a very different personage in *Paradise Lost:*

> High on a throne of royal state, which far
> Outshone the wealth of Ormus and of Ind,
> Or where the gorgeous east with richest hand,
> Showers on her kings barbaric pearl and gold,
> Satan exalted sat, by merit raised
> To that bad eminence. . . .

This was no bad eminence, however, for President Patton. He deserved his place not only by administrative ability but also by great services as a defender of the faith. His manner on this occasion was dignified. As each man received his degree, he was saluted with applause from the gallery. He then turned and shook hands with President Patton. After the degrees had been conferred, Dr. Patton made a brief address and introduced the president of the United States. Mr. Cleveland was the only one without hood or gown. Dr. Thayer of Harvard sat next to me. During the previous exercises he whispered, "Don't you think that Grover looks bored?" I replied, "No, he looks awe-stricken!" When he rose to address that academic audience, so different from the ordinary political gatherings he was used to, it seemed to me that he fairly shook in his boots. But the reception that was given him encouraged him. When a thousand students try to make a noise, they usually succeed. And they succeeded now. The president stood for quite a time before the applause subsided. Then he began in a voice that fairly trembled. But he had hardly spoken a single sentence before the applause was renewed. He found that the audience was with him. It was just before the presidential election. Bryan was running on the free-silver ticket. There was danger that the Democratic party would be carried over to the side of practical repudiation of national obligations. Mr. Cleveland had not before uttered himself. It soon became evident that he had chosen this occasion to stand for financial honor and public faith. With his ponderous rhetoric he yet combined a clear head and an indomitable courage. The applause soon changed his uncertain manner into one of strength and boldness. His voice grew large and oratorical. He was moved himself, and he swayed his hearers. I have never seen an academic audience so carried away. Grover Cleveland must have thought it the greatest success of his life. I do not wonder that he has since concluded to make his residence in Princeton. That night there was a torch-light procession with transparencies, one of which read, "Send your boys to Princeton, Grover!" As Mr. Cleveland had only girls, he nudged his wife as she sat by his side. She evidently took the hint, for now a son has been born to them in Princeton.

For twenty-three years I had occupied the old family mansion on South Carolina Street. It was never large enough for my purpose. Six children and two servants filled up all the rooms. I had no proper study. The little reception room, ten feet by twelve in size, adjoining the parlor and with a piano banging only a step or two away, was my only place for work. Here I wrote my *Systematic Theology* and *Philosophy and Religion*. I lugged books by the hundred to and fro between Clinton Street and Trevor Hall. There was no spare room. When a friend stayed with me overnight, some member of the family was obliged to give up his bed. I longed for a larger and better house, but I could see no way to get it. The seminary was in debt, and what money was contributed seemed needed for other things. Hattie's ill health, however, made a change at last absolutely indispensable. In case of sickness there was no possibility of heating the upper rooms, and there were no accommodations for a nurse. At last, to cap the climax, an undertaker bought the premises next door and set up his business there. The hearse drove into his backyard, and coffins were put into it under our windows. The shades occasionally flew up and revealed a corpse in the process of embalming. As my wife was in a nervous state, all this was trying. The street, moreover, was gradually becoming a business street. Doctors' offices and boardinghouses took possession of it. We felt that we must leave that address and move elsewhere.

I followed the method of Mr. Spurgeon and committed the case to God in prayer. I told him that it was his matter as much as mine; that my usefulness required a change; that he must show the way. I tried at first to collect money from friends. But the responses were discouraging. At last it occurred to me that the seminary possessed a fund which it might use. In Dr. Robinson's time there had been a president's house. This had been sold at his departure. The proceeds did not belong to the endowment funds of the seminary. But they had been used for this purpose. Why should they not now be restored, together with twenty-four years of interest? This would put us in possession of $23,500 which might be applied to the purchase of a lot and to the building of a new president's house. Our trustees fell in with the suggestion, and a lot a hundred feet wide was secured on Sibley Place. Plans were drawn by Messrs. Fay and Dryer. I had myself made many plans, and the whole interior design was my own. The architects did little more than put on the outward dress. One fundamental idea of mine was that there should be no room which did not have at least one dimension of twenty feet. To carry out so large a scheme, I found, would take more money than we had at our disposal. But good friends made up what was lacking. Mrs. Hedstrom of Buffalo gave $2,000, Mr. Huntley of Batavia, $500. Mrs. John B. Trevor of Yonkers gave $250 for dining-room furniture, and Mr. George A. Woolverton of Albany $250 for a hall window. Other additions were made by our board of trustees. Ground was broken October 21, 1895. Work proceeded through the entire winter and spring, the building after it was enclosed being heated by steam, and only two days exclusive of Sundays were lost on account of inclement weather. So vigorously was the enterprise prosecuted that May 12, 1896, I gave a lunch to the board of trustees in the still unfurnished house, and on May 21 following, just seven months after first breaking ground, I moved into the house and took possession. The total cost of the property was $28,751.99 ($8,000 of which was paid for the lot).

As the house was the Lord's gift to me, I resolved to devote it to the Lord. The motto over the sideboard in the dining room is really the motto of the house: *Christo Deo Salvatori*. At the luncheon aforesaid I expressed my thanks to the board and, in addition, to Mr. Fay, the architect, and Mr. Townson, the chairman of the building committee, both of whom had during the preceding seven months given to the work so much of their time and labor. I then called upon my pastor, Rev. J. W. A. Stewart, D.D., to offer prayer and lead the company in consecrating the house to the service of Christ and his church. I have tried to find a motto for every important room and to make all of these mottoes expressive of some religious idea. In the vestibule the motto is the Greek Χαιρε, or "Welcome." In the reception room: "Worth is Warrant for Welcome hither." In the guest chamber: "The friends we've tried are by our side." On the mantel in the dining room: "Brown bread and the gospel is good fare." In the hall: *Alere flammam*—"Cherish the flame." In the drawing room: "Yet in our ashen cold is fire yreken"—a line from Chaucer's *Canterbury Tales*. In the library: *Inter silvas Academi quaerere verum*—"Within the woods of Academus seek the truth"—a line from one of the *Epodes* of Horace; *Numen lumen, astra castra*—"God our light, and heaven our home"; "The love of learning, the sequestered nooks, and all the sweet serenity of books"—a couplet from Longfellow's "Morituri Salutamus"; "My Library was Dukedom large enough"—Prospero's saying in Shakespeare's *Tempest*. In my room the motto is *Sit nox cum somno, sine lite dies*—"May night bring sleep, and the day no strife"—a line from Martial. In Hattie's chamber: *Unum amore, more, ore, re*—"One in love, in habit, in speech, in deed." In the sitting room: *La sua voluntà è nostra pace*—"His will is our peace"—a line from the *Paradiso* of Dante; "True to the kindred points of heaven and home"—from Wordsworth's poem "To a Skylark"; *Aperto vivere voto*—"Live with open vow"—let your purpose in life be frankly disclosed; say out what is in you; let your light shine; confess Christ and he will confess you.

I doubt whether any house has been held more strictly to its purpose than has this one since we entered it. It is a place for the entertainment of students and friends of the seminary and for doing good to others by bringing them under social and Christian influences. During the first year of our occupation we entertained at meals of one sort or another 494 persons. We had each class of the seminary by itself—the wives of members of the class being included. We had one lunch party for ladies which included more than a hundred guests. The seminary and university professors were at one time or another invited. All lecturers before the seminary stayed with us. President Timothy Dwight of Yale was with us, and we made a luncheon in his honor which most of the Yale graduates attended. Drs. Behrends, Morehouse, Elmendorf, Brown, Mead, Jones, Tupper, Gifford, Butler, Harper, McVicar, Fox, MacArthur, Wilkins, Waffle, Upham, and Judson appear already on our list, though at this present writing (November 14, 1897) only a year and a half has elapsed since the opening. I think I may reasonably hope that the house will not only promote Christian affection among the members of our seminary and denomination but also that it will be the means of drawing to our institution in the future the interest and contributions of those who are able to give. As for ourselves, no one can tell how much of a help and comfort it has been. Work has been easier now that I have had a pleasant place to do it in. The quiet of Sibley Place has been a rest and refreshment to my wife, and it will greatly prolong her life. As I get older, I need more to have my outward surroundings favorable. The students of the seminary call my house "The White House." I suppose it is an allusion to the president's house at Washington. But I am sure there is a hundred times more peace here than can be found there. The Lord seems to have given us his peace, and he gives, not as does the world, but in full measure, pressed down, and running over.

Yet we have had our measure of trial—not as much as others have endured, yet enough to call for patience and faith. None of our children has been taken from us by death; no one of them has disgraced us by a disreputable marriage or by any serious disregard of our injunctions. During the period of their education we have often been straitened in our resources, but we have never come to actual want—always some way of relief has been opened to us. For eleven years after our marriage we had almost no sickness. In 1872 Charles had peritonitis, and in 1876 John had scarlet fever; and, indeed, these illnesses left some permanent marks behind them.

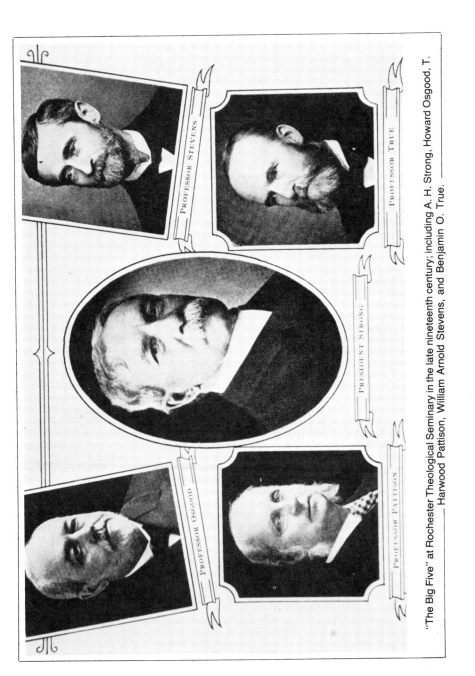

"The Big Five" at Rochester Theological Seminary in the late nineteenth century; including A. H. Strong, Howard Osgood, T. Harwood Pattison, William Arnold Stevens, and Benjamin O. True.

But neither Hattie nor I was seriously ill until 1879. In fact, I never but once in my life had even a headache, and then it lasted but a few minutes. But in the early summer of 1897 I made an excursion to Irondequoit Bay, rowed around among the weeds, caught malaria from the semi-stagnant water, and soon after was prostrated with fever which threatened to become typhoid pneumonia. Some experiences of that time are worth recording. It had been a theory of mine that illness was a sort of vacation when one could pray and be good. I found myself unable to pray and extraordinarily wicked. Instead of being trustful and submissive, I was unbelieving and rebellious. I concluded that during sickness was no time to make one's peace with God and that special gifts of God's Holy Spirit were needed to make sickness of any spiritual benefit.

Never before did I know what it was to be mastered by my thinking instead of being able to master it. I was swept away as by a flood. I was on the edge of delirium. I was alarmed lest I should lose myself altogether. But I had no power to stop or check the rush of ideas. My mind seemed in a state of preternatural exaltation. This was not always unpleasant. Colors would flash before me—reds and greens so vivid that they took my breath away. The brilliancy seemed to pierce me like a knife, till the pleasure became intolerable pain. Then, and only then in all my life, I seemed to myself to be a poet. Fragments of songs suggested themselves to me and sang themselves over and over in my ears. I began the composition of a sonnet which surpassed anything that Milton or Wordsworth ever wrote. I solemnly resolved to write it down as soon as I could use a pen. Unfortunately, when I could write, every vestige of the sonnet had vanished from my memory. I had a homeopathic physician, and I spent whole days and nights in constructing an elaborate refutation of homeopathy—an argument so ingenious and amusing that I fully intended to give it to the world. But when I got well, I could not remember even the general course of my reasoning. Incipient delirium is dream-life, with the added *consciousness* that all is a dream, while dream-life proper never knows that it is unreality and illusion.

After about six weeks, my physician permitted me, at my earnest request, to have what I had had an insane craving for, namely, a dinner of beefsteak and beer. I went out to Canandaigua

Lake to convalesce and there rowed across the lake and back when I ought rather to have been in bed. The result was that I found myself in bed for another six weeks. The relapse was even more disagreeable than the original sickness. Those were not the days of trained nurses, and the care of a very ugly patient fell upon my patient wife. I recovered at length; and when September came, I was able feebly to begin my work in the seminary once more. The result in Hattie's case was not so happy. I have always feared that the strain upon her connected with my illness was the real cause of her own illness that followed only two or three months after my recovery. But before I tell of that, I will complete the account of my own sickness by mentioning an attack of "La Grippe" which I had in 1891 and which prevented my attending the Vassar commencement at which Katy graduated. It began in June with what seemed to be a slight cold but almost immediately became complete prostration accompanied by fever. This time I had learned wisdom by experience. From the very first I had a trained nurse. The comfort and peace which she brought into the house can hardly be described in words. My sickness disappeared almost as suddenly as it came. In three weeks I was walking out again. And these two illnesses are all that I can mention. I have always had the gift of sleeping at a moment's notice. A long night's sleep is my specific for all the ills to which flesh is heir. A daily nap, when I can take it, helps to break the nervous strain of my work. Although I am obliged to be more careful and sparing in my diet than I was in earlier years, I feel perfectly well. I tire somewhat more quickly than of old, but I manage to take more rest. I have concluded that, for me, stimulants of all sorts hinder far more than they help. I have greater strength and better spirits without them.

Mamma's history from 1879 until now has not been so cheering. In September of that year, directly after I myself got well, Katy was taken down with pneumonia, and for a month her mother cared for her. The result was that Hattie was worn out. In November following she had a fainting fit which greatly alarmed us. Dr. Ely prescribed brandy, and this drove her wild. In January I took her to the Clifton Springs Sanitarium. There she grew worse rather than better. Mr. Rockefeller offered to pay our expenses if I would take her south. We went to Aikin, South Carolina, in

February and March. We had pleasant company. Mr. and Mrs.
George Ellwanger and Mr. and Mrs. Chauncey B. Woodworth
were with us. Mamma improved considerably. It was as good as a
sea voyage to be flopped about on a southern railroad, and the dry
air of the pines was fragrant and balmy. But we came home too
soon. We reached Rochester in a snowstorm. Mamma had
recovered something of her strength, and she resumed her care of
the house, of which Mary had temporarily taken charge. But she
was not wholly well. In the autumn she spent three weeks in
Dansville under the care of Dr. Jackson. In 1884 Laura was born. In
March, 1888, Mrs. Rockefeller kindly invited Mamma to take Mary
and Laura and accompany her to Washington and to Asheville,
North Carolina. There they all stayed for a month together. Katy at
that time was in college. In 1892, Mary was married. From
September, 1893, to June, 1894, Katy was in Europe, and Mamma
had sole charge of the housekeeping. This, I now think, was too
much of a burden for her after all she had been through.

But our foresight is not as keen as our hindsight. In November,
1894, when Katy was in New York visiting Charles and Bessie,
Mamma was seized with a series of shocks which at first we thought
to be a sort of incipient paralysis but afterwards proved to be less
serious than that. Katy was at once summoned home, and she
reached us on the morning of Thanksgiving Day. She became
housekeeper and manager, her mother's comfort and companion,
and the light and life of the household generally. As Mamma's case
did not seem to improve, another journey south was resolved upon.
Mr. Rockefeller again furnished the means, or it never could have
been undertaken. Lakewood was tried but was speedily abandoned.
Dr. Weir Mitchell in Philadelphia was consulted and pronounced
her illness a case of cerebral meningitis. He advised a more
southerly air and more varied surroundings. Katy therefore took
her mother successively to Jacksonville, De Land, and St.
Augustine. After six weeks at hotels, Mamma set her face
homeward, convinced that she was better off at home than abroad.
They came back by way of Richmond and Fortress Monroe. But in
the homeward journey the grippe seemed to get hold of Hattie, and
not long after her return she became desperately ill. Perhaps it was
the culmination of a trouble that had been long coming on. At any

rate there were two months of great anxiety. We had a trained nurse for night service. Yet Mamma seemed to get worse and worse. Dr. Biegler at last told me I must send for the absent children as he did not think there were many chances of life. Charles came from the San Remo in New York and John from Mount Auburn in Cincinnati. Mary would have come from Ogdensburg, but her state of health prevented. The children had some words with Mamma, which they feared might be her last, she was so nearly unconscious. But from that time there seemed to be a slight change for the better. Slowly fear in our minds gave place to hope. When we found that we could lease the Lapham house on Canandaigua Lake for the summer and that a present of five hundred dollars from Mrs. Rockefeller would enable us to pay for it, we told Mamma, and the news seemed to put new life into her. She set herself to get ready for moving into the country. Taking her trained nurse with her, she took possession the middle of May. Charles visited us there. John and Lide spent August with us. By September Mamma was measurably well.

I have told the story of Mamma's illness at length in order to remind the children of what she has passed through. But I have not been able to set before them the long watchings and anxieties of these last eighteen years, the hope deferred, the many fears that have possessed us. Nor could I, even if I had the most skillful pen, describe adequately the patience and even heroism with which Mamma has borne the lengthy trial. Compelled, as she has been for weeks together, to sit motionless, unable to read or sew or talk, and waiting for what she knew not, it is a wonder that she has preserved so much of her cheerfulness and vivacity. It is no wonder that at times her heart has failed her, but these times grow fewer, and I have hope that in her case the Scripture may be fulfilled and at the evening time it may be light. She has always had a small opinion of her own gifts and abilities, but there are very few women of so much native genius. Nobody that I have ever known writes better letters than she; she took the prize at Lake Placid the other day for the best poem, when a great many bright people competed; men and women alike regard her as a most interesting talker; she would be a leader in society if she had her health. May she long be preserved to me and to her children! Surely the faithful care she has given us deserves its reward. I know that the children appreciate the fact that they have one of the best of mothers. And as for my unworthy self, I can only repeat to her the words of Robert Browning's poem "Rabbi Ben Ezra":

> Grow old along with me!
> The best is yet to be,
> The last of life, for which the first was made:
> Our times are in his hand
> Who saith, "A whole I planned,
> Youth shows but half; trust God:
>   see all, nor be afraid!"

When I was twenty-one years old, life seemed sad and mysterious; I had no desire to live; I expected soon to die. Though my view of life brightened as I went on, I never quite got rid of the idea of an early death, until after a curious experience in Cleveland. There I began one of the years with a premonition that I should never live to see its end. Month after month, however, passed by, and I was still in the land of the living. December came, and the last week of December, and I still lived. In the middle of that last week a farmer called with a buggy to take me to the quarterly meeting of the Association with his church. All the way into the country and all the way home I was waiting for the horse to run away, throw me out, and break my neck. But I reached home in safety. The last day of the year and the last night of the year arrived. I went to bed in peace, and I waked in safety. When I came down on that first morning of the new year, my wife said that my countenance wore a look of extreme disappointment. It taught me not to trust in premonitions.

When James Russell Lowell reached the age of seventy, he said that he felt like an old cow trying to bite a big pumpkin; somehow "he didn't seem to git no kind of purchase on nothin'." I am only sixty-one, and I am not as far gone as James Russell Lowell was at seventy, but I have no great expectations of the future. Sometimes I seem to myself to have finished my best work. The *Systematic Theology* cannot be rewritten without making an entirely new book of it, and although I see much that might be done in the way of improvement, I doubt whether it will be worthwhile to write a new treatise. *The Great Poets and Their Theology* has been completed, and the critics have yet to tear it to pieces. I do not believe I can greatly alter it for the better. It would please me to collect and publish my essays on ethical monism, my address at the Convocation of the University of Chicago on "Modern Tendencies in Theological Thought,"[5] and my paper on "Christianity and Evolution."[6] Other papers written since I printed my *Philosophy and Religion* might be added to those I have mentioned, and they might together make a book of considerable size. If I should die before accomplishing this, I trust one of my sons will do it for me. I do not feel that I have a great deal to live for. I am as vigorous in my teaching as ever, but I well know that my strength must soon decline and work must become more and more of a burden. When I attended the party given to Mrs. Abelard Reynolds on her hundredth birthday, I asked one of the ladies present if she would choose to live so long, provided the choice were left to her. She hesitated a moment and then said: "I would prefer to have someone else choose for me." And so I prefer that God should choose whether my life is to end soon or late, for I know that "all things work together for good to them that love God."

I have been greatly blessed in my own soul, in my home, in my church, in my work. God has been faithful to all his promises. If I had been more prayerful and more obedient, I might have accomplished more, and I might have enjoyed more. My mind in these later days turns very often to the words: "If thou take forth the precious from the vile, thou shalt be as my mouth." I appreciate more highly than ever the dignity of being a mouthpiece of almighty God, a channel through which he communicates his truth to others, and I see, as I never have before, that only personal holiness is the condition of safety, of knowledge, and of power. Cousin Lillie's sad aberration of mind and the dropping away of one friend of my early days after another make me wonder sometimes how long my pleasant home and my prosperous work will last. But a second thought teaches me that with that matter I have really nothing to do. My business is to work while it is day, remembering that the night cometh when no man can work. Life may soon be over:

[5] *Christ in Creation,* pp. 137-162.
[6] *Ibid.,* pp. 163-180.

> Yet be it less or more, or soon or slow,
> It shall be still in strictest measure even
> To that same lot, however mean or high,
> Toward which Time leads me, and the will of Heaven;
> All is, if I have grace to use it so,
> As ever in my great Task-Master's eye.[7]

I wish to close this autobiography with my testimony to the goodness and mercy of God. In spite of my unfaithfulness to him, not one word of all his promises has failed. I rejoice that my hope rests not upon the strength of my resolves, for they are weak and brittle as spun glass, but on his eternal purpose and grace. And as he has called me into his kingdom, has made me partaker of Christ, has made me his minister, so I believe that what he has done for me already is the pledge of infinitely more that he will do for me in the eternity that is to come. I have never had any fear of death since I gave my heart to the Savior. Whether it comes soon or late, I feel certain that it will only usher me into his presence and make possible a larger and nobler work in his service. I have tried to preach his gospel here, but it has been with weak heart and stammering tongue. There will be grander utterance hereafter. Those whom God has called into the ministry of Christ are called for eternity. To the principalities and powers in heavenly places shall be made known through the church the manifold wisdom of God. His servants shall serve him forever. There will be work to do for all who love him, and heaven is only the world of more abundant life where all our highest desires and aspirations find their complete satisfaction.

> The high that proved too high, the heroic
>   for earth too hard,
> The passion that left the ground to lose
>   itself in the sky,
> Are music sent up to God by the
>   lover and the bard;
> Enough that he heard it once: we shall
>   hear it by and by.[8]

---

[7] John Milton, "On His Having Arrived at the Age of Twenty-Three," lines 9-14.
[8] Robert Browning, Abt Vogler, 10. 5-8.

I do not long for death, for life here is thus far increasingly pleasant. But I know that the life beyond is better than the life of earth. Therefore all the days of my appointed time will I wait till my change comes. I put my future into the hands of God, believing that he will perfect that which concerns me. I only ask that my children may follow me in the faith and service of Christ, so that when I finally appear before him, I may say, "Here am I and the children whom thou hast given me." Then unto him that loved us and washed us from our sins in his own blood and made us to be a kingdom of priests unto God and his Father, unto him shall be glory and dominion, forever and ever. Amen.

9

Later Additions

Ten years have passed since I began this autobiography. They have been years of continuous work but also of unbroken health and fairly good spirits. I have enjoyed life more during the past year than ever before, and I think I have accomplished more than in any previous year. Prince Bismarck said that the first eighty years of one's life are always the happiest. If he meant to intimate that the later years are necessarily unhappy, he was mistaken. Particularly if he is a teacher, it is true that only in his later life does he begin to receive the best of his reward. His pupils begin to appreciate what he has done for them; he acquires confidence in the conclusions at which he has arrived; he sees the visible proof that his work has not been in vain.

In the theological seminary we have seen great progress. When I took charge of the institution thirty-four years ago, its property and endowments amounted to less than $200,000. They now amount to over $2,000,000. Brother Henry has pledged $87,500 for the building of a new dormitory to be called the Alvah Strong Hall, a noble proof of his family affection and a great addition to our seminary equipment.[1] This edifice is now going up, and if I can see it completed and furnished and paid for, I shall regard it as one of the crowning evidences of God's favor. It is a great comfort to me that my son John has for two years been by my side as a professor in the seminary. His prayerful and affectionate spirit has won the hearts of the students and has given them an object lesson in the Christian life.

I have not apostatized from the faith, nor have I ceased to teach the unity and sufficiency of Scripture, righteousness as the fundamental attribute of God, the fall of man and original sin, the deity, preexistence, virgin birth, and physical resurrection of our Lord Jesus Christ, his omnipresence in nature, in humanity, in history, and in the hearts of his people, the regenerating work of his Holy Spirit, and his future Second Coming to judge the world and to reward the faithful. I believe that the teaching of these truths has won for me the confidence of the churches and the favor of God. Let others teach as they will, I propose to walk in the old paths and to hand down to my successors the old gospel.

I have now completed the revision and enlargement of my *Systematic Theology,* which has already passed through seven editions, each edition embodying successive corrections and supposed improvements. During the twenty years since its first publication in 1886, I have collected much new material. My philosophical and critical point of view has somewhat changed. While I still hold to the old doctrines, I interpret them differently because I seem to myself to have reached a fundamental truth which throws new light upon them all. This truth I have tried to set forth in my book *Christ in Creation,* which was published in 1899, as my

[1][Note added by Strong in 1909]: This gift was increased when it became evident that the cost of the edifice would be larger, and it finally amounted to $140,000. As the building actually cost $160,000, of which Mr. J. D. Rockefeller gave $12,500, and I had guaranteed the trustees against a deficit, this left $8,413.50 for me to pay, and I gave my note bearing interest for that amount, which I still owe at this writing, June 25, 1909. [Note added later by Strong]: But my son Charles relieved me of all anxiety on this account by paying the last of my debt, $6,000, namely, so that my own contribution to the building was finally reduced to $2,413.50.

previous book *The Great Poets and Their Theology* was published in 1897.[2]

That Christ is the one and only Revealer of God in nature as well as in Scripture is in my judgment the key to theology. This view implies a monistic and idealistic conception of the world, together with an evolutionary idea of its origin and progress. But it is the very antidote of pantheism in that it recognizes evolution as only the method of the transcendent and personal Christ, who fills all in all and who makes the universe teleological and moral from its center to its circumference and from its beginning until now.

Neither evolution nor the higher criticism has any terrors to one who regards them as parts of Christ's creating and educating process. The Christ in whom are hid all the treasures of wisdom and knowledge himself furnishes all the needed safeguards and limitations. It is only because Christ has been forgotten that nature and law have been personified, that history has been regarded as an unpurposed development, that Judaism has been referred to a merely human origin, that Paul has been thought to have switched the church off from its proper track even before it had gotten fairly started on its course, that superstition and illusion have come to seem the only foundation for the sacrifices of the martyrs and the triumphs of modern missions. I believe in no such irrational and atheistic evolution as this. I believe rather in him in whom all things consist, who is with his people even unto the end of the world, who governs and guides all history, and who has promised to lead those who love him into all the truth.

Philosophy and science are good servants of Christ, but they are poor guides when they rule out the Son of God. As I reach my seventieth year and write these words on my birthday, I am thankful for that personal experience of union with Christ which has enabled me to see in science and philosophy the teaching of my Lord. But this same personal experience has made me even more alive to

[2] [Note added by Strong, apparently in 1909]: Mr. Arthur L. Lesher, 670 Broadway, New York, one of our noble trustees, gave me $1,500 to defray the expense of putting copies of my *Theology, Outlines, Great Poets,* and *Christ in Creation* into the libraries of the principal colleges and theological seminaries in this country and in Europe. As I gave away as many as sixty copies of the *Theology* to personal friends, the total bill of the Publication Society was $2,166, leaving me $666 to pay, which I paid in June, 1909.

Christ's teaching in Scripture, has made me recognize in Paul and John a truth profounder than that disclosed by any secular writers—truth with regard to sin and atonement for sin that satisfies the deepest wants of my nature and that is self-evidencing and divine.

I am distressed by some common theological tendencies of my time because I believe them to be false to both science and religion. How men who have ever felt themselves to be lost sinners and who have once received pardon from their crucified Lord and Savior can thereafter seek to pare down his attributes, deny his deity and atonement, tear from his brow his crown of miracle and sovereignty, relegate him to the place of a merely moral teacher who influences us only as does Socrates by words spoken across a stretch of ages passes my comprehension. This is my test of orthodoxy: Do we pray to Jesus? Do we call upon the name of Christ, as did Stephen and all the early church? Is he our living Lord, omnipresent, omniscient, and omnipotent? Is he divine only in the sense in which we are divine, or is he the only begotten Son, God manifest in the flesh, in whom is all the fullness of the Godhead bodily? "What think ye of the Christ?" is still the critical question, and none are entitled to the name of Christian who, in the face of the evidence he has furnished us, cannot answer that question aright.

Under the influence of Ritschl and his Kantian relativism, many of our teachers and preachers have swung off into a practical denial of Christ's deity and his atonement. We seem on the verge of a second Unitarian defection that will break up churches and compel secessions in a worse manner than did that of Channing and Ware a century ago. American Christianity recovered from that disaster only by vigorously asserting the authority of Christ and the inspiration of the Scriptures. We need a new vision of the Savior like that which Paul saw on the way to Damascus and John saw on the isle of Patmos to convince us that Jesus is lifted up above space and time, that his existence antedated creation, that he conducted the march of Hebrew history, that he was born of a Virgin, suffered on the cross, rose from the dead, and now lives forevermore, the Lord of the universe, the only God with whom we have to do, our Savior here and our Judge hereafter. Without a revival of this faith our churches will be secularized; mission enterprise will die out; and the candlestick will be removed out of its place as it was with the seven churches of Asia and as it has been in our own times with the apostate churches of New England.

I am now beginning to print the revised and enlarged edition of my *Theology* in the hope that its publication may do something to stem this fast advancing tide and to confirm the faith of God's elect. It is probably the last important work that I can do, and it will occupy the most of two years. But I consider it the best service I can render to the kingdom of God. I have no doubt that the vast majority of Christians still hold the faith that was once for all delivered to the saints and that they will sooner or later separate themselves from those who deny the Lord who bought them. When the enemy comes in like a flood, the Spirit of the Lord will raise up a standard against him. I would do my part in raising up such a standard. In spite of the supercilious assumptions of modern infidelity, I would avow anew my firm belief, only confirmed by the experience and reflection of a half century, in the old doctrines of the Christian church. I believe that these are truths of science as well as truths of revelation, that the supernatural will yet be seen to be most truly natural, and that not the open-minded theologian but the narrow-minded scientist will be obliged to hide his head at Christ's coming.

The universal presence of Christ, the Light that lighteth every man, in heathen as well as in Christian lands, to direct or overrule all movements of the human mind, gives me confidence that the recent attacks upon the Christian faith will fail of their purpose. It becomes evident at last that not only the outworks are assaulted but also the very citadel itself. We are asked to give up all belief in special revelation. Jesus Christ, it is said, has come in the flesh precisely as each one of us has come, and he was before Abraham only in the same sense that we were. Christian experience knows how to characterize such doctrine, as soon as it is clearly stated. The new theology will be of use in enabling even ordinary believers to recognize soul-destroying heresy even under the mask of professed orthodoxy.

I would hasten the day when at the name of Jesus every knee shall bow. I believe that if any man serve Christ, him the Father will honor; and to serve Christ means to honor him as I honor the

Father. I would not pride myself that I believe so little but rather that I believe so much. Faith is God's measure of a man. Why should I doubt that God spoke to the fathers through the prophets? Why should I think it incredible that God should raise the dead? The things which are impossible with men are possible with God. When the Son of man comes, shall he find faith on the earth? Let him at least find faith in me, his professed follower. In the conviction that the present darkness is but temporary and that it will be banished by a glorious rising of the Sun of righteousness, I am giving the new edition of my *Systematic Theology* to the public with the prayer that whatever of good seed is in it may bring forth fruit and that whatever plant the heavenly Father has not planted may be rooted up.

In two sermons during the last two years I have tried to give my testimony. In Cleveland at the Baptist Northern Anniversaries in May, 1904, I delivered an address on "Our Denominational Outlook," and at the Baptist World's Congress in London in July, 1905, I preached the sermon in Spurgeon's Tabernacle to four thousand people. I have given an account of these stirring occasions in papers written especially for the purpose, so that I shall not speak of them here. The most effective address of my life was perhaps that given to the Ecumenical Missionary Conference in New York City in April, 1900. Only now and then have I really enjoyed public speaking. On these occasions, however, I have felt that I had a message to deliver and the power of God seemed given to me to deliver it. I am hopeful, however, that in another sphere and in a future life the desire to proclaim the honor of my Savior and my King will be permitted to express itself more freely and fitly than has been given me here. I believe that every power will find fit employ in that eternal world of joy, and even if I have not been able worthily to preach in this world, I shall still have a chance to make of myself a great preacher in the world to come. And so I leave my seventy years of past life behind me gladly, believing that my times are in his hands. With the great apostle I can say that "forgetting the things that are behind and stretching forward to the things which are before, I press on toward the goal, unto the prize of the high calling of God in Christ Jesus."

Augustus Hopkins Strong with his son John Henry Strong, at the left of the photograph, and John Henry Strong's son William Strong, at the right. The photograph was taken in Strong's house at 17 Sibley Place in 1913.

Second Addition
Added June 28, 1908, As I Am Approaching My Seventy-second Birthday and Am Preparing for a Year's Absence in Europe

I now begin to question whether my work in the seminary is not done. After thirty-six years of teaching, during which I have not been absent from a single class exercise on account of ill health, I feel the need of rest, and the board of trustees has given me a leave of absence for a full year. The chariot wheels have at times dragged heavily, though at other times my lecturing has been as successful as ever. I remember the presidents of Yale. Dr. Woolsey resigned his presidency at seventy, and he enjoyed an honored and useful old age. Dr. Dwight did the same and is reaping the same reward. But Dr. Porter, good man that he was, was overpersuaded by his friends; he held on to his office until he was seventy-five; then he was practically forced to resign. I would not have such an experience, and I therefore am inclined at present to end my connection with the seminary one year from this time. I delay the announcement of this determination, only in order that I may not act under the influence of any temporary depression or without giving the seminary authorities time to offer advice.

When I speak of depression, I would not leave it to be inferred that my inveterate equanimity has forsaken me. I am still without any known organic weakness. I need more sleep than usual, and I am disinclined to any great new enterprise. But I am hale and hearty; I enjoy life and talk; there is much of literary acquisition and production which is agreeable to me. In going abroad I have the purpose of reading *Les Trois Monsquetaires* and *La Divina Commedia,* thus combining the frivolous and the severe:

> *Wo Starkes dich und Mildes paarten*
> *Da gibt es einen guten Klang.*

In other words, I would like to find recreation in learning a little more French and Italian; and if only I could get command of them orally, I would think myself fortunate.

In my foreign tours hitherto, six in number, I have always had a definite scheme of travel. This time I have none. I do not care where

I go or what I do. Charles promised to meet Mamma and Laura with me in Paris, and I tell him that he can do with us for two months whatsoever he pleases. If we can see something of the south of France in the fall and reach Rome by the first of November, I shall be content. One great object of the journey will be to give Mamma an exit from her long seclusion. For twenty years she has been shut into the house. New sights and sounds, I trust, will draw her out of herself and will convince her that she can yet see something of society and can enjoy life.

For a time at least I am disposed to leave theology and philosophy behind and to go back to the solid ground of nature. Yet it would not be true to say that I doubt my theology. Indeed, I am more and more convinced that I have taught the essential truth, by which all are to be judged at the last day. I am willing to make my *Systematic Theology* my monument. Now that the last volume of the work is coming from the press, I feel grateful that Mr. Arthur L. Lesher has enough confidence in it to give me $1,500 to put a copy of it into the library of every important college and theological seminary in this country and Great Britain. I only desire that those who are studying the great problems may be compelled to take account of what I have written. I hope that, in these days of storm and stress, the work may anchor our Baptist denomination in the old faith and may give to our theology its old emphasis upon the deity and atonement of Christ.

But before I leave theology and philosophy behind me, I wish to add one eleventh milestone to the ten which I have already marked in this autobiography. It has to do with the unity and sufficiency of Scripture. My later thought has interpreted the Bible from the point of view of the immanence of Christ. As I have more and more clearly seen him in human history, I have been led to recognize an evolutionary process in divine revelation. No age and no race of man has been left without its witness to the truth. Christ is the Light that lighteth every man. As Hebrew history is the work of Christ, so is Hebrew Scripture. As the history is his work in spite of its imperfections, so the Scripture is his work in spite of its imperfections. Both are like the human eye, to which we do not refuse to attribute designing intelligence simply because it is not a perfect optical instrument.

I am prepared now to acknowledge all that the higher criticism can prove as to the composition of the sacred documents at the same time that I see in them the proof of a divine as well as a human authorship. Inerrancy in matters not essential to their moral and religious teaching is not to be claimed. And yet the Bible, taken as a whole, and interpreted by Christ's teaching and Spirit, is our sufficient rule of faith and practice. We shall never outgrow it but shall ever find it able to make us wise unto salvation. It will always be our textbook, not of science or philosophy, but of religion.

The eleven forward steps of my doctrinal progress may well be concluded by a twelfth, which has even more to do with my personal religious experience. It is my new conviction of a present God and Savior. The immanence of God has been to me for some years the immanence of Christ, and Christ's all-encompassing power and goodness has been to me the open secret of the universe. But of late I have been impressed as never before that God is *here* and *now*. He that comes to God must believe that He *is* and that He *is* the rewarder of those who diligently seek him. These present tenses have a new meaning to me. And the kingdom of heaven is within us, and we are citizens of it today, without waiting for the future. If we ask in faith for things according to God's will, we already *have* the things which we desire of him. We seize the triumph from afar, and faith is the very substance of things hoped for, the evidence of things not seen. Robert Browning said well that "there shall never be one *lost* good." But I go further and say: "There shall never be one real good *desired* that is not actually attained." Nay more, the soul even here and now, possessing in Christ the present God, possesses all things in him. The Lord is our inheritance, and even in this life we sit with him upon his throne, wield his power, and are made rulers of the world.

When Schleiermacher lay upon his deathbed, he said, "I feel constrained to think the profoundest speculative thoughts, and they are to me identical with the deepest religious feelings." So for me my philosophy and my religion have been one thing, indeed, my philosophy has grown out of my religion. I have tried to express in my *Theology* the impression Christ's presence and greatness and life have made upon my soul.[3] To me Christ is all and in all. The best proof to me that Scripture is inspired is this: that I find recorded there what I have felt in my own heart. Deep answers unto deep. The outer word answers to the inner word, and both are recognized as expressions of Him who is the eternal Word of God.

I leave behind me two packages of manuscripts which I think may be worth publication in separate volumes. One contains the main addresses which I have delivered during the past ten years, and the other contains the sermons which I have most used. I do not regard either of these collections as supremely valuable, and yet they present in more popular form than does my *Theology* the essentials of my doctrine. I leave to my children the verdict as to their worth and as to the propriety of publishing them.

The only deaths in our family circle have been those of Bessie Rockefeller Strong, Charles's wife, after seventeen years of married life, and of Virginia Strong, John's daughter, aged only eight months. Charles has his Margaret left to him, a most engaging child. Mary has her Robert, Alan, and George; John his William and Elizabeth; Kate her Grenville, John, and Richard. Laura is engaged to marry Edmund H. Lewis of Syracuse. Cora lives apart from us in Dansville, more happy in a quiet country town than in the city. When I consider the trials that have come to so many others, I can but think that the lines have fallen to us in pleasant places. We have a goodly heritage in this world, and there is more to follow, even an exceeding and eternal weight of glory.

> Through many dangers, toils and snares
>   I have already come;
> 'Tis grace hath brought me safe thus far,
>   And grace will lead me home.
>
> Yes, though this heart and flesh should fail
>   And mortal life shall cease,
> I shall possess within the veil
>   A life of joy and peace.

---

[3] This sentence is unclear in the original manuscript. The editor has substituted the word "impression" for the original "experience of" to attempt to clarify the sentence.

This earth shall soon dissolve like snow,
The sun forbear to shine,
But God, who called me here below,
Will be forever mine.[4]

Third Addition
Added July, 1917, As I Am Approaching My Eighty-first Birthday and Am Reviewing the Ten Years Just Past

The year in Europe which I anticipated nine years ago was actually spent abroad. In hope that complete change of scene and new objects of interest might divert my wife from her melancholic seclusion, I engaged *appartements de luxe* on the steamer to Cherbourg, and with Laura to keep her company we took all our meals on board at the elegant Ritz Restaurant instead of the regular table. On the way we stopped at Plymouth to take with us a trained nurse, an Englishwoman, who had been highly recommended to me. Charles met us at the station in Paris, where we arrived after an exhausting night's railway ride, and he entertained us sumptuously at a quiet private hotel for several days. An auto drive in the Bois de Boulogne seemed to do Mamma good, and her talks with Charles, after the meals in our private parlor, pleased her, for she had not seen him since last year. He took us then to Glion in Switzerland, and we spent a month with him and Margaret. Kate and Carl came. With them Laura visited Chamonix, and with these three I, leaving Mamma and her nurse with Charles and Margaret, made a memorable journey to southeastern France, visiting Lyons, Orange, Avignon, Arles, Nîmes, Aigues-Mortes and Carcassonne, all of which I have described in my *Miscellanies, I:* 392-424.

Leaving Charles and Margaret at Glion, our party of four, including my wife, her nurse, Laura, and me, went by the Simplon Pass to Milan and then to Cadenabbia on Lake Como, to spend the month of October, 1908. It was near the end of the season for tourists, but the weather was like our Indian summer. The cypresses about the villas and the distant snows of the Alps were lovely features of the landscape. But it grew cold, and we packed our trunks for Rome. There we lodged at the Hotel Eden and had rooms

[4] "Amazing Grace."

overlooking the grounds of the Villa Borghese, while the roof garden gave Mamma a noble view of St. Peter's and the whole city of Rome. We had hoped to interest Hattie in the galleries and churches, but she refused to see them. Only twice during the whole winter did she consent to leave the hotel, and then only by carriage to visit St. Peter's and at another time St. Paul's without the walls. Three or four times she went down to the table d' hôte, but almost always she had her meals alone with her nurse in her room. Indeed, the plan of amusing her proved to be a complete failure. Her interest in her surroundings grew less and less. She became homesick and longed to return to Rochester. Laura and I were compelled to give up all sight-seeing outside the city, so that Perugia and Urbino, Siena, Assisi, and Ravenna were left unvisited. Fortunately I had in years before seen Florence, Parma, Bologna, and Pisa. Our stay in the Eternal City was enlivened by some entertainments given by President Whittinghall of the Baptist Theological Seminary, by Dr. Jesse Benedict Carter of the American School of Classical Studies, and by Mr. Griscom of the United States Embassy, and of these Laura and I gladly availed ourselves. But Mamma's progress was all downward; and when Charles offered to bring Margaret and go home with us by way of Naples, she accepted his offer, and we all sailed for New York in March, though we had expected to stay in Italy till June. So my seventh foreign tour lasted only eight months instead of a full year.

I must connect with this the sad story of Mamma's further decline until she passed away from earth altogether. For thirty years she had hardly gone out of the house and had never gone to church. She shut herself into her room when we entertained guests, whether on an anniversary or family occasions. Her mind became finally unbalanced, so that she saw sights that had no foundation in reality. Yet on November 6, 1911, we celebrated our Golden Wedding and gave thanks that we had been permitted to live together for fifty years. This anniversary happily came before her worst symptoms had shown themselves, and she seemed to enjoy the occasion. But there was a bodily disease, curbed indeed by successive operations, though at last so diffused through her whole system as to make further operations useless. The end came on July 8, 1914, when she was almost reduced to a skeleton. Her death was painless. She was unconscious. In any event she would have been without fear, for she had faith in Christ. She had been a conscientious and devoted wife and mother, had given her strength to her husband and children, and in all her illness had been lovingly cared for by them. I honor her memory. She was a heroine who fought a good fight, and when she died, she left us all desolate. At the funeral all the children but Charles were present. The Scripture was read by Dr. Wallace, and prayer was offered by Dr. Stewart. There was no music. The remains were placed in brother Henry's mausoleum at Mount Hope, which he has generously shared with me, and there they rest in peace, "till the day dawn, and the shadows flee away."

Now I must take up the history of my children where I left it ten or more years ago. After the death of his wife Bessie, November 14, 1906, Charles continued his residence abroad, vibrating between Glion and Paris, until at last he bought ground at Fiesole, near Florence, and built there a villa. For Margaret's education he put her in school at Southwold in Sussex, on the eastern coast of England. The teachers were Newnham graduates, and when Margaret was ready for college, Charles took her to Newnham where she spent a year. She did not care for further college work; and when the war came on, she devoted herself to her father and depended on him mainly for instruction. She has therefore lacked associates of her own age. Most of her life has been spent with people older than she. Charles had been professor of psychology in Columbia University since 1903, with liberty to teach in New York or to conduct his researches in philosophy abroad. But several years ago he thought it best to resign this professorship, since it was purely honorary and he did not need the salary or the title—an act of chivalry similar to that other resignation of his Harvard fellowship, after marrying the daughter of the richest man in the world, in order that his poorer friend Santayana might have the benefit of it—Charles little suspecting that this resignation might consign him to poverty and so straiten him for means that his wife's health might be affected thereby. There was a sense of honor of which I am proud!

Charles is clearheaded and conscientious, and his writing is a model of lucid statement. His book, *Why the Mind Has a Body,* has been greatly praised for its simple, concise, and intelligible style—a merit so rare in philosophical writing.[5] But Charles lacks the imagination and emotional elements necessary to the attainment of the highest truth. I do not see that he has changed his views of Christ and of Christianity or that he now accepts Christ as his divine Lord and Redeemer. I had hoped that his recent paralysis and confinement to bed in the sanitarium at Val-Mont might open his eyes to his human weakness and need. I have great pity for him and great faith that Christ will yet reveal himself to him, for his filial loyalty and his persistent search for truth touch my heart. I believe that these traits are signs of Christ's working in him, though he is as unconscious of their Author as was Saul on his way to Damascus. And so I rejoiced last year in our church's action in reversing the excluding vote by which twenty-five years ago it had separated him from its membership. I was conscientious then in approving that excommunication. I now see more clearly that the Light that lighteth every man is Christ, and I live in hope that before I die Charles will see "the light of the knowledge of the glory of God in the face of Jesus Christ."

Mary has been a sort of mother to her younger sisters and has taken Hattie's place as housekeeper during their early years. She has proved herself a wise counselor and a great helpmeet to her husband. Of late years I have put Cora's affairs into her hands, contenting myself with paying the quarterly bills. I have ordered in my will that a fixed salary be paid her for the time and labor she bestows. Her three sons have all shown ability in scholarship. Robert, at his graduation from Harvard, hopes for a commission in the artillery service; Alan, though not yet graduated, has already sailed for France as a prospective aviator; only George, from being under age and from illness, strengthens his body by service in an instruction camp. Mary's husband, Dr. Robert G. Cook, is a tower of strength in Canandaigua, as superintendent of Brigham Hall, deacon in the Congregational Church, and man of influence in all social and municipal affairs. He united with the church several years ago.

John is a son after my own heart, in that his affections give him access to theological truth, so that he sheds abroad the influence of

---

[5] Charles Augustus Strong, *Why the Mind Has a Body* (New York: Macmillan Company, 1903).

an evangelical faith and a spiritual life. His two pastorates in Cincinnati and in New Britain were succeeded by eight years of work as professor of New Testament interpretation in our seminary. Here his presence was a joy to me, and he won the confidence of the students by his insight into the meaning of Scripture and his earnest exposition of it. When the tone of seminary life changed at my resignation of the presidency, John began to feel that direct work for the salvation of souls was more to his taste than merely teaching others to do it. A call from the Eutaw Place Baptist Church in Baltimore, sent to him when he was in Europe and though the church had never seen him, seemed to him a call from God, and he has now had three full years of a successful pastorate with that people. But John is more spiritual than are the churches of our day. He excels in personal religious work rather than in popular oratory. He needs opportunity to teach New Testament truth, unhindered by any church's itching ears or commercial ambitions. I trust that God will open the way. The loss of his little daughter Virginia in 1906 was followed by the birth of Emilie in 1908. William, his son, is a model of physical height and vigor—six feet three—and he is spending his summer in farming at William B. Hale's, before entering college at Princeton. He has poetical gifts, and with larger reading of the best authors and greater maturity of judgment he may make himself a name as a writer. Elizabeth, the oldest daughter, has the attraction of a born society woman, though she is only fifteen years of age. John has reason to be proud of his versatile and brilliant wife and of his interesting and promising children.

Katy has made of herself an object lesson as pastor's wife and general manager of affairs. Her college training makes her equal to presiding at meetings or teaching classes of young men. Her children, Grenville, John, and Richard, are all bright and well trained. I expect much from them in the future. Grenville has the gentlemanly characteristics and the poise of judgment which argue his ability to command. John is a natural thinker and philosopher, with gifts for abstract reasoning. Richard is affectionate and docile, sure to be a comfort to his parents. Nurture, in all these three children, has matched whatever nature bestowed. They have not been permitted to grow up wild, but as cultivated members of the human family. They owe much of this not only to the training, but also to the example, of their keenly observant and well-balanced father. Carl has a versatility and a command of his resources which would make him an excellent college president.

When I speak of Laura, I take the opportunity of saying that her marriage to Edmund on June 1, 1910, is simply a specimen of the good sense of my children in their matrimonial alliances. I doubt whether five better matches can be found elsewhere. The whole lot, when met together, form a homogeneous and loving company. Edmund Lewis is no exception. He has made his way to the front in his profession, as assistant to the attorney general of this state, and he is now patriotically seeking the position of judge advocate in our army. If health is granted him, he may yet become famous as a lawyer and a statesman. His clear and winning address carries conviction, while his face is a very mirror of sincerity. The loss of little Katherine Strong Lewis at the age of six months leaves the parents still with two pretty children, Mary Strong Lewis, born in 1913, and Janet Heffron Lewis, born in 1915. Laura has literary gifts which I hope she will transmit to them. She has a nervous organization which makes it important that she should be preserved from undue anxiety and labor, and with that in view I have now for some time paid the salary of a competent nurse to help her in her care for the children. Her year in Paris in the school of the Misses Ferris gave her a knowledge of the French language which would enable her to earn her own living by teaching. There was a social culture in that school which made Laura a mistress in any company. But confinement to the French and absence of suitable diversion made her homesick. When I came with Charles and rescued her, it was an unspeakable relief. I only wish that I could endow her with a large fortune so that she might be *une grande dame.*

Cora has been a problem to me ever since her fifteenth year. Her case is one of arrested development. At the age of forty-seven she is still very much of a child. Yet she has some command of language and some affectionateness of spirit. These are accompanied by an inveterate unwillingness to subject herself to discipline. Gifts of drawing and painting are unused, because she remembers that on a single occasion long ago they were laughed at. Her fear that the nervous twitching of the muscles of her face will be seen keeps her from attending church and makes her prefer the darkness of the picture shows. I have thought it best to humor her and to permit her to live apart from the family with a single companion whom she likes, while I pay the bills. I have made provision for her expenses after my death, so that she will never come to want. Mary will care for all her real needs. I am glad that her tastes are simple and that in spite of some childish ideas with regard to prayer, her self-centered life has still some conscious hold upon God and God's promises.

My account of my wife and children leads me to mention some of the tours I have made during the last twelve years. In 1905 I sailed on the Leyland Line from Boston, with Dr. and Mrs. Mabie and their daughter, for Liverpool, to deliver the sermon before the Baptist World Alliance in London. That sermon, two hours long, some say, is printed in my *Miscellanies,* I: 40-73—a great sermon indeed, yet not coming up to the four-hour standard of the old Puritan divines. It was delivered in Spurgeon's Metropolitan Tabernacle before an audience of four thousand people. I was ill and weak, but the singing of "All Hail the Power of Jesus' Name" by some hundreds of Welshmen, to the tune "Diadem," gave me heart, and I survived the greatest effort of my life. In 1907 I went over to France to bring Laura back from her school, and Charles, who a few months before had lost his wife, met me in Rouen, and together we took a bicycle tour in Normandy and Touraine, which I have chronicled in an article on "The Châteaux of France" in my *Miscellanies,* I: 362-391. In Paris I took up Laura, and we went to Beauvais, Cologne, Bonn, Weimar, crossed to Dover and Canterbury, and after a couple of weeks for rest at Sandford-on-Thames, near Oxford, we sailed from Southampton for home.

My seventh European tour was with Mamma and Laura. This I have already described at the beginning of the present appendix. In the four following years I made four successive summer journeys to England, Scotland, and Wales. I had heard that Andrew D. White, after his Berlin ambassadorship was over, gave himself a vacation in England, with the ambition of seeing with his own eyes all of the thirty-seven English cathedrals. He was handed on from one bishop or dean to another, was most hospitably entertained, and was enabled to study English architecture with first-class authorities and assistants. I became fired with the same ambition. So in 1910 I made a summer tour with my son John, in which we ascended Snowdon, visited Llandudno, Bangor, Beaumaris, Ludlow Castle, and Hereford, sailed down the Wye, saw at Bristol the Müller orphan houses and the Baptist College, inspected the Roman remains at Bath and Wells, explored the country of Lorna Doone, Lynton, Clovelly and Tintagel, Exeter, Winchester, Portsmouth, and the Dickens House, and sailed for home from Southampton, having seen eight cathedrals in all.

The ninth tour was with Robert Cook, Jr., in 1911. We landed at Plymouth, saw Truro Cathedral, went to Penzance and Land's End, and then in Wales visited Llandaff and St. David's. Salisbury, Chichester, Southwark, St. Paul's, and Westminster Abbey followed—eight more cathedrals. On the Isle of Wight we saw Ventnor, Freshwater, and the Tennyson Memorial Cross facing the great Atlantic, Carisbrooke Castle, where Charles the First was confined, Stonehenge and the Roman remains from Silchester preserved at Reading. We visited Margaret at Southwold. She joined her father and us a little later in London, and we sailed for home together from Liverpool. My tenth tour was with Carl in 1912. This time we landed in Liverpool, visited Manchester with its wonderful Rylands Library and City Hall, Sheffield, Nottingham, Norwich, and Bedford, with its memorials of John Bunyan. We saw something of Cambridge, Beverly, York, Alnwick, Hexham, and made a special examination of the Roman Wall which I have described in my *Miscellanies*, I: 335-361. Then we went to Edinburgh, St. Andrews, the headquarters of the golf industry, Balmoral and Aberdeen, not omitting Loch Leven, where Mary, Queen of Scots, was confined in 1567, making her escape in 1568, as related in Walter Scott's *Abbot*. We went northward from Aberdeen to Inverness, and, by way of the Caledonial Canal, to Oban, Glasgow, Carlisle, Liverpool, and home—having seen six cathedrals on our way.

In my eleventh and last English tour, in 1913, Charles met me in Liverpool, and we saw the last four of my English cathedrals. They were Newcastle, Southwell, Wakefield, and St. Asaph's. To have completed the list of thirty-seven was a gratification, somewhat childish perhaps, but nonetheless real. The study of architecture is a great delight to me, especially in its historical connections. Of course I did not in each case have the dean at my side to pour his learning into me. But I had all the more opportunity to make discoveries of my own. Charles did not think my investigations as restful as he could desire, for I tired him out. We had a lovely journey together notwithstanding. In Newcastle we met Mr. Lindsay and his family, and on the steamer going home I tried to make Charles acquainted with Miss Jean. But he was proof against all mediating efforts, and I concluded that it was best to leave him to his own devices. I had accomplished my ambition in the matter of cathedrals and now had something to brag of. But I grieve to say that this was the first part of my last visit with Charles. The war has come to make our coming together difficult.

After my return from Europe in 1909, I continued to teach for three years. But it was with considerable effort. Increasing deafness made it impossible to permit discussion in my classes, for I could not hear the questions that were put to me. I therefore confined myself to lecturing, and this pouring forth without response became irksome. I resolved to close my connection with the seminary when I had completed my fortieth year of service. In 1911 I gave notice to the trustees that in another year I should offer my resignation of my presidency and of my professorship of systematic theology. This I did in 1912, resolving in my own mind that I would no longer exert my influence in seminary affairs. The later course of events leads me to question whether in this resolve I did not make one of the great mistakes of my life. I was a trustee of the seminary as well as its president, and my resignation of the presidency did not relieve me from my duty as trustee. It was my duty as trustee to do all I could to ensure a right succession and to care for the doctrinal and spiritual future of the institution. I felt that my son John was the man who ought to take my place. But, at that time, to advocate John's claims seemed to me to savor of nepotism, and I therefore studiously abstained from mentioning his name. I think I could then have secured his election, but I made it a point of honor to be silent. I let the opportunity slip by, and I mourned over the result.

The committee on nominations appointed by the trustees in 1911 was a conservative one. It embraced the names of Drs. MacArthur, Rhoades, Villers, and Barbour. The natural procedure would have been to elect first a president, and then a professor of systematic theology, allowing the president elect to have a voice in the choice of his cabinet. If I had used my influence as trustee, I could have secured the nomination of my son as president and then the nomination of a sound man as professor. But I neither influenced the committee, nor did I attend the meetings of the board of trustees. The result was that the election of a president was postponed for another year, and Dr. Cross was elected professor of systematic theology. He had been mentioned for this position but had declined to say whether he believed in the preexistence, deity, virgin birth, miracles, objective atonement, physical resurrection, and omnipresence of Jesus Christ, and the committee had resolved not to nominate him. Learning of this and rejoicing, I had confidentially told the secret to Dr. Stewart, whereupon he wrote to Dr. Cross and drew from him a letter so stating his position that a strong radical minority of the board urged his claims and secured his election, in spite of the objections of the nominating committee.

This same committee next year proposed Dr. Mullins for president, but the radical element in the board had learned its strength and prevented his election. The presidency went vacant for several years, but at last Dr. Barbour was called to fill it. The result of the election of Dr. Cross has been the resignation of some members of the committee and the withdrawal of others from active service. I regard that election as the greatest calamity that has come to the seminary since its foundation. It was the entrance of an agnostic, skeptical, and anti-Christian element into its teaching, the results of which will be only evil. Its view of Scripture as only the record of man's gropings after God instead of being primarily God's revelation to man makes any systematic theology impossible and any professorship of systematic theology to be only a history of doctrines. The election of Dr. Cross was followed by the election of Professors Robins, Parsons, and Nixon, who sympathize with his views. These men, with Professor Moehlmann, soon gave evidence in their utterances that a veritable revolution had taken place in the attitude of the seminary toward fundamentals of the Christian faith. Whether Dr. Barbour, with his compromising spirit, will have power to keep our students true to Christ and to his gospel, in spite of so many radicals in his faculty, is a most serious question. I can only commit the case to Christ's hands in the confidence that my mistake in absolving myself from responsibility, since it was conscientious, will be in some way overruled for the good of Christ's cause.

My resignation from the seminary left me free for literary tasks, and Mamma's increasing weakness made these my only relief from anxiety and care. Plenty of work was thrust upon me. My *Systematic Theology* in three volumes had been published in 1909. A new edition of my *Philosophy and Religion* followed in 1911. After I left the seminary, one of my students presented me with a typewritten copy of stenographic notes of my remarks at our noon prayer meetings during the preceding year. I revised these and had them printed in a book entitled *One Hundred Chapel-Talks to Theological Students.*[6] Then came in 1912 the publication of my *Miscellanies, Historical and Theological,* in which I gathered up, in the hope of saving from oblivion, many addresses, essays, and sermons, most of them produced during my presidency of the seminary.[7] Dr. Trumbull of the *Sunday School Times* induced me to put a chapter of my *Systematic Theology* into a booklet entitled *Union with Christ.*[8] In 1914 I had printed *Popular Lectures on the Books of the New Testament,* from a typewritten stenographic report of my lectures to a large Sunday School class twenty years before.[9] These, of course, I revised and brought down to date. But my special new work was *American Poets and Their Theology,* printed in 1916.[10] Upon this I spent much time and reading, with a view to rectify the judgment of young people as to the theology taught by the poetical writers most generally accepted in our time. It was a great question whom to include as the ninth poet admitted to my Hall of Fame. I wavered between Whitman and Wilkinson. Old friendship for my classmate urged me to choose him. I wrote

---

[6] *One Hundred Chapel-Talks to Theological Students, Together with Two Autobiographical Addresses* (Philadelphia: The Griffith and Rowland Press, 1913).

[7] *Miscellanies: Historical and Theological* (Philadelphia: The Griffith and Rowland Press, 1912).

[8] *Union with Christ: A Chapter of Systematic Theology* (Philadelphia: American Baptist Publication Society, 1913).

[9] *Popular Lectures on the Books of the New Testament* (Philadelphia: The Griffith and Rowland Press, 1914).

[10] *American Poets and Their Theology* (Philadelphia: The Griffith and Rowland Press, 1916).

complete essays, one on Whitman and another on Wilkinson. But I was compelled at last to recognize in Whitman a breath of real poetry which I could not find in Wilkinson and to acknowledge that Whitman was by far the more widely known. So with great regret I decided to take up Whitman for severe treatment and to set Wilkinson aside as more of a rhetorician and critic than a poet. I have sent out this last book on my eightieth birthday, with many prayers that it may carry light and blessing into every college and seminary library in the land.

The printing of my books has not been a source of great revenue. I have published them, not for financial gain, but as my testimony to Christ and his truth. I have usually defrayed the initial expense of plates and printing, in hope of subsequent returns. Yet I suppose I have made $5,000 out of them, and last year 2,260 volumes in all have been sold. They may in the future bring greater returns, possibly $1,000 a year to my literary executors. Fortunately my financial circumstances have improved, so that I do not need to depend on my books for support. God has been very good to me in this matter of finance. While I have been somewhat lavish in expenditure and have thought it necessary to my station to live well as to dress and food and travel and entertaining, I have at times been greatly straitened for means. When I had three children away at school at one time, little needs of the household were with difficulty met, and the quarter's bills were perforce permitted to go over to the next three months unpaid. The gift of Kodak stock from my dear brother Henry, amounting in all to 200 shares, has been the foundation of a small fortune. By investing the dividends in new stock instead of spending them, I have at last increased the 200 shares to 500, which in some years, at 5 or 6 percent, has yielded an income of $20,000 to $25,000. I think of this provision for my old age, and for the future of my children, with profound gratitude to God and to my brother Henry. I have resolved not to strive for further accumulation of resources but to give my surplus income to my children and to missionary and educational work at home and abroad.

The death of my first wife, so soon after my resignation from the seminary, was followed by a period of depression on my part such as I had never before known. Sister Julia remained as my housekeeper, but the house seemed empty and desolate. My long anxiety with regard to Hattie's mental and physical condition had worn me out. I felt the need of change, and since it was dangerous to combat the cold of winter, I determined at once to go south. But I started too early, reaching De Land early in October. There I found unendurable heat, poor quarters, and poor food. The College Arms Hotel was not yet open, and I was compelled to live at the worst hotel I had ever experienced. The result was that I lost all strength and courage. There was no proper companionship. I had almost literally jumped from the frying-pan into the fire. I think I should have died then and there, far away from home, if I had not persuaded Mrs. Marguerite G. Jones of Rochester to come down and share my lot. On the last day of December she arrived, and on the next morning, January 1, 1915, we were married at the College Arms Hotel by Mr. Colebrook, pastor of the De Land Baptist Church, and one of my former pupils at Rochester. Dr. Lincoln Hulley, president of the John B. Stetson University, and Mrs. Hulley were the only witnesses. I can truly say that the coming and the care of Marguerite saved my life, for I had spent many days in bed before her coming, and I was ill for quite a long time after. But with that New Year's Day I began to mend.

My first acquaintance with Marguerite dates back to a visit I made to Orange, New Jersey, twenty years ago. I was seeking additions to our seminary funds. Dr. Dickinson was then pastor of the Orange Baptist Church, and he arranged for me an interview with Mr. John Jay Jones after I had preached on the Sunday morning. I then only remarked the gracious and favoring influence of one of whom I had no thought as a future wife. A result of that interview was, as I believe, his making our seminary one of his residuary legatees and our ultimately receiving from his estate more than $600,000. Years passed, and he too passed away. His widow might have contested his will and might have deprived the seminary of a large part of his bequest. She showed instead so disinterested a desire to carry out his wishes that I was deeply impressed with her generous and Christlike spirit. After his death she came to Rochester, made it her home, and became an active and useful member of our First Baptist Church. I knew of her benevolent activities and of her missionary spirit. Her knowledge of eastern lands gained in a tour round the world seven years before impressed me with her intelligence. In my sorrow and illness my mind turned to her. She and I were in financial respects equally well off, so that a matrimonial alliance between us need work no loss to my children. She took pity on my condition, accepted my proposals, and became to me a ministering angel, for whose sympathy and support I have never since ceased to be profoundly grateful.

The announcement of our marriage was a surprise to many friends, though I had given a little previous notice of it to my brother, my sisters, and my children. I thought it desirable to make the children better acquainted with Marguerite, and I therefore engaged parlor and sleeping rooms for them all at the new Willard Hotel, in Washington, so that we might have a whole week together as a family party. That party was so delightful a reunion that we resolved to make it an annual affair. I have made these family parties an occasion for exhortations to the children to hold together and for explanations of my intention to distribute my property equally to the four children, Mary, John, Kate, and Laura, Charles being in need of nothing from me, and Cora being provided for by funds left by me to trustees for her benefit. I cannot express my gratitude for the kind and helpful way in which my marriage has been received by my children, and Marguerite has equal joy in knowing that she has gained and not lost by her union with me. She has made these family parties memorable by her hospitality. Our second party indeed took place in Rochester in our own house, which we had refurnished and redecorated in 1915 at an expense of over five thousand dollars. The party was accompanied by a reception for those who knew either us or our children—162 guests accepted our invitation and we received regrets from 52 others. This was on May 25, 1916. We had previously, on December 9, 1915, at the inauguration of President Barbour, entertained at dinner Drs. Peabody, Bruce, Vedder, Dickinson, Riggs, Mullins, Trotter, McClure, G. Anderson, T. D. Anderson, Fosdick, Bryan, Horr, Crannell, and Mathews. Both Katy and Laura helped us, and I doubt whether there was ever a more distinguished company of Baptist guests. We have begun indeed a series of entertainments for relatives, ministers, missionaries, and humble workers in the churches, which I trust will do something to revive the spirit of brotherhood and further the interests of Christ in the world. In May, 1916, I counted up the number of guests who had taken meals or refreshments in my house during the twenty years since it was opened, and I found that it was 7,305. Dividing this by 20, to learn how many had been entertained each year, I had an arithmetical surprise, for it was exactly 365, or one for each day in all those twenty years.

Until 1914 all my longer tours had been European, and there had been eleven of them. The twelfth was American, to Nassau and Cuba. Robert Cook, Sr., was in need of a change, and I invited him and Mary to accompany me. We sailed for the Bahamas from New York. A voyage of three days brought us to Nassau, that tropical island which the Gulf Stream keeps always warm. There Mr. Eastman's yacht met us and entertained us. The brilliant hues of the palms and the flowers and the waters were a novelty and a delight. The color line seems to have been obliterated between the races, and the colored man is as much respected as the white. English roads and schools and government have made the island a charming place of resort. The cab driver looked at the two statues of Columbus and Queen Victoria and supposed that Queen Victoria was Columbus's second wife. But black men are policemen and judges here. The great hotel can accommodate nearly a thousand guests, but it is built of wood, and fire would quickly sweep it away. From Nassau we sailed for Havana, stayed a week, visited Matanzas with its famous cave of stalactites, and returned home by way of Key West, Miami, Palm Beach, De Land, and St. Augustine, not forgetting to call on brother Henry and sister Hattie at Augusta, Georgia. We have been absent only six weeks, but we had seen in Havana the union of old Spain and young America.

My thirteenth tour was also American. It followed immediately upon our first family party at Washington and took us from Philadelphia through the Panama Canal to San Diego and San Francisco. I have described this journey to Panama and California in a special paper entitled "Circumnavigating the United States." This has never yet been published, though it gives some vivid impressions of the great canal, of the two Expositions, and of our return by way of the Canadian Pacific. We made a study of the Roman Catholic missions in California, which convinced us of the futility and short life of sacramental propagandism. Most of these mission buildings are in ruins, and their altars have few communicants or none. Romanism made its converts slaves of the priests, instituted no education, became secularized, avaricious, and immoral. When the Indian died and the white man took his place, the estates of the Roman church became ranches for Yankee thrift and money making. But the people were free, and California has a great future before it.

It was in part the desire to see Oriental Baptist Missions and to contrast them with those of Rome that prompted us in 1916 to plan and carry out a scheme for visiting our missions in Japan, China, and India. My graduates had for years begged me to inspect their fields of labor; but until I resigned my work of teaching, I could not go. Since Marguerite had made the tour some years before, her company was an additional inducement, for she could serve as guidebook and encyclopedia. Rev. Louis Agassiz Gould, a former pupil of mine in the seminary, and a former missionary in China, was my courier and secretary. We started from home on September 11, 1916, went to Los Angeles by way of the Grand Canyon of Arizona, and sailed from San Francisco on September 30 for Honolulu and Yokohama. I have described this tour in my forthcoming book, *A Tour of the Missions,* so that I do not need now to enter into details.[11] Suffice it to say that we had a royal reception everywhere. It was like being met by a brass band at every landing place or station, conducted through files of uniformed students, to halls where hundreds were assembled whom we were expected to address through an interpreter who repeated in the native language what we said in English. Imagine us sight-seeing all day, riding in sleeping cars all night, and filling up the waiting times by writing letters on the platforms of railway stations. Mr. Gould had laid out a program for us that would have exhausted the Angel Gabriel. Yet by consuming a sufficient amount of energy and coffee, I survived and enjoyed it all, though I did more work than I had ever done in the same time before.

Java is blazing hot, for it is south of the Equator. Returning to

---

[11] *A Tour of the Missions: Observations and Conclusions* (Philadelphia: The Griffith and Rowland Press, 1918).

Hong Kong brought us into what seemed by comparison an Arctic temperature. I was clothed for heat and not for cold. Cutting wind and driving rain, with no fires, gave me a chill. I took to my bed, lost all appetite, and began to think my end was near. China was at the close of the coldest winter it had known for many years. The doctors told me I was in no condition to go north to Peking. So, to save my life, I gave up seeing northern China and Korea, and took the Japanese steamer *Tenyo Maru* at Hong Kong for Yokohama, Honolulu, and San Francisco. We landed in San Francisco on the very day of President Wilson's war address to Congress, having had a voyage of twenty-seven days with no submarines to molest or make us afraid. After one week in port, we spent a fortnight with brother Henry and his wife in Santa Barbara, and two weeks in Pasadena completed our stay in California. We returned to Rochester by way of Salt Lake City and Colorado Springs, reaching home on May 19, after our eight months' tour in the Orient, a tour which cost us $12,287 and which cost me thirty-six pounds of flesh. Under the care of Dr. Witherspoon and Alvah Miller, however, I have begun to mend, having regained eighteen pounds of what I had lost, and with a voracious appetite hoping to regain eighteen pounds more.

May 22-29 was the week of our third family party. Mary and Robert, John and Lide, Kate and Carl, Laura and Edmund were all here, Charles and Margaret being absent in Switzerland, and Cora coming only at the weekend. Our trunk, full of gifts and bric-a-brac from the Orient, was rescued from the customs office by payment of $153 and was opened by the children, the treasures being exposed for exhibition in the reception room. It was a hilarious and delightful time. On Saturday morning, all being assembled for prayers and the doors being shut, I gave a lecture on family unity and impoverished myself for three months by giving to each one of the four children a check for $500. It was worthwhile to see their loyalty and affection to us and to one another. There is a proper family pride. It is a safeguard against many dangers, and I wish to cultivate it.

The only other great event, and one to which all else has been for the past year tending, has been our journey to New Haven to attend my sixtieth class anniversary at Yale. On the way thither we stayed a day and a night at Miss Colgate's in Yonkers, and Marguerite and I made addresses to four hundred women at their annual missionary meeting in the Warburton Avenue Church. We then went to Vassar and attended the commencement exercises, though we found everything much changed since the death of Dr. Taylor. A new regime has risen which "knows not Joseph," and a new denomination of Christians has been put, as I think treacherously and unwisely, in control of that great institution. From Poughkeepsie, we went at Miss Spelman's invitation to Pocantico and were charmingly entertained at luncheon by her and Mr. Rockefeller, who personally took us in his motorcar thirty-two miles to the Belmont Hotel in New York. There we stayed for three days, going on Saturday, June 16, 1917, to New Haven and taking the rooms reserved for us for the commencement week at $25 a day. Mr. and Mrs. Levi Holbrook soon came and took the room adjoining ours. From that time Holbrook assumed control, arranged for the class dinner, and paid all the expenses thereof, as I myself had done ten years before.

On Tuesday evening nine of our class of 1857 sat down, the survivors of 104 who had graduated sixty years ago, and the representatives of twenty who are still living. They were Beard, Cone, Doster, Holbrook, Huntington, Seymour, Woodruff, Wheeler, and I. Marguerite and I were placed in the seats of honor. Doster and Woodruff each brought a son; Huntington brought a son and daughter besides his wife. Holbrook, Wheeler, and I also had our wives with us, so that the entire company numbered seventeen. No grace was said. Mrs. Holbrook afterwards remarked that her husband did not request me to ask a blessing for fear it would throw a gloom over what ought to be a happy occasion. I thought it a sad indication of a very common view of religion held even by Christian people, namely, that religion is a mournful thing to be kept out of sight whenever possible instead of being the joyful recognition of the Giver of every good and perfect gift. But the dinner was superb; lobster and champagne were constituent parts of it; we ate as if it were our last meal on earth, and since we were all over eighty years of age, it was wonderful that any of us were able to attend the alumni dinner next day. Five of us, however, did sit down there: Beard, Holbrook, Huntington, Seymour, and I. At the close of the dinner the night before, I had told them that I proposed to call a class meeting up beyond and was hopeful that many of the old fellows, such as Holmes and Butler, Scoville and Tyler, Hand and Smith, Barrows and Brown, Eaton and Edwards, Hubbell and Jackson, Wells and Wilson, would then answer to their names. Why not? Is not God the Author of these ties which bind us so closely together on earth? And will he not respect the work of his own hands?

We made our homeward journey by way of Lake Mohonk, where we spent Sunday, Monday, and Tuesday. The grounds were ablaze with peonies and roses, and the vegetation never seemed more beautiful. We took the ride to Minnewaska, for I had never before seen it. A motorcar took us on Tuesday evening, in spite of a threatening thunderstorm, to Poughkeepsie, and the morning of June 27 found us at breakfast in our own house at 17 Sibley Place, thankful that we were alive, and promising ourselves that we would not soon wander again. Since then I have been resting, settling bills, entertaining relatives, and, above all, striving to complete this appendix to my autobiography. I have wished to do this while my memory of events was clear, and the revival of old scenes has been a comfort to me. Names and dates, however, sometimes escape me, and it would not be wonderful if my children found that some of my descriptions were sadly mixed. Only such as I have, can I give them.

My doctrinal views have not changed during these last ten years. They have rather grown more definite and settled. If I have made progress at all, it is in the way of personal appropriation of truth which had been previously held as a matter of theory. I have come, for example, to apply to myself what I regard as Christ's promise of spiritual resurrection and to believe that I have been raised with Christ from the death of trespasses and sins and am the continual recipient of his life-giving presence and power. God in Christ, here and now, is my comfort and joy. I project this experience into the past and see that Christ joined me to himself, though I was unconscious of it, at my conversion, that he has been progressively revealing himself to me, and that all my Christian life has been a leading of his Spirit, so that I can truly say, "Not I live, but Christ liveth in me." Is not this the preliminary "rapture of the saints"? I protest that I have never sought a place or made an address or written a book on my own motion or in my own strength but that I have been thrust forward and compelled to do it by a superior power, which I believe now to be the power of Christ. "He leadeth the blind by a way that they know not." All my successes have been Christ's successes, not mine. Mine have been the failures, because of my unbelief and sin. "Oh, that I had hearkened to his commandments! Then had my peace been as a river, and my righteousness as the waves of the sea!" I commend this experience to my children and to my grandchildren. May they from the very beginning let Christ be all and in all, their leader, their inspiration, and their life!

Because my life is so connected and identified with the life of Christ, I can cease from vain regrets from the past and from all fears for the future. I am sorry for those who mourn continually over the loss of past gifts and who cannot look with joy on the prospect of death. Much of our modern poetry has in it this element of sadness. Tennyson can write:

> Tears, idle tears, I know not what they mean,
> Tears from the depth of some divine despair,
> Rise in the heart, and gather to the eyes,
> In looking on the happy autumn-fields,
> And thinking of the days that are no more.[12]

Paul has no such "divine despair," and Jesus tells us that "greater things than these shall ye see." Thomas Moore can see only solitude and desertion in his old age:

> Oft, in the stilly night,
>   Ere Slumber's chain has bound me,
> Fond Memory brings the light
>   Of other days around me;
>   The smiles, the tears,
>   Of boyhood's years,
>   The words of love then spoken;
>   The eyes that shone,
>   Now dimmed and gone,
>   The cheerful hearts now broken!
> Thus, in the stilly night,
>   Ere Slumber's chain has bound me,
> Sad Memory brings the light
>   Of other days around me.

---

[12] Alfred, Lord Tennyson, *The Princess: A Medley*, 4. 21-25.

When I remember all
The friends, so linked together,
I've seen around me fall,
Like leaves in wintry weather;
I feel like one
Who treads alone
Some banquet-hall deserted,
Whose lights are fled,
Whose garlands dead,
And all but him departed!
Thus, in the stilly night,
Ere Slumber's chain has bound me,
Sad Memory brings the light
Of other days around me.[13]

Robert Burns gives us the comfort of the wife who grows old along with her husband, but she sees no hope beyond the grave:

John Anderson, my jo, John,
When we were first acquent,
Your locks were like the raven,
Your bonnie brow was brent;
But now your brow is beld, John,
Your locks are like the snow;
But blessings on your frosty pow,
John Anderson, my jo!

John Anderson, my jo, John,
We clamb the hill tegither;
And mony a canty day, John,
We've had wi' ane anither:
Now we maun totter down, John,
And hand in hand we'll go.
And sleep tegither at the foot,
John Anderson, my jo.[14]

No one of these speaks of reunion with the loved and lost or of a resurrection from the dead. Christ tells us of something better: "I go to prepare a place for you"; "Because I live, ye shall live also"; "Where I am, there ye shall be also"; and the old hymn expresses the exact truth:

[13] Thomas Moore, "Oft, in the Stilly Night."
[14] Robert Burns, "John Anderson."

And when I'm to die
"Receive me," I'll cry,
For Jesus has loved me,
I cannot tell why;
But this I do find,
We two are so joined,
He'll not be in glory,
And leave me behind.

The more common verse has the same meaning:

If Christ and we are one,
Why should we doubt or fear?
If he in heaven has fixed his throne,
He'll fix his members there.

So I look forward to death as not the end but only the beginning of true life, of unfettered progress, of satisfied affection, of holy service. "Eye hath not seen, nor ear heard, neither hath entered into the heart of man, what God hath prepared for them that love him." "Faithful over a few things" here, we shall be "rulers over many things" there.

And every power find sweet employ
In that eternal world of joy.

In joining us to himself, Christ has made all things to be ours. We shall enter into the joy of our Lord and shall see the greatness of God's salvation. For union with Christ makes all things work together for our good and for that triumph of his cause which is more to us than any personal advantage. So, in view of death, I can say with Paul: "To depart and to be with Christ is far better" than to abide forever in this world of sin and sorrow; and I conclude this testimony with the words of that same apostle:

"Thanks be unto God for his unspeakable gift!"[15]

---

[15] In his later years Strong spent the winters in Pasadena, California. He traveled and lectured in Europe in 1920. He delivered the William Cleaver Wilkinson Lectures at the Northern Baptist Theological Seminary in Chicago, November 3-9, 1921. He died in Pasadena on November 29, 1921. His funeral was in Rochester on December 5, 1921, and he was buried in Mount Hope Cemetery in Rochester.

Appendix A

GENEALOGY OF THE STRONG FAMILY
from Professor Dwight's History
with pages indicated

	1630	
1st generation pages 16, 17	Elder John Strong of Northampton, 1605–1699—94 eighteen children	Abigail Ford of Dorchester died 1688—80 sixteen children
	1662	
2nd generation 4th child page 19	Jedediah Strong of Coventry, Conn. 1637–1733—96 fourteen children	Freedom Woodward of Northampton, 1642–1681—39 thirteen children

1688

| 3rd generation
3rd child
page 770 | Jedediah Strong, Jr.
of Lebanon, Conn.,
1667–1709—42 | Abiah Ingersoll
of Northampton,
1663–1732—69
eight children |

1730

| 4th generation
7th child
page 858 | Ezra Strong
of Marlboro, Conn.
1702–1785—83
twelve children | Abigail Caverley
of Colchester, Conn.
1715–1788—73
twelve children |

1757

| 5th generation
3rd child
pages 893, 894 | Philip Strong
of Warren, Conn.
1735–1787—52
fifteen children | Rhoda Payne
of Warren, Conn. (?)
1739–1825—86
fifteen children |

1798

| 6th generation
10th child
page 911 | Ezra Strong
of Scipio, N.Y.
1777–1846—69
six children | Betsey Dunning
of Warren, Conn.,
1777–1852—75
six children |

1834

| 7th generation
4th child
page 912 | Alvah Strong
of Rochester, N.Y.
1809–1885—75
four children | Catherine Hopkins
of Rochester, N.Y.
1808–1877—68
four children |

1861

| 8th generation | Augustus Hopkins
Strong
of Rochester, N.Y.
1836–
six children | Harriet Louise Savage
of Rochester, N.Y.
1839–1914
six children |

GENEALOGY OF THE HOPKINS FAMILY, SUMMARIZED

1633

1st generation	John Hopkins	Jane (Strong?)
	of Hartford	of Boston (?)
	1613(?)–1654—41	died (?)
	two children	two children

1664?

2nd generation	Stephen Hopkins	Dorcas Bronson
	of Hartford	of Farmington
	1634–1689—55	died 1697—(57?)
	six children	six children

1683

3rd generation	John Hopkins	Hannah (Rogers?)
	of Waterbury	of Waterbury ?
	1665–1732—67	died 1730—(70?)
	eight children	eight children

1717

4th generation	Stephen Hopkins	Susannah Peck
	of Waterbury	of Wallingford
	1689–1769—80	died 1755—75
	six children	six children

1747

5th generation	Stephen Hopkins	Dorothy Talmadge
	of Waterbury	of Long Island,
	1719–1796—77	1st wife
	six children	died 1761—35 (?)
		five children

1771

6th generation	Samuel Hopkins	Mary Miles
	of Goshen	of Wallingford
	1748–1818—70	died 1811—58
	six children	six children

1803?

7th generation	Mark Hopkins	Almira Stanley
	of Mt. Morris	of Goshen,
	1778–1832—54	died 1817—29
	seven children	seven children

1834

8th generation	Catherine Hopkins	Alvah Strong
	of Rochester, N.Y.	of Rochester, N.Y.
	1808–1844—69	died 1885—76
	six children	six children

MY CHILDREN AND GRANDCHILDREN

1834

7th generation	Alvah Strong	Catherine Hopkins
4th child	of Rochester, N.Y.	of Rochester, N.Y.
page 912	1809–1885—75	1808–1877—68
	four children	four children

Nov. 6,
1861

8th generation	Augustus Hopkins	Harriet Louise Savage
1st child	Strong	of Rochester, N.Y.
page 912	of Rochester, N.Y.	1839–1914—
	1836–	six children
	six children	

Mch. 22,
1889

| 9th generation pages 912, 913 | Charles Augustus Strong b. Nov. 28, 1862, | Bessie Rockefeller b. Aug. 23, 1866, d. Nov. 14, 1906. |

| 10th generation | Margaret Strong, | b. June 11, 1897. |

June 2,
1892

| 9th generation | Mary Belle Strong b. Aug. 29, 1864 | Robert George Cook, b. Aug. 4, 1864. |

| 10th generation | Robert Strong Cook, Alan Augustus Cook, George Elmendorf Cook, | b. Feb. 11, 1895; b. August 17, 1896. b. March 10, 1898. |

June 20,
1894

| 9th generation | John Henry Strong, b. Dec. 7, 1866, | Eliza Livingston McCreery, b. Oct. 1, 1867. |

| 10th generation | William McCreery Strong, Elizabeth McCreery Strong, Virginia Strong, Emilie Strong, | b. April 9, 1898; b. April 8, 1902 b. Jan. 6, 1906, d. Aug. 28, 1906. b. July 4, 1908. |

| 9th Generation | Cora Harriet Strong, b. Feb. 10, 1870. | |

Jan. 16,
1900

9th generation   Kate Louise Strong   Charles Grenville
                   b. Feb. 10, 1870,   Sewall,
                                              b. Aug. 4, 1872.

10th generation Grenville Strong   b. Jan. 11, 1902
                 Sewall,
                 John Ives Sewall,   b. Sept. 15, 1905,
                 Richard Benson   b. Feb. 11, 1908.
                 Sewall,

June 1,
1910

9th generation   Laura Rockefeller Edmund Harris Lewis
                   Strong   b. Syracuse, N.Y.
                   b. June 19, 1884,   August 30, 1884.

10th generation Mary Strong Lewis,   b. Aug. 17, 1913
                 Jane Heffron Lewis,   b. June 6, 1915
                 Katherine Strong   b. Aug. 6, 1916
                 Lewis   d. Feb. 6, 1917
                 Laura Margaret Lewis b. Oct. 7, 1919

Appendix B

ENGLISH CATHEDRALS

Strong did not explain why he chose to conclude his *Autobiography* with this list of English cathedrals, just as he had not tried to explain in 1913 why it had meant so much to him to tour every one of them. One cannot help wondering, however, whether that illustrious style called Baptist Gothic which gave birth to such American monuments as the University of Chicago and Riverside Church has at least a few of its origins in those tours of English cathedrals which Theodore D. Bacon and Augustus Hopkins Strong made with so much gusto in the summer of 1859.

Bangor	Lincoln	St. Asaph's
Birmingham	Liverpool	St. David's
Bristol	Llandaff	St. Paul's
Canterbury	Manchester	Salisbury
Carlisle	Newcastle	Southwark
Chester	Norwich	Southwell
Chichester	Oxford	Truro
Durham	Peterborough	Wakefield
Ely	Ripon	Wells
Exeter	Rochester	Westminster Abbey
Gloucester	St. Albans	Winchester
Hereford		Worcester
Litchfield		York

Appendix C

The Strong Family Papers

The collection in which Strong's *Autobiography* was found had been unavailable to the public and to most of the Strong family until Mrs. Emilie Strong Smith inherited it in 1978. Mrs. Smith appointed Crerar Douglas curator of the collection, authorizing him to catalogue it and edit the *Autobiography* and the items listed below. She then placed the catalogued collection and the edited materials, which have been organized in typescript volumes of about two hundred pages each (with prefaces and notes), in the library of the American Baptist Historical Society in Rochester, New York.

The following individuals made possible the completion of the project: Rosalie B. Douglas, who transcribed and typed the edited materials from the original manuscripts; Elizabeth de Cuevas, granddaughter of Charles Augustus Strong; William H. Brackney of the American Baptist Historical Society; Norman E. Tanis, Director of University Libraries, California State University, Northridge; Dennis C. Bakewell, Special Collections Librarian, California State University; and Jerome Richfield, Dean of the

School of Humanities, California State University, who provided extra time for research in 1981.

The historical context of most of the papers will be evident to readers of Strong's *Autobiography*. Further light on the significance of Charles A. Strong's papers is provided by the writings of Charles Strong's lifelong friend George Santayana. Santayana's portrayal of Oliver Alden in *The Last Puritan,* for example, is an interpretation of the life and thought of Charles Strong. Their own writings, however, show that the Strongs were more complex than Santayana thought Puritans should be.

I. LETTERS AND PAPERS OF AUSGUSTUS HOPKINS STRONG

Vol. 1: *Early Writings*
Vol. 2: *American Letters, 1854-1863*
Vol. 3: *Letters from Europe, 1859*
Vol. 4: *Letters from Europe and the Near East, 1859-60*
Vol. 5: *Unpublished Lectures and Sermons, 1886-1910*
Vol. 6: *Letters to John Henry Strong, mostly 1916-1921*
Vol. 7: *Later Writings, 1918-1921*
Vol. 8: *Miscellaneous Notebook Materials*

II. LETTERS AND PAPERS OF HARRIET SAVAGE STRONG (one volume)

III. EARLY LETTERS OF CHARLES AUGUSTUS STRONG

Vol. 1: *Letters from Exeter, 1877-1879*
Vol. 2: *Letters from Exeter, 1879-1880*
Vol. 3: *Letters from Europe, 1881*
Vol. 4: *Letters from Europe, January-June, 1882*
Vol. 5: *Letters from Europe, June-December, 1882*
Vol. 6: *Letters from Europe, 1883*
Vol. 7: *Letters from Harvard, 1884-1885*

Index of
Principal Persons

381